TRANSPORTATION DEMAND ANALYSIS

McGraw-Hill Series in Transportation

Consulting Editor
Edward K. Morlok, *University of Pennsylvania*

TRANSPORTATION DEMAND ANALYSIS

Adib Kanafani

University of California, Berkeley

McGraw-Hill Book Company

New York   St. Louis   San Francisco   Auckland   Bogotá   Hamburg
Johannesburg   London   Madrid   Mexico   Montreal   New Delhi
Panama   Paris   São Paulo   Singapore   Sydney   Tokyo   Toronto

This book was set in Times Roman by Benj. H. Tyrrel.
The editors were Julienne V. Brown, Kiran Verma, and Susan Hazlett;
the production supervisor was John Mancia.
The drawings were done by ANCO/Boston.
Halliday Lithograph Corporation was printer and binder.

TRANSPORTATION DEMAND ANALYSIS

Copyright © 1983 by McGraw-Hill, Inc. All rights reserved.
Printed in the United States of America. Except as permitted under
the United States Copyright Act of 1976, no part of this publication may be
reproduced or distributed in any form or by any means, or stored in a data base
or retrieval system, without the prior written permission of the publisher.

1 2 3 4 5 6 7 8 9 0 H A L H A L 8 9 8 7 6 5 4 3

ISBN 0-07-033271-1

Library of Congress Cataloging in Publication Data

Kanafani, Adib K.
    Transportation demand analysis.

    Includes bibliographies and index.
    1. Transportation planning.   2. Demand (Economic
theory) I. Title.
HE152.5.K36 1983   380.5'068   82-13015
ISBN 0-07-033271-1

CONTENTS

PREFACE

Demand analysis is one subject that occupies a prominent place in the transportation literature. However, much of the material on this topic is to be found dispersed throughout the literature on broader topics such as transportation planning. Thus, in spite of the abundance of material written in this field, the absence of a consolidated book on this subject has left transportation demand analysis with little recognition as a field of study by itself, quite aside from having rendered teaching and researching it cumbersome. For a number of years, I have felt the need for a single text that would encompass the whole topic of demand analysis and that would present it within a meaningful framework. This book aims to do that. It is also intended for the professional who is interested in transportation planning and some aspects of engineering.

The book is written primarily as a textbook for a first-year graduate program in transportation or related fields such as city and regional planning and economics. It is also meant to serve as a source pool for users of transportation demand analysis by providing the theoretical and methodological information needed for the practicing analyst to apply the more practical tools of the trade, such as packaged computer programs and analysis systems. Having attempted to include the latest developments in the field, I feel that the book can serve as a reference for the researcher interested in exploring different means of improving the state of the art.

This book is organized in a unique way. Chapters follow a conceptual framework that underlies the work, reflecting the author's suggestions for a course outline. Demand analysis as an exploratory analysis that aims at explaining travel or shipping behavior within a given paradigm furnishes the framework. The paradigm is that of microeconomic demand and supply theory but fundamental alterations to that theory are essential for its applications to transportation. The scope includes passenger and commodity transportation, and the geographical context is divided into urban and interurban settings. Chapter 2 introduces a quick but intentionally thorough overview of microeconomic demand theory. It is presented in general terms since specific references to transportation appear in the rest of the text. Chapter 3 follows with an introduction of the concepts of supply. Here the discussion is specific to transportation. Regardless of what particular interests the reader has within the field of transportation demand analysis, Chapters 2 and 3 should be read before subsequent chapters. Chapter 4 introduces the principal concepts of urban passenger transportation demand. It is a basic chapter, one which should be read before Chapters 6 and 7, which deal with specific methods of travel analysis that are common in the urban passenger case. Special attention is given to choice analysis, with Chapter 5 devoted to the subject. Choice analysis is important in all aspects of demand analysis although it is predominant in the urban passenger case. Chapter 5 covers more than Chapter 4, specifically for urban applications. For the reader who is not quantitatively inclined, or for situations in which the instructor finds that the class lacks adequate preparation in probability and statistics, it would be appropriate to follow the sequence of Chapters 4, 6, and 7 for covering urban passenger transportation. Again, the material in Chapters 6 and 7 that deals with trip distribution and mode and route choice applies to urban as well as nonurban travel. However, since most of the developments in these areas have been through urban travel analysis, the material is presented as a part of the urban sequence of chapters. The reader of Chapters 8 through 10 will find applications of these methods to interurban travel of both passengers and commodities. The conventional sequence of models used in urban travel analysis—trip generation, distribution, mode choice, and route choice—is presented in Chapter 4 as one of the approaches to urban travel analysis. Less emphasis is placed on trip generation than on the other methods, since it does not follow the overall conceptual framework of choice and utility maximization that results from adopting a microeconomic demand theory logic.

The nonurban chapters of the book deal with passenger travel and commodity transportation. Chapter 8 introduces the principal ideas of intercity travel demand analysis and serves as a preface to the more detailed Chapter 9, which deals specifically with air transportation. This was done for two reasons. First, more work has been done in air transportation demand analysis than for any other type of intercity travel, and second, the methods and models presented in Chapter 9 can be used as an example of what might be done in other modal contexts. The instructor interested in doing this can supplement the material with notes on specific applications of demand analysis to other modes of travel. Finally, Chapter 10 provides the principal ideas and methods of commodity flow analysis. It presents both a microeconomic framework using the shipper as an analysis unit, and a macroeconomic one based on interindustry analysis extended to the multiregional dimension.

In a course in which there is little or no emphasis on urban travel, a sequence of readings might be as follows: Chapters 1, 2, 3, 8, 9, and 10, with Chapter 5 added if there is interest in stochastic choice modeling, and with Chapter 7 included if there is interest in network flows and assignments.

Even though an attempt has been made to make the text complete, such is usually a virtually impossible task. The references at the ends of chapters are intended to give the students additional information. Considerable flexibility is left for the instructor in presenting the material. While I have presented perhaps somewhat rigidly my own paradigm for demand analysis, the instructor can either adopt and present what is here or use it only as a backdrop for presenting his or her own approach.

Since it is probably impossible for me to extend acknowledgments to all those who have helped me with this writing endeavor, which has now taken a number of years, I will attempt to mention only those who have had the strongest influence on my thinking of the subject and on my productivity in writing about it. Since I have taught this material for over a decade now, both at the University of California at Berkeley and at the Universidad de Los Andes in Merida, Venezuela, it must be said that without doubt, the scores of students of mine who have managed to learn the subject from unfinished drafts deserve a lot of credit. In particular, I can single out the students of the past two years who have been very helpful in pointing out errors and inspiring writing improvements in the final drafts of the text. My colleagues at the Institute of Transportation Studies have also extended valuable advice and encouragement: Geoffrey Gosling, Edward Sullivan, and Carlos Daganzo all read and commented on earlier drafts of parts of the book. My teaching assistants have also been very helpful in suggesting improvements, and in composing exercise problems: Greig Harvey, Redha Behbehani, Huey-Shin Yuan, and Atef Ghobrial all worked with me on teaching the material from the notes that preceded this book. My friend Richard de Neufville from the Massachusetts Institute of Technology read earlier drafts and provided invaluable support and encouragement during the early phases of my writing. Bonnie Berch and Sylvia Adler typed the manuscript and often improved my English considerably. The support of the Institute of Transportation Studies of the University of California at Berkeley was important for the completion of this project.

Finally, all the members of my family contributed to this writing project in many more ways than they think. To all of them I give my gratitude. Most of all, I thank my wife Karin who put up with years of unsettled ambiance created as a result of the project that had not yet been completed. Without her, this work would have never been done, nor would it have been inspired. I dedicate this book to her, therefore, only as a part of the gratitude that I wish to give.

Adib Kanafani

TRANSPORTATION DEMAND ANALYSIS

INTRODUCTION

The need for transportation stems from the interaction among social and economic activities dispersed in space. The diversity of these activities and the complexity of their patterns of interaction result in numerous determinants of transportation needs. The reasons people need to travel are endless; they range from the indispensable quest for food and shelter to the voluntary exercise of mobility for its own recreational value. Commodities are also shipped from place to place for a myriad of reasons, stemming from the economic necessities of production and consumption and from the pursuit of economic advantage and gain.

This diversity of patterns of socioeconomic interaction and the resulting complexity in the evolution of transportation needs indicate that formal and systematic analyses are essential for understanding the relationships between the spatial distribution of activities and transportation. This is the main objective of *transportation demand analysis,* and the topic of the following chapters.

The motivation for transportation demand analysis is indeed strong, for its is an essential activity in transportation planning. It provides a framework for estimating the needs for transportation and for forecasting the volumes of traffic that will use transportation facilities. This forecasting is essential for the design of transportation facilities and for the evaluation of their economic feasibility.

The rest of this chapter is devoted to a discussion of the concept of *demand for transportation* and to the definition of *transportation demand analysis* and its role in transportation systems planning.

1.1 THE DEMAND FOR TRANSPORTATION

The first step in the study of the relationship between socioeconomic activities and transportation needs is to adopt a meaningful measure of these needs. The need for transportation is manifested in the form of traffic volume, whether it be the flow of automobiles on a road, passengers on a flight, or tons of cargo on a train. However, the volume of traffic by itself may be a misleading indication of the true need for transportation, because it represents a need that is tempered by the availability of transportation services. Clearly, the traffic volume in a congested transportation facility that is operating at capacity cannot be taken as a manifestation of the true need for transportation, for it does not include additional traffic that might flow into the facility if additional capacity were available to carry it. If the addition of capacity leads to an increase in traffic volume, then obviously the potential traffic is greater than the traffic volume originally observed.

It can be seen from this example that a single measurement of traffic volume is not sufficient to express the need for transportation. What is required is to specify completely the different levels of volume that would occur at different service levels. For this reason, the concept of *demand* as it is understood in economic theory is adopted to express the need for transportation. In economics, demand is expressed by a series of numbers, referred to as a *demand schedule* or *function,* describing the levels of consumption of a particular good at various price levels. Transportation demand is defined in much the same way. To transport people and goods consumes time and energy, for which a cost is incurred. The traffic volumes that would occur at different levels of cost represent the demand for transportation. The evolution of specific volumes at specific transportation facilities represents an interaction of the demand for transportation with the service characteristics of these facilities. Such characteristics are often referred to as *supply* characteristics, and hence the notion of demand and supply interaction in transportation demand analysis. The economic concepts of demand and supply and their applicability to transportation demand analysis are discussed in greater detail in Chap. 2. It suffices to mention here that the demand for transportation results from the spatial interaction of socioeconomic activities and that the flow of traffic at transportation facilities results from the interaction of this demand with the supply, or service, characteristics of these facilities. Therefore, demand and volume are different things and should not, in general, be used synonymously.

The demand for transportation is usually defined for specific users and specific temporal and spatial settings. One may speak, for example, of the demand for transportation by commuters between two locations in an urban area during the average day of the week, or of the demand for daily shipment of food products from a growing area to a marketplace during a particular month of the year.

1.2 TRANSPORTATION DEMAND ANALYSIS

Transportation demand analysis is the process of relating the demand for transportation to the socioeconomic activities that generate it. In this process, the type, level, and location of human activities are related to the demand for movement of people and goods between the different points in space where these activities take place. The results of this analysis are relationships, often in the form of models, between measures of activity and measures of transport demand. Since, as mentioned in the preceding section, transportation demand is itself expressed by a relationship between traffic volumes and transportation cost characteristics, the results of transportation demand analysis become, then, relationships between traffic volumes, on the one hand, and transportation system characteristics and socioeconomic activity levels on the other. Such relationships are often referred to as *transportation demand models*. Their construction and use is discussed in detail in the following chapters.

It is important to note here that demand analysis is distinct from traffic forecasting. The main purpose of demand analysis is to achieve an understanding of the determinants of the demand and of the manner by which they interact and affect the evolution of traffic volumes. Whether one can use the results of demand analysis to forecast future traffic volumes will depend on the amount of confidence the forecaster has in understanding these effects and on the forecaster's ability to project the various exogenous factors that appear in a transportation demand model. It is true that demand models provide a major input into the forecasting process, but it should be recognized that there are limitations to their power as forecasting tools. The strength in forecasting is not in the models or procedures used, but in the methodology applied and in the logic used to project exogenous factors. The analyst might well find it reasonable to use models of demand analysis for short-term forecasting in order to study the impacts of changes in the demand and supply environments of transportation. But as the term of forecasting becomes longer, it is unlikely that the same models will continue to be of as much relevance.

Historic Perspective

Transportation demand anaylsis must be as old as organized transportation itself. The complex and elaborate networks constructed by ancient civilizations must have come about after some sort of analysis of transportation requirements. The formal study of the relationship between the distribution of resources and socioeconomic activities and the requirements of transportation is not a recent development either. As early as the middle of the nineteenth century, Kohl (1850) studied the relation between the geography of resources and the shape of transportation networks. In what might be considered the earliest formal transportation demand analysis, he discussed the impact of the characteristics of the then available technologies of transportation on traffic, thus recognizing the interaction between demand and supply. The earliest form of the now commonly known gravity model was suggested by Ravenstein (1885) for the study of migration patterns between cities and by Lille (1891) while analyzing railroad network planning. In the scientific tradition of his time, Lille proposed *the law of travel (das Reisegesetz)* to explain the interaction between point dispersed over space. Lille's law is also similar to the gravity model of spatial interaction, discussed in detail in Chap. 6.

During the first half of the century, a number of sociologists and social geographers contributed to the developments of transportation demand analysis. The works of Reilly (1929) on retail gravitation, Stewart (1948) on demographic gravitation, Stouffer (1940) on interaction over space, and Zipf (1946) on the gravity model of intercity travel represent the more significant contributions of the time and constitute a foundation that continues to underlie much of the work in demand analysis to this day. Two significant developments followed. The first, of particular relevance to urban transportation, dealt with explaining the relationship between urban land use and travel activities. Seminal in this regard was the work of Mitchell and Rapkin (1954). The relationship between land use and transportation continues to occupy a significant segment of the research community in the field, although the more recent developments in disaggregate, individual demand analysis seem to have overshadowed the land-use approach. The second significant development was probably spurred by the work of Beckmann, McGuire, and Winsten (1955). Here the microeconomic paradigm of demand and supply was articulated to include transportation. Equilibrium between demand and supply was explicitly modeled. This work provided a significant background to much of what followed in transportation demand analysis. The microeconomic ideas of demand continue to underlie most modern work in the field. Throughout this book, we shall see repeated reference to this idea, explicitly or implicitly. Chapter 2 attempts to introduce it and comment on its validity as a paradigm for the study of transportation.

The development of transportation planning as a distinct and major activity toward the middle of this century provided the medium for accelerated developments in transportation demand analysis. A number of large urban transportation studies carried out in cities of various sizes provided a sizable empirical base for further study of transportation demand and its relation to socioeconomic activities. Transportation demand models and land-use models were developed in tandem. In these urban studies, the emphasis was placed on passenger transportation; the study of commodity flows was to follow.

The more recent developments in demand analysis include numerous conceptual as well as analytical advances. First, and probably most significant, has been the adoption of what has become commonly known as the *behavioral approach*. Here the fundamental assumptions of microeconomic theory became explicit propellers of analytical developments. The traveler or shipper is considered a rational person attempting to maximize the utility that can be derived from socioeconomic activities including travel and transportation. Utility maximization models were now used to derive models of trip generation, of mode and route choice, and of shipper behavior. Travel demand need not be related directly to indicators of land use but can be derived directly from postulates regarding the user's socioeconomic characteristics and the set of activities available within the physical and economic environments. A closely related development, and one which follows logically, is the study of the quantification of human attitudes towards attributes of demand and supply. The main thrust of this work is attempting to quantify aspects of traveler behavior that have typically been considered strictly qualitative, such as psychological characteristics of the perception of transportation system attributes, and preferences that cannot be expressed on cardinal scales. The works of Hensher (1976), Nicolaidis, Wachs, and Golob (1977), Recker and Golob (1976), and Kitamura (1981) represent samples of the research that has become quite popular in recent years. There is no doubt that these attempts will lead to a better understanding of the nature of transportation demands; they will increase the explanatory power of demand models. The ability to quantify aspects of demand and utility have intrigued economists and social welfare students for decades, for our ability to quantify these will help us deal with problems of resource allocation that currently defy explicit solutions. However, it must be added that until our ability to project or forecast attitudes and preferences improves, the use of an attitudinal model for forecasting transportation demand and transportation impacts will not materialize. Whether we can expect to develop this ability or not is of course a matter of speculation and a subject of debate among social scientists. The transportation demand analysis methods that can be used in planning will always be limited by the state of the art in forecasting. However, this does not preclude the need for research into the nature of demand, for the best chance to improve forecasting ability is to improve the understanding of the phenomena to be forecast.

A second important feature of the recent developments in demand analysis is the recognition that travel and shipping decision processes have important random elements. Even if people behave in a rational manner and do so consistently, there will always be certain perturbations that cause behavior not to repeat itself exactly when the decision process is repeated. Either due to the inability of the modeling schemes to represent all causes of these perturbations, or because the behavior process itself is not very well defined, even in the mind of the decision maker, the models of demand now contain random elements. The incorporation of stochastic analysis into demand modeling and the introduction of probability and statistics as tools for the analysis have certainly advanced the state of the art. Recent advances in the methods of model estimation and validation, and in survey design, have reduced the costs of transportation studies and can be said to have improved the analyst's confidence in the prediction needed for planning. The works of Daganzo (1980), Lerman and Manski (1978), and McFadden (1974) are examples of the recent advances in the science of statistics and probability as applied to transportation demand analysis. Our statements about transportation are no longer laws as in the days of Lille, but they are qualified statements of probability that are based on empirical evidence and that explicitly recognize the limitations of generalization and conjecture.

Outlook for Transportation Demand Analysis

When thinking about the outlook for transportation demand analysis, two things come to mind. The first is that changes in the methodology and the process of transportation planning will occur and will continually alter the role that demand analysis plays in it. The second is that changes in the state of the art of demand analysis itself will always occur, partly as a consequence of its changing role in planning and partly due to the momentum that the recent analytical developments are likely to have.

If one were to characterize the recent changes in transportation planning processes simply, then one would select the most salient features, of which two suggest themselves. The first is that transportation planning, in most of its settings, has increasingly been recognized as a process that is primordially a political process. The contribution of analysis, whether quantitative or qualitative, is gauged by the ability to integrate the results of the analysis into the political debate which is at the heart of transportation planning. Gakenheimer (1976) characterizes the evolution of urban transportation planning and suggests that the current (in 1976) status then was one of stalemate in which the role of analyses was left in a rather questionable state. It is fair to say that more recently, the role of demand analysis has come to be recognized as simply one of providing analytical content to assessment of policies and to prediction of consequences. The results of the traffic forecast no longer play a central role in the decision-making process that shapes transportation actions, for decision makers have finally come to realize that the results of these forecasts are endogenous to their process and a subject of their decision making. The second, and interestingly related, fundamental change that has occurred recently in transportation planning is that in most settings the policy questions that arise have been altered by circumstances. In most settings one can find that the question of growth and expansion of transportation systems has taken a secondary position and that more of the concern of planners has been diverted to issues relating to expanding the capabilities of existing systems to cope with transportation requirements or to alter the demand by influencing some of its determinants. These changes can perhaps be attributed to two primary causes, even at the risk of oversimplifying an admittedly complex problem. One is that in some settings social awareness of some of the external impacts of transportation systems and transportation activities has risen to unprecedented levels. Society now more than ever before questions the wisdom of increasing the magnitude of transportation activities and systems in order to cope with unrestrained forecast demands. Typical of this has been the tendency in the United States to question the need for freeway construction in central urban areas. Another cause is that the more recent changes in the economic environment of many societies have forced them to rethink existing paradigms regarding transportation and its role in economic activities. Factor prices have altered making fundamental changes in the relative costs of activities. The ability to pay, and the wisdom of paying, transportation costs had to be reconsidered.

With the transportation planning process in a state of flux it is rather difficult to project the role that demand analysis and forecasting will play in the future. That transportation analysis will always play a role is unquestionable. The need will always exist for analysis to improve the planners' understanding of how transportation phenomena occur. The extent to which quantitative analysis will directly influence planning decisions is more elusive to project.

At the analytical level it is possible to anticipate some developments in the coming years by identifying those recent developments that have had, or are likely to have, significant impacts on methodological developments. Work on the statistical calibration of transport models with disaggregate data will probably continue in the near future. One can expect further improvements in traffic survey design and further reduction in the sizes of data bases, and hence reductions in the cost of transportation studies to result from these developments. This will probably be coupled with an increased dependence on inexpensive micro-computer technology. Much of the quantitative work involved in demand analysis will become a desk activity for the transportation planner, thereby facilitating the work itself and, more important, making it possible for the planner to test rapidly large numbers of scenarios, policy options, or structural hypotheses.

Whether totally new paradigms for travel analysis will emerge is not easy to predict. In urban passenger travel it is possible, and certainly desirable, that new approaches emerge. Until that happens it will not be possible to tell whether the marginal improvements achieved in the field represent the most that can be done. An area of promise is in the application of the concept of time budgets to travel analysis. Although by no means a recent development, it can be noted that this area has generated renewed interest in recent years. The work of Burns (1979), and Golob, Beckman, and Zahavi (1981) represents examples of a return to the idea that urban travel behavior occurs within a set of time, as well as budget constraints on human urban activities. These authors seek to identify regularities in the way by which urban travelers allocate their time to activities including transportation and in the way by which the spatial dimension affects this process. Much of the recent work in this area appears to build on the original work of Hägerstrand (1970), in which human activities are represented in a space-time framework. A potentially profitable extension of this type of work would be the application of scheduling ideas to travel behavior. This is particularly relevant now as many urban societies begin to look into options for temporal shifts in their activity patterns, such as the staggered work hour and the flextime options. An understanding of the manner by which human activities are scheduled might provide a very useful complement to the utility maximization paradigm in travel demand analysis.

The following chapters of this book present the various aspects of transportation demand analysis using its current state of the art and conceptual framework. The methods discussed in these chapters are by and large proven methods that have been used in some form of transportation analysis. The more recent methods presented may not have been applied in actual transportation planning activities, but they are much farther along than speculative ideas. The more novel methods of stochastic choice analysis or of multiregional input-output analysis applied to transportation represent methods that are just now becoming well known and entering the realm of application. This book should therefore be seen only as a starting point for setting new trends in transportation demand analysis.

REFERENCES

Beckmann, M., C. B. McGuire, and C. B. Winsten: "Studies in the Economics of Transportation," Yale University Press, New Haven, Conn., 1955.

Burns, L. D.: "Transportation, Temporal and Spatial Components of Accessibility," Lexington Books, Lexington, Mass., 1979.

Daganzo, C. F.: Optimal Sampling Strategies for Statistical Models with Discrete Dependent Variables, *Transp. Sci.,* vol. 14, no. 4, pp. 324–345, 1980.

Gakenheimer, R., and W. C. Wheaton: Priorities in Urban Transport Research, *Transportation,* vol. 5, no. 1, pp. 73–91, March 1976.

Golob, T., M. J. Beckmann, and Y. Zahavi: A Utility Theory Travel Demand Model Incorporating Travel Budgets, *Transp. Res.,* vol. 15B, no. 6, pp. 375–390, December 1981.

Hägerstrand, T.: What about People in Regional Science, *Papers Region. Sci. Assoc.,* no. 24, pp. 7–21, 1970.

Hensher, D.: Market Segmentation as a Mechanism in Allowing for Variability in Transportation Behaviour, *Transportation,* vol. 5, pp. 257–284, 1976.

Kitamura, R.: A Stratification Analysis in Work Trip Mode Choice, *Transp. Res.,* vol. 15A, pp. 473–485, 1981.

Kohl, J. G.: "Der Verkehr, und die Unsiedelungen der Menschen in Ihrer Abhangigkeit von der Gestaltung der Erdoberflache," Urnoldische Buchhandlung, Leipzig, 1850.

Lerman, S., and F. Manski: Sample Design for Discrete Choice Analysis of Travel Behavior: The State of the Art, U.S. Department of Transportation, Report DOT-TSC-UMTA-MA-06-0049-78-8, 1978.

Lille, E.: "Das Reisegesetz und Seine Anwendung in Eisenbahnfart," Commissions-Verlag von Spiegelhagen und Schurich, Vienna, 1891.

McFadden, D.: Conditional Logit Analysis of Qualitative Choice Behavior, in "Frontiers in Econometrics," ed. by P. Zarembka, Academic Press Inc., New York, pp. 105–142, 1974.

Mitchell, R. B., and C. Rapkin: "Urban Traffic, a Function of Land Use," Columbia University Press, New York, 1954.

Nicolaidis, G. C., M. Wachs, and T. F. Golob: Evaluation of Alternative Segmentation for Transportation Planning, *Transp. Res. Rec.*, no. 649, pp. 23–31, 1977.

Ravenstein, E. G.: The Laws of Migration, *J. Roy. Stat. Soc.*, vol. 48, pp. 167-227, 1885.

Recker, W., and T. F. Golob: An Attitudinal Mode Choice Model, *Transp. Res.*, vol. 10, pp. 299–310, 1977.

Reilly, W. J.: Methods of Study of Retail Relationships, University of Texas Bulletin, no. 2944, 1929.

Stewart, J. Q.: Demographic Gravitation, Evidence and Application, *Sociometry*, vol. 11, nos. 1, 2, pp. 32–58, 1948.

Stouffer, S. A.: Intervening Opportunities; a Theory Relating Mobility and Distance, *Am. Soc. Rev.*, vol. 5, no. 6, pp. 845–867, 1940.

Zipf, G. K.: The P^1P^2/D Hypothesis on the Intercity Movement of Persons, *Am. Soc. Rev.*, vol. 11, no. 6, pp. 677–686, 1946.

DEMAND THEORY

2.1 THE DEMAND FOR TRANSPORTATION

Consider the hypothetical situation in which there are two towns in a rural setting, separated by a distance of rugged, mountainous terrain, and not connected by a road or any other means of transport. The first of these towns A is an agricultural production center where a surplus of food products is generated. The second town B is an industrial town with no food production. It is easy to see that town B would make a good market in which to sell the food products produced at A, if it were possible to bring these products to B at a reasonable cost. In the situation as it is, an enterprising merchant, from either A or B, might carry a small quantity of highly prized food products, say on muleback, and transport them with rather great difficulty between A and B. The selling price of these commodities would have to be quite a bit higher than their price at the production center A in order to make up for the time the merchant has to spend on the journey and for the loss and deterioration of these food products that are incurred during the journey either due to their perishability or simply to the dangers of a long trek through the mountainous jungle. Consequently with the high selling price at B there will only be a few people who can afford, or who would be willing to pay for, the high price of the imported foodstuffs. Consider now a second situation in which a trail or clearing is established between A and B, such that it is now possible to use horse-drawn carriages for transport. The travel time is now cut in half from what it was in the muleback case, and the deterioration of products in transit is further reduced. It now pays for the merchant to reduce the selling price at B, and hence sell the foodstuffs to more people. The amount of traffic between A and B is increased. Consider now a third scenario in which a primitive road is built between the two towns in such a way as to permit small trucks to operate. This further reduces the transportation cost and permits the merchant (or by now merchants) to transport larger quantities at relatively lower costs. The selling price in *B* can now be reduced further, and more people will be able to buy the products. The traffic between *A* and *B* will again increase. One can now imagine further improvements to the road leading to further reductions in transport cost, and, as before, to increases in the traffic between *A* and *B*.

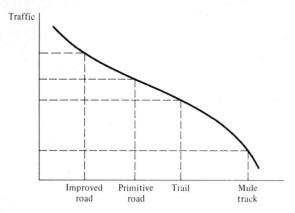

Figure 2.1 Effect of transportation system on traffic.

The evolution of traffic volume between *A* and *B* as described in this example can be shown graphically as in Fig. 2.1. The increase in traffic resulting from the improvement in the transportation system is a direct result of the increase in the amount sold at *B* that is brought about by the reduction in the selling price. Now if a traffic counter had been placed along the route between the two towns, the conclusion that would be drawn from the traffic counts in the first case would be that there is not much traffic between the two towns and that perhaps there is not much demand for transportation. As the road is built and improved, the observer will be forced to change the conclusions and, in the last case, may in fact have to admit that the demand for transportation between the towns is indeed high. This suggests that the demand for transportation between *A* and *B* depends on the type of transportation system that connects them and that demand can be increased by improving it. This conclusion is wrong and demonstrates the danger of confusing traffic flow with demand.

This example serves to illustrate the following fundamental aspects of transportation demand.

Demand and Traffic Are Two Different Things

The curve shown in Fig. 2.1 represents one demand condition but many traffic conditions. If we were to convert the horizontal axis of the figure to represent the "cost" of transportation (the cost is reduced as the transportation system is improved), then we would see that the curve represents a relationship between traffic volume and transportation cost (see Fig. 2.2). As the cost is reduced, the traffic volume increases, and vice versa. It is this relationship that reflects the demand for transportation and not any of the single traffic volume values, for it is easy to see that any such single value could come from an unlimited number of curves such as the one shown.

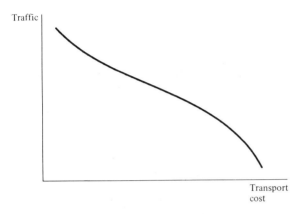

Figure 2.2 Effect of generalized cost on traffic.

We can then define the demand for transportation as a potential for traffic flow. This potential is itself related to the production and consumption activities at A and B, or indeed, in general, to any socioeconomic activities.

The "transportation cost" to which we converted the horizontal axis of Figure 2.1 is a very generic cost and includes all the attributes that in this particular case make for the difficulty of transporting the foodstuff between A and B. It includes the actual money cost of transportation when relevant, the value of the time involved, the deterioration of the commodities being shipped, and the discomfort and inconvenience of the journey; it is usually referred to as *generalized cost*, a term which is defined in greater detail in the next chapter. It suffices now to think of it as a resistance to the movement between A and B. With demand defined as a potential and transportation cost thought of as a resistance, we can now draw an analogy with electric circuits; the actual amount of traffic flowing between A and B (the current) is resulting from the interaction between a demand (potential) and a transport cost (resistance). This analogy is helpful in understanding the concept of transportation demand but is of limited value when attempting to characterize this phenomenon in a behavioral economic way.

Transportation Demand Is a Derived Demand

While the volume of traffic on the road between A and B is affected by the condition of the road and by the transportation cost, it is also affected by the market for foodstuffs in B. Indeed, if the demand for these products in B is low or nonexistent, then there would be no traffic flow between A and B, no matter what improvements are made to the road. Likewise, for the same road conditions, given by any particular location on the horizontal axis of Fig. 2.2, more or less traffic will flow, depending on the amount of demand for foodstuffs that exists in B. For this reason, we say that the demand for transportation between A and B is *derived* from the demand in B for foodstuffs imported from A. Indeed, there is little point in transporting these commodities simply for the sake of transportation, no matter how inexpensive this might be.

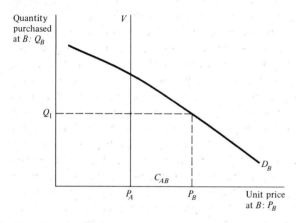

Figure 2.3 Relation between the demands for a commodity and for its transportation.

To see how the demand curve for transportation can be deduced directly from the demand for the goods themselves at B, consider the curve D_B as shown in Fig. 2.3. This curve represents the demand at B for the goods and is a relation between the quantity purchased Q_B and the unit price of the goods P_B. To convert this to a relationship between the amount transported V and the cost of transportation C_{AB}, we need simply recall that the price at B must equal the price at A plus the transportation cost,

$$P_B = P_A + C_{AB} \tag{2.1}$$

Thus by translating the vertical axis in Fig. 2.3 by an amount equal to P_A which we can assume constant for this example, we obtain a relation where the quantity shipped V is given as a function of the cost of transportation C_{AB}. Algebraically, if we let the demand for the goods in B be given by a function

$$Q_B = Q(P_B) \tag{2.2}$$

and if we define the demand for transportation by another function

$$V_{AB} = V(C_{AB}) \qquad (2.3)$$

then it is evident from Fig. 2.3 that the following relation exists always:

$$V(C_{AB}) = Q(P_A + C_{AB}) \qquad (2.4)$$

which means that knowledge of the demand for goods $Q(\cdot)$ is sufficient to which determine the demand for transportation $V(\cdot)$.

In a more realistic situation, the relationship between the demand functions $Q(\cdot)$ and $V(\cdot)$ may be more complex than this, depending on the structure of the market for the products and the marketing process used. In complex market conditions, transport flows of commodities often are the result of an optimization process in which a producer, or producers, tries to achieve an objective such as maximizing net revenues. Analysis of these situations in described in Chap. 10.

The relationship between transportation demand and the demand for socio-economic activities can be extended to all forms of transportation, whether it be transportation of goods or of people. The demand for shopping trips in an urban area is derived from the demand for shopping, air travel demand for vacation trips is derived from the demand for recreation at particular destinations, and so forth.

Because of this strong relationship between the demand for transportation and the demand for socioeconomic activities, it is essential for the study of transport demand to develop an understanding of the way in which the phenomena of demand arise and to develop a methodology for their analysis. For this purpose the classical approach of microeconomics is adopted and then modified as appropriate for its application in transportation. The remainder of this chapter is devoted to a brief introduction to microeconomic demand theory and to its application to transportation demand.

2.2 MICROECONOMIC DEMAND THEORY

In microeconomic theory, demand is approached at two levels: an individual level, referred to as *consumer demand,* and an aggregate level, referred to as *market demand.* The latter is obtained simply by aggregating, or summing, all individual consumer demands, although it is often studies directly at an aggregate level without explicit attention to individual consumers. This dichotomy is important in applying demand theory to transportation: individual demand analysis may be useful when the application deals with microscopic prediction of individual traveler behavior in a transportation system, and aggregate market demand is useful when predicting the behavior of total transportation systems in a microscopic way. This distinction, often referred to as aggregate versus disaggregate modeling of transport demand, is more important in the case of urban transportation where microscopic analysis is common.

Consumer Demand

The term *consumer* is defined either by an individual who is independently making decisions about the amounts of the various commodities available to consume during a specific period of time, or a household who for all practical purposes can be assumed to make these decisions as one unit. The theory is concerned with understanding and characterizing the factors that affect consumption behavior, with the purpose of developing demand relationships for all commodities of interest. The following basic assumptions are made in consumer demand theory:

1. The consumer has a choice. In an environment where people do not have choices as to the way they wish to spend their resources on consumption goods, there would be little need for a demand theory to predict such choice. Choice in this regard means that the consumer can vary the amounts of the various commodities consumed and can vary the amount of money out of the total budget that is to be spent on particular commodities or groups of commodities. For example, the consumer can purchase and consume more food and less clothing, more recreational trips and less food, and so forth.

2. Every consumption good possesses certain characteristics that give utility, or satisfaction, to the consumer. These utilities are different for different consumers and are usually thought of as returns from the consumption process. It is important to note that it is these characteristics of the goods rather than the goods themselves that are assumed to generate the utility. This concept is relevant in the application of the theory to transportation, for then it implies, for example, that it is not the specific modes or routes of a trip that are subject to choice, but that their characteristics such as travel time and travel cost are. This concept, referred to as *abstract commodities,* is from Lancaster (1969) and its application to transportation is seen at various locations in the following chapters.

3. The consumer has a consistent preference structure that is based on the relative utilities of the various goods available. This preference structure applies to goods that are alternatives in the sense that the consumption of one does not necessarily imply the consumption of another in a given proportion. Goods for which the consumption pattern is defined in terms of the relative quantities are usually grouped together and referred to as *bundles of goods.* The choice then becomes one between these bundles. The economic terms used to describe these two situations are *competitive goods* for the situation where a choice truly exists between consumption alternatives and *complementary goods* in the other case. In transportation one can talk about the choice between automobile trips and bus trips as competitive modes, whereas when dealing with air travel, air trips and airport access trips are bundled together as complementary.

Preference is defined on the basis of the utility that each good, or bundle of goods, gives to the consumer. It does not imply directly that the consumer always chooses the good with the higher utility, for the choice is affected by the prices of the alternatives and by the budget of the consumer. The preference structure is assumed to be consistent, in the sense that it is stable over some period of time, and transitive. Stability implies that if one good is preferred over another, then this will continue to be the case, except if changes occur in the characteristics of the consumer. Usually one talks of the preference structure of an individual of given socioeconomic characteristics (such as age and income). In transportation it is easy to see how the preferences of travelers, e.g., with respect to mode choices, may be affected by their socioeconomic characteristics. Stability implies that as long as an individual belongs to a particular socioeconomic group, the relative utilities of goods will not change and hence the preference will remain the same. Another assumption of consistency is transitivity, which implies that relative preference can be transferred from one group of goods to another. For example, given three goods X, Y, and Z, the preference of X over Y and Y over Z directly implies the preference of X over Z.

4. The consumer is assumed to be insatiable. This means that for any given goods, more is always better than less. The utility function describing the manner by which the utility accrues from consumption cannot be decreasing. Realistically, this cannot be interpreted to mean that a consumer will in fact consume an unlimited quantity of a good. What it means is that given the choice between two quantities of the same goods the consumer will always opt for the larger quantity. In reality, the issue of infinite consumption does not arise, since budget and time constraints will always provide a meaningful bound. This is particularly the case in transportation where, notwithstanding the budgetary limits on the cost of travel, the time consumed is also limited.

5. The choice of the consumer is limited by a budget constraint. Consumption of goods requires the expenditure of money and possibly other resources such as time. The consumer does not possess an unlimited supply of these resources and consequently does not have an unlimited choice. Given a group of goods from among which the consumer is making a choice, and given a limit on the amount of money and time that the consumer is able to allocate to this group of goods, the consumer will choose a combination of goods that will maximize the utility without violating any of the budgetary constraints that are present. It is from this basic principle of consumption behavior that most demand relationships are derived. How this is done is the subject of the remainder of this chapter and of much of what follows later on.

Preference and indifference The preference relationship between goods cannot be discussed without reference to particular quantities of these goods. For example, consider the case of two goods X and Y. A consumer will always relate a particular quantity x of X to a particular quantity y of Y and will either prefer one over the other or be indifferent between them. Thus the analysis of preference deals with quantities of goods, although there is no need for these quantities to be measured in any particular system of units. But one can still speak of comparing, e.g., 5 kg of oranges with one pair of shoes, or six shopping trips by bus with one trip to the movies by automobile. The specific units used are not very important, particularly since these units can always be converted into monetary terms by multiplying each by the unit price.

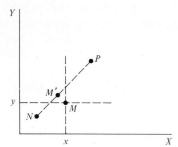

Figure 2.4 Generation of two points of indifference.

Returning to the example of two goods X and Y, the quantities consumed of these goods can be represented on a two-dimensional diagram (x, y) which is referred to as a *consumption field* (see Fig. 2.4). Any point in this field, such as point M, would then represent a given combination of quantities x and y of the two goods in question. This combination of goods (x, y) gives the consumer a certain level of consumption utility which is the combined utility of the two quantities. It is easy to see that any point in the consumption field which represents more of both X and Y would be preferred to point M and that, conversely, M would be preferred to any point that represents less of both. It is possible then to say definitely that point P is preferred to point M and that point M is preferred to point N, i.e.,

$$P > M > N \qquad (2.5)$$

In moving within the field from a point in the lower left-hand quadrant, such as N, to a point in the upper right-hand quadrant, such as P, one would then be moving from a point inferior to M to a point superior to it. Somewhere along this path, then, there must be a point such as M' which is equivalent to M. Such a point would represent a combination of goods X and Y that is neither preferred to M nor inferior to it. At this point we say that the consumer is *indifferent* between the two choices, in the sense that the consumer considers these two points completely exchangeable in all respects. Tracing the locus of all such points in the consumption field (X, Y) results in a line referred to as the *indifference curve*. Such a curve is shown as curve I in Fig. 2.5.

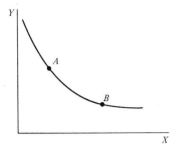

Figure 2.5 Indifference curve between goods X and Y.

What the indifference curve shows, then, are all the combinations of X and Y among which the consumer is indifferent. In other words any two points along curve I in Fig. 2.5, such as points A and B, will lead to exactly the same utility to the consumer.

It is also useful to think of the indifference curve as the trace of a three-dimensional function $U(x, y)$ which gives the utility of consumption in terms of the quantities of goods X and Y. Any one indifference curve would represent the projection on the consumption field of a given value of U. The indifference curve is thus referred to also as an *isoutility curve*.

For goods of which more is always better or at least as good as less, the indifference curve would always be convex to the origin in the consumption field. Consequently, it would also follow that indifference curves will not cross. A consumption field on which a number of indifference curves are shown would then look as shown in Fig. 2.6. The farther from the origin an indifference curve is, the larger is the utility implied, Thus curves $I_1, I_2, \ldots, I_n$ have the following preference relationship:

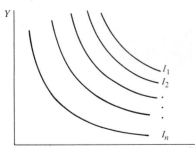

Figure 2.6 A consumer's indifference map.

$$I_1 > I_2 \cdots > I_n \tag{2.6}$$

Such a representation is referred to as an *indifference*, or *utility*, *map*, and describes completely the preference structure of the consumer with respect to the two goods in question. The map also describes the manner by which the consumer is willing to substitute one good for another; consider, for example, curve I_1 in Fig. 2.6. The slope of that curve represents the relative rate of change of y and x, and can be represented by either dx/dy or dy/dx. This slope is called the *marginal rate of substitution* and has the interpretation as the number of units of X that the consumer is willing to give up in order to receive one unit of Y, or vice versa, while maintaining the same level of consumption utility. Now, let $U(x, y)$ be the utility function, and let the constant utility generated at indifference curve I_1 be given by $U(x, y) = U_1$. Since U is constant, then the total derivative of U must vanish:

$$dU(x, y) = dU_1 = 0 \qquad (2.7)$$

$$dU(x, y) = \frac{\partial U}{\partial x} dx + \frac{\partial U}{\partial y} dy = 0 \qquad (2.8)$$

which gives

$$\frac{\partial U/\partial x}{\partial U/\partial y} = -\frac{dx}{dy} \qquad (2.9)$$

which says that the marginal rate of substitution between two goods is equal to the ratio of their marginal utilities. The *marginal utility* of a good is the rate of change of utility with the quantity consumed of that good. Since the assumption of insatiability implies that the marginal utility of any good is always non-negative, the result in Eq. (2.9) implies that the marginal rate of substitution is negative, which is expected since the consumer will always give up some of one good for some of the other but never both at the same time.

It will be useful to extend this example to the general case where there are n goods X_i $(i = 1, 2, \ldots, n)$. The consumption utility function $U(\cdot)$ is now an n-dimensional function

$$U(X) = U(x_1, x_2, \ldots, x_n)$$

The indifference map in this case is a map in an n-dimensional space Ω in which every point is defined by the consumption vector $X = \{x_1, x_2, \ldots, x_n\}$. For a given level of utility $U(X) = U_0$, the locus of all points X defines an indifference surface for which Eq. (2.9) also holds for every pair of commodities. To see this consider that at $U(X) = U_0$, a constant,

$$dU(X) = dU_0 = 0$$

$$= \sum_i \frac{\partial U}{\partial x_i} dx_i \qquad (2.10)$$

Holding all x_i fixed except two, say x_m and x_n, then

$$0 = \frac{\partial U}{\partial x_m} dx_m + \frac{\partial U}{\partial x_n} dx_n \qquad (2.11)$$

which is the same as the result in Eq. (2.9).

It is important to note that the utility function is assumed to have certain regularity properties, including differentiability at all points. In particular, the assumption of insatiability implies that $\partial U / \partial x_i \geq 0$ for all i. In addition it is normally assumed that the second derivatives of U, $\partial^2 U / \partial x_i\, \partial x_k$, exist and are continuous for all i and k. The second derivative may have any sign, although a common assumption is that it is negative, implying that marginal utility from consumption is decreasing.

Choice under a budget constraint The choice of a consumption pattern is not solely determined by the indifference map of a consumer. Indeed, if this were the case, then the assumption of insatiability would imply infinite consumption of all goods under consideration. The choice is normally constrained by a number of limitations on the resources required for the consumption activity. Most important of these are the budget constraints that limit the amount of money a consumer can, or will, allocate to a group of goods. Other limitations include the time available and in some cases the space available. It is common to consider the monetary budget constraints only in microeconomic demand theory, since these are usually the most critical ones. In applying the theory to transportation other constraints become important and cannot be ignored, for example, the time spent in transportation is usually limited and its limitations affect travel demand. As we shall see further on, time can be either considered by itself or incorporated into monetary budget constraints by transforming it into money terms using the concept of the value of travel time.

Assuming that all prevailing limitations can be represented by the monetary budget constraint for the purpose of exposition, we can look at the process by which the consumer chooses a consumption pattern. Given a vector of unit costs $\mathbf{P} = \{p_1, p_2, \ldots, p_n\}$, which represents for each good the cost of acquiring one unit, and given a total budget B that the consumer can or will allocate to the group of goods in question, only consumption vectors that satisfy

$$\sum_i x_i p_i \leq B \qquad \text{or} \qquad \mathbf{PX} \leq B \qquad (2.12)$$

can be chosen. In other words, the total amount of money spent on a consumption vector $\mathbf{X}$ cannot exceed the budget B. If we consider the n-dimensional preference space Ω, then we can see that Eq. (2.12) divides this space into two regions, one feasible region where choice can occur and one infeasible region where the budget constraint prohibits choice. The insatiability assumption implies that in order to maximize the utility of consumption, the consumer needs to maximize consumption itself. Since the utility function is assumed to be continuous and differentiable with respect to all x_i, it follows that the consumer will choose a vector $\mathbf{X}^*$ for which Eq. (2.12) becomes

$$\sum_i x_i^* p_i = B \qquad (2.13)$$

Depending on the exact shape of the U function, there may be one or more such $\mathbf{X}^*$ vectors. In general, with the assumption of a strictly convex utility function and with the implied assumption of constant unit costs p_i, there is a unique vector which meets the condition of Eq. (2.13). This vector is referred to as the *optimal consumption vector,* which represents the actual consumer choice implied by all the assumptions made so far regarding consumer behavior.

To arrive at the same result in a more formal way we restate the basic principle of consumer choice under a budget constraint as follows: given a vector of goods from which a consumer is to chose, a utility function $U(X)$, and given a vector of unit costs $\mathbf{P}$ and a budget $B,$ the consumer will chose that vector of goods $\mathbf{X}^*$ which will maximize $U(X)$ subject to the constraint $\mathbf{PX} = B$. The analytical formulation of this principle is to construct a lagrangian L:

$$L = U(x_1, x_2, \ldots, x_n) - \lambda \sum_i p_i x_i \qquad (2.14)$$

where λ is a Lagrange multiplier. The derivatives of L must vanish at $\mathbf{X}^*$, so that

$$\left. \frac{\partial U}{\partial x_i} \right|_{x_i = x_i^*} - \lambda p_i = 0 \qquad i = 1, 2, \ldots, n \qquad (2.15)$$

which implies that for a consumption vector $\mathbf{X}$ to be optimal from the consumer's point of view, it should satisfy the relationship

$$\frac{\partial U}{\partial x_i} = \lambda p_i \qquad i = 1, 2, \ldots, n \qquad (2.16)$$

for any good for which a nonzero consumption quantity x_i exists. This means that the choice will be made in such a way that the marginal utility of each good is proportional to its unit cost. This relationship can also be translated by dividing Eq. (2.16) for one good i by the same equation for another good k:

$$\frac{\partial U / \partial x_i}{\partial U / \partial x_k} = \frac{p_i}{p_k} \qquad \text{for all } i \text{ and } k \qquad (2.17)$$

Recognizing the left-hand side of Eq. (2.17) as the ratio of marginal utilities which from Eq. (2.9) is equal to the marginal rate of substitution, the following general result is obtained: the optimal consumption vector of a consumer is chosen such that the marginal rate of substitution between any pair of goods is equal to the ratio of their unit costs.

To illustrate this result in a more concrete way, we revert back to the two-good example. Consider a consumer in a situation where there are only two goods X_1 and X_2. A utility function $U(x_1, x_2)$ can, as before, be traced by indifference curves as on Fig. 2.5. Let the unit cost vector $\mathbf{P} = \{p_1, p_2\}$ represent the unit costs of goods X_1 and X_2, respectively. Note that the use of the notation $\mathbf{P}$ for unit cost is because in most cases in consumption analysis these unit costs to the consumer are the prices of the respective goods. We are using the term *cost* rather than price in order to permit a generalization which is important in the application to transportation, as we shall see later on.

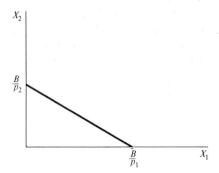

Figure 2.7 A budget line with fixed unit prices.

If the consumer has a budget B allocated to these two commodities, then the optimal choice would be made in such a way that $p_1x_1 + p_2x_2 = B$. This budget constraint can be shown graphically on an indifference map as in Fig. 2.7. It is a line with intercepts B/p_1 and B/p_2, respectively, showing the quantities that could be obtained if the whole budget were spent on X_1 and X_2. Thus, the line, referred to as a *budget line,* has a slope which is equal to the ratio of the prices p_1/p_2. It divides the indifference region into two subregions, one to the upper right side, which is the infeasible or unaffordable region, and the other to the lower left side, which is the feasible or affordable region. If we now combine the indifference map of Fig. 2.6 with the budget line of Fig. 2.7 as shown in Fig. 2.8, then we can see the graphic interpretation of the optimality conditions of Eq. (2.17).

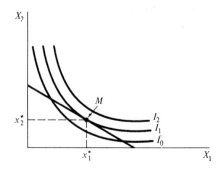

Figure 2.8 Optimal consumption pattern with two goods.

Figure 2.8 shows that I_1 is the highest indifference curve that can be reached without leaving the feasible budget region. It can also be seen that any point on that indifference curve other than its tangency point with the budget line will fall in the infeasible region and will imply a total consumption cost that exceeds the budget. This tangency point M represents the optimal consumption choice (x_i^*, x_2^*) that is represented by indifference curve I_1.

Changes in income and in price If the income of the consumer increases so that it is possible to augment the amount B, then changes will occur in the optimal consumption pattern. An increase in the budget, say from B to B' as shown on Fig. 2.9, will result in a shift of the budget line without a change in its slope, as

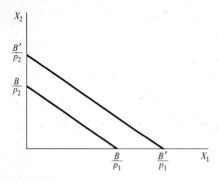

Figure 2.9 Increase in income or in budget.

long as the unit costs remain unchanged. In general, such an increase will result in changes in all quantities x_i, but the direction of such changes cannot be determined a priori without knowledge of the indifference map. Two situations can be illustrated using the two-good example. These are shown in Figs. 2.10 and

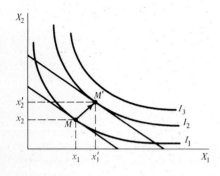

Figure 2.10 Income effect with two normal goods.

2.11. In the first situation (Fig. 2.10) an increase in the budget from B to B' results in an increase in the quantities of both goods, as indicated by the displacement of the optimality point from $M(x_1, x_2)$ to $M'(x_1', x_2')$. With the increased budget the consumer can afford a higher utility level, as indicated by the shift from indifference curve I_1 to I_2. In the second situation (Fig. 2.11) the same

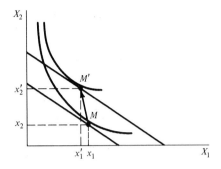

Figure 2.11 Income effect with one inferior good.

increase in budget results in an increase in the quantity consumed of goods X_2 but a decrease in the quantity of X_1. This is shown by the displacement from M (x_1, x_2) to $M'(x_1', x_2')$, where x_1' is less than x_1 and is obviously the result of the shapes of the indifference curves in this case. From the slope of these curves it can be seen that the marginal utility of good X_2 is considerably higher than that of X_1 and that along any one indifference curve, the consumer would give up a considerable amount of X_1 in return for a relatively small amount of X_2. In such a case, it is customary to refer to X_1 as an *inferior good* and to X_2 as a *normal good*. This definition is only relevant when comparing goods and is a measure of the relative marginal utilities. As we shall see later on, a more general definition of inferior and normal goods is based on the so-called income elasticities of the demand.

It should come as no surprise that the consumption of some goods might decrease if the income of the consumer increases. This is particularly relevant in transportation demand analysis when dealing with the demand for bus transportation as an alternative to auto transportation. In the example of Fig. 2.11, X_1 could very well represent the number of bus trips made by a consumer during a given period of time and X_2 the number of auto trips. It is common for people to reduce their utilization of public transportation and increase their private auto use as their incomes increase.

If the consumer's income and budget remain unchanged but the prices of the commodities do change in such a way that their relative values remain the same, then an effect exactly similar to that of income change will take place. This can easily be seen by considering the two-good example. If the prices of X_1 and X_2 change in the same proportion, then their relative values will remain the same. This means that the price ratio, which is the slope of the budget line, will not change. What will change are the intercept points B/p_1 and B/p_2, giving the same effect as that shown in Fig. 2.9.

If the price of only one good changes while that of the other remains the same, then the effect that takes place will be different from the previous case. The change in one price will alter the relative prices of the goods in question. As seen in Fig. 2.12, the slope of the budget line changes, with the intercept point B/p_1 increasing as p_1 declines.

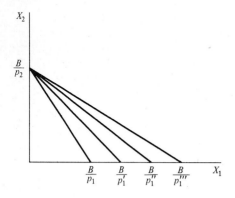

Figure 2.12 Effect on budget line of price change.

The effect of such a price change on the consumption pattern can be illustrated by the diagram in Fig. 2.13. As the price X_1 falls, the budget line RS rotates

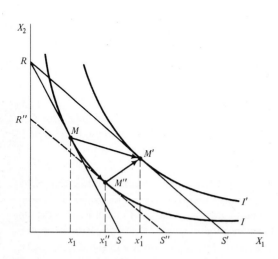

Figure 2.13 The combination of income and substitution effects.

to RS', where S' represents the new, higher intercept point on the X_1 axis. The decrease in price thus shifts the budget line to the left and enables the consumer to achieve a higher utility level, as indicated by the shift of the optimal consumption point M on indifference curve I to M' on indifference curve. I'. This movement from M to M' implies that the consumption of at least one of the goods increases, but not necessarily of both. To see why this is the case, we consider resolving the movement from M to M' into two components. The first component is represented by shifting the budget line to $R''S''$, which has the same slope as the line RS', thus incorporating the effect of the change of price but which is tangent to the first indifference curve I. The second component is obtained by shifting the new line $R''S''$ parallel to iself up to RS'. The first component would result from compensating the decrease in the price of X_1 in such a way as to keep the consumer on the same indifference curve I, the implication being that the compensation will leave the consumer with the same purchasing power. The effect of this component is to move the consumption point from M to M'', clearly indicating a shift from X_2 to X_1. This is referred to as the *substitution effect,* which always results in an increase in the consumption of the good whose price has fallen relatively. The second component is a translation of the budget line from $R''S''$ to RS', which is equivalent to an increase in income. The effect of this shift, referred to as the *income effect,* is to move the consumption point from M'' to M'. Whether this will result in an increase in the consumption of one or both of the goods depends on their relative utilities and can be determined as in Figs. 2.10 and 2.11. In this particular case the shift from M'' to M' causes an increase in both x_1 and x_2, implying that both goods are normal.

In Fig. 2.14a and b is shown a situation where good X_1 is inferior, and consequently the income effect results in a decrease in x_1. Two conditions can

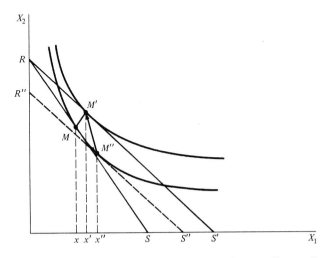

Figure 2.14a The case of an inferior good. (a) Income effect smaller than substitution effect.

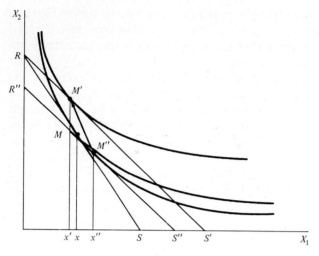

Figure 2.14b The case of an inferior good. (b) Substitution effect smaller than income effect.

arise here. The first, in Fig. 2.14a, is when the substitution effect is larger than the income effect, so that there is a net increase in x_1. This can be seen by comparing the substitution effect $(x'' - x)$, which is positive, to the income effect $(x' - x'')$, which is negative. The first is larger than the second with the net result that x_1 will increase. The second condition, in Fig. 2.14b, is when the opposite is true, so that the substitution effect $(x'' - x)$ is less than the income effect $(x' - x'')$, resulting in a net decrease in x_1. It may appear curious that the consumption of a good decreases despite the fact that its price has fallen. This phenomenon is referred to as the *Giffen paradox*, which occurs when a good is strongly inferior with respect to another. Again, the formalization of the definition of inferiority in this case can be made using the values of income elasticity and price elasticity, as we shall see later on. The Giffen paradox, where the consumption of a good decreases with a lower price or increases with a higher price, may occur in transportation when comparing public and private modes of travel. It is sometimes argued that reducing the price of urban transit travel can cause a decrease in ridership, since potential travelers might allocate the increased purchasing power caused by the price decrease to acquire and use private means of transportation. The extent to which this is true in general is uncertain. What is more likely is the situation in Fig. 2.14a, where the income effect is smaller than the substitution effect. The same, or similar, phenomena do occur in air transportation where consumers may be faced with choices among different services at different prices. The income effect in the case of low-excursion-fare travel may or may not be smaller than the substitution effect, and the effect of changing the relative prices of different fare packages may not be obvious without a detailed study of the demand. (See Chap. 9.)

It should be relatively easy to see from Fig. 2.14 that proportionate changes in all prices and income will result in no change in the optimal consumption patterns. The price increases will tend to reduce consumption of all goods available, and the income increase will have the opposite effect. If these changes are proportionate, i.e., if all variables change by the same factor, then the effects will cancel out and no change will occur in the optimal consumption pattern. This property is quite fundamental when deriving demand functions using the utility maximization principle. It implies that when the utility functions are smooth and differentiable, the demand functions are homogenous. This is an important property, as we shall see later on in this chapter.

Consumer demand functions With this basic theory of consumer behavior we can now proceed to a formal definition of a demand function. Looking back at any of Figs. 2.10 to 2.14 we can see that the actual quantity of a good, say x_1, that is consumed depends on the location of point M. This in turn depends on the price, not only of X_1 but also of the other good in question X_2. The location of M also depends on the budget level B and on the exact shape of the indifference curves, or the utility function $U(X)$. Any functional relationship that would give the quantity consumed x_i of any good i in terms of all these factors is called a *demand function* for good i. In general it is not necessary to include all these terms explicitly in the demand function. Since we know from theory that the following condition must be satisfied

$$\frac{\partial U}{\partial x_i} = \lambda p_i \qquad (2.18)$$

we can eliminate the explicit reference to $U(X)$ in the demand function and presume that the prices in the demand function will suffice. The constant parameters of the demand function will implicitly include $\partial U / \partial x_i$ or some function of it. The demand function becomes then a relationship between the quantity x_i and the prices of all goods, the income or budget, and a set of parameters that stands for the utility function of the individual consumer:

$$x_i = X_i (B, p_1, p_2, \ldots, p_n) \qquad (2.19)$$

where X_i is a well-defined function for each good i and for an individual consumer with a given utility function. A very fundamental property of demand is shown in this function. The demand for a good i is not only a function of its cost but also of the costs of all other goods that can be considered substitutes. This property is quite relevant when applying this theory to transportation demands. The demand for air traffic is not independent of the cost of driving; the demand for urban mass transit is not unrelated to the price of gasoline that an auto driver would incur; the demand for rail transportation of commodities is not independent of the rate structure of the trucking system, and so forth.

The concept of demand function can be illustrated graphically by looking at two-dimensional projections. The most commonly used such projection is the cost consumption curve which shows the relation between x_i and p_i for fixed values of all other variables. For a normal good, the cost consumption curve would be decreasing, which is the most common form of demand functions.

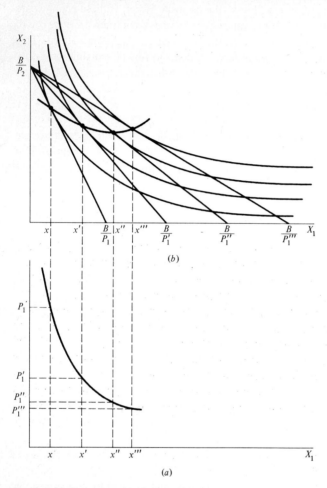

Figure 2.15 Generation of price-consumption curve.

Figure 2.15 shows how such a curve can be derived from the indifference map by varying the cost of the good. In Fig. 2.15a, an indifference map is shown for the two-good example. With a given budget B the optimal consumption point M changes as the cost p_1 of X_1 changes. The locus of all such points M is the curve from which a cost consumption relationship can be extracted as shown in Fig. 2.15b. Note that the consumption curve for X_2 as affected by the cost of X_1 could just as easily have been generated from the same diagram in Fig. 2.15a.

Characterization of consumer demand functions We shall limit the discussion in this section to demand functions represented as relationships between a quantity x_i, unit cost p_i, and income I or budget B, assuming all other factors fixed. This will facilitate graphic interpretation of the concepts. Demand as a relationship between quantity and cost can be characterized by specifying a functional form. This is usually done empirically by analyzing statistics of x, p, and the other variables involved. Normally, socioeconomic characteristics of the consumer are introduced as proxies for the budget B and for the utility functions. The sensitivity of demand with respect to any of these variables can then be measured by the derivative of this function with respect to the variable. Another measure of the sensitivity of the demand function is the elasticity which is defined with respect to any variable v in the function as

$$e_v = \frac{\partial x / x}{\partial v / v} = \frac{\partial \log x}{\partial \log v} \tag{2.20}$$

which graphically would be the slope of the demand curve if it were drawn on logarithmic scales. The advantage of elasticity over the ordinary derivative is that it is dimensionless and independent of the units used for x or any of the variables in the function. This facilitates comparison of the sensitivities of the demand to any of the factors that affect it. When v is the cost, then elasticity is referred to as the *cost elasticity* or *price elasticity:*

$$e_i = \frac{\partial x_i / x_i}{\partial p_i / p_i} \tag{2.21}$$

When v is the consumer's income I, then the elasticity

$$e_I = \frac{\partial x_i / x_i}{\partial I / I} \tag{2.22}$$

is referred to as the *income elasticity,* and so forth. One can define the elasticity with respect to any variable in the demand function.

What the elasticity shows is the ratio of the percentage changes of demand and the variable in question, but only for small percentage changes. Thus as the price of a normal good i increases by 1 percent, then the quantity consumed will decrease by e_i percent. Note that for a normal good the price elasticity is negative and the income elasticity positive. For an inferior good, income elasticity may be negative, as explained by the situation in Fig. 2.11. The price elasticity of an inferior good may be positive, although as mentioned earlier this does not occur frequently.

When the demand function for a good contains explicit reference to the characteristics of other substitutes, the elasticity of the demand with respect to any of these is referred to as a *cross-elasticity*. Thus we can talk of the elasticity of the demand for good i with respect to the unit cost of good j as a cross-elasticity. In transportation this is a useful definition when there are alternative transportation options, such as modes, for which there are specific demand function. For example, it is common in urban transportation to formulate the demand function for, say, automobile trips on the basis of not only the attributes of automobile travel (time, cost, etc.) but also the relevant attributes of alternatives such as bus and rail travel. Thus, in transportation, unlike other microeconomic applications, cross-elasticities are not limited to price variables but apply to all relevant attributes of the system.

Thus, using the notation of Eq. (2.19), we can see that the cross-elasticity of the demand for good i can be defined with respect to the cost p_j of any of the substitute goods j as follows:

$$e_{ij} = \frac{\partial x_i / x_i}{\partial p_j / p_j} \qquad (2.23)$$

In a transportation application, this might, for example, refer to the cross-elasticity of the demand for air trips with respect to the price of competing bus services or with the cross-elasticity of the demand for automobile trips in a urban area with respect to the fare charged on an alternative rail transit system. Normally, then, one would expect these cost cross-elasticities to be positive due to the substitution effect. Cross-elasticities can be expected to be positive when goods are true substitutes for one another, so that if the price of one increases, then the consumption of the other will also increase.

When the elasticity is less than unity, demand is said to be *relatively elastic*. These definitions apply to elasticity taken in its absolute value and are the same regardless if one is speaking of a positive (e.g., income) elasticity or a negative (price) elasticity.

Some basic properties of consumer demand functions Demand functions that are derived by maximizing utility subject to a budget constraint must satisfy some basic properties that arise from the optimization process. First, the budget constraint itself can be written in terms of the demand functions of Eq. (2.19):

$$\sum_i p_i x_i(B, p_1, p_2, \ldots, p_n) = B \qquad (2.24)$$

Differentiating this with respect to the budget B, yields

$$\sum_i p_i \frac{\partial x_i}{\partial B} = 1 \qquad (2.25)$$

Multiplying all terms by $x_i B / B x_i$ yields

$$\sum_i \frac{p_i x_i}{B} \frac{B}{x_i} \frac{\partial x_i}{\partial B} = 1 \qquad (2.26)$$

Note that the first half of this expression $p_i x_i / B$ is the share of the budget spent on good i and the second is the budget elasticity (or the income elasticity) of the same good. Hence, if we define S_i as the budget share of good i and I_i as the income elasticity of the demand for i, then a basic property of the demand function becomes

$$\sum_i S_i I_i = 1 \qquad (2.27)$$

which means that, taking the expenditures as weights, the weighted average of a consumer's income elasticities is unity. Another related basic property can be obtained by differentiating the budget constraint Eq. (2.24) with respect to p_i and converting the resulting equation to elasticities to yield

$$\sum_i e_{ij}S_i = -S_j \tag{2.28}$$

where e_{ij} is the cost (price) and cross-elasticities of the demand for good i. This says that taking the expenditures as weights, the weighted average of the elasticities of demand for all goods with respect to the price of one good is equal to the proportion of income spent on that good.

Another property of demand related to the price and income elasticities of the demand for one good is that the income elasticity equals the sum of the cost (price) and cross-elasticities. This can be derived directly from the homogeneity property which was discussed earlier and which can be stated as follows:

$$X_i(B, p_1, p_2, \ldots, p_n) = X_i(\lambda B, \lambda p_1, \lambda p_2, \ldots, \lambda p_n) \tag{2.29}$$

where λ is a constant multiplier. Differentiating this equality with respect to λ and then setting $\lambda = 1$ gives

$$B \frac{\partial x_i}{\partial B} + p_1 \frac{\partial x_i}{\partial p_i} + \cdots + p_n \frac{\partial x_i}{\partial p_n} = 0 \tag{2.30}$$

which can be converted to elasticities by dividing by x_i to yield

$$I_i = \sum_{ij} e_{ij} \tag{2.31}$$

This result is referred to as the *Slutsky-Schultz relationship*, which has some interesting implications, among them a direct corollary that applies when there are only two goods. If we consider Eq. (2.28) when there are only two goods i and j combine it with Eq. (2.30), it can be shown that the following conditions result:

$$I_i = e_i + \frac{x_j}{x_i}(1 - e_j)$$

and $$\tag{2.32}$$

$$I_j = e_j + \frac{x_i}{x_j}(1 - e_i)$$

Since x_i and x_j are nonnegative quantities, this corollary states that if the price elasticity of one good is greater (less) than unity, then the income elasticity of the other must be less (greater) than its price elasticity. It is important to remember that this result is only applicable when there are only two substitutable goods in the consumer's choice. Loosely interpreted, this result can be taken to mean the following: if a consumer is faced with two goods, a necessity and a luxury, where the demand for the necessity has a price elasticity less than unity, and the demand for the luxury has a price elasticity larger than unity, then the income elasticity of the demand for the necessity is less than its price elasticity, and the income elasticity of the luxury is larger than its price elasticity. The value of this result in transportation applications is limited, if only because there are few situations that can be characterized by a two-good model. One such situation is that of a firm considering the choice between communications and air transportation as substitutable alternatives. If we consider that air transportation is a luxury when compared to communications (telephones, telex, etc.), then it might be postulated that the demand for air transportation is relatively price elastic and for communications relatively price inelastic. In this case, the income elasticity of the first is larger than its price elasticity, and the opposite is true for the second. One would then expect that if the firm's income (or budget) increased in the same proportion as, say, the price of air transportation, a net increase in air traffic generation would result; but if the firm's budget increases in the same proportion as the cost of communications, then a net decrease in its purchases of communications services would result. This example serves to recall the income and substitution effects discussed earlier. The decrease in communications would in this case be due to the substitution effect which would cause the firm to shift to more air travel. Recall that if the firm's budget increases together with the prices of both air transportation and communications in the same proportion, then nothing will change in its consumption pattern [see Eq. (2.29)].

Example To illustrate the derivation of demand functions by utility maximization we consider the following utility function in the case of two goods:

$$U = x_1^{\alpha_1} x_2^{\alpha_2}$$

where x_1, x_2 are the quantities of each good and α_1, α_2 are constant parameters.

A budget B limits the combinations of x_1 and x_2 to

$$B = p_1 x_1 + p_2 x_2$$

where p_1 and p_2 are the unit prices. Maximizing U subject to the budget constraint can be done by setting

$$x_2 = \frac{B - p_1 x_1}{p_2}$$

then substituting in U to obtain

$$U = x_1^{\alpha_1} \left(\frac{B - p_1 x_1}{p_2} \right)^{\alpha_2}$$

and setting $\partial U / \partial x_1 = 0$, which yields

$$x_1 = \frac{\alpha_1 B}{(\alpha_1 + \alpha_2) p_1}$$

and by symmetry

$$x_2 = \frac{\alpha_2 B}{(\alpha_1 + \alpha_2) p_2}$$

These two demand functions exhibit unitary price elasticities and no cross-elasticity. It is easy to see that they do satisfy the budget constraint. It is also possible to see that at optimality the ratio of the prices p_1/p_2 is equal to the ratio of the marginal utilities

$$\frac{\alpha_1/x_1}{\alpha_2/x_2}$$

It should now be mentioned that the properties of demand functions discussed so far, which are a direct result of the utility maximization model, are all formulated in terms of relationships between the various elasticities of demand. In other words, they all represent relationships between the parameters of the demand function. They therefore provide for a potentially substantial reduction in the number of unknown parameters that must be estimated when calibrating demand functions. We shall discuss this further later on in this chapter when considering the empirical estimation of transportation demand functions.

Not all demand functions are derived by maximizing utility functions subject to budget constraints. Indeed, this method, although theoretically quite appealing, is of quite limited use in transportation demand analysis. The reason for this is quite simple: it is not in general possible to specify a utility function. As mentioned earlier, utility is something that we are able to quantify only on an ordinal scale. Considerable psychometric research has yet to be conducted before capabilities are developed for articulating cardinal utility functions in transportation systems analysis. Recent work in attitudinal measurements in transportation will provide a foundation for such a development, but until a workable methodology for the construction of utility models is available, the practical use of utility maximization in demand analysis will continue to be limited.

The alternative approach to demand modeling is an ad hoc one. It consists of specifying a priori forms of demand models and using empirical analysis to verify their validity. The justification for this approach is that if assumptions regarding the form of the utility function must be made in order to proceed with the derivation of a demand function, then there is little point in not assuming the form of the demand function itself directly. The more commonly used functional forms in demand analysis are discussed in the next paragraphs together with some of their elasticity properties.

Some empirical demand functions and their properties   There are many forms that can be taken by demand functions. Three are most commonly used in practice, particularly in applications to transportation demand. These are (1) the linear, (2) the multiplicative, and (3) the exponential forms. Hybrid forms combining any of these three are also to be found in transportation applications. Each of these forms has its behavioral interpretation, and while empirical evidence is necessary for its validation, the choice must be based on a logical postulation of the causal realtionships involved. Thus the linear demand function implies that all the factors that affect traffic, such as income, cost, and travel time, have independent additive effects. The multiplicative form on the other hand implies that the effects are not independent but do interact. Different forms are common for different transportation applications, as will be seen in the relevant chapters that follow. In this section we take a look at these three functional forms and briefly discuss their properties.

The *linear* demand function implies independent effects. For example, considering the following travel demand function relating trips T to cost p and income I:

$$T = \alpha_0 + \alpha_1 p + \alpha_2 I \qquad (2.33)$$

where α_0, α_1, and α_2 are constant parameters. We can see that the effect of p on T, as measured by $\partial T/\partial p$, is the constant α_1 and is independent of the value of I. The proportional effects, or the elasticities, are not constant, however,

$$e_p = \frac{\partial T/T}{\partial p/p}$$

$$= \frac{p}{T}\alpha_1 \qquad (2.34)$$

which is not constant but depends on the values of p and of T, which in turn

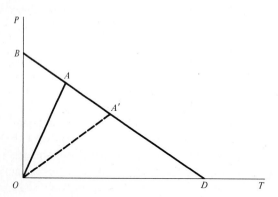

Figure 2.16 Geometric interpretation of elasticity for linear demand.

depends on the value I. This variability can be illustrated graphically as in Fig. 2.16. A projection of the demand curve is drawn on the Tp plane for a given value of I. This projection has a gradient α_1. If we take a ray from the origin to any point on the demand curve, such as OA to point A, then we can see that the elasticity of demand with respect to p at point A and as given by Eq. (2.34) is the ratio of the slopes of line OA and the demand curve itself BD. At point B the elasticity is infinite and at point D it is zero. At point A' where line OA' bisects BD, the elasticity is equal to unity. Point A' has some interesting implications;

it is the point that divides the demand curve into two equal regions, one in which demand is relatively elastic and one in which it is relatively inelastic; it is also the point at which the product pT, showing total expenditures, is maximized.

When the demand function has a *multiplicative* form

$$T = \alpha_0 p^{\alpha_1} I^{\alpha_2} \tag{2.35}$$

it implies that there is interaction between the effects of its variables. To see this, we look at the effect of p on T as measured by $\partial T/\partial p$ as an example:

$$\frac{\partial T}{\partial p} = \alpha_0 \alpha_1 I^{\alpha_2} p^{\alpha_1 - 1}$$

$$= \alpha_1 \frac{T}{p} \tag{2.36}$$

Clearly, this effect is dependent on the value of T and hence is not independent of the value of I. Thus the effects of p and I are interacting.

The interesting property of the multiplicative demand function is that its elasticity with respect to any of its variables is constant. Notice that the function can be linerarized by logarithmic transformation. The elasticity of T with respect to I, for example, is

$$\frac{\alpha T/T}{\alpha I/I} = \frac{\alpha \ln T}{\alpha \ln T} = \alpha_2 \tag{2.37}$$

The same is true of the elasticity with respect to p which would be equal to α_1. Thus, while the straight effects are not independent, the elasticities, which can be thought of as proportional effects, are constant and independent of one another. This property has led to the prevalent use of this form of demand model in transportation application. There is however no a priori reason why demand elasticities should be constant. Indeed, it may be argued that the contrary is more likely, as we shall see in later chapters. The use of multiplicative demand functions in transportation is simply a matter of convenience.

The *exponential* demand function combines features of the two previous types. It implies interaction between effects, and results in variable demand elasticities:

$$T = e^{\alpha_0 + \alpha_1 p + \alpha_2 I} \tag{2.38}$$

The effect of I, for example, is given by

$$\frac{\alpha T}{\alpha I} = \alpha_2 T \tag{2.39}$$

which is clearly not independent of the value of p. The elasticity of demand with respect to a variable, e.g., p is given by

$$\frac{\alpha T/T}{\alpha p/p} = \alpha_1 p \tag{2.40}$$

which, interestingly, is proportional to p itself. The same is true of any other variable in an exponential demand function. The postulation of demand elasticities that are proportional to the variables concerned is not uncommon in transportation applications. This is not always done for all variables, however, and the resulting form is a combined multiplicative and exponential function. The pure exponential function arises in transportation demand modeling when postulating certain properties of travel. For example, the entropy formulation of trip distribution models, discussed in Chap. 6, often results in an exponential demand function. Some utility maximization approaches also result in an exponential demand function.

A more common functional form, however, is the combined multiplicative and exponential function:

$$T = \alpha_0 I^{\alpha_2} e^{\alpha_1 P} \tag{2.41}$$

where an a priori assumption is made that income elasticity is constant but that price elasticity is not. This hybrid form is commonly used in transportation demand analysis and will be seen again in various contexts in later chapters.

It should be noted that none of these demand functions possesses any of the properties of Eq. (2.28) and (2.31). The parameters for these functions are usually estimated empirically without any of the restriction implied by the properties of utility-maximizing demand functions. There is no reason, however, why these restrictions cannot be used even when dealing with empirical demand functions, for they do come from basic properties, such as Eq. (2.28), that should hold whether there is a utility-maximizing process or not.

Another method of a priori specifying the functional form of the demand function is to estimate the form empirically, as well as the parameter values of the demand function. This is done by reverting to a transformation of the variables of the form:

$$X' = \begin{cases} [(X + \mu)^\lambda - 1]/\lambda & \lambda \neq 0; X + \mu > 0 \\ \ln (X + \mu) & \lambda = 0; X + \mu > 0 \end{cases} \tag{2.42}$$

This transformation allows different functional forms in the untransformed variables depending on the value of λ. Thus when $\lambda = 1$, the transformation is linear and so is the demand function; when $\lambda = 0$, the transformation results in a function linear in the logarithms, which is the multiplicative function; when $\lambda = 2$, the demand function becomes quadratic, and so forth. The use of μ, which is a location parameter, is to ensure that $(X + \mu)$ does not become negative. If all variables X are known to be positive, then it is possible to eliminate μ and to simplify the transformation to

$$X' = \begin{cases} (X^\lambda - 1)/\lambda & \lambda \neq 0 \\ \ln X & \lambda = 0 \end{cases} \tag{2.43}$$

which is referred to as the *Box-Cox transformation*. By including μ or λ, or both, in the estimation of model parameters it is possible to determine empirically an appropriate functional form of the demand function.

Gaudry and Wills (1978) and Hensher and Johnson (1979) have a method to the estimation of transportation demand functions. It is to be while this method does expand the scope of the ad hoc approach specification, it does not add any behavioral power to demand modeling. Furthermore, it does limit the functional forms to those that can be derived from the transformation. Thus a mixed multiplicative-exponential model cannot be estimated directly with this method; it would have to be specified a priori. The estimation of transformation parameters does require simplifying assumptions in order to extract from data both model structure and parameter values. Given the complexity of the estimation procedures required to apply this method, it is probably preferable to simply specify demand models a priori and estimate their parameters using available data.

Market Demand

So far we have discussed the demand function of an individual consumer, who as mentioned earlier could be a single individual, a household, or a single firm attempting to maximize consumption utility subject to an income or budget constraint. In reality, we are often interested in the behavior of a total market, not of a single consumer. This is particularly true in the case of transportation demand analysis, for a major motivation is forecasting total traffic. The traffic generated by a single individual or household is only of limited interest in transportation planning. Therefore, a way must be found for passage from individual demand to market demand.

If all individuals in a market had the same utility function, the same income or budget, and faced the same prices or costs, then the market demand function would simply be the individual function multiplied by the number of individuals. This situation is of course purely hypothetical. Indeed, if all individuals in the system were that similar, then there would be no need for a theory; everything could be predicted from the observation of a single individual. On the other hand, if all individuals in society had significantly different utility functions, budgets, and costs, then demand analysis would be intractable, because it would involve the analysis of immense amounts of data and very cumbersome computations. While this scenario is likely to be closer to the truth than the first one, there are most probably large groups of individuals whose behavioral characteristics are sufficiently close that, for the purposes of demand analysis, they can be considered similar. All consumers in such a group could be represented reasonably well by a single individual.

To develop some of the fundamental properties of market demand functions, we assume a market made up of segments, each of which is homogenous in the sense that all its members have the same utility function and income or budget. We assume for now that prices are the same for the entire market, although this assumption can be relaxed in order to account for possible price discrimination between segments or for possible differences in the perception of prices that may in fact be the same. Using the same notation as before, we consider the market demand function as the sum of individual demand functions:

$$X_i (I, p_1, p_2, \ldots, p_n) = \sum_k X_i^k (I^k, p_1, p_2, \ldots, p_n) \qquad (2.44)$$

where X_i^k is the demand for i by market segment k, I is the total market income, and I^k is k's income. It is easy to see from Eq. (2.44) that the following relation exists between segment and market price elasticities:

$$e_{ij} = \frac{\sum_k e_{ij}^k X_i^k}{\sum_k X_i^k} \qquad (2.45)$$

where e_{ij} is the market price or cross-elasticity of the demand for i with respect to the price of j, and e_{ij}^k is the corresponding elasticity for market segment k. This says that the market elasticity is the weighted sum of segment elasticities where the weights are the quantities demanded by each segment.

The same relationship can be derived between income elasticities if it is assumed that the market is homogenous with respect to income. In other words, if the following relationship exists between segment and total market incomes:

$$I^k = \alpha_k I \qquad \text{with} \sum_k \alpha_k = 1 \qquad (2.46)$$

where α_k remains constant, then Eq. (2.45) will also hold for income elasticities. Furthermore, if Eq. (2.46) is valid, then the properties discussed earlier, and shown in Eq. (2.25) and (2.28) for individual demand functions, will also hold for market demand.

The existence of a market utility function, or as it is often referred to, a *social welfare function*, that is well-defined, continuous, and convex to permit an optimization at the market level cannot be demonstrated. Market demand functions that are considered the result of a utility optimization process are obtained by aggregating individual demand functions that are themselves derived from utility maximization. Alternatively, of course, market demand functions can be specified using the ad hoc empirical approach mentioned earlier.

Aggregation of individual demand functions The most straightforward method of moving from individual to market demand functions is simply to sum the segment functions as shown in Eq. (2.44).

An extension to this summation approach is to obtain the market function by integrating the density functions of the variables that differ from one segment to the other over the ranges of these variables. Thus, if the individual demand function is a known function of prices and income, such as $X_i^k (I^k, p_1, p_2, p_3, \ldots, p_n)$, and if the segments are distributed over income strata according to a frequency function $f(\eta)$, then market demand can be given by

$$X_i (p_1, p_2, \ldots, p_n) = \int_I X_i(I, p_1, p_2, \ldots, p_3)f(\eta) \, d\eta \qquad (2.47)$$

This approach can be used for any stratifying variable for which the frequency function of the market segments is known. The method is sometimes referred to as the *stratification approach* and has been employed in demand analysis for many years, perhaps starting with its use by Pareto in 1895. The procedure may use distributions that are observed empirically and estimated statistically or specified a priori on the basis of theoretical considerations or computational advantages. For example, in numerous applications the income distribution has been assumed to follow a gamma density function [Kanafani (1972)].

Aggregation by entering segment averages of the demand function variables in the market function is commonly used. The method has serious pitfalls, however, for it is known that the function of averages of variables is not in general the same as the average of functions. In other words if segment demand functions $X_i^k (I^k, p_1, p_2, \ldots, p_n)$ are aggregated to a market demand function by replacing I^k with the average over all segments I and multiplying the function by the number of segments in the population, then in general a function would be obtained that is not equivalent to the sum of all the segment demand functions:

$$SX_i (I, p_1, p_2, \ldots, p_n) = \sum_{k=1}^{s} X_i^k (I_n, p_1, p_2, \ldots, p_n) + \Delta \quad (2.48)$$

where Δ is an error referred to as the *aggregation bias*. When the functions X_i^k are linear in all their variables, Δ vanishes, and hence this aggregation method works only for linear demand functions. Given that most functions used in transportation demand analysis are not linear, this aggregation method is not suitable, but its simplicity has always been a strong temptation to use it. Other aggregation methods have been developed for specific transportation applications. We shall see some of these in later chapters.

The essence of the aggregation problem is to reduce the magnitude of the analysis. In order to avoid having to analyze the behavior of every individual, one aims to identify as a sample a small group of individuals whose behavior is then observed. If these individuals are selected carefully so that they do represent the total population, then their individual demand models can be considered acceptable proxies for larger segments of the population and can be combined to give a market demand function.

The uses of demand elasticity As a measure of the response of demand to changes in the variables that affect it, elasticity can be a useful tool in demand analysis. However, care should be excercised to avoid pitfalls that can easily arise in interpreting elasticity values. Theoretically, it should be clear from Eq. (2.20) that elasticity is a relation between differentials and that it is only valid for infinitesimally small changes in variables:

$$e = \frac{\partial x / x}{\partial v / v} = \lim_{\Delta v \to 0} \frac{\Delta x / x}{\Delta v / v} \quad (2.49)$$

The use of elasticity values to interpret real changes should be recognized as an approximation and should be avoided when these changes are large. Elasticity, as a relation between differentials, is valid at the points at which it is defined.

Theoretically, therefore, elasticity is in fact of rather limited use. Its use to interpret the impacts of changes in demand variables should be recognized as an approximation and should be avoided for large changes.

To illustrate the discrepencies that can arise when using demand elasticity to interpret the effects of changes, we consider the following example.

Example Let the demand for air trips T between two cities be given by the following function of the air fare p: $T = Kp^\alpha$, where K is a constant, and α is the price (fare) elasticity of demand. Suppose the $\alpha = -2.0$, suggesting that the percentage change in traffic is twice the percentage change in price. Let the fare be doubled, i.e., increased by 100 percent. The elasticity of -2.0 would imply that this would cause traffic to decrease by 200 percent, whereas a simple calculation would show traffic will actually decrease by a factor of 4 or by 300 percent. It is clear then that elasticity values cannot be used to predict the impacts of such large variations in variables. What magnitudes of changes can be interpreted using elasticity values depend on the form of the demand function and on the elasticity values themselves. (See Prob. 2.1.) What discrepancies can be tolerated will of course depend on the nature of the application. Clearly when a demand function is known, then it should be used to predict the impacts of changes.

Another source of discrepancy in interpreting elasticity values results when they are calculated by comparing discrete changes in variables. This can be done either empirically or by calculating such changes from a given demand function. Such an elasticity is referred to as an *arc elasticity,* as contrasted to *point elasticity,* which is given by Eq. (2.20). For observed or calculated changes Δx and Δv, one definition of arc elasticity is

$$e_{\text{arc}} = \frac{\Delta x/x}{\Delta v/v} \tag{2.50}$$

There are two problems inherent in this definition. One is that arc elasticity will differ from point elasticity, the difference increasing as Δv (or Δx) increases. The second is that inconsistent results can be obtained; when a change in a variable V is reversed, its effect on the dependent variable X will not be the same as the original change. We can illustrate these problems with the following example.

Example Suppose the demand for trips T is given by the following function of fare P:

$$T = 1000p^{-2.0}$$

Suppose further that an initial condition is given by $P_0 = 10$ for which $T_0 = 10$. A change in fare to $p_1 = 15$ results in traffic decreasing to $T_1 = 4.4$. The arc elasticity calculated using Eq. (2.50) will be

$$e_{\text{arc}} = \left(\frac{4.4 - 10}{10}\right) \Big/ \left(\frac{15 - 10}{10}\right) = -1.12$$

When the change is reversed so that $p_0 = 15$ and $p_1 = 10$ for which $T_0 = 4.4$ and $T_1 = 10$, the elasticity becomes

$$e_{\text{arc}} = \left(\frac{10 - 4.4}{4.4}\right) \Big/ \left(\frac{10 - 15}{15}\right) = -3.82$$

These values are different, and they are both different from the point elasticity of -2.0. A closer approximation is obtained when the arc elasticity is defined as

$$e_{\text{arc}} = \frac{\Delta \ln x}{\Delta \ln v} \tag{2.51}$$

which for the above example will equal -2.05, which is closer to the true value of $e = -2.0$. Another approximation can be obtained by using the following definition of arc elasticity:

$$e_{\text{arc}} = \frac{(x_1 - x_0)(v_1 + v_0)}{(x_1 + x_0)(v_1 - v_0)} \tag{2.52}$$

which for the above example yields a value of -1.94. Equation (2.51) or (2.52) should always be used for computing elasticity rather than Eq. (2.50). Using these definitions, the problem of inconsistency does not occur when reversing changes in variables.

In addition to its use in predicting changes in demands, elasticity, with respect to supply variables, is used to predict changes in the resources consumed. For example, the elasticity of trip demand with respect to price is useful in predicting changes in total expenditures; the elasticity with respect to travel time is useful in predicting changes in total time spent on travel, and so forth. To see this, consider the price (or cost) elasticity e_p. The total expenditures E when there are x trips are given by

$$E = xp \tag{2.53}$$

Differentiating with respect to price p gives

$$\frac{\partial E}{\partial p} = p \frac{\partial x}{\partial p} + x$$

$$= x \left(\frac{p \partial x}{x \partial p} + 1\right)$$

$$= x(1 + e_p) \tag{2.54}$$

This is a rather useful result. We can see that since e_p is negative, price and expenditures will vary in the same manner when $|e_p| < 1$; and in opposite manner when $|e_p| > 1$. Thus for a relatively inelastic demand an increase in price will result in an increase in total expenditures and vice versa. When X refers to transportation offered by an operator for a fee, such as in the case of airline or railroad traffic, then E will be the operator's revenue. An operator, such as an airline, would then be quite interested in a good estimate of the fare elasticity in order to determine whether an increase in fare, for example, would result in an increase or a decrease in total revenues. Note that when $|e_p| = 1$, E will remain invariant to changes in p, as can be seen from Eq. (2.54).

Demand, revenues, and benefits The demand function has a wider interpretation than simply a relationship between quantity and price. As seen in the previous paragraphs, there is a relationship between the demand function and the function describing total expenditures, or revenues, as the case may be. In addition, there is a direct interpretive relation between demand and the user benefits that may accrue from the consumption activity in question. In this section we shall explore these relationships.

Consider a demand function $X = X(p)$ where p represents the cost or price of consuming one unit of X. As shown in Fig. 2.17, such a demand function can

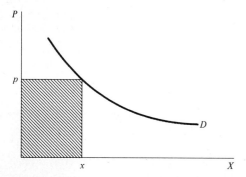

Figure 2.17 Total expenditures.

be used to compute total expenditures, or operator revenues, at any point as

$$E = pX(p) \tag{2.55}$$

as the product of the coordinates of the demand function in the XP plane.

The demand function can also be used to determine the value of p for any given value of X. Such a value would represent the average expenditure, price, or average operator revenue $AE(x)$

$$p = AE(x) = X^{-1}(x) \tag{2.56}$$

For the special case when the demand function is linear, the total expenditures E vary parabolically with X, as can be ascertained from Fig. 2.18. The total revenue reaches a maximum at the point when

$$\frac{\partial E}{\partial x} = 0$$

$$\frac{\partial [pX(p)]}{\partial x} = X \frac{\partial p}{\partial x} + p$$

$$0 = p(1 + 1/e) \qquad (2.57)$$

which occurs when $e = -1$. Thus total expenditures or operators' revenues are maximized at the point where the demand elasticity equals unity. This is the same as point A' in Fig. 2.16, the point where the price is half the value at which consumption X vanishes. Figure 2.18 also shows the corresponding curve of

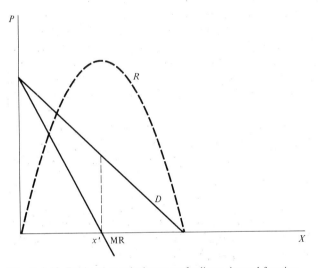

Figure 2.18 Total and marginal revenue for linear demand function.

marginal expenditures which are positive up to point x' and then negative indicating declining total expenditures or revenues. This curve is often referred to as the *marginal revenue curve* and is commonly used in analyzing pricing policies. We shall see it again in the next chapter on supply analysis. It is important to note, however, that this curve, the marginal revenue, is a plot of $\partial E/\partial x$ and should not be confused with $\partial E/\partial p$ as derived in Eq. (2.54). The two are easily related. The revenue and marginal revenue functions can take on different forms depending on the demand function itself. Using Eq. (2.54) or (2.57) one can generate these functions for a variety of cases (see Prob. 2.1).

Using Eq. (2.56) we can interpret the demand function as one that gives the average price paid or cost incurred by each consumer. Figure 2.19 shows such

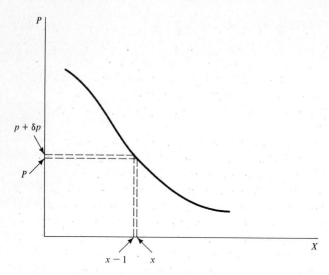

Figure 2.19 Benefits measured by willingness to pay.

a demand function where two points are identified, (x, p) and $(x - 1, p + \delta p)$. These points imply that with a price p there are x consumers willing to pay that price, or one consumer (in the case of an individual demand funciton) willing to pay the price x times. When the price rises to $p + \delta p$, then the number x drops by one unit. The interpretation of this is that the consumption of the xth unit is worth a price p, but not a price $p + \delta p$. The consumption of the $(x + 1)$st unit is worth at most $p + \delta p$, and so forth. Thus the value p for any given x represents the maximum worth of the consumption of the xth unit and is considered to be the user benefit accruing from this consumption activity. In the transportation context, $X^{-1}(x)$ gives the user benefit derived from a trip, as measured by the amount of price, or cost, that the trip maker is willing to incur. It is therefore the amount of user benefit that is accrued at the margin as X changes from $(x - 1)$ to x. Hence the function $X^{-1}(x)$ is referred to as *marginal benefit function.* Referring to Fig. 2.19, it can be seen that if the value of the ordinate of the curve gives the benefit to the xth user, then the area under the curve between the origin and the value $X = x$ will equal the sum total of all the user benefits. This value is given by

$$B(x) = \int_0^x X^{-1}(r) \, dr \qquad (2.58)$$

It is common to subtract from this value an amount equal to $X^{-1}(x)$, which is the cost actually incurred by all users when the total volume is x. THis leaves what might be considered the net benefit to users, a value referred to as the *consumers surplus* (CS):

$$\mathrm{CS}(x) = \left[\int_0^x X^{-1}(r)\, dr \right] - x\, X^{-1}(x) \qquad (2.59)$$

Consumer surplus is often used in evaluation as a measure of the net user benefit accruing from the operation of a transportation system for which the demand is known.

To summarize, the demand curve when drawn on an XP plane represents a relationship between quantity consumed X and unit price or cost p. It also represents the average expenditure or revenue that is obtained at any value of X. The product of the coordinates of the demand curve gives the total expenditure or revenue from which a marginal revenue curve can be derived by differentiation. The demand curve also represents the marginal benefits accruing to consumers or to consumers of a transportation facility. The area under the curve between the origin and a point $X = x$ represents the total benefits accruing from the consumption of x units.

Demand, supply, and equilibrium Knowledge of the demand function alone is not sufficient for the prediction of quantity consumed, nor of any of the other variables associated with it. The demand function is a relation between quantity demanded and price, and in order to determine the quantity demanded, the price must be known. Conversely, if the quantity demanded is known, then the demand function will permit the determination of that price which brings about that quantity. The framework used for dealing with this question is that of *equilibrium*, a concept which has been used in economic analysis since the middle of the nineteenth century. Equilibrium is said to be achieved when the factors that affect the quantity demanded $X(p)$, and among them the price, and the factors that determine the quantity supplied $S(p)$, also among them the price, result in both these quantities being equal statically or converging toward equality dynamically.

In order to apply the concept of equilibrium, we need to introduce the *supply function*. As with the demand function, the supply function is a relation between quantity S and price P, among other variables, but it represents the mechanism by which the quantity is produced or offered in a market. Thus the supply function can represent the quantity of goods a producer is willing to offer at a given price: tons of farm products at a given market price, airline seats at a given air fare, and so forth. It can also represent the price that must be charged or the cost that must be incurred in order to offer a certain quantity: the air fare that an airline must charge in order to break even in a particular market, the price demanded by the supplier of a scarce commodity, and so forth.

The simplest form of equilibrium is when the following conditions exist:

$$x = X(p) \qquad (2.60a)$$

$$s = S(p) \qquad (2.60b)$$

$$x = s \;\rightarrow\; X(p_0) = S(p_0) \qquad (2.60c)$$

The price p_0 is that price at which the quantity demanded x equals the quantity supplied s. This static equilibrium in the case of one good can be extended to a

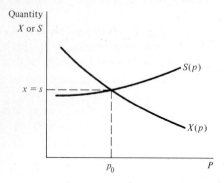

Figure 2.20 Static equilibrium of demand and supply.

whole market of many goods. It is shown graphically in Fig. 2.20 in which for illustration the supply function is shown to be an increasing function. The exact shape of the demand and the supply functions and the existence and uniqueness of static equilibrium will depend on the type of market involved. A discussion of the demand and supply equilibrium question in transportation is the subject of the next chapter.

The dynamic equilibrium concept starts with the basic notion that the quantity supplied S during a time period t will depend on the price during the previous period. The price charged during period t will also depend on the price charged during the previous period and on whether the demand exceeds the supply or not. These two notions are expressed as

$$x_t = X(p_t) \tag{2.61a}$$

$$s_t = S(p_{t-1}) \tag{2.61b}$$

$$p_t = p_{t-1} + \phi(x_{t-1} - s_{t-1}) \tag{2.61c}$$

where ϕ is a parameter that is supposed to be positive to indicate that when demand exceeds supply, the price will tend to rise, and vice versa. A special case of this dynamic equilibrium formulation is when Eq. (2.61c) is replaced by

$$x_t = s_t \tag{2.62}$$

This case is referred to as the *cobweb model* and implies that equilibrium is achieved by price oscillations until Eq. (2.62) is satisfied. As shown in Fig. 2.21a and b, these oscillations will either converge to a static equilibrium or will diverge indefinitely depending on whether the curve is steeper or flatter than the supply curve, respectively. The case of the diverging oscillations is not a realistic model of market systems, for it is rarely observed that prices will oscillate widely

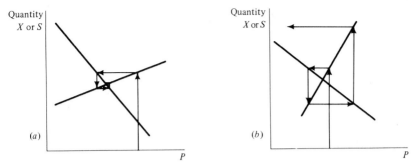

Figure 2.21 The cobweb model of dynamic equilibrium. (*a*) Converging; (*b*) diverging.

for long periods of time. Equation (2.61*a*) provides a more robust model, for with a sufficiently small ϕ a static equilibrium will be achieved.

Example The following numerical example serves to illustrate equilibrium between demand and supply and how this equilibrium is achieved in the dynamic model. Consider the following static demand function:

$$X(p) = 10{,}000 - 50p$$

X might be number of daily air trips in a particular market and p air fare in dollars. Consider also the following supply function:

$$S(p) = 200p - 20{,}000$$

This supply function could refer to the number of daily seats offered by the airlines at a given fare level. It could also be interpreted as a direct result of an airline cost function which determines the price that must be charged in order to supply a given number of seats, $p = 100 + 0.005s$. The demand and supply functions can be solved directly for a static equilibrium, which clearly exists and is unique in this linear case since $\partial X/\partial p < 0$ and $\partial S/\partial p > 0$. At $p = p^*$ static equilibrium is achieved:

$$x = X(p^*) = S(p^*) = s$$

the solution of which is $p^* = 120$, and $x = s = 4000$.

This equilibrium solution can be shown to be unstable according to the cobweb model since $\partial S/\partial p > \partial X/\partial p$. However, a dynamic demand and supply system according to Eqs. (2.61*a*) to (2.61*c*) can be found that would lead to an equilibrium solution. Suppose the following dynamic system is used with $\phi = 0.002$:

$$x_t = X(p_t) = 10{,}000 - 50p_t$$
$$s_t = S(p_{t-1}) = 200p_{t-1} - 20{,}000$$
$$p_t = p_{t-1} + 0.002\,(x_{t-1} - s_{t-1})$$

An iterative solution method is applied with initial prices $p_0 = 100$, $p_1 = 100$. This solution converges to the static equilibrium value in about 12 to 14 iterations, depending on how accurately one compares the results. Table 2.1 shows the solutions at various steps and demonstrates the convergence of the system.

Table 2.1

Time period	p	x	s
0	100	—	—
1	100	5000	0
2	110	4500	0
3	119	4050	2000
4	123.1	3845	3800
5	123.2	3840	4620
6	121.6	3918	4638
7	120.2	3990	4326
8	119.3	4034	4038
9	119.3	4034	3864
10	119.7	4107	3864
11	120.1	3995	3932
12	119.8	4011	4020
13	120.0	3997	3956
14	119.9	4001	4012

The extent to which such oscillations in price and quantity occur in reality cannot be ascertained empirically, because it is usually not possible to differentiate between random fluctuations and significant variations that result from an equilibration process. In this particular example, the fluctuations in price after the third iteration can hardly be considered significant, let alone observable empirically. It seems a safe position to adopt that if a static equilibrium exists, then it can be considered a valid representation of a dynamic system at a given point in time. What is more intriguing is the question whether such an equilibrium exists at all. This of course depends on the nature of the demand and supply functions and will be treated in more detail in the next chapter.

2.3 APPLICATIONS OF DEMAND THEORY TO TRANSPORTATION

Microeconomic demand theory provides a very useful framework for the analysis of transportation demand. Obviously, there are some distinctions between transportation and other consumption activities which require making some modifications and adaptations of this theory when it is applied to transportation. But as a framework, it is probably superior to any other. There are numerous references in the literature to the problems involved in applying microeconomic demand theory to transportation [see, for example, Manheim (1980)]. Often the severity of these problems is exaggerated, leading to suggestions that other frameworks be used for transportation demand analysis, such as optimization techniques, simulation, and purely empirical analyses.

The difficulties cited in the adaptation of microeconomic demand theory center on three basic characteristics of transportation demand. The first is that transportation demand is derived from the demand for other social and economic activities. In other words, the actual travel or shipping activities do not generate utility per se, and hence the utility maximization model is not appropriate. This is of course true, for it is rather rare that transportation is undertaken for its own sake. However, if it is accepted that the trip itself permits the trip maker to partake of a socioeconomic activity that generates utility and that transportation is simply a means to overcome the spatial separation between the origin and the destination of the trip, then transportation can be thought of generically as an opportunity cost to be incurred as a component of the total cost of the consumption activity, or whatever socioeconomic activity is involved. The utility function is then to be thought of as a function of the number of trips and associated socioeconomic activities. The cost of transportation, or, more generally, the attributes of the transportation system that affect the resources that must be committed to the trip, can then be included in either the cost function or the budget equation or incorporated as negative (or positive) contributions to the utility function. Theoretically there is no reason why the framework of microeconomic demand theory cannot accommodate this adaptation of the utility maximization model. In practical terms the issue is less important since in most transportation applications the ad hoc approach is used for the determination of demand function.

In this regard, an important distinction must be made in thinking about transportation demand analysis. This is the distinction between passenger and commodity transportation. In the case of passenger demand, the utility function cannot really be quantified, and the ad hoc approach is common. The many idiosyncrasies of the individuals making travel decisions can only complicate and obscure any utility maximization model, especially at the aggregate market level. Stochastic demand models are therefore widely used for analyzing passenger travel demand, as we shall see in subsequent chapters. In the case of commodity transportation, on the other hand, shipping can be considered an integral part of a production process where inputs and outputs are spatially separated. The framework of optimization of a production process provides powerful tools for dealing with commodity transportation demands. In this case an isomorphism between demand theory and production theory can be utilized to better interpret the utility function, which in this case can actually be quantified as its counterpart, the production function. This isomorphism between production theory and commodity transportation demand theory is an important reason why combining passenger and commodity demands into one set of "abstract" users of transportation, differing only in their respective values of user attributes, is not appropriate. While it is done for the convenience of the analyst, it does force passenger travel demand into the same isomorphism with production theory, which is really only appropriate for commodity transportation. The process by which the utility of socioeconomic activities of potential trip makers accrues is not well understood, nor is it likely to be to such an extent as to allow drawing analogies with production theory. Besides, even though commodity shipping decisions are made by people, it is conceptually and ethically unappealing to combine passenger and commodity transportation demand within the same model.

The following chapters will show how for passenger transportation demand the identification of trip purpose is an important means of stratifying demands and accommodating the notion that they are in fact derived rather than pure demands. For commodity transportation, the distinction between commodity types and production activity types will accomplish the same thing.

Another aspect of transportation demand that is sometimes thought to limit the extent to which it lends itself to the microeconomic paradigm is the inability to store, or stockpile, transportation. In classical theory it is assumed, correctly, that goods can be stockpiled in order to accommodate fluctuations in demand, and hence they can be supplied when demanded. In transportation this cannot be done to the same extent, and hence transportation services are in a sense supplied, sometimes whether they are demanded or not, e.g., empty seats on airplanes, highways operating well below capacity. This is a supply issue and is the subject of the next chapter. However, it is important to note here that the inability to store transportation is not completely true. Indeed, many of the resources that are used up in transportation can be "stored" until the transportation service is actually consumed. For example, for systems such as highways and airports, the fixed costs are incurred regardless of traffic, but the variable traffic-related costs are not. Airplane seats are flown regardless of whether they are filled or not, but the traveler's travel cost, and indeed travel time, is saved until the trip is actually made. The mere scheduling of transportation services is a type of stockpiling whereby services are offered when needed.

The crucial difficulties that are faced in applying microeconomic demand theory to transportation are methodological and have to do with the specification of appropriate demand models and with the experimentation needed to validate such models. Transportation behavior, particularly in the case of passenger travel, is subject to many more uncertainties than other consumption activities. In urban transportation a typical urban household has an enormous number of choices to make when considering the possible combinations of location, trip-making rate, modes, routes, and times of travel. The complete quantification and modeling of all these choices and of the process of travel decision making is replete with conjectures, uncertainties, and assumptions. Microeconomic demand theory is nowhere near being an adequate theory of the behavior of a sociotechnical system such as transportation. Consequently what we find is a predominance of stochastic models of transportation demand where randomness represents, to a large degree, our ignorance. An added difficulty is with experimentation, which in the case of transportation is extremely handicapped for two reasons. One is that the transportation system is of a large magnitude with a long gestation period. Thus by the time effects begin to stabilize, influencing factors would have changed again to elude the assessment of impacts. The other reason is that controlled experimentation with people is not easily performed. It is difficult to control experiments completely, and in many cases information about behavior in hypothetical situations represents conjecture on the part of the subject surveyed.

The following chapters are devoted to the analysis of transportation demand. The application of microeconomic demand theory is exposed in specific cases such as urban passenger transportation, nonurban passenger transportation, and commodity transportation. Microeconomic analysis of sectoral transportation requirements is also introduced as a framework for analyzing commodity transportation demands. The methodological issues involved will be discussed in the appropriate chapters dealing with specific segments of the analysis.

Problems

2.1 Consider three demand functions with constant price elacticity: one for relatively inelastic demand; one for relatively elastic demand; and one for demand with unit elasticity. For each of these, draw in sketch from the following functions:

    (*a*) Average revenue

    (*b*) Marginal revenue

    (*c*) Total revenue

2.2 The volume of traffic along a corridor is plotted against the price of travel during three different years t_1, t_2, t_3:

    (*a*) Could a demand function be estimated by running a regression line through these points? Why or why not?

    (*b*) What events could have caused such a series of observations?

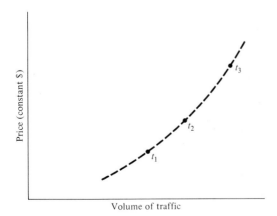

2.3 In city A, the demand function for a commodity is given by

$$q = a - b \cdot P$$

where q is the quantity purchased, P is the unit sales price in A, and a and b are nonnegative parameters.

The commodity can be supplied from either city B or city C. In B, the unit price for the commodity is P' and in C, the price is P''. From B, the commodity can be shipped to A by truck, and from C, it can be shipped by rail. The quantities shipped from either city will naturally depend on the transportation costs.

(a) Derive the demand functions for transportation on the links BA and CA.

(b) What are the transport cost-elasticities on each link?

(c) What are the transport cross-elasticities between the two links?

2.4 In the community of Shopperville, there is a population of households that can be assumed homogenous in that they have similar socioeconomic characteristics. There are three shopping centers located at varying distances from Shopperville. For all practical purposes, these shopping centers can also be assumed identical, except for their distances to Shopperville.

Suppose that you are interested in calibrating a model of the demand for shopping travel by the residents of Shopperville. What observations would need to be taken, and under what conditions, to allow the calibration of a true demand model, if such a thing is possible?

2.5 The demand for travel by automobile in an urban corridor is given by the following function:

$$V_A = \alpha t_a^\beta t_b^\gamma p_b^\delta p_a^{\phi + \theta I}$$

where V_a = total number of vehicle trips per day

t_a, t_b = corridor travel times by automobile and by bus, respectively

p_a, p_b = average costs by automobile and bus, respectively

I = average annual household income

$\alpha, \ldots, \phi$ = parameters

(a) Determine the cost-elasticity of the demand.

(b) Identify the signs of all the parameters of the model that would be expected a priori.

(c) If $\beta = -2.0$, $\gamma = +0.10$, and $\delta = +0.9$, what change will take place in traffic volume if travel times on both the automobile and the bus rise by 10 percent simultaneously with an increase in 20 percent in the bus tariff?

(d) Can this model be used to evaluate the revealed value of time of travelers in the corridor?

2.6 In a travel survey of households, it was found that trip making occurs according to the following law:

$$P(x|r) = \frac{e^{-\lambda_r}\lambda_r^x}{x!}$$

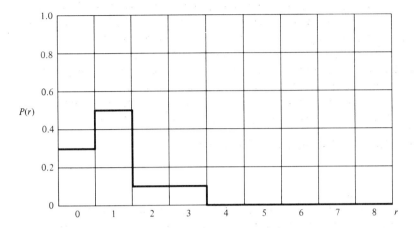

where $P(x|r) =$ conditional probability of making x trips given that the household owns r cars

λ_r = a value derived for households with r cars

$\lambda_0 = 2$, $\lambda_1 = 3$, $\lambda_2 = 5$, $\lambda_3 = 8$, otherwise $\lambda = 0$

If the distribution of car ownership among the households is as shown on the graph, find the expected number and the variance of trips generated by a household.

REFERENCES

Beckmann, M. J., C. B. McGuire, and C. Winsten: "Studies in the Economics of Transportation," published for the Cowles Commission for Research in Economics by Yale University Press, New Haven, 1955.

Baumol, W. J.: "Economic Theory and Operations Analysis," Prentice-Hall, Inc., Englewood Cliffs, N. J., 1977.

Gaudry, M. J., and M. J. Wills: Estimating the Functional Form of Travel Demand Models, *Transp. Res.,* vol. 12, pp. 257–284, 1978.

Heggie, I.: "Transport Engineering Economics," McGraw-Hill Book Company, New York, 1972.

Hensher, D. A., and L. W. Johnson: External Structure of Variables in Individual Choice Models of Travel Demand, *Intern. J. Trans. Econ.,* vol. 6, no. 1, pp. 51–61, 1979.

Johnson, L. W.: Utility Maximation, Demand Systems, and Functional Form in Transport Demand Analysis, *Transp. Plan. Technol.,* vol. 5, pp. 247–255, 1979.

Kanafani, A.: An Aggregative Model of Trip Making, *Transp. Res.,* vol. 6, no. 2, pp. 119–124, 1972.

Koppelmann, F.: Guidelines for Aggregate Travel Prediction Using Disaggregate Choice Models, *Transp. Res. Rec.,* no. 610, pp. 19–24, 1977.

Lancaster, K. L.: "Introduction to Modern Microeconomics," Rand McNally, Chicago, 1969.

Manheim, M.: "Fundamentals of Transportation Systems Analysis," MIT Press, Cambridge, Mass., vol. 1, 1980.

Quandt, R. E.: "The Demand for Travel: Theory and Measurement," D. C. Heath, Lexington, Mass., 1970.

Wold, H., and L. Jureen: "Demand Analysis," John Wiley & Sons, Inc., New York, 1955.

THREE

TRANSPORTATION SUPPLY

In the previous chapter, we introduced the transportation demand function as a relationship between traffic flows and a set of variables that represents the determinant of transportation demand and supply. The demand variables describe the social and economic activities that give rise to transportation needs; the supply variables describe different aspects of the cost and level of service by which such needs might be met. In this chapter, we focus on the supply variables and discuss how they are influenced by transportation technology, by the operating policies of the system, and by the level and nature of traffic using the system. The discussion is limited to supply analysis only as it relates to supply-demand equilibrium and the problem of traffic estimation and forecasting. Supply analysis has a scope that extends much wider than this; it is an important part of most transportation planning and policy analyses, many of which have concerns that extend well beyond traffic forecasting. For example, transportation supply analysis is an important element in technology assessment and evaluation, in environmental impact studies, and in the development of regulatory and institutional policies.

3.1 FRAMEWORK FOR SUPPLY ANALYSIS

The *supply function* is defined in classical microeconomic theory as a function that gives the quantity of a good that a supplier is willing to offer in a market at a given price. It is then, like the demand function, a relationship between quantity and price. This definition is adequate for most analysis of consumption in microeconomic demand theory since the price is indeed the most important supply variable affecting consumption. This, however, is not the case in transportation, where there are three important departures from conventional consumption that require modification of the definition of supply:

1. In transportation, the supplier is often not well-defined, and consequently supplier behavior cannot be studied explicitly. For example, in intercity highway transportation, the transportation system is supplied on such a large and aggregate scale that for any specific traffic activity, it is impossible to identify

a supplier who can determine an appropriate capacity to offer at a given price. Indeed, if there are no tolls imposed, then the user of the highway system is paying for it in a rather indirect way through regular taxes, fuel taxes, and other indirect costs. There are situations, of course, where a supplier is identifiable and where the classical economic definition of the supply function is appropriate. Examples of this would include air transportation, where the airline is the supplier of at least a major component of the transportation service, and urban bus transportation, where there is an operator who is capable of making supply decisions on a short-term basis.

2. In transportation, there are nonmonetary aspects of supply that are as important, if not more so, than the price charged by the operator. Travel time in many types of transportation is a most important attribute of supply. Microeconomic theory does not provide a satisfactory way of readily dealing with the many attributes of transportation within its classical framework of supply.

3. Much of what determines the attributes of transportation supply is a result of user rather than supplier behavior. Many of the important aspects of transportation level of service that directly affect the evolution of traffic flows depend on how travelers use the available transportation systems and cannot therefore be considered as supply attributes determined by a "supplier." For example, in urban passenger transportation, travel time is determined largely by the travelers' choice of route. In rural highway transportation, the travel time and vehicle operating cost incurred by an automobile traveler depend primarily on speed which, within limits, is largely at the discretion of the driver.

For these reasons, it would be inappropriate to restrict the definition of transportation supply to the microeconomic concept of a quantity offered by a supplier at a given price. For purposes of demand analysis and traffic estimation, we are concerned with defining supply by the set of all attributes of transportation that have a bearing on the quantity and nature of transport activities that actually take place. This extends well beyond the monetary price or cost of transportation to other attributes that directly or indirectly represent resources expended in the transportation system, although they may not be quantifiable or convertible to monetary cost. The selection of appropriate attributes depends on the type of transportation in question. Thus, in urban automobile transportation, the travel time, operating costs, delays in transit, and the availability and cost of parking may be sufficient to describe transportation supply; whereas in intercity air transportation, travel time, air fares, other ground costs, airport delays, aircraft types, frequency of service, schedule of service, load factor, and passenger service quality may all be necessary descriptors of transport supply. There is no need to adopt a single framework for the definition of supply for all types of transportation. Such a framework is likely to be complicated and to confuse the important aspects of transportation analysis.

The evolution of transportation supply characteristics depends on four major influences:

1. *Technology*. The technical characteristics of the transportation system affect its performance. In particular, the operating cost of a system depends largely on the type of technology used. Other important aspects of supply depend directly on technology, such as capacity and speed.
2. *Operating strategy*. The manner by which the technology is utilized to deliver a particular transportation service depends on the behavior and objectives of the operator. For example, the strategy used in expanding system capacity in response to increases in traffic loads is a strong determinant of many important supply attributes in scheduled systems such as airline and bus transportation. Operator's behavior also determines the extent to which operating costs are recovered and the manner by which this is done. This is the pricing mechanism which translates the operating cost function into a user cost function as we shall see later on.
3. *Institutional requirements and constraints*. Transportation operating strategies and pricing policies are often subject to requirements and constraints that are imposed by a regulatory process or necessitated by prevailing market conditions. For example, in a regulated transportation system, the pricing strategy that the operator can apply might be determined by governmental institutions, as might the capacity offered or the type of equipment used. These same influences on operator behavior might be necessitated by market structure. For example, pricing in a competitive market would be totally different from that in a monopolistic or an oligopolistic market.
4. *User behavior*. Some aspects of transportation supply are dependent on the behavior of the users of the transportation system. The manner by which the shipper of commodities actually uses the available transportation services often determines the overall shipping costs: the shipper can vary inventory levels, shipment sizes and frequencies, and packaging methods. Urban travelers can also influence their supply attributes by choosing routes and travel speeds and by adopting such means of travel as car and van pools.

These four influences interact together to result in what might be considered the supply function, which describes the supply attributes from the user's viewpoint and as they relate to the nature and magnitude of traffic flows. Figure 3.1 shows a structural diagram indicating the major interactions between these influences. Transportation technology as operated by the operator and as influenced by the institutional and market environment can be described by a *performance function*. This performance function may be considered analogous to the operator's or supplier's cost function. This cost is transformed into a user cost by the application of a specific cost recovery scheme such as pricing or taxation. Also influenced by user behavior, user cost function may be considered the supply function for the purposes of transportation demand analysis. An important aspect

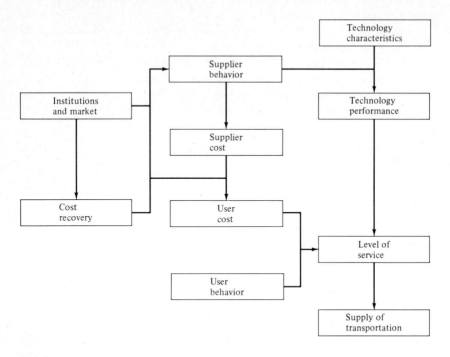

Figure 3.1 Influences on the supply of transportation.

of user behavior as it affects the user cost function is the manner by which users *perceive* the costs incurred. Since the perceived costs may sometimes be different from the actual costs, and since the travel or shipping decisions are made on their basis, the transformation of supplier or operator cost functions into user cost functions should include the appropriate corrections.

In order to clarify these relationships, it is worthwhile perhaps to identify and describe the role of each of the major actors in the process. There are four major actors:

1. *The supplier.* This refers to the person or entity who actually supplies the transportation service. It could be a highway department whose role is to construct and maintain a highway system, or a firm who owns a number of trucks that are used to offer freight services. The supplier incurs a cost that is directly related to the performance characteristics of the technology employed, although as mentioned earlier, the cost is also affected by the other actors and influences in the process. The supplier may or may not be involved in the operation or the regulation of the transportation service in question. For example, in many countries, airports are planned and built by a central

government agency but are operated by local authorities. Often the operations of such airports are regulated by yet another government agency. The costs incurred by the supplier are recovered directly if the supplier is the same as the operator, or indirectly when other actors intervene in the operation and pricing of the system. For example, the costs incurred by a highway department are recovered indirectly through taxation and sometimes by tolls that are collected by an operator. In the case of airlines, the supplier and operator are the same entity, namely the airline, and the costs are recovered directly through fares and other charges.

2. *The operator.* This is the person or entity actually concerned with the operations of the transportation system and with the day-to-day decisions regarding the specific characteristics of the service such as scheduling and routing. The operator is often also involved in recovering system costs from the users through direct charges. For some transportation systems, the operator and the supplier are the same entity, but more commonly they are different entities which together provide the transportation service, with the supplier providing the basic infrastructure and the operator responsible for the operation and maintenance of the system. This applies to public as well as private transportation; for example, in air transportation, the basic infrastructure that may be supplied by a government agency is supplemented by the airline services provided directly by the airlines. The total system is operated by the local airport authorities as well as by the airlines. Thus, we can see that the roles of supplier or operator can be played by more than one entity. Indeed, in most transportation systems, the supplier is more than one entity, with the infrastructure often supplied by a public entity, whereas operating components of the system are supplied by carriers or other types of operators. In private automobile transportation, the highway system is supplied by the public highway agency, whereas the automobile and its appurtenances are supplied by the operator, who is also the user in this case.

3. *The user.* Here we consider the person or entity who actually makes the travel decision. In passenger transportation, this is the traveler or the passenger, and in goods transportation, it is the shipper, the forwarder, or the receiver. The importance of the user in supply analysis is that the costs incurred, or perceived as incurred, by the user are relevant in the supply function. The same is true of all the other levels of service attributes that have a bearing on the travel decision: the ones perceived by the user are the ones relevant in supply analysis. For this reason, it is common to refer to *user travel time functions* or *user cost* functions in the analysis.

   Another important aspect of the user in supply analysis is that user behavior will often influence the cost and other levels of service attributes, as mentioned earlier. Thus, the supply function to be employed in demand analysis and traffic estimation is a specifically defined function that represents the synthesis of supplier and operator costs, and their methods of recovery, as well as the impact of user behavior on these costs and the user's perception of them.

4. *The regulator*. This refers to the entity which exercises some sort of control on the operation of the system or on any of the linkages between the actors involved in transport supply. Regulation can be of a technical, operational nature when it relates to requirements concerning the manner by which the transportation technology is to be adapted, delivered, or operated. It can also be of an economic nature when it relates to requirements concerning the manner of cost recovery, the methods of pricing, and in some cases, the amount and nature of transport services supplied to users. Regulation can affect all three previously mentioned actors. For example, in designing and building the airport infrastructure, the responsible public agency (the supplier) has to meet certain engineering norms and standards; the airport authority operating the airport system must follow safety rules, as must the airlines operating their aircraft at the airport. Both these latter actors have to follow certain rules concerning the manner by which they charge their customers for the service.

It is important to note the existence of a functional hierarchy among the four actors. This hierarchy begins with the supplier, whose technology determines basically the type of transportation to be supplied. This is followed by the operator who adapts and articulates the technology in responding to traffic conditions and to influences from the prevailing environment of the system. Finally, there is the user who "receives" the transportation service thus offered. All three actors are influenced in their behavior by the regulator. This functional hierarchy also applies to the cost and other levels of service attributes. The supplier's costs can affect the operator's, which in turn will affect the user's. These costs, as well as the relationships between them, are influenced by the fourth actor: the regulator. In the following sections, we shall present illustrations of these roles in the development of transportation supply functions for different types of transportation supply. Before that, a brief review of the concept of transportation cost might be in order.

3.2 COSTS AND COST FUNCTIONS

The cost of transportation is a complex, multidimensional attribute that represents the resources that must be expended in order for transportation to take place. These resources are expended by the supplier, the operator, or the user. The scope of transportation cost extends beyond the monetary components to include characteristics such as the value of time spent in travel, the loss of value of goods while in transit, and the cost of the inconvenience and discomfort of traveling under some conditions. For this reason, it is common in transportation analysis to refer to *generalized cost* in order to reflect this multidimensionality. Attempts are also often made in transportation analysis to transform all cost components to a single system of units, usually monetary units. This is done by attaching monetary values to units of the other cost components, such as a dollar value for 1 h of travel time or of delay time.

In most analyses involving cost, including transportation supply analysis, one is interested in a relationship between the cost of the system and its output. For example, in analyzing the operating cost of a bus line, one would wish to have a relationship between the cost and the amount of seat-kilometers. Such a relationship between cost and output is referred to as a *cost function*. There are many types of cost functions that can be developed depending on the types of analysis at hand. A total cost function relates the total cost of the system to its output. A total cost function $C(x)$ relates the total cost of the system C to its output x. An average cost AVC function is obtained by $AVC(x) = C(x)/x$, and relates the cost per unit to the output of the system. The marginal cost MC function $MC(x) = \partial C(x)/\partial x$ relates the gradient of the cost function to output and represents the cost of marginally increasing the output of the system.

Cost functions that represent a system with a fixed capacity are referred to as *short-run functions*. When the capacity of the system is expanded as the output level increases, then the resulting cost function is referred to as a *long-run function*. The distinction between the two is quite important since in the long-run case opportunities might exist for optimizing the compatibility between system capacity and output, with the result that average costs are reduced or kept from increasing as output increases. An example of this is the case of a highway cost function. The total cost as a function of traffic volume for a one-lane facility might look as shown in Fig. 3.2a. The rapid increase in cost at higher volumes indicates that the capacity of the highway is reached or exceeded, and there is significant congestion. The average and marginal cost functions for such a system would look as shown in Fig. 3.2b, where again due to congestion, average and marginal costs rise sharply as congestion sets in. These functions would be referred to as short-run functions since they represent a facility with a fixed capacity. If, however, we consider the result of adding a lane to the highway in question and if we combine the total cost curves for the one-lane and the two-lane facilities, then we can represent both by a cost function which shows both the costs and the implication of a transition from a one-lane to a two-lane capacity. Such a curve, shown in Fig. 3.2c, would be referred to as a long-run cost function. The corresponding average and marginal cost functions shown in Fig. 3.2d illustrate the advantages of capacity expansion as output increases. While all the functions in Fig. 3.2c and d imply a transition from the one-lane to the two-lane facility when output reaches V, the value at which the two corresponding cost curves are equal, such a transition can occur at any other point since facility expansion is not based solely on cost considerations. In any case, the resulting envelope of the two short-run cost functions would represent the long-run function.

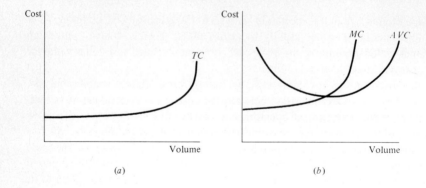

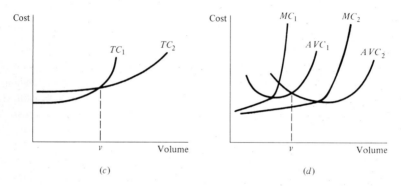

Figure 3.2 Highway Transportation Cost Functions. (*a*) Short-run total cost; (*b*) short-run average and marginal costs; (*c*) long-run total cost; (*d*) Long-run average and marginal costs.

In most transportation applications, the transition from a short-run to a long-run cost function occurs in rather large increments, reflecting the indivisibilities of transportation capacity. The example of Fig. 3.2*c* and *d* shows this clearly. The addition of a lane to a highway facility results in a quantum increase in capacity. Thus, while, theoretically, long-term functions are often considered smooth and differentiable, in most transportation applications this is not the case, and the phenomenon of indivisibility has to be taken into consideration.

3.3 THE SUPPLY FUNCTION

The supply function relates the attributes of the transportation system, as they are experienced by the users, to the level of output of the system. In other words, it is a function representing a causal relationship which is the reverse of that of the demand function. The demand function shows how the traffic volume is affected by the level of service attributes of the transportation system, and the supply function shows how these attributes are influenced by the traffic volume using the system. In order to facilitate equilibrium analysis and traffic estimation, one normally uses the same variables to describe traffic and level of service in both these functions. If we think of most levels of service attributes as components of transportation cost, then the supply function would be analogous to a user average total cost function, since it is the average cost incurred by each unit of traffic which will determine actual traffic volume that is to materialize. For the same reason, it is important to think of the supply function as giving the relation between traffic and the *perceived* cost of travel. This is particularly important when incorporating individual operating costs in automobile transportation into the supply function, for it is fairly well known that individual vehicle owners typically underestimate the actual costs of driving their vehicles. The issue of perceived costs is also important when dealing with the supply functions for scheduled collective modes such as buses and airplanes. It is also fairly well known that passengers find waiting time more of an inconvenience than line-haul time. In other words, the perceived costs of equal amounts of time in waiting and in transit are usually different. In general, it is through empirical observations that the demand analyst is able to verify the extent to which perceived and actual values of transportation attributes differ. Demand and supply model parameters estimated from data would normally represent user behavior and consequently would implicitly take into account the question of user perception of attributes.

We have said so far that the supply function is analogous to an average total cost function. Whether it is a short-run or a long-run function depends on the operator behavior and on whether system capacity is modified as the level of traffic changes. A typical example of a supply function used in highway traffic analysis is shown in Fig. 3.3 as the perceived user average total cost function.

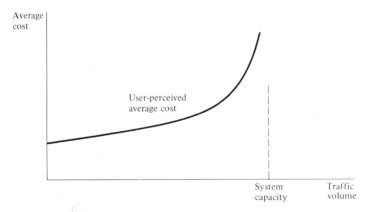

Figure 3.3 A transportation supply function.

This function would be a composite including the actual out-of-pocket costs incurred by the users of the highway, the value of travel time involved, and the cost value of the discomfort and inconvenience of traveling on the highway, particularly as the traffic volume increased. Note that the supply function in Fig. 3.3 would be related, and in part derived from, the corresponding highway cost function shown in Fig. 3.2b. How this is done is the central focus of transportation supply analysis and the subject of the rest of this chapter.

Link Supply and System Supply

It is useful in transportation supply analysis to distinguish between the supply function for an isolated link and that for a system. This distinction is important since in most transportation applications one is concerned with the supply characteristics of a system composed of a group of links, each representing a particular route, mode, or facility.

A *link supply function* relates the traffic and supply characteristics for a single, isolated transportation facility, which may be a route between two points, by a particular mode. The highway function given in Fig. 3.3 could, for example, represent a link supply function for a given stretch of highway connecting two well-defined points between which all the traffic of interest flows. A link supply function is valid for only a single transportation technology. Thus, if automobiles as well as buses are operated on this highway facility, then a different supply function would be needed to describe the characteristics of each. It is possible to combine both supply functions into one that would then represent a system supply function for the given highway considered as a system including automobile and bus transportation facilities.

A *system supply function* represents a transportation system that might be composed of a group of links operating in series or in parallel. In the case of series aggregation, the system is composed of facilities that must all be used in order to connect a point of origin and a point of destination. In the case of parallel aggregation, the system may be composed of different facilities constituting options that are available simultaneously to the potential user. The aggregation of link supply functions into system functions can be demonstrated by the example shown in Fig. 3.4a to d. In Fig. 3.4a is shown a situation where two links are connected in series to make up a transportation system serving between A and B. The individual link functions for these two links are added vertically to make up the system supply function as shown in Fig. 3.4b. In Fig. 3.4c, the two links serve in parallel between A and B. In this case, the system supply function is obtained by summing the curves horizontally as shown in Fig. 3.4d. To interpret this physically, we can think of the supply function S as giving average user travel cost. The vertical addition for series aggregation implies the addition of the costs on links 1 and 2 in order to arrive at the cost between A and B. The horizontal addition for parallel aggregation implies that for any given value of average user

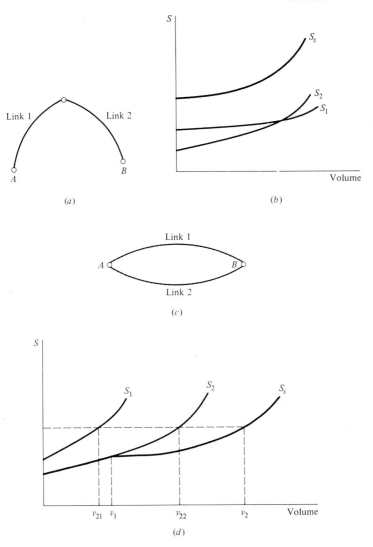

Figure 3.4 Aggregation of link supply into system supply functions. (*a*) Links in series; (*b*) series aggregation; (*c*) links in parallel; (*d*) parallel aggregation.

cost S, the traffic volume would be the sum of the volumes carried by links 1 and 2 since they are operating in parallel.

If we let the supply function be given by $S(v)$ where v is the traffic volume and S, for example, the total average user cost, then for series aggregation, the system supply function S_s would be obtained by the addition of the link functions S_1 and S_2:

$$S_s(v) = S_1(v) + S_2(v)$$

The situation is not as straightforward in the case of parallel aggregation, for implied in such an aggregation is some rule for allocating total traffic v among the links serving in parallel. Such a rule can be simple when the number of links in parallel is small, say less than four, but will require analysis of transportation choice when the alternatives are numerous. For example, in the two-link case shown in Fig. 3.4c and d, the allocation rule is that all traffic will use link 1 as long as it is cheaper than link 2, i.e., up to a volume v_1. After that, traffic is allocated in such a way that the average cost on both links is equal, so that if the volume is v_2, the allocation will be v_{21} to link 1 and v_{22} to link 2 such that $v_{21} + v_{22} = v$ and $S_1(v_{21}) = S_2(v_{22})$. Obviously this is one of many allocation rules that can be used depending on the nature of the system on hand. It is important to note that different allocation rules will result in different system supply functions. Different rules are usually applied depending on whether the choices are among modes, routes, destinations, or combinations of these. In such cases, the construction of the appropriate supply function becomes an integral part of equilibrium analysis. How this is done is seen at various places in the following chapters.

Components of the Supply Function

In general, the supply function gives the level of service attributes that affect the realization of traffic volumes, as they are affected by these volumes. As mentioned in a previous section, these attributes result from the interaction between the four players involved in the delivery and use of transportation services: the supplier, the operator, the user, and the regulator. The important components of the supply function are different for passenger and for commodity transportation.

For passenger transportation, it is common to take into account the following attributes in a supply function:

1. *Total travel time*. This may be broken down into its components, such as access time, waiting time, transfer time, and line-haul transit time. Of course, not all of these components are relevant in all cases.
2. *Total travel cost*. This is also broken down into components such as out-of-pocket money cost, vehicle operating cost, implicit costs such as indirect taxes, and terminal costs associated with some modes such as parking in the case of private automobile transportation.
3. *Schedule inconvenience*. For some scheduled modes, such as airplanes and trains, a given schedule of services may constitute a level of inconvenience since a potential user may not be able to use the service at exactly the desired time. This inconvenience can be measured by the headway between services, although this is only an approximation until one knows exactly when each user's desired time of travel is. It is common in transportation analysis to consider schedule inconvenience as a part of waiting time and a component of total travel time, but it is more appropriate to keep it separate since in

general potential users may not actually wait for transportation services that might not be offered at the most convenient time. For some cases, frequent services have the additional marketing appeal in that they give the potential users more options for travel. This is an attribute of supply that may be taken into account in addition to whatever waiting time one might be able to identify, as is sometimes done in analyzing demand and supply in regional and short-haul air transportation.

4. *Discomfort and inconvenience of travel.* This is an attribute that is easily identifiable as having an impact on the realization of traffic, although it is usually not easily quantifiable. One can include this attribute in supply functions in some cases, however. For example, in air travel analysis, different functions are built for jet and for nonjet aircraft when it is believed that the additional level of comfort of jet aircraft would represent a lower average total cost of travel to the user, *ceteris paribus.*

For commodity transportation similar attributes are included in the supply function:

1. *Total travel time.* This is a broken down into line-haul time and terminal times at trip ends including loading and unloading, as well as access to the line-haul mode and delays.

2. *Total transport cost.* This is also broken down into line-haul freight rate, terminal costs including those for access and egress from the line-haul mode, and terminal storage costs at trip ends. In some cases, the freight rate covers all transport costs including insurance and taxes. However, when the user is the same as the operator, then vehicle operating costs, insurance, and taxes all become identifiable components of the total cost of transportation.

3. *Service frequency.* As in the case of passenger transportation, increased service frequency is analogous to reduced transport cost. In the case of commodity transportation, more frequent service can result in reductions in inventory levels and hence in storage costs for the shippers. The effect of service frequency should be considered over and above any delays in transportation that may be identified as a part of the total travel time.

4. *System reliability.* This usually refers to the ability to predict the performance of the system in advance, such as being able to anticipate the arrival of shipments, or the state of the goods being shipped. This ability, which increases with the reliability of the system, will often result in reduced inventory level and hence shipper costs. The reliability of the system can be quantified as variations in the system attributes such as time, cost, and safety.

5. *Preservability.* This can be an important attribute for some types of commodities. It is related to the risk of deterioration of the commodity while in transit. For perishable goods, deterioration will occur at a certain rate while in transit, depending on the manner in which the goods are packaged and carried. For example, fruits carried in a refrigerated truck will deteriorate at

a slower rate than in an unrefrigerated one. Consequently, the refrigeration of a truck is analogous to a reduction in the total cost of transporting the goods, *ceteris paribus*. Of course, another component of total cost, the freight rate, is usually higher for the refrigerated truck.

It is important to note that not all of these attributes of transportation level of service are relevant for technologies and in all applications. Indeed, one should try to simplify the analysis by including only those attributes that are relevant to the issues at hand. Furthermore, there is little point in including in the analysis of transportation supply, variables that cannot be measured adequately, or the value of which does not change appreciably within the context of the analysis. In urban traffic analysis, for example, it is often common to limit the supply function to a travel time function when dealing with network flows and the choice of routes for a particular mode of travel. In air travel analysis, air fares and service frequencies are often the only variables used in the supply function.

3.4 SELECTED TRANSPORTATION SUPPLY FUNCTIONS

In developing a morphology of transportation supply functions, there are three fundamental distinctions that can be made between types of transportation systems. The first is whether it is transportation of passengers or of commodities. The second is whether it is urban transportation or regional transportation (inter-urban, rural, etc.). The third is whether it is transportation by an individual mode, such as private automobile, or collective mode, such as bus or airplane. These distinctions are important because they result in basic differences between supply functions. The distinction between passenger and commodity transportation is meaningful since the important attributes of transportation level of service, and the manner by which they are perceived and quantified, differ. In the case of commodity transportation, the conversion of level of service attributes into a single monetary cost equivalent is considerably more straightforward than in the case of passengers. The distinction between urban and nonurban transportation is useful since the magnitudes of the relevant supply variables differ significantly. Attributes that may be important in urban transportation may be insignificant at the nonurban level where travel distances are so much longer and travel activities less frequent. The distinction between individual and collective modes of transportation is important because the evolution of supply differs significantly. In the case of individual transportation, the operator and the user are one and the same, whereas in the case of collective transport, they are distinct entities. Thus, in structuring the supply function for a case of individual transportation, we may seek to study the relation between the supplier and the user directly, whereas in collective transportation, the intermediate influence of the operator's behavior may have to be taken into account. An important aspect of operator behavior in this regard is scheduling. Collective means of transport are normally scheduled, whereas individual means are not. This means that an important aspect of level of service, namely schedule frequency, is present in the supply function for collective but not for individual transportation.

Using these three distinctions, we obtain a simple taxonomy of transportation for the purpose of supply analysis. Such a taxonomy is shown in Fig. 3.5. Notice

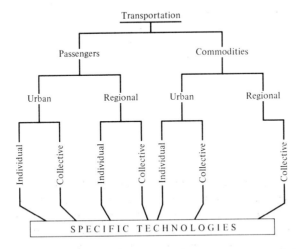

Figure 3.5 A simple taxonomy for transportation supply analysis.

that the tree is not complete because individual modes of transportation are left out for commodity transportation at the regional level. This is merely a simplification introduced, since it is not common to undertake long-distance regional transportation for commodities at the individual level. It is in fact rare in urban transport as well, for most commodity transport is carried out in conjunction with some collection-distribution activity whereby commodities are consolidated and hence transported collectively. For each of the branches identified in the taxonomy, a number of specific technologies can be considered. The supply functions for these technologies will differ in their specific technical and operational parameters but will share the same fundamental structure. In the following sections, we shall look at supply functions for some of these types of transportation.

Urban Highway Transportation

We first consider an urban highway connecting two well-defined points of origin and destination and serving individual automobile traffic, as well as a bus system. For each of these two modes, we can develop a link supply function and then aggregate these in parallel to arrive at a system function for the given highway.

Starting with the individual automobile mode, we are interested in the average, perceived user cost function. In order to construct such a function, we follow the hierarchy shown in Fig. 3.1. At first, we identify the players involved in the delivery and use of the transportation in question. We identify a supplier who in this case would be a governmental agency responsible for the construction and maintenance of the highway infrastructure. The operator and user in this case are the same: the individual vehicle driver. The regulator may be another agency responsible for maintaining a specific operating condition on the highway (speed limit, signaling, etc.).

Starting with the supplier, we identify the supplier's cost function by taking the total cost of construction and converting it into an equivalent annual cost using the appropriate economic accounting and taking into consideration the life of the facility and the appropriate discount rate. To this cost must be added the cost of maintenance, which can depend on the volume of traffic using the facility. Figure 3.6a shows a typical cost function for such a case. The linear total cost

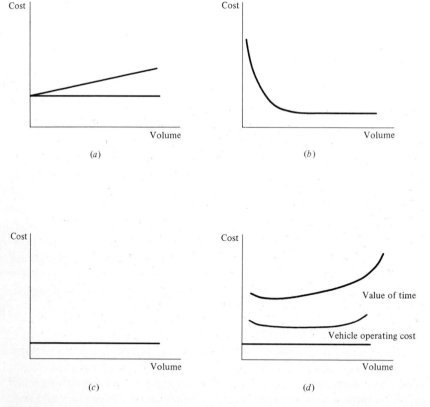

Figure 3.6 Urban highway supply function. (a) Supplier's total cost; (b) supplier's average cost; (c) cost recovery by taxes; (d) automobile user supply function.

function suggests no scale economies in the construction and maintenance of urban highways, a result recently suggested by the empirical work of Keeler and Small (1977). The total cost function can now be converted into an average cost function as shown in Fig. 3.6b. In order to translate this supplier cost into a user cost, the cost recovery scheme must be defined. There are normally two types of schemes used in cost recovery in urban automobile transportation: a direct and an indirect. The first is in the form of tolls paid by each user, and the second in the form of taxation. Both can be used simultaneously, as is the case in toll facilities in the United States, where a user paying a toll on a highway is also assessed the gas tax and other vehicle registration and operation taxes. Assuming for this example that if tolls are used, then they are fixed with respect to traffic volume, then the conversion of the supplier cost function into a user function will result in a simple invariant value representing the tax and whatever toll is charged. This is shown in Fig. 3.6c.

To this user cost must be added other components of cost that result from the operation of the vehicle on the highway. The first is the cost of operating the vehicle. This is a component which varies with volume as shown in Fig. 3.6d. At first, the cost declines with increasing volume, showing the effect of reduced travel speed on operating cost. But at higher volume, the operating cost increases again due to congestion, stop-and-go driving conditions, and increased brake use.

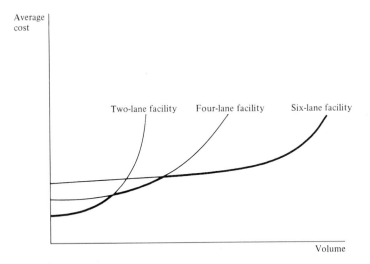

Figure 3.7 Long-run highway supply function for automobile travel.

The other component to be added is the value of travel time and the associated discomfort and inconvenience of travel. The relation between this component and traffic volume is also shown in Fig. 3.6d. At first, it increases slightly with volume, showing the result of speed reduction on travel time. But at higher volumes, congestion results in rapid deterioration of speed and a sharp increase in travel time and in the inconvenience of travel. The resulting curve shown in Fig. 3.6*d* represents the addition of the three major components of average user cost: taxes and tolls, vehicle operating costs, and the value of travel time and inconvenience. This curve would then be the link supply function for individual automobile transportation. Note that this is a short-run function, for there is no facility expansion. A long-run function incorporating the effects of increasing the capacity of the highway by adding lanes might look as shown in Fig. 3.7, in which the curve for each level of capacity is derived in the same manner as in the above example, and then the envelope of these curves, identified on the basis of the timing of capacity expansion, results in the long-run supply function.

Supply Function for Bus Service

The construction of a supply function for bus service on the highway link is considerably more complex than for individual travel. For one thing, there is the additional influence of the behavior of the operator, who at any traffic level has numerous operational options regarding fleet size, schedule frequency, and the spacing of bus stops. Operator behavior in collective transportation modes has not been the subject of as much research and modeling as user behavior. Consequently, the construction of supply functions for this type of transportation still depends on making many simplifying assumptions. Considerable work on this subject has been done by Morlok (1976, 1980).

To construct a supply function for the highway link example, we begin with the identification of players. First, the supplier can be thought of, as in the previous case, as the governmental agency responsible for the construction and maintenance of the highway infrastructure. The operator would be a private or public bus company that is entrusted with day-to-day operation of the bus service. The regulator is a political entity that may influence the manner by which the operator costs are recovered from users, namely by regulating the fare levels. The users are the actual bus riders traveling along the highway.

The supplier's cost function is the same as in the previous case, although in practice care should be exercised in developing a highway construction and maintenance cost function by taking a realistic mix of automobiles and buses into account. It is likely that due to their heavier weight buses may cause higher maintenance costs. Usually in representing cost functions buses are converted into automobile equivalents by multiplying by an appropriate factor (usually between 1.2 and 2.0). The recovery of the supplier's cost depends on the type of entity that is entrusted with the operator of the buses. If the operator is a private company, then taxes and tolls would be the means of recovery. If, on the other hand, the operator is another public agency, then it often happens that it is exempted from these charges, and no recovery of supplier cost is made. This is often seen as a form of indirect subsidy to public transportation. Thus we can start directly with the operator's cost function, and we can include a component for tolls and taxes, assuming that these are applied to the bus company. We can assume for simplicity that this component of cost is fixed.

The next step would be to add the operating cost of the buses themselves, including both direct and indirect costs. Here it is important to distinguish between short-, medium-, and long-run costs. Short-run costs imply that the number of buses and the frequency of service does not vary, regardless of the traffic volume. This is not realistic, since the bus company will at least be able to adjust the schedules even if no additional buses are acquired. In the medium-run function, one can assume that schedules and operating strategies can be modified according to traffic volume. In the long run, it can be assumed that the fleet size and the route structure can also be modified. For a single link it should suffice to look at the long-run costs since it can be assumed that a bus company can, without expanding its fleet, adapt by modifying the allocation of buses between links of its service network. The total operating cost would have a functional relationship to traffic volume as shown in Fig. 3.8a, from which the average cost

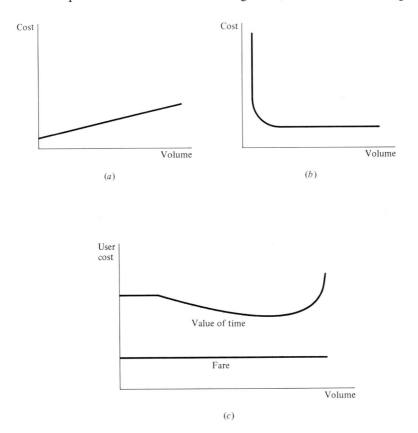

Figure 3.8 Urban bus service supply system. (a) Operator's total cost; (b) operator's average cost; (c) supply function.

function can be derived as in Fig. 3.8*b*. Examples of these functions have been derived by Morlok (1976) showing an average cost per passenger kilometer of approximately $0.15, once the volume on the line exceeds about 500 passengers per hour. We shall intentionally avoid reference to specific cost figures, since such figures are likely to be valid only for the specific systems for which they are obtained and for a short period of time.

Cost recovery for transit operations is usually a subject of considerable government regulation. It is more common than not for bus fares to be set by a public agency and to bear little direct relation to the actual operator's average cost function. Ideally, one would want to transform this latter into a user price function with a pricing scheme that would achieve some operating objective, such as complete cost recovery, partial cost recovery, or profit maximization. Assuming that fares are set politically at some level, e.g., equal to average operating cost at high traffic volume, then the operator's cost function of Fig. 3.8*b* can be transformed into a price function as in Fig. 3.8*c*. This latter would make up the first component of the user average cost function or the supply function.

To this must be added a component representing the value of travel time and the associated inconvenience and discomfort of travel. The relation between this cost component and the volume of traffic is shown in Fig. 3.8*c* and reflects a particular operating policy of the bus system. The value of travel time and inconvenience starts out at a certain level depending on the minimum schedule frequency that the operator deems feasible on the route even with very little traffic. The value of time is made of two components, travel time and schedule delay time. As the traffic increases, the capacity of the system at this minimum service frequency is approached, and the operator begins to increase the frequency of service on the route. This will result in a reduction in schedule delay, and hence the value of time and inconvenience of travel. This reduction continues as the service frequency is increased until either of two limits is approached. Either the ability of the operator to add services on the route is limited, or the capacity of the highway is approached and congestion begins to occur. Either of these two would result in an increase in travel time, the first resulting in passengers having to wait longer due to buses being full, and the second resulting in the travel time of each bus increasing due to congestion. It is possible, of course, for both of these phenomena to occur simultaneously, but it is to be noted that congestion on a highway due solely to increased bus volumes occurs only when the passenger traffic volume is very large. A single lane serving buses can normally carry about 1000 buses per hour if it is a freeway lane; this would translate into approximately 50,000 passengers per hour. Even when the lane is in a facility with limited access, large volumes of passengers can be carried before congestion occurs. The result of the addition of the fare and the value of time and inconvenience would represent the total of the user average cost and hence the supply function for the service, as shown in Fig. 3.8*c*. Note that this is a link supply function and does not include any other access links that may be serving the same traffic.

System Supply Function

If we are interested in a supply function for the highway taken as a system which serves both automobile and bus traffic, then it is possible to combine the two link supply functions for these services to obtain a system supply function. This can be done by parallel aggregation of the functions shown in Figs. 3.6d and 3.8c. It is important to note that when doing this aggregation, similar units of traffic volume need be used and that the congestion effects calculated for each mode take into account the presence of the vehicles of the other mode on the same highway. For traffic measurement, it is possible to convert either mode into passenger flow rates. For taking congestion effects into consideration, some assumptions about the traffic mix can be made, or more accurately, an iterative procedure can be used in order to match the traffic on each mode that is implied in the system supply function with the traffic mix assumed in calculating travel times in each link supply function. This is usually done in the analysis of transportation networks and using computer-based algorithms.

In order to do the parallel aggregation of the link supply functions, it is necessary to adopt a traffic allocation rule. The simple equilibrium assumption can be made in this case, although as mentioned earlier, this is just one of many traffic assignment rules that can be used. More on this subject is discussed in Chap. 7 which deals with route choice analysis. The equilibrium assumption will lead to a horizontal addition of the two supply functions as shown in Fig. 3.9.

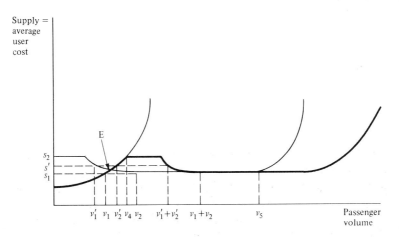

Figure 3.9 System supply function for highway serving automobile and bus traffic.

However, due to the fact that one of the two link functions, that of the bus service, is not convex, the aggregation is not quite as straightforward, as discussed in a previous section, and merits some discussion. Referring to Fig. 3.9, it can be noted that as long as the traffic volume is below v_4, the level at which the automobile supply function equals that of the bus with minimum service frequency, all the traffic will be allocated to automobiles according to the equilibrium assumptions. This is so because the equilibrium point E where the two functions cross does not represent a stable equilibrium. If the traffic volume at E is all served by the bus, then it would pay for some of the traffic to shift to the automobile, thus incurring a lower average cost as indicated by the lower value of the automobile supply function to the left of E. This shift would also result in a deterioration of the service by bus and an increase in the average cost for that mode and would therefore precipitate further shift to the automobile until all the traffic uses that mode to the exclusion of the bus, for which the supply function would be now have reached a value S_2. The same is, of course, true for any traffic volume less than at E. For any point to the right of E and less than a volume v_4, the same would occur if the traffic or any part of it is served by the bus: it will be cheaper for some passengers to shift to the automobile in order to take advantage of the lower supply function to the left of E. This shift will cause a deterioration of the bus level of service and will precipitate more shift until point E is reached, which, as we saw above, is not a stable equilibrium point. At volumes larger than v_4, a simple horizontal addition of the two link supply functions will result in the system function. Notice that the decreasing portion of the system supply function decreases faster than the bus link function, since the system function represents the addition of the decreasing bus function to an increasing automobile supply function. For example, at a value of system supply of S', the system can handle a total volume of $v_1' + v_2'$ as shown in Fig. 3.9. At a supply value of S_1, the system can handle either a volume of v_1 on the automobile link alone or that in addition to a volume on the bus service of v_2.

It is important to note again two features of the system supply function in this case. The first is that the function is not convex, due to the nonconvexity of the bus link function. The second is that the function is a result of the assumptions

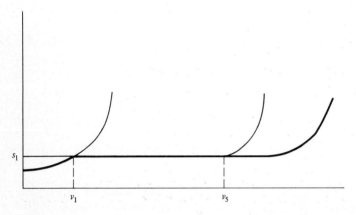

Figure 3.10 System supply function when bus service frequency is not reduced at low traffic volumes.

made in the aggregation concerning user bahavior as well as operator behavior. If, for example, the operator is assumed to operate at a high frequency level in order to attract passenger traffic even when actual traffic is below v_4, then the bus link function would have a different shape and the aggregation would result in a different system supply function even when maintaining the same equilibrium assumptions. Compared to Fig. 3.9, the supply function for an operator who does not reduce service frequency when traffic volume declines would look as shown in Fig. 3.10. The simple horizontal addition would apply throughout the range of volumes, and the resulting system function would be convex.

Intercity Air Transportation

In order to demonstrate the construction of a supply function for a case of intercity air transportation, we consider a simple system consisting of two airports serving two cities at some distance. The supply of passenger air transportation between these two airports is represented by the perceived user average cost function. In long-distance air travel, this function is dominated by the air fare, which depends directly on the cost recovery scheme used by the airline providing the service and is influenced by regulation and market characteristics. However, in order to see this supply function in the same perspective used for other types of transportation, it is worthwhile to discuss the role played by each of the actors involved in providing transportation in this case.

First we can identify two suppliers. The first is the airport authority which builds the airport infrastructure, and the second the government which often plays a major funding role in airport construction. These two suppliers incur costs that are normally directly recovered from the airlines and the passengers via taxes and charges. In the United States, it is customary for airports to charge the airlines landing fees and other space rentals in order to recover the cost of operating the airport and of servicing the debt used to finance construction. The government charges the airlines taxes in the form of registration fees and the like and charges passengers taxes assessed on the basis of the values of the air fares (usually at a rate of 8 percent). These supplier costs are then recovered directly and appear as fixed components in the cost functions of the airlines and of the passengers. We can then identify two operators. The first is the airport authority, which may adjust the operating procedures in response to traffic conditions, such as by raising landing fees during peak hours or by assessing passenger head taxes or tolls in order to aid in the recovery of operating costs. The second is the airline, which incurs an operating cost in addition to the charges paid to the airport and the taxes paid to the government. The airline cost function usually shows economies of scale and a decreasing average cost at low volume, after which average costs become constant until such a point when congestion effects begin to appear and the average costs rise again due to delays. The airline costs are in principle recovered through air fares, which in the case of long-distance air travel will make up the major component of the user's supply function.

In addition to air fares, and any direct fees and charges paid to the airport, the users incur a travel time and inconvenience cost. This component of the supply function usually decreases with volume, indicating a reduction in schedule delays, but then increases again as congestion effects appear. The supply function for the users might look as shown in Fig. 3.11, which is drawn to illustrate how

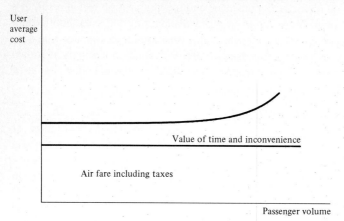

Figure 3.11 Supply function for long distance air travel.

the air fare is a predominant component of total average cost for long-distance air travel. For example, for a 3000-km trip, the air fare might be of the order of $300 and the travel time approximately 4 h. At a value of travel time of say $8 h, the total value of time for the trip would be $32. If one adds to that a delay time of 2 h due to either congestion or the inconvenience of schedules, then the total value of travel time including delay would be on the order of $40, or about 12 percent of the total trip cost. In the case of short-haul travel, say for a trip of 300 km, the picture would be different. The air fare might be of the order of $40 and the travel time about 1 h. If we add another 2 h due to congestion or to schedule delay, then the total time value for the trip would be about $24, which is nearly 50 percent of the total trip cost. The supply function for a short-haul air service might look as shown in Fig. 3.12.

Given the example of long-distance air travel, we assume that the air fare alone represents the user supply function. In this case, in order to construct this function, we would need to understand the process by which the air fare is determined. This depends largely on two factors. The first is whether the fare is regulated by a government institution or not. The second, in the case of un-regulated fares, is the structure of the market in which the service is being offered. In particular, it is important to know whether the market is that of a monopoly where one airline determines the fare that best suits its objectives, or whether the market is competitive in which the fare is set according to the lowest level offered by any airline in the market and is not at the discretion of any single airline, at least in principle. This provides us with a good example of how pricing and market structure affect the supply function in transportation.

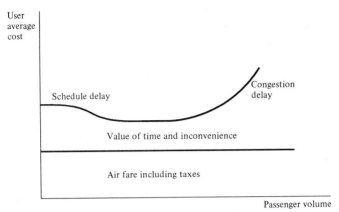

Figure 3.12 Supply function for short-haul air travel.

Consider first a *monopoly* where there is only one airline in the market and where the fare is not regulated. For the airline to maximize profit from the service, it would be necessary to charge a price such that the marginal revenue equals the marginal cost. It follows directly that the price charged will depend on the nature of the marginal revenue function, and hence the demand function. An example of this situation is shown in Fig. 3.13. The airline's average and mar-

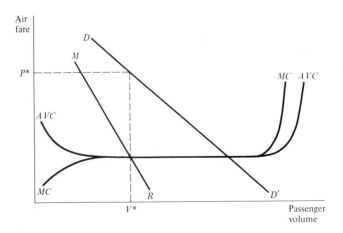

Figure 3.13 Airline fare in a monopoly market.

ginal cost functions are shown as AVC and MC, respectively, and the demand and marginal revenue functions are shown as DD' and MR, respectively. The point at which the profit-maximizing rule of marginal revenue equaling marginal cost corresponds to an air fare equal to p^* and a volume of V^*. In this case, there is no supply function in the conventional sense but a supply *point*. The price is fixed at p^* and will change only if the demand, and hence the marginal curve function, changes.

The other market condition is that of *perfect competition*, in which the price is fixed in the market and is not influenced by the behavior of any individual airline. From the point of view of constructing the supply function, this situation is similar to that when the fare is fixed by a regulatory action. The situation is depicted in Fig. 3.14, where the fixed air fare is given by p. The average and

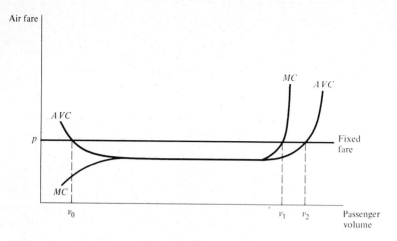

Figure 3.14 Supply of air transportation in a competitive market.

marginal cost functions for an airline are shown on the same diagram. At the point where the marginal cost MC equals the fixed price, which in this case would also be the average and marginal revenue, the airline will offer a supply of v_1. Offering any volume other than v_1 would be also profitable but would not generate maximum total profits. If the airline offers more than v_1, then profits will decrease until at v_2 they will vanish since the airline's average cost will equal the fare. For a profit-maximizing airline, then, in a perfectly competitive market, it can be said that the supply function is the same as the airline's marginal cost function. Of course, if the average cost of the airline is larger than the fixed fare, at all levels of volume, then this airline will not be able to operate profitably in the market. The airline in Fig. 3.14 can offer profitably a capacity for anywhere between v_0 and v_2 passengers.

The above two examples are intended to illustrate the impact of pricing, market structure, and the regulatory environment on the evolution of the supply function for collective transportation modes. Also, in the case of a monopolistic market, the nature of the supply may not be described by a function in the conventional sense. The price depends on the cost function of the supplier and on the demand function as well. Changes in the nature of the demand function will affect the price charged, and hence the supply of transportation.

PROBLEMS

3.1 The following graph shows the demand and cost functions related to an urban mass transit system. Indicate the following graphically:

(a) The tariff and traffic volume resulting from a strategy to maximize total revenues to the transit company.

(b) Tariff and traffic levels resulting from a strategy to maximize the profits of the transit company.

(c) Tariff and traffic levels resulting from the strategy to maximize usage subject to the constraint that operating variable costs must be covered.

(d) Tariff and traffic levels resulting from the strategy to maximize total net benefits (to society!).

(e) Which of the above strategies yields the highest consumer surplus?

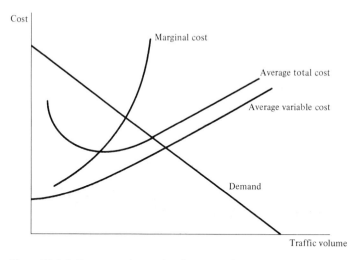

Figure P3.1 Influences on the supply of transportation.

3.2 Given a region with communities A, B, C, and D connected by the highway network shown below with distances indicated in kilometers. A product is to be made of wood, steel, and labor. For each ton of the product 0.8 t of wood and 0.2 t of steel and 100 worker-hours of labor are necessary.

Transport costs are as follows:

	Terminal	Line-haul
Wood	$20.00/t	$0.20/t·km
Steel	$30.00/t	$0.40/t·km
Product	$50.00/t	$0.60/t·km

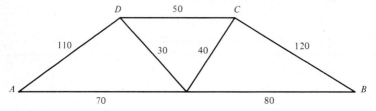

Figure P3.2 Highway transportation cost functions. (*A*) Short-run total cost; (*B*) short-run average and marginal costs; (*C*) long-run total cost; (*D*) long-run average and marginal costs.

Resources are available at the following locations, at the indicated cost per ton,

	A	*B*	*C*	*D*
Steel	$20	$25	—	—
Wood	—	—	$300	$450
Hourly wage rates	5.00	4.00	5.00	5.50

Demand for final products exists at *B*, *C*, and *D* and is expressed by a demand function of the general form

$$q_i = a - bp_i$$

where q_i = quantity of the product sold in the *ith* market
p_i = price in the *ith* market

In particular

$$q_b = 240 - 0.160p_b$$
$$q_c = 240 - 0.240p_c$$
$$q_d = 100 - 0.050p_d$$

The product is manufactured under conditions of constant returns to scale and is produced at only one location.

(*a*) Where will production occur, assuming that location is determined by an economic calculus?

(*b*) What quantity of resources will be shipped from each source?

(*c*) What quantity of product will be shipped to each market?

(*d*) What are the link demands for transportation (in tons)?

3.3 The network shown below indicates the transportation costs between the three cities *A*, *B*, and *C*. These costs are in dollars per ton for the movement of potatoes. Potatoes are produced only in city *A* and are demanded only in cities

B and C. The quantity produced in A is very large so that there is no limit to the ability to meet the demands in B and C.

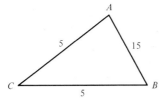

Figure P3.3 A transportation supply function.

The production cost per ton in A is \$5.00 and the demands for potatoes in B and C are given by the following demand functions:

In B: $q = 50 - 2.5p$

In C: $q = 100 - 10p$

where q represents the quantity purchased in tons and p represents the price per ton of the sale of potatoes.

(a) Calculate the quantity of potatoes purchased in each of the cities B and C.

(b) Compute the flows (in tons of potatoes) on the links of the network.

REFERENCES

Florian, M., and M. Gaudry: A Conceptual Framework for the Supply Side in Transportation Systems, *Transp. Res.*, vol. 14B, no. 1/2, pp. 1–8, 1980.

Heggie, I.: "Transport Engineering Economics," McGraw-Hill Book Company, New York, 1972.

Keeler, T., and K. Small: "On the Environmental Costs of Various Transportation Modes," Institute of Urban and Regional Development, Berkeley, Calif., 1977.

Manheim, M. M.: "Fundamentals of Transportation Systems Analysis," vol. 1, MIT Press, Cambridge, Mass., 1979.

Morlok, E. K.: Supply Functions for Public Transport: Initial Concepts and Models, in *Traffic Equilibrium Methods*, ed. by M. Florian, Springer Verlag, New York, pp. 322–367, 1976.

_____: "Introduction to Transportation Engineering and Planning," McGraw-Hill Book Company, New York, 1978.

_____: Types of Transportation Supply Functions and Their Applications, *Transp. Res.*, vol. 14B, no. 1/2, pp. 9–28, 1980.

FOUR

URBAN PASSENGER TRAVEL DEMAND

This chapter is devoted to demand analysis in the case of urban passenger transportation. It contains a discussion of the general framework for the analysis including its purpose, scope, and limitations. It also contains a discussion of the basic approaches to demand analysis and the fundamental assumptions upon which they are based.

Urban travel demand analysis, while not the oldest, is probably the most advanced field of transportation demand analysis. It received considerable attention as a major analytical input into the urban transportation planning studies of the 1950s and 1960s. Although the policy issues have now changed, there remains considerable public interest and involvement in urban transportation planning, and travel demand analysis continues to be required as a policy analysis tool. However, the shift in issues facing urban transportation planning has rendered many of the demand analysis techniques available of limited value and has forced transportation analysts to adapt these techniques.

4.1 DEMAND ANALYSIS IN URBAN TRANSPORTATION PLANNING

Transportation demand analysis is useful in addressing a variety of policy issues and in providing important quantitative inputs in urban transportation planning. Generally two types of questions can be answered with the aid of demand analysis.

The first is when strategies related to the supply of transportation are to be evaluated. Demand analysis is used in this case to assess the impacts of these strategies on urban traffic movements, traveler benefits, and nontraveler impacts. The types of transportation strategies that can be so assessed are quite varied. They include high-investment options, such as construction of new urban freeways or transit systems, and low-investment options, such as traffic management schemes, parking allocations, or exclusive bus lanes in commuting corridors.

The second case is when alternative land-use plans are to be evaluated. In this case, demand analysis provides the link between the land-use patterns and transportation demands, and, given an actual or postulated transportation system, provides estimates of the resulting traffic movements and their related impacts.

It should be noted that in the first case, the pattern of socioeconomic activities that create the demand for transportation is not taken as a policy variable. In other words, it is assumed fixed and exogenous to the analysis, and only the supply of transportation is considered endogenous. On the other hand, in the second case, the supply of transportation may be assumed fixed and only the determinants of transportation demand are varied. In this manner, demand analysis cannot directly account for the long-term mutual effect between demand and supply. To do this requires an iterative feedback process where only one of the two factors is changed at a time. This is a lengthy process for which efficient methodology is not yet readily available.

Limitations of Demand Analysis

Although a very useful tool in urban transportation planning, demand analysis has limitations that are important to recognize. Most significant are the theoretical limitations stemming from the inability to apply the elements of a demand theory fully. Urban transportation models are usually based on hypotheses concerning the behavior of urban travelers, which are empirically validated by observing trip behavior. In other words, it is not possible to conduct "controlled" experiments or laboratory tests to ascertain how travelers would behave under hypothetical situations. Consequently, demand models are constructed on the basis of observations of traveler behavior under existing transportation supply conditions. They are therefore valid only when applied to situations that are not too different from those under which the analysis was performed. Furthermore, they are valid only in the short run, since they do not consider the long-term effects of changes in traveler behavior.

There are also limits to the need for demand analysis in transportation planning. Demand analysis is useful for forecasting traffic movements and associated impacts resulting from changes in the socioeconomic environment or in the transportation supply system. In planning situations where these kinds of changes are not envisaged in the short run, or where detailed predictions of traffic flows and user benefits are not required, it is not necessary to conduct demand analysis. Also there are planning situations where the problems of traffic forecasting are not sufficiently complex to warrant the use of demand models. This is particularly the case when very simple networks are involved, or where the possible configurations of the system are not numerous. It is very important to recognize in transportation planning those situations where demand analysis is not necessary, for by avoiding it considerable savings in time and cost can be accrued.

4.2 FRAMEWORK FOR DEMAND ANALYSIS

In structuring a framework for urban transportation demand analysis, it is necessary to make the following two definitions: (1) an operational definition of what constitutes an *urban* area and urban transportation, and (2) a delineation of the scope of the analysis and the necessary level of detail to which it has to be carried out.

Definition of Urban Transportation

Urban areas can be defined in many ways depending on the purpose of the definition. In most urban transportation studies, it is necessary to extend the limits of a study area beyond the political or administrative boundaries of a city. Clearly, in order to account for all important traffic movements, one needs to extend the area of interest to include all areas of residence that generate traffic to the city of interest. In many large metropolitan areas, this extension brings the urban transportation study area of one city into the economic and social zone of influence of another, and the definition loses its meaning for the purpose for which it is intended. It is important to realize that in transportation demand analysis one is concerned with the important traffic movements and not with the few commuters who travel exceptionally long distances. Consequently, it is sufficient to define an urban area for the purposes of transportation demand analysis as the region including all the major economic activities in a city and its suburbs, plus all the residential areas where it is known that most people engaged in these economic activities live. Such a definition should not require a traffic study in itself. It should be made simply on the basis of qualitative knowledge of the urban area under study.

Urban transportation of interest in demand analysis includes the travel activities that take place in an urban area on a regular daily or weekly basis. These activities can include in some instances travel activities generated outside the area of interest. However, for the purpose of demand analysis, the occasional long-distance trip or the infrequent through trip is not of much interest, and there is little need to construct complicated demand models for their analysis.

The Scope of Urban Transportation Demand Analysis

In order for demand analysis to be efficient and effective, it is necessary to limit its scope. The factors that affect the demand for and the supply of transportation are not only numerous but are also mutually dependent. Consequently, simplifications have to be made if demand analysis is to be manageable. For example, the demand for automobile transportation depends on automobile ownership and affects the supply of transporation. Conversely, the acquisition of means of transportation, particularly automobiles, depends among other things on the availability of transportation facilities. The simultaneous analysis of these factors can become intractable, and the resulting models are likely to be forbiddingly complex.

The scope of demand analysis in this and the following chapters is limited to the relationship between travel activities, on the one hand, and demand and supply factors on the other. The first is considered the endogenous variable in the models developed, and the last two are considered exogenous factors. Long-run locational decisions as well as decisions concerning the acquisition of means of transportation are not included in the analysis that follows, not because of their unimportance, but because of the practical necessity to limit the scope. The purpose of the analysis is to construct meaningful relationships between the factors that affect travel activities. These relationships are used mainly for estimating traffic and its impacts. However, they can also be used, in the appropriate context, to study other transportation-related phenomena such as the long-term locational trends. Thus, while the limitations placed on the scope of demand analysis may appear quite constraining, the fact is that when properly applied, individually or within larger analytical frameworks, transportation demand models can be quite useful in conducting many types of transportation planning analyses.

Appropriate Levels of Detail

The purpose for which demand analysis is performed determines the level of detail to which it needs to be carried out. Transportation planning analyses vary considerably in their nature and detail. For example, when the purpose of the analysis is the design of alternative transportation facilities, e.g., transit stations or roadway intersections, then traffic estimates are required with a high level of detail, both spatially and temporally. In other words, hourly or even shorter variations in traffic are important design parameters. On the other hand, when the purpose of the analysis is to assess the economic impact of systemwide alternatives, such as network configurations or land-use patterns, then traffic estimates on an annual or seasonal basis may be sufficient. The spatial detail also varies according to the purpose of the analysis. For traffic engineering studies, estimates of movements on a block-by-block basis may be necessary, whereas only movements within broadly defined traffic corridors may be sufficient for large system evaluations.

Transportation demand analysis is not particularly suited for responding to highly detailed estimation requirements. As the level of detail increases, the applicability of transportation demand models decreases. The reason for this stems from the basic characteristics of demand models, which as with all models, are based on the principle of generalization. As the problem at hand becomes more detailed and specific, it becomes less amenable to generalizations, and specific calculating schemes, such as computer simulation models or simple algebraic tools, become more suitable for the analysis. Demand models that are constructed and calibrated specifically for such detailed analyses are not likely to be useful in other situations and cannot therefore be considered a part of a general methodological framework for transportation demand analysis.

The choice of level of detail is not made solely on the basis of the needs of the analysis. Importantly, the level of detail is also chosen on the basis of the behavioral characteristics of the system being analyzed.

In urban transportation, the majority of travel activities occur in daily cycles, with differences between weekdays and weekend days. On weekdays, work and shopping travel activities occur with relatively stable and known hourly patterns. The same is true of the mostly personal and recreational travel activities during weekends. Consequently, there is little need to perform demand analyses at a finer level of temporal detail than the daily. The spatial level of detail should also be chosen according to the characteristics of the urban structure and the transportation network at hand. The abstraction of analysis networks and traffic zones is an important step in setting up an empirical framework for urban transportation demand analysis and is discussed separately later in this chapter. However, suffice it to mention here that demand analysis should be concerned with the major travel activities of importance to the planning problems in question and should not be cluttered with detailed analyses of special cases or minor traffic movements.

4.3 FUNDAMENTALS OF URBAN TRAVEL DEMAND ANALYSIS

The basic approach to the analysis of urban travel demand is that of microeconomic demand theory. The principle of utility maximization can be shown to underlie most, if not all, behavioral hypotheses regarding urban trip behavior, albeit most often implicitly and not explicitly. This principle is quite a powerful one and is used to derive most urban travel demand models. Naturally, in order to implement the principle of utility maximization, it is necessary to make and test meaningful hypotheses concerning the structure of the utility functions, and the relationship between their components and the travel activities of interest.

Basic Hypothesis

The basic hypothesis used in deriving transport demand models is shown schematically in Fig. 4.1. It postulates that the demand for urban transportation is linked directly to the demand for urban activities and is derived from them. Activities such as work, shopping, personal business, and recreation are chosen from a set called the *activity demand set*. This set contains all the urban activities that an individual or a household would have a demand for and depends on the socioeconomic characteristics. For example, the activity demand set of a household would depend on the size of the household, its combined income, the number of people employed, and so forth.

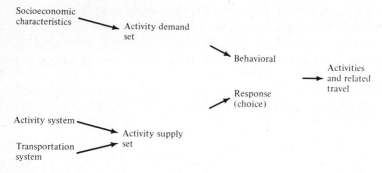

Figure 4.1 Basic hypothesis of urban travel demand.

Naturally, not all the activities included in the demand set of an individual or a household are undertaken. The number of activities undertaken depends on the availability of opportunities for doing so. In the most general sense, availability is not only measured by mere presence, but by presence at a certain distance or transportation cost. Thus an *activity supply set* is defined on the basis of the urban land-use pattern and the characteristics of the transportation system. This set includes, for each potential traveler, the totality of urban activities available at different transportation costs. It is of course not infinite, as might be theoretically conceived, but is made to include those activities that are reasonably within the domain of the urban traveler and that are likely to enter the choice process.

The juxtaposition of the activity demand and supply sets creates an environment for the traveler where a choice can be made with regard to which and how many urban activities to undertake and, consequently, which urban trips to make. It is this choice process that underlies most urban transportation demand analyses and which has been the subject of considerable research.

Thus while in demand analysis it is customary to relate travel to socioeconomic characteristics and to transport system attributes directly, it should be recognized that this is based on the postulate that these relations contain implicitly the more fundamental relations between activity demands and supplies from which transportation demands are derived. Transportation is not simply a function of land use but of the land-use system including the land users.

The important behavioral assumptions of demand analysis are related to the process of choice. It is usually postulated that the urban traveler faces a series of choices regarding the urban activities and related travel. These choices are assumed to relate directly to the demand and supply sets. In other words, in choosing a destination for a particular trip purpose, the traveler is in fact choosing an activity from among those found in the intersection of his or her demand and supply sets, and bases this choice on the activity attributes and the transportation system attributes. In most analyses, these two sets are assumed independent. As mentioned before, the mutual dependence between demand and supply in transportation is usually not taken into consideration in short-run analysis.

Choice in Urban Trip Making

In urban travel demand analysis, the trip-making process is fundamentally represented as a choice process whereby travelers choose the various atrributes of their travel activities. These choices are, as mentioned earlier, strongly related to the choices of the urban activities themselves. *Trip purpose* represents the nature of the urban activity in question, e.g., work or shopping; *trip frequency* implies a certain level of participation; and *trip destination* is itself the location of the activity.

Most urban travel demand analyses are structured for different trip purposes separately. In other words, it is usually assumed that the demands for different activities, such as shopping, recreation, and so forth, are independent. This is clearly an assumption made for the sake of simplification, for it is quite likely that an urban traveler may trade off trips by different purposes in the process of optimizing the use of available resources. While theoretical constructs have been proposed for dealing with this trade-off problem, a working methodology does not yet exist.

For any given trip purpose, the choices involved in trip-making decisions are the following:

1. How many trips to make during a given period of time, e.g., on an average weekday
2. What destination to choose for each trip
3. What mode of travel to use
4. Which of the available routes between the origin and the destination to use
5. At what times to make these trips, e.g., A.M., P.M., during peak or off-peak periods

The understanding of this choice process and its successful modeling are essential for the conduct of urban travel demand analysis. The process is quite complex since it involves a number of decisions about travel activities that are obviously not unrelated. Empirically, it is virtually impossible to verify assumptions regarding the exact nature of this process without detailed questioning of individual trip makers, and even then with very limited success.

The two major questions concerning the structure of the choice process are: (1) whether the choices are dependent or independent; and (2) if they are dependent, whether they are made simultaneously or sequentially in some order. The resolution of these questions has important implications for the modeling of the choice process and for the resulting transportation demand models.

In the case of the first question, the independence assumption implies that the choice of each of the trip attributes is made independently of the others, e.g., the choice of destination is independent of the choice of mode. This implication leads to a model structure where the probability of a mode-destination combination, for example, is simply the product of the independent probabilities of the destination and the mode choices. The dependence assumption on the other hand implies that the choice of one attribute may depend on the values of the other attributes of the trip, e.g., the choice of destination is not independent of what mode is being considered, or vice versa. In such a case, a conditional probability structure is defined in which the choice of one attribute is conditional on a postulated choice of another. Alternatively, a simultaneous probability structure has to be defined, as is discussed later on.

The independence assumption is likely to be unrealistic in most urban travel cases. For example, it would be unrealistic to assume that the choice of destination for a trip is independent of what mode is being considered or chosen, because different sets of destinations may be accessible by different modes. The opposite is also true, and the same applies to other choices. It would be equally unrealistic to assume that the choice of route is independent of the trip destination or of the mode. On the other hand, it may be possible to assume for the purposes of demand analysis that the more important, long-term choices related to trip activities may be made first and independently of the other choices. For example, the destination of a work trip may be selected, whether by choice or not, independently of the other attributes of the work trip, which are then determined on the basis of the destination. In such a case, it may be said that the choice of destination is independent of the other choices, but the reverse is not true.

It seems, therefore, reasonable to assume that the choices are in general not independent, but that there exists a hierarchy in the dependence of the less important choices on the more important ones.

This directly brings up the second question of whether the choices are made simultaneously or sequentially in some order, a question about which one cannot be as conclusive. The assumption of simultaneous choices is conceptually the most general in the sense that it recognizes the possibility that the transportation attributes of all alternatives available to the traveler affect the choice of any one of them. However, this assumption implies that a trip maker takes all these factors into consideration for every trip-making decision. In a complex, multimodal urban transportation network, the number of possible combinations of alternatives and their attributes can be so numerous as to exceed the realistic limit of human discrimination. In such cases, the simultaneous decision process becomes extremely difficult, if not impossible.

The sequential assumption, on the other hand, implies that a certain hierarchy exists among the choices and that the more important ones are made first. Two factors go into making this a more realistic assumption and one that is likely to be closer to the true trip-making decision process.

The first concerns the issue of traders versus nontraders, or captive versus noncaptive travelers. This issue is related to the situations where a traveler does not have a choice with regard to a particular attribute of the trip. For example, a traveler to whom an automobile is not available, and who originates from an area where the only alternative is a bus, has little choice of mode for trips. Except for the short walking or bicycle trips, the traveler's mode is already "chosen" to be the bus, and the other attributes of the trip are chosen on the basis of this choice. This can also occur in route choice where only one route can realistically be assumed to exist between an origin and a destination, particularly by public transport modes.

The other factor determining the hierarchy of trip-making decision is related to long-term versus short-term decisions. For work trip purposes, in particular, the choice of destination is a long-term decision not likely to change from day to day. However, other attributes of a work trip such as choice of mode or route may change from day to day. In such a case, it can be seen that a hierarchy exists where the choice of destination comes first and is followed by the choices of the other trip attributes, and made conditional on the destination choice.

These two factors are major considerations in postulating a theory of urban travel behavior. Most urban travelers make trip decisions that are somehow constrained, and therefore they are nontraders with respect to some aspects of their trip choices. Furthermore, the hierarchy of long-term trip decisions is also present in most urban travel, not only in work trips. Therefore, the assumption that a hierarchy exists and that trip-making decisions are made sequentially has a behavioral appeal. However, the analytical difficulty that is caused by this assumption is the question of which sequence to adopt in modeling urban traffic. This question has been subject of considerable debate in urban transportation analysis. Most of this debate is polemic, for while it is difficult to know which sequence to assume in the analysis, it is easy to realize that no one sequence prevails in all urban trips. Furthermore, it is extremely difficult to stratify urban trips into categories where specific sequences prevail. Consequently, the choice of modeling strategy should be made on empirical grounds.

4.4 APPROACHES TO URBAN TRAVEL DEMAND MODELING

There are two basic approaches to modeling urban travel demand: (1) the direct approach, and (2) the structured choice model approach. The first involves a direct application of the concepts of microeconomic demand modeling of Chap. 2 in deriving models of the number of trips demanded by individuals. The second, recognizing the multiplicity of choices available to the urban trip maker, involves structuring a series of models of choice and then combining them to predict the total number of trips of various types. In the end, both of these approaches will lead to the same result, because they both have the same objective: predicting the number of trips made in an urban area as a function of demand and supply characteristics. Both these approaches can be applied at the individual (*disaggregate*) level and the market (*aggregate*) level.

The Direct Approach

A demand function is postulated relating the number of trips made by an individual to a set of demand and supply variables. In urban transportation, it is necessary to specify many attributes of the trip in order to select the appropriate demand and supply variables. The following attributes need to be identified: purpose, origin, destination, mode, route, and time of day. Given that, in general, cross-elasticities may exist between the demands for trips with different attributes, the demand function will include a rather large number of variables. Let X_{ijmrt}^P be the number of trips made by an individual during a given period of time for purpose p, from origin i to destination j, by mode m, route r, and at time of day t. The demand function will then be

$$X_{ijmrt}^P = X(\mathbf{D}^P, \mathbf{S}_{ijmrt} \qquad \text{for all } i, j, m, r, t) \qquad (4.1)$$

where $\mathbf{D}^P$ = a vector of demand variables for trip purpose p
  $\mathbf{S}_{ijmrt}^P$ = a vector of supply variables for trips with attributes
        given by i, j, m, r, and t

Note that if all the cross-elasticities are to be allowed in the model, then the number of variables can be immense. If there are I possible origins, J destinations, M modes, R routes, and T time periods, and if there are, for example, d demand variables for each trip purpose and s supply variables of interest, then the total number of variables in the demand function for each trip purpose would be $d + sIJMRT$. The number of model parameters will be at least as much. In the quite realistic situation when $d = s = 3, I = 1, J = 5, M = 3, R = 2$, and $T = 3$, the number would be 273. Clearly, this is a situation which contradicts the whole purpose of using a model. For this reason, it is customary to make simplifications by assuming away many of the cross-elasticities in the model, thereby reducing the number of variables. Notice that in the example of Eq. (4.1), one such simplification is already made, namely the elimination of the cross-elasticities of the demand for different trip purposes. This is a common procedure since the demand variables for trips with different purposes are likely to be different: the demand for work trips depends on the type of employment, but the demand for shopping trips may depend on the size of the household. If all cross-elasticities are eliminated, then a simple model is obtained as follows:

$$X_{ijmrt}^P = X(\mathbf{D}^P, \mathbf{S}_{ijmrt}) \qquad (4.2)$$

The number of variables corresponding to the above example would be only six in this case. This, however, does not represent any significant saving in the complexity and extensiveness of the demand modeling effort, unless one further assumption is made, namely, that the functional forms of all these models are identical. Without this assumption, it would be necessary to construct and calibrate a demand model separately for each set of attributes, resulting again in a very large number of models for which data are usually unobtainable, particularly at the individual level.

Further simplifications can be made by aggregating trips under one or more of the attributes. For example, it is customary to construct demand functions for trips over all time periods, thus eliminating the t index from X_{ijmrt}, and to deal with total daily trips for a typical weekday or a weekend day. Trips are often also aggregated over all routes, thus eliminating one additional index r in the demand function. The trips thus estimated are then distributed among the available routes using a trip-assignment model. This approach implies that the total demand for trips is not elastic with respect to the attribute that is eliminated. For example, when the route attribute is eliminated, the implication is that the trips will occur regardless of which route is actually taken. They are then all assigned to the alternative routes in the trip-assignment analysis. The extreme of such a simplification is when all attributes are suppressed except the trip origin, resulting is a model for all trips made by an individual or by a group from a given origin. Such a model is called a *trip-generation model*. Notice that by eliminating trip attributes, it becomes difficult to include variables of transportation supply. The trip-generation model would then be as follows:

$$X_i^P = X(\mathbf{D}^P) \tag{4.3}$$

It is possible, in order to improve the behavioral content of such a model, to include an overall measure of the accessibility of the origin location i as a proxy for transportation supply.

Another level of simplification is when origins and destinations are left in the model, resulting in what is referred to as the *origin-destination demand model* or a *generation-distribution model:*

$$X_{ij}^P = X(\mathbf{D}^P, \mathbf{S}_{ij}) \tag{4.4}$$

In this case, the supply variables represent aggregate measures for all modes, routes, and times of day. These distribution models are rather common in urban travel demand analysis. They are described in more detail in Chap. 6. Trips estimated from X_{ij}^P are then distributed among the modes and routes available, again implying that the total origin-destination demands are inelastic with respect to the characteristics of specific modes and routes.

One of the earliest direct demand models was proposed by Kraft and Wohl (1967) who applied a simplified version of it to the derivation of optimal tolls for an urban freeway bridge in the San Francisco Bay Area. The Kraft-Wohl model had the following formulation:

$$q(ij|p, h) = \alpha_{ph}(Y_i)^{\beta_{ph}}(P_i)^{\gamma_{ph}}(E_j)^{\delta_{ph}}\prod_y c(ij|p, y)^{\theta_{phy}}\prod_y f(ij|p, y)^{\phi_{phy.}} \tag{4.5}$$

where $q(ij|p, h)$ is the trip volume for purpose p and time of day h; Y_i is the income measure for residents in zone i; P_i is a population measure for zone i; E_j is an employment measure for zone j; $c(ij|p, y)$ is the travel time or congestion for trips with purpose p made at time y; between zones i and j; and $f(ij|p, y)$ is the toll or fare for travel between i and j for purpose p at time period y; and all the other elements of the equation are constant parameters. Kraft and Wohl suggested that the supply variables c and f be accumulated for all routes and modes serving any given ij pair, thus implying a horizontal aggregation of link supply functions.

Models of the Kraft-Wohl type had limited applications in urban travel demand analysis. An example of such applications is the set of direct demand models calibrated for the Boston metropolitan region by Domencich, Kraft, and Valette (1968). One of their results is the following model:

$$V_{ijt} = PE_j t_{ijt}^{-0.59} c_{ijt}^{-0.32} HS_i^{2.5} Y_i^{-0.04} ED_j^{0.03} PBE_j^{-0.79}$$

where V_{ijt} is the daily number of shopping trips made by one household between zones i and j by the transit mode; t_{ijt} is the total travel time between i and j by transit; c_{ijt} is the corresponding total travel cost; HS_i is the household size averaged for the zone of origin i; PE_j is the total retail employment in zone j as a proportion of the total retail trade in the region; ED_j is the retail trade employment density in zone j; and PBE_j is the employment in personal business in zone j as a proportion of the total regional employment in personal business. The absence of any cross-elasticities between modes is noted in this model. Also noted is the fact that the model is calibrated on aggregate zonal level data on income and household size. It is thus a market demand function obtained by using the population averages of the variables.

The Sequenced Choice Approach

When it is formulated as in Eq. (4.1), the direct demand model discussed in the previous section implies a simultaneous choice process in which the number of trips X_{ijmrt} is decided by the trip maker on the basis of all the attributes of all the alternatives simultaneously. Simplifications such as in the models of Eqs. (4.2) and (4.3) imply that a sequential process is followed. The trip generation of Eq. (4.3) implies that the number of trips is first decided on and then the other attributes selected such as destination and mode. The generation-distribution model of Eq. (4.4) implies that the number of trips and the destinations are decided first, and then other attributes such as mode and route are selected. Further simplifications of the general direct demand model reflect the postulation that a sequenced choice process takes place in the trip-making behavior.

The *sequenced choice approach* to modeling travel behavior is an attempt to model explicitly the choice processes that take place in order to predict trips X_{ijmrt}. Notwithstanding the fact that different sequences can be postulated for the trip-making process, there are two ways by which the process can be modeled. These two methods differ in the way by which the total number of trips generated is modeled. In the first method, a trip-generation model is defined first as in Eq. (4.3). The trips generated X_i^P are then distributed among the alternatives available for mode destination and route choices, using models of travel choice. This method is common in practice and has become a part of the widely distributed computer-aided planning system referred to as the *Urban Transportation Planning System* (UTPS) (DOT, UMTA, 1976).

To illustrate this method, we suppose that the sequence postulated is that of destination choice, followed by mode choice, and then followed by route choice. We simplify the illustration by ignoring the choice of time of day, and we ignore the trip-purpose index, assuming the analysis is for a single purpose without any loss of generality. The UTPS process proceeds with a trip-generation model:

$$X_i = X_i(\mathbf{D}_i) \tag{4.6}$$

The trips thus generated as distributed among the available destinations according to some distribution model which gives the proportion of trips $p(j)$ that would be made to each destination j:

$$X_{ij} = X_i p(j|i) \tag{4.7}$$

The trip-distribution model $p(j|i)$ breaks the trips X_i down among the destinations according to the relative attraction of each and the values of some aggregate supply measure averaged over all modes and routes. The trip interchanges between origins and destinations X_{ij} are then distributed among the available modes on the basis of a mode-choice model that gives the proportions of trips that will take each of the available modes on the basis of the values of a supply function for each. This supply function represents an aggregate over all routes, or as the case is often in practice, according to the supply values of the best available route for each mode. This mode split results in

$$X_{ijm} = X_{ij} p(m|i, j) \tag{4.8}$$

The modal trip interchanges thus generated are finally distributed among the available routes for each mode using a trip-assignment model which again simulates the choice of route on the basis of supply variables for each modal route connecting every origin-destination pair:

$$X_{ijmr} = X_{ijm} p(r|i, j, m) \tag{4.9}$$

Note that as the process proceeds from trip generation to trip distribution, to mode choice, and then to assignment, it becomes possible to specify the supply variables in the models more exactly since more of the attributes of the trips in question are being defined. In the applications of the UTPS process it is common to adopt a sequence similar to the one illustrated here, or one in which mode choice precedes destination choice. In all cases, trip generation is analyzed first, yielding a given number of trips that are to be allocated among the alternatives available. Trip assignment is usually carried out last since the selection of routes requires a detailed specification of their supply characteristics which can only be done once the modes and origin-destination pairs are defined.

The major drawback of this method is in the implication that total travel demand is not elastic with respect to the attributes of the supply system and that trips are generated on the basis of demand variables only. The UTPS process forces, as it were, a number of trips generated through the urban transportation network. Attempts to correct this are made by either incorporating aggregate measures of supply in the trip-generation model, or by a feedback that would allow modifying trip-generation rates on the basis of transportation supply. Some of these attempts are described in the next chapter which deals with trip-generation analysis.

The alternative approach to modeling travel demand with the sequenced choice method is to reverse the modeling sequence and to start with a set of conditional choice models. At each stage in the sequence the conditional choice model provides a means of obtaining the expected supply characteristics for use in the choice model in the stage following. Finally, trip generation is modeled on the basis of demand variables and supply variables based on the expectations over all the alternatives. We illustrate this method by the same example in which a hierarchy of choices is postulated where destinations are chosen first, followed by modes, and then by routes. Starting with the last choice in the hierarchy, that of routes, it is possible to construct a conditional choice model giving the proportions of trips for any given mode and destination combination that would select each of the routes available for those modal interchanges:

$$P(r|m, i, j) = g(\mathbf{S}_{ijmr} \text{ for all } r \in R_{mij}) \tag{4.10}$$

where P is the proportion of all trips, from i to destination j by mode m that would select route r; $g(\cdot)$ is a route choice function; $\mathbf{S}_{ijmr}$ is a vector of supply variables for route r; and R is the set of all routes available for trips by mode m from i to destination j.

At this point, these conditional route choice proportions can be used to calculate the weighted average, over all routes, of the supply characteristics for each mode to each destination. Note that this weighted average is the actual average of the supply attributes and is an accurate measure only when the choice model is deterministic, i.e., when $p(r|m, j)$ is a deterministic proportion rather than a stochastic measure of probability. In a stochastic choice model, the expected values of the perceived supply attributes are used, since they are supposed to influence choice. The modification of this process for use in stochastic choice models is discussed in the next section.

The conditional choice proportions can now be used to provide a weighted average of the supply characteristics for any destination-mode combination mj as follows:

$$\mathbf{S}_{mij} = \sum_r \mathbf{S}_{mijr} p(r|mij) \tag{4.11}$$

With these weighted supply values, it is possible to proceed to the next level in the conditional choice hierarchy by modeling the conditional choice of mode:

$$p(m|ij) = f(\mathbf{S}_{mij}, \text{ for all } m \in M_{ij}) \tag{4.12}$$

where $f(\,\cdot\,)$ is a mode choice function, S_{mij} is as obtained from Eq. (4.11), and M_{ij} is the set of modes available for travel between i and j. In the same manner, the weighted average of the supply characteristics to any destination can be obtained by weighing over all modes as follows:

$$S_{ij} = \sum_m S_{mij} p(m|ij) \tag{4.13}$$

The destination choice model can now be based on these weighted supply values:

$$p(j|i) = h(S_{ij}, \text{ for all } j \in J_i) \tag{4.14}$$

where $h(\,\cdot\,)$ is a destination choice function; S_{ij} is as obtained from Eq. 4.13; and J_i is the set of all destinations available to travelers from i. The weighted average of all supply values for travel from i can now be obtained in the same manner:

$$\begin{aligned}
S_i &= \sum_j S_{ij} p(j|i) \\
&= \sum_j \sum_m \sum_r S_{mijr} p(r|mij) p(m|ij) p(j|i)
\end{aligned} \tag{4.15}$$

Using this weighted supply model, a trip-generation demand model can be specified for trips generated in i:

$$X_i = X(\mathbf{D}_i, \mathbf{S}_i) \tag{4.16}$$

which unlike the conventional trip-generation model of the UTPS process includes a supply vector.

Note that all the models of choice in Eqs. (4.10), (4.12), and (4.14) can include demand as well as supply variables. The specific functions used in the choice models of route, mode, and destination may be different. Chapters 5, 6, and 7 are devoted to a discussion of these types of models.

In order to illustrate this method, a simple example is given below.

Example Given a transportation system serving an area in which there are three possible destinations for a given trip purpose. The system is made of two modal networks, each serving between the origin and each of the three destinations via two routes.

The travel times and travel costs on the network are given as t_{jmr} and c_{jmr} for destinations j, modes m, and routes r. Note that $j = 1, 2, 3; m = 1, 2;$ and $r = 1, 2$.

$$t_{jmr} = \begin{cases} m = 1 \begin{cases} r = 1 \\ r = 2 \end{cases} \\ m = 2 \begin{cases} r = 1 \\ r = 2 \end{cases} \end{cases} \begin{array}{ccc} j=1 & j=2 & j=3 \\ \left[\begin{array}{ccc} 25 & 36 & 45 \\ 16 & 24 & 36 \\ 28 & 25 & 62 \\ 22 & 16 & 44 \end{array}\right] \end{array}$$

$$c_{jmr} = \begin{cases} m = 1\begin{cases} r = 1 \\ r = 2 \end{cases} \\ m = 2\begin{cases} r = 1 \\ r = 2 \end{cases} \end{cases} \begin{array}{ccc} j=1 & j=2 & j=3 \\ \begin{bmatrix} 10 & 6 & 20 \\ 10 & 6 & 20 \\ 5 & 4 & 15 \\ 5 & 4 & 15 \end{bmatrix} \end{array}$$

Also given is a vector of attractiveness attributes A_j for the destinations $A = \{100, 50, 150\}$.

A hierarchy of choices is postulated in order to proceed with the estimation of traffic flows from an origin i to the three destinations j by each of the modes and routes. The hierarchy assumed is such that destination choice is first, and using that, the choice of mode is made on the basis of which route is chosen.

The sequenced choice process begins by modeling the choice of route conditional on mode choice. Let the conditional route choice model be given by:

$$p(r|m, j) = \sum_l \frac{t_{mjr}^{-1}}{\sum_l t_{mjl}^{-1}} \qquad \text{for all } m, j$$

This model bases route choice only on travel times, since as can be seen from the c_{jmr} table, travel cost is invariant with respect to route in this particular example. This could be a situation where the costs c_{jmr} represent tolls and other fees which are the same for each mode regardless of the route taken. Applying the conditional route choice model using the t_{jmr} table given above, we obtain the following route choice proportions for each mode and destination combination:

$$p(r|m, j) = \begin{cases} m = 1\begin{cases} r = 1 \\ r = 2 \end{cases} \\ m = 2\begin{cases} r = 1 \\ r = 2 \end{cases} \end{cases} \begin{array}{ccc} j=1 & j=2 & j=3 \\ \begin{bmatrix} 0.39 & 0.40 & 0.44 \\ 0.61 & 0.60 & 0.56 \\ 0.44 & 0.39 & 0.40 \\ 0.56 & 0.61 & 0.60 \end{bmatrix} \end{array}$$

As an example of this calculation, consider $p(2|1, 3) = (t_{1,3,2})^{-1}/(t_{1,3,2})^{-1} + (t_{1,3,1})^{-1} = (36)^{-1}/(45^{-1} + 36^{-1}) = 0.56$. These route choice probabilities can now be used to estimate the weighted average travel time for each mode and destination combination:

$$\hat{t}_{mj} = \sum_r t_{mjr} \, p(r|m, j) \qquad \text{for all } m, j$$

This calculation applied to the t_{mjr} table given above results in

$$\hat{t}_{mj} = \begin{bmatrix} 20 & 30 & 40 \\ 25 & 20 & 50 \end{bmatrix}$$

A mode choice model can now be applied to predict the conditional choice of mode for each destination. Let the choice model be given by:

$$p(m|j) = \frac{e^{V(m,\ j)}}{\sum_m e^{V(m,\ j)}} \quad \text{for all } j$$

where $V(m, j)$ is a linear choice function of the travel time and travel cost given as

$$V(m, j) = -0.2t_{mj} - 0.1c_{mj}$$

Note that since the travel costs in this example do not differ among the routes, $c_{mjr} = c_{mj}$. Were they different, then it would be possible to estimate a weighted average cost c_{mj} applying the same weighing method used for travel time. Note also that the mode choice model used in this example is the commonly used *logit model*. The derivation of the logit model is discussed in the next chapter. The calculated $V(m, j)$ values for this example are then

$$V(m, j) = \begin{bmatrix} 5 & 6.6 & 10 \\ 5.5 & 4.4 & 11.5 \end{bmatrix}$$

for which the mode choice model yields the following conditional choice proportions:

$$p(m|j) = \begin{bmatrix} 0.62 & 0.11 & 0.80 \\ 0.38 & 0.89 & 0.20 \end{bmatrix}$$

Note that conditional choice proportions must always satisfy

$$\sum_m p(m|j) = 1 \quad \text{for all } j$$

The weighted average values of the time and cost functions $\hat{V}(j)$ for each destination can now be calculated from

$$\hat{V}(j) = \sum_m V(m, j)\, p(m|j)$$

which yields the following:

$$\hat{V}(j) = [5.19,\ 4.64,\ 10.3]$$

On the basis of these values, it is possible to construct now a destination choice model such as the following gravity type model:

$$p(j) = \frac{A_j V_j^{-2}}{\sum_j A_j V_j^{-2}}$$

This is also a commonly used model of destination choice (trip distribution) as we see in Chap. 7.

The calculated values of $p(j)$ are

$$p(j) = [0.50, 0.31, 0.19]$$

At this point, it is possible to calculate all the unconditional and joint proportions of choice using the following fundamental relationships:

$$p(m, j) = p(m|j)\, p(j) \qquad \text{for all } m, j$$

$$p(r, m, j) = p(r|m, j)\, p(m, j)$$

$$= p(r|m, j)\, p(m|j)\, p(j) \qquad \text{for all } m, j, r$$

Applying this last relationship results in the following $p(m, r, j)$ matrix:

$$p(m, r, j) = \begin{cases} m = 1 \begin{cases} r = 1 \\ r = 2 \end{cases} \\ m = 2 \begin{cases} r = 1 \\ r = 2 \end{cases} \end{cases} \begin{array}{ccc} j = 1 & j = 2 & j = 3 \\ \begin{bmatrix} 0.121 & 0.0136 & 0.067 \\ 0.189 & 0.0204 & 0.085 \\ 0.084 & 0.108 & 0.015 \\ 0.106 & 0.168 & 0.023 \end{bmatrix} \end{array}$$

for which $\sum_j \sum_m \sum_r p(m, r, j) = 1$, and from which marginal proportions can be obtained for any route, mode, or destination.

This matrix of choice proportions can also be used to calculate the weighted average of the cost or time or their combination $V(\cdot)$ for any trip from the origin in question. Such an expected value can be used as an aggregate supply measure that can be used in a demand function to estimate the total number of trips generated. Applying the figures used in this example, and using $V = -0.2t - 0.1C$ as the measure of generalized transport cost, we obtain the following:

$$\hat{V} = \sum_j \sum_m \sum_r (-0.2t_{mjr} - 0.1C_{mjr})p(j, m, r) = 5.99$$

Supposing the demand for trips from an origin i is given by

$$X_i = 10000\hat{V}^{-1.5}$$

then this would give a total trip generation of 681 trips, which can now be allocated among all the modes, routes, and destinations according to the $p(j, m, r)$ matrix, giving the following estimates of traffic in the transport system:

$$X_{ijmr} = X_i p(j, m, r) = \begin{cases} m = 1 \begin{cases} r = 1 \\ r = 2 \end{cases} \\ m = 2 \begin{cases} r = 1 \\ r = 2 \end{cases} \end{cases} \begin{array}{ccc} j = 1 & j = 2 & j = 3 \\ \begin{bmatrix} 82 & 9 & 46 \\ 129 & 14 & 58 \\ 57 & 75 & 10 \\ 72 & 114 & 16 \end{bmatrix} \end{array}$$

Note that in this example, the supply attributes t_{jrm} and C_{jmr} are assumed fixed and not dependent on the amount of traffic. In general, this is not totally correct since with any link in a transport system, one is likely to encounter time and cost functions that are increasing with traffic. In route choice analysis in particular, it is necessary to adjust the supply variable used on the basis of traffic flow estimates. This is discussed further in Chap. 7 dealing with mode and route choice analyses. In the sequenced choice approach, the effect of increasing travel time and cost is somewhat reduced since the choice models would tend to reduce the proportions of choice of those links whose costs or times have increased. Nonetheless, a complete model system for urban travel estimation, including route choice analysis, would normally involve an iterative feedback process in order to deal with this equilibration process. For this reason, it is common to apply the sequenced choice approach exclusive of the route choice analysis and without iteration. Modal flows estimated for each origin-destination pair are then assigned to network routes using an iterative trip-assignment method.

In the example presented above, it was considered that i represents a particular origin location in which there is an aggregate market demand for trips given by $X_i = 10{,}000 \hat{V}_i^{-1.5}$. The same sequenced choice approach could have been applied if i referred to an individual traveler whose demands for trips were also related to $\hat{V}_i$ in some fashion. The distinction between the aggregate market demand and the individual demand is important when structuring the specific choice models to be used in the analysis, as we shall see in following chapters.

4.5 URBAN TRIP GENERATION

Trip generation refers to a class of demand analyses that deal with the total numbers of trips made by individuals or households. It is a simplification of the demand models of the direct approach discussed earlier in this chapter following the general structure of Eq. (4.3). By looking at numbers of trips typically aggregated over all modes, destinations, and routes, the implied assumption is that these numbers represent an equilibrium between the demand for transportation and the supply conditions prevailing in the transportation system at the time observations are made. As such, trip-generation analysis is aggregate in nature even if it is considered at the individual or household level. Forecasting trip patterns using trip-generation models implies that either the demand is inelastic with respect to supply conditions or that these conditions will not change appreciably between the time of analysis and the time of the forecast. As mentioned earlier, attempts to deal with this have been made by including some aggregate measures of supply that can change during a planning period. Such measures as household accessibility to various parts of a transportation network or to various urban activity locations have been used. But the aggregate nature of supply measures specified at the level of trip generation does by necessity limit their applicability to policy analysis and planning.

Trip-generation analysis has conventionally been divided into two types. The first, *trip production* refers to the number of trips made by an individual or a household, or aggregated over a group of households such as by zone of residence. The second, *trip attraction*, refers to the number of trips made to a particular urban location or activity. Trip attractions are normally considered only at the aggregate zonal level. The distinction between trip production and attraction is not really founded on the basic concepts of demand theory nor of travel behavior. While a trip-production model can be thought of as a demand model in the sense that it reflects an individual's or a group's propensity for trip making, the trip-attraction model has no such interpretation. Observations of trip production are in fact observations on the trip-distribution (destination choice) process. Their analysis is better done as a part of trip-distribution analysis. Trip-attraction analysis can be useful on its own when dealing with major facilities such as shopping centers and recreation facilities. In such cases, it may be necessary to study the traffic requirements of these facilities without having to do a complete origin-destination study. In this section, we deal with trip generation primarily in the context of trip production.

Factors That Affect Trip Generation

Most empirical studies of trip generation seem to reveal that person-trip production (trips by all modes of travel) is influenced mainly by two factors, which curiously enough are themselves related. The first, and apparently more important, is the car ownership, and the second is income. These two socio-economic indicators themselves reflect other trip-maker characteristics that influence trip demands. For example, it is not difficult to imagine that the number of trips made by a household is strongly influenced by the number of people in that household (the household size). But it is also easy to see that for any given income class, the larger the household, the higher is its car ownership likely to be.

The relationship between trip making and income and car ownership has been investigated rather thoroughly by the Federal Highway Administration (FHWA) of the U.S. Department of Transportation (DOT) (1975). Tables such as Table 4.1 have been derived for city after city in the United States. They all show essentially the same trend. Table 4.1 shows average daily person-trips per household for Sacramento, California, in 1970, for selected income classes and stratified by car ownership. To the extent that these average figures can be considered representative of typical trends, they do illustrate quite clearly the importance of both income and car ownership on trip making. Such numbers can only be used for illustration, of course, for it is clear that they are rather aggregate and refer to one particular city at one particular point in time. However, the fact that similar tables can be drawn up for many other cities indicates that at least the trends shown are meaningful statements regarding the effect of income and car ownership on travel demand.

Table 4.1

Household income	Cars owned by household			
	0	1	2	3 +
0–3000	1.24	4.66	6.00	5.40
6–7000	4.78	7.12	9.26	12.14
10–13500	5.38	9.16	11.13	15.41
25,000 +	6.75	9.24	12.00	13.62

Source: U.S. DOT FHWA (1975).

This is not to be taken to mean that income and car ownership alone can explain travel demand. Indeed, as Table 4.2 shows, family size has effects on trip making similar to those of income. The table shows 1973 data for Miami, Florida.

Table 4.2

Family size	Cars owned		
	0	1	2 +
1	1.0	2.9	5.6
2	1.9	4.5	5.9
3	2.9	6.2	7.7
4	4.1	8.5	10.7
5	5.8	10.2	13.7

Source: Ibid.

The effects of household size and income appear to be similar, but this can, of course, be very misleading. If household size increased and income remained unchanged, then one would expect trip demands to decline due to the effective reduction in the wealth of the household.

Another factor that has been observed to influence trip generation is the nature of the occupation of the head of a household. Households where the occupation of the head is managerial, professional, or sales-related generate more person-trips than households with the same size but where the occupation of the head is in clerical, craft, or labor categories. The differences have typically not been very large, and perhaps not significant when compared with other factors such as income or car ownership [see, for example, Hutchinson (1974)].

The effect of socioeconomic factors on trip generation can be more meaningful when evaluated separately for trips with different purposes. Early studies of trip generation seem to indicate that families with higher income tend to make proportionately more non-work-related trips than families with lower income. For example, the figures in Table 4.3 show the distribution of trips among three trip purposes for five income groups. The data comes from the city of Wichita Falls, Kansas, and are reported by the U.S. DOT, FHWA (1975). These results are likely to be typical of many urban area trip-generation patterns: low-income households are likely to generate more home-based work trips relative to other trip purposes than high-income households.

Table 4.3 Percent distribution of trips among trip purposes

Income group	Home-based work	Home-based nonwork	Non-home-based
Low	21	55	24
Medium	16	59	25
High	14	59	27

Source: Ibid.

The distribution of trips among trip purposes is also likely to be influenced by the car ownership of a household. Households without cars are likely to generate predominantly essential trips such as home-based work and shopping, whereas households with multiple car ownership would be expected to generate a proportionately higher number of other types of trips such as nonwork trips and non-home-based trips.

What is clear from all this is that there are a number of socioeconomic factors that affect trip generation and that they are all likely to be interrelated to one degree or another. Given this interrelationship between factors, one is inclined to question the validity of the linear trip-generation models so commonly used in transportation planning.

Trip-generation characteristics can also be analyzed on a mode-by-mode basis, the implication being that the demand functions for trips by mode are unrelated or that mode choice occurs prior to the decision regarding the number of trips to make. Such an analysis reflects the impact of the socioeconomic characteristics of the household on both the number of trips generated and on their distribution among modes. In general, it is found that public transport system use declines with income and with car ownership, and increases with residential density. An example of such an analysis is in Table 4.4, which shows some results from the San Francisco Bay Area.

Table 4.4

	Total person-trips			Percent distribution of person-trips by mode		
Household classification	Trips/ household	Persons/ household	Trips/ person	Auto	Transit	Walk or other
Residential density class						
Under 10 DUs/acre*	9.0	3.3	2.7	81.9	4.9	13.2†
10–30 DUs/acre	7.3	2.9	2.5	67.0	13.8	19.2†
Over 30 DUs/acre	6.8	2.0	3.4	41.9	21.0	37.1†
DU structure class						
Single unit	10.4	3.6	2.9	77.3	5.7	17.0
2–19 units	6.6	2.5	2.6	66.6	11.7	21.7
20 or over units	6.1	1.8	3.3	60.4	12.0	27.7
Income class						
Less than $5,000	5.5	2.3	2.4	59.9	10.6	29.6
$5,000–$7,000	8.1	3.0	2.7	72.4	7.9	19.7
$7,000–$9,000	9.2	3.3	2.8	75.3	6.0	18.7
$9,000–$12,500	11.2	3.6	3.1	77.3	5.8	16.9
$12,500 and over	12.6	3.7	3.4	80.2	5.6	14.2
Car availability class						
No cars	3.9	1.9	2.0	17.9	30.5	51.5
One car	8.1	3.0	2.7	73.1	7.5	19.5
Two cars	11.4	3.7	3.1	80.4	4.6	15.0
Three or more cars	14.2	4.2	3.4	85.5	3.5	11.0

* DU = dwelling unit

† Walk only

Source: Kollo and Sullivan (1969).

Some interesting characteristics are illustrated by Table 4.4. The number of trips per household seems to reflect socioeconomic characteristics: it increases with income and car availability and decreases with residential density and density of dwelling units. But the number of trips per person does not seem to vary as much. This indicates that the increase in household trip generation may be due to the increase in household size which itself may be reflected in socioeconomic characteristics such as income and car availability and type of dwelling. Another interesting phenomenon illustrated by Table 4.4 is the effect of the socioeconomic characteristics on mode selection. It is interesting to note that while the number of trips generated by a household does not decrease too rapidly with residential density, there is a marked decrease in the percentage of automobile trips and a corresponding marked increase in the percentage of walking and public transport trips.

Models of Trip Generation

Trip generation has typically been analyzed with two types of models. The first is a simple linear model where the trips generated by a household or a group of households are a function of a number of socioeconomic characteristics. These models have typically been calibrated using regression analyses from data obtained from origin-destination surveys. In order to permit the incorporation of socioeconomic variables that do not necessarily vary in a continuous manner, or whose impacts are far from being linear, the regression models are often stratified on these characteristics or specified with dummy variables that describe discrete classes of them. Alternatively, trip-generation rates based on cross-classifications of households into socioeconomic classes are estimated from survey data and are used as models of trip generation.

There is really no fundamental difference between these two methods. They both attempt to relate trip generation to some attributes of the tripmakers. In regression models, the explanatory variables are taken to be continuous and variable within relatively large ranges. In estimating the parameters of these regression models, assumptions are made, such as the linearity and normality of the error terms. Nonlinearities can be dealt with using more general estimation techniques than linear regression, by variable transformations, or by combining continuous and discrete variables using dummy variable regressions. On the other hand, in cross-classification analysis, the explanatory variables are taken to vary discretely, and no assumptions are needed regarding ranges or the linearity of effects for the explanatory stratifiers. In order to evaluate the significance of trip-generation rates using cross-classification, some distributional assumptions are needed such as the normality of unexplained variations.

Regression models of trip generation This approach involves setting up models, usually linear, that relate the trips generated to the socioeconomic characteristics of the tripmakers. The generation models can be specified and estimated as individual demand models, say at the household level, or as aggregate market demand functions typically at a zonal level. In the latter case, households are grouped according to some geographic classification on the basis of "traffic analyses zones" and assumed to be homogeneous for the purposes of modeling trip generation. At the zonal level, averaged values of the explanatory variables are used to estimate average trip-making rates for the zone.

The zonal regressions for trip generation are usually estimated separately for different trip purposes, and attempts are made to select explanatory variables appropriately for each trip purpose. These attempts are often not very meaningful since the zonal regressions are so aggregate that averages of variables are meaningless in some cases. The following is an example of a trip-generation model calibrated from zonal data from the San Francisco Bay Area by Kollo and Sullivan (1969):

Home-based work trips:
  Average weekday trips per zone $= -193 + 1.54$ (number of employed residents)

Home-based personal business trips:
  Average weekday trips per zone $= 317 + 0.26$ (zonal population)

Trip-generation regression models can also be specified and estimated at the disaggregate household level. Usually a model structure similar to the aggregate case is used, except that household-related socioeconomic indicators and trip-making rates are used. Clearly, the disaggregate regressions are a more accurate representation of true demand models. Aggregating household into groups, whether by zone of residence or any other factor, will tend to mask the variations in trip-making rates that exist between the aggregated households. The result is that zonal regression models will give misleadingly good "fit" to data, since these models have to explain only the variations between zones. As an illustration of this, consider the following two models calibrated on the same data set by the U.S. DOT (1967). The first is an aggregate zonal model where the trip-generation rates of 143 zones were related to one zonal socioeconomic indicator, namely the number of cars per zone. The second is a disaggregate model where the trip generation of 5255 households was regressed against two household socio-economic indicators: the number of cars per household and the number of persons per household over 5 years of age. The results of the two regressions are shown in Table 4.5, and they clearly illustrate the potentially misleading good fit that one can obtain with aggregate models of trip generation. The first model with an $R^2 = 0.95$ explains 95 percent of the variations in trip-generation rates on the basis of variations in the numbers of cars in zones and estimates trip making with a standard error of 17.6 percent. Such results are considered very good and the model appears to be quite significant. The second model on the other hand is only capable of explaining 36 percent of the variations of trip-generation rates between households, even after adding the number of persons per household as a second explanatory variable after car ownership. The standard error of the estimate is close to 75 percent. This shows that the variations of trip-making rates among households are large compared to those among zonal averages. Hence, a zonally aggregated trip-generation model is not explaining all the variations, and possibly not even most of them. For this reason, and because survey data usually yield household information, there is no point in aggregating the data and applying zonal trip-generation models. Trip generation should be conducted at the disaggregate household level. In forecasting future tripmaking, it is sometimes necessary to aggregate household trip estimates since many of the socioeconomic variables on the basis of which traffic is forecasted, are often only projected at the aggregate level. The aggregation of demand model obtained from disaggregate trip-generation analysis would then follow the procedures mentioned in Chap. 2 for moving from individual to market demand functions.

Table 4.5 Zonal and household trip-generation models

Aggregate model: $T = 36.03 + 5.09$ (cars/zone)
$R^2 = 0.95$; standard error of estimate 17.6%

Disaggregate model: $T = 0.69 + 1.39$ (persons/household)
$\qquad\qquad\qquad\qquad + 1.94$ (cars/household)
$R^2 = 0.36$; standard error of estimate, 74.9%

Source: U.S. DOT, FWHA (1967).

Category analysis Category analysis, or cross-classification analysis, is a method whereby households are grouped into subsets on the basis of one or more socioeconomic characteristic. All the households in a given subset are assumed to be homogeneous and hence to have similar trip-generation rates. Hence, the average rates for the households in a subset are used as a model of trip generation for households whose socioeconomic characteristics define the subset in question. It is important then that the cross-classification of households be done on the basis of as many socioeconomic variables as possible and using relatively small ranges in order for the homogeneity assumption to be valid. The advantage of this method over the regression models of trip generation is that assumptions regarding the functional form of the effects of the various factors on trip generation are not necessary and that socioeconomic variables which do not vary in a smooth, continuous fashion can be incorporated readily into the generation model. Binary variables such as sex and availability of certain types of transportation in the area can be easily incorporated in category analysis by using them as stratifiers. Table 4.6 is an illustration of a cross-classification of households for trip-generation analysis. The data are cross-classified on the basis of two socioeconomic variables: car ownership, which is broken down into four categories (no cars, two cars, and three or more cars), and number of persons per dwelling unit, which is broken down into seven categories starting with one and ending with eight or more persons per dwelling unit. The numbers shown in the table are fairly typical of cross-classification at this level: trip-generation rates increase with both socioeconomic variables. It is easy to see, however, that the increase in both cases is not linear. At this coarse stratification, it is likely that considerable variations will exist in the trip-generation rates of households within a cell. The use of average values will then result in an error, and the nonlinearity of effects implies that the estimates of trip rates on the basis of average values will be biased estimates. In order to assess the severity of the aggregation problem in a cross-classification, it is possible to perform an analysis of variance. With this analysis, one would compare the variations within groups and between groups. Under some statistical assumptions, it is possible to use tests such as the F test to assess the significance of the grouping.

Table 4.6 Typical cross-classification of household trip generation rates

Persons per household	Autos per household			Weighted average
	0	1	2 +	
1	1.03	2.68	4.37	1.72
2	1.52	5.13	7.02	4.38
3	3.08	7.16	9.40	7.46
4	3.16	7.98	11.73	9.10
5 +	5.20	9.18	13.39	11.78
Weighted average	1.60	6.62	10.85	6.58

Note: Cell entries are average daily person-trips by household for Madison, Wisconsin, in 1962.
Source: U.S. DOT, FHWA (1967).

Aggregation errors are rather common in trip-generation analysis, whenever households are grouped into classes on the basis of some socioeconomic characteristics, or some spatial unit such as zone of analysis. Figure 4.2 illustrates the source of this type of error. Households with given income levels are interviewed in order to determine their trip-generation rates. For two groups of households, one with low income and one with high income, the frequency distributions of trip-making rates are shown. The sharp decline of the trip-frequency curve for low-income households indicates that the variations in trip-making rates within this class of households are relatively low. On the other hand, the rather spread-out frequency function for trip rates for the high-income households suggests that an average trip rate for this class of households may not be meaningful. The data

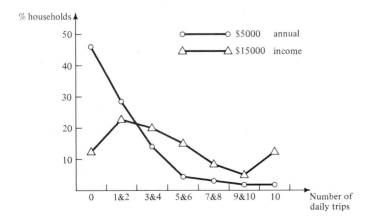

Figure 4.2 Frequency function of trip generation rates.

shown in Fig. 4.2 were obtained from the San Francisco Bay Area, but they are rather typical and illustrate a phenomenon that is common in trip generation.

4.6 SUMMARY

This chapter has been devoted to an introduction to the general principles on which urban travel demand analyses are based. The scope of demand analysis is limited to the relationship between travel demands and the characteristics of the urban activity system, including the socioeconomic activities and the transportation supply system available. Long-term trends in these activity systems are not accounted for directly in the demand models used for traffic estimation and policy analysis. Such long-term trends are usually assessed by long-range transportation-planning process using the travel demand models as a part of a more complete set of analyses.

    Urban travel behavior is likely for the most part to consist of a sequential choice process in which a potential trip maker considers the supply attributes of destinations, modes, routes, and times of travel, and then elects to make a set of trips. The direct approach to modeling urban travel demands is not suitable for estimating this type of behavior and can only be useful as an approximate method giving general orders of magnitude at an aggregate level.

    There is an extensive body of methodology dealing with the analysis of the major choices made in urban travel: destination choice, mode choice, and route choice. Trip-generation analysis deals with the demand for trips aggregated over modes, destinations, or routes, or all of these. The following three chapters deal with the methods of urban travel demand analysis. Chapter 5 introduces the methods of choice analysis. This is followed by trip-distribution analysis in Chap. 6, and mode and route choice analysis in Chap. 7.

PROBLEMS

4.1 The following aggregate demand model is an applied version of the product form:

$$V_{ijm} = a_m \left(\prod_{k=1}^{n} p_{ijk}^{b_{mk}} \right) \left(\prod_{k=1}^{n} t_{ijk}^{d_{mk}} \right) \left(P_i P_j \right)^{e_m} \left(\epsilon_i \epsilon_j \right)^{f_m} \left(Y_{ij} \right)^{g_m}$$

where V_{ijm} = volume of travel between i and j by mode m
$\quad\quad\; p_{ijk}$ = price of travel between i and j by mode k
$\quad\quad\;\; n$ = number of modes available
$\quad\quad\; t_{ijk}$ = travel time between i and j by mode k
$\quad\; P_i, P_j$ = population at i and j, respectively
$\quad\; \epsilon_i, \epsilon_j$ = employment at i and j, respectively
$\quad\quad\; Y_{ij}$ = mean income at i and j together
a, b, d, e, f, g = mode-specific constants

(*a*) For four modes, how many different coefficients would have to be estimated?

The following table contains partial results of a regression analysis using this model for two modes (auto and commuter rail) and two purposes (work and nonwork).

		Elasticities or cross-elasticities of V_{ijm} with respect to						
Purpose	Mode	Rail cost	Auto cost	Rail time	Auto time	Income	Employ-ment product	Pop. product
P1	M1	E1	0	−4.376	0	Not used	0.893	Not used
	M2	E2	−0.358	0.844	−3.410	Not used	1.067	Not used
P2	M3	−3.003	0	−2.636	0.056	0.465	Not used	0.854
	M4	0.185	−0.929	0.458	−1.364	1.523	Not used	0.794

(*b*) Which set of elasticities and cross-elasticities do you think is for personal trips? Which set is for business trips? Explain your answer.

(*c*) Identify which mode is rail and which mode is auto for each trip purpose.

(*d*) What information, if any, do you have about the signs and magnitudes of the elasticity and cross-elasticity which should appear in the blanks marked E1 and E2?

4.2 According to probability theory, the distinction between simultaneous and sequential models is trivial. The joint distribution is just the product of a marginal and a conditional distribution. So, for a destination–mode choice problem:

$$p(d, m) = p(d) \cdot p(m|d)$$

If we were studying 15 possible destinations and 3 possible modes to each destination, the joint model would have 45 alternatives for each observation, while the sequential model would have 15 alternatives for the destination model and 3 for the mode choice. Thus, a sequential model is much more tractable. Yet, many researchers have argued strongly in favor of simultaneous models for cases with a high degree of simultaneity among choices. Why should it make any difference how the models are estimated?

4.3 A number of sources in the literature postulate a hierarchy for household travel decision making which distinguishes longer-range choices from day-to-day choices. This hierarchy might be summarized as follows:

(*a*) Within the mobility block, which decisions do you think are simultaneously made, which are sequentially made, and which are independent of the others?

(*b*) Within the travel block, how many trip purposes would you model in order to capture each unique decision-making process? What choices would you model for each trip purpose? Do you think these choices are made simultaneously or sequentially (within each trip purpose)? Do you think the choice processes for the different trip purposes are independent?

Long range or "mobility" decisions	Choice of work place Choice of residence Auto ownership Choice of primary mode to work

$$\downarrow$$

Short-range or "travel" decisions	Day-to-day work mode choice
	Nonwork frequency, destination,
	    mode, time, and route choices for
	    each nonwork trip purpose

4.4 The following models of trip generation were obtained from a regression analysis of the results of a travel survey. In the transcription of the results from computer output, a number of errors were committed. Identify the errors that appear in the following:

(a) Zonal trip productions for shopping trips:

$$T = 30.9 + 91.0X_1 - 0.7X_2 + 0.3X_3 - 0.9X_4$$

where T = total daily trip products by zone
    X_1 = number of dwelling units in each zone
    X_2 = median income in each zone
    X_3 = number of households per zone
    X_4 = accessibility of the zone

(b) Household trip productions for work trips

$$T = 20.0 + 1.5X_1 - 0.7X_2 + 1.3X_3$$

where T = total daily trip products per household
    X_1 = household income
    X_2 = number of persons employed in the household
    X_3 = population of the zone

4.5 (a) Consider a system with 1000 persons living at node i; two destination nodes a and b; and two travel modes, highway h and rail r. The generalized travel costs and the links for each mode are shown in the accompanying figure. The probability that an individual chooses to travel to destination j, given that he or she travels in mode m, is given by

$$p(j|m) = \frac{A_j/c_{jm}}{\sum_k A_k/c_{km}}$$

where A_j = attractiveness of location j
    c_{km} = generalized travel cost to destination j via mode m

The probability of choosing mode m, given that the trip is going to destination j, is given by

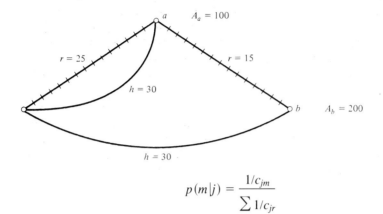

$$p(m|j) = \frac{1/c_{jm}}{\sum_r 1/c_{jr}}$$

(*b*) Suppose all 1000 individuals in a population choose to travel. Calculate the total number of rail passengers and the total number of trips to destination *a*.

(*c*) Suppose that each person chooses to travel with probability

$$p(t) = 1 - \exp\left(\frac{-0.1\sum_j\sum_m A_j}{c_{jm}}\right)$$

How many rail passengers will there be?

REFERENCES

Ben-Akiva, M.: Structure of Passenger Travel Demand Models, *Transp. Res. Rec.*, no. 526, pp. 26–42, 1974.

——, and T. J. Adler: Joint Choice Model for Frequency Destination, and Travel Mode for Shopping Trips, *Transp. Res. Rec.*, no. 569, pp. ——, 1976.

Domencich, T., and D. McFadden: "Urban Travel Demand; a Behavioral Analysis," A Charles River Associates Research Study, American Elsevier, New York, 1975.

Domencich, T., G. Kraft, and P. Valette: Estimation of Urban Passenger Travel Behaviour; an Economic Demand Model, *Highway Res. Rec.*, no. 238, pp. 64–78, 1968.

Fleet, C. R., and S. R. Robertson: Trip generation in the Transportation Planning Process, *Highway Res. Rec.*, no. 240, pp. 11–27, 1968.

Hutchinson, B. G.: "Principles of Urban Transportation Planning," McGraw-Hill Book Company, New York, 1974.

Kollo, H. P., and E. C. Sullivan: "Trip Generation Model Development," Bay Area Transportation Study Commission, BATSC Technical Report, no. 229, 1969.

Kraft, G., and M. Wohl: New Directions for Transportation Demand Analysis and Forecasting, *Transp. Res.,* vol. 1. pp. 205–230, 1967.

Mitchel, R. B., and C. Rapkin: *Urban Traffic, a Function of Land Use,* Columbia University Press, New York, 1954.

McGinnis, R.: *Social Structure and Urban Travel Behaviour,* Dissertation, Ph.D., University of California, Berkeley, 1975.

U.S. Federal Highway Administration: *Guidelines for Trip Generation Analysis,* Bureau of Public Roads, Washington, D.C., 1967.

U.S. Federal Highway Administration: *Trip Generation Analysis,* Washington, D.C., 1975.

FIVE

ANALYSIS OF TRAVEL CHOICE

Choice is a fundamental component of the trip-making decision process. As the discussion of urban travel demand illustrated, the potential trip maker is often faced with a choice among a number of alternative arrangements of trip attributes such as destination, mode, and route. This is also true in nonurban travel behavior and applies to both passenger travel decisions and shipper decisions regarding the transportation of commodities. Modeling travel choice is therefore an important function in transportation demand analysis and often a prerequisite to successful traffic estimation. Choice is a complex process about which not much is well known. Empirical evidence is very scarce since the possibilities of controlled experimentation are very limited. Nonetheless, simplifications are made to permit the analysis of travel choice using manageable quantitative models.

One simplification often made is that the choice process is deterministic and reproducible. In other words, if a potential traveler is repeatedly faced with the same set of alternatives, then the choice made will consistently be the same. This deterministic assumption has been at the foundation of most models of travel demand, at least during the first decades of their development. Trip-distribution models, diversion models of mode choice, and most techniques of traffic assignment are based on the assumption that the choice process is a deterministic one. Another important simplifying assumption is that there is a decision rule that is used by the potential traveler and that this rule is consistent and stable, much in the same way individual preference behavior is assumed to be in microeconomic demand theory. This assumption permits the structuring of well-defined decision rules that are based on demand and supply characteristics of the traveler and of the alternatives available.

It is possible to relax both of these assumptions by adopting a stochastic model of choice. Such a model would be based on the postulate that the choice process itself is not deterministic but subject to random influences that cannot be completely accounted for. These influences can stem from inconsistencies in the behavior of choice makers either due to lack of information regarding the attributes of the alternatives available or to stochastic fluctuations in the manner by which these attributes are perceived. The stochastic nature of choice could also be the result of the absence of a rational and consistent decision rule. Of course, there is no way of finding out precisely what the sources of randomness are, and the postulation of stochastic choice models remains at best a means of hiding our ignorance of the true factors about travel behavior. Stochastic models do provide a far superior means for predicting travel behavior than deterministic models: they are conceptually more appealing and are better corroborated by empirical evidence.

5.1 MEASUREMENT OF CHOICE

Although choice can be reflected by the number of people choosing each alternative, a more appropriate measure is the *proportion* of a population that makes each choice. Using proportions as measures has the advantage that it permits the analysis of choice independent of the total number of people in a population. Proportions are meaningful in the case of deterministic choice at a market level only. For deterministic choice at an individual level it suffices to identify the alternative chosen using some meaningful rule. In the case of stochastic choice, the proportions are thought of as probabilities measured over a population and a choice set. Stochastic choice probabilities can be measured at an aggregate market level, indicating for each alternative the probability that it is the choice of an individual chosen at random from the population, when the sampling is defined over a given period of time during which it is postulated that a choice will be made. At the individual level, the choice probability of an alternative defines the number of times the alternative is chosen by the individual relative to the total number of times a choice is made if the individual faces exactly the same choice environment. It can be thought of as the outcome of a Bernoulli trial such as the toss of a dice or the flip of a coin.

Deterministic Choice

We begin with the simplest case: the case of *deterministic choice* at the individual *(disaggregate)* level. An individual traveler is faced with a set of alternatives I. Each alternative $i \in I$ is described by a function $V(i)$, which is referred to as the *choice function*. $V(i)$ contains all of the demand and supply variables that have a bearing on the merits or demerits of the alternative. It is most common to construct $V(i)$ assuming that it is a linear function of the demand and supply variables or of some simple combinations of them. In other words, a commonly used form of the choice function is

$$V(i) = \mathbf{A}_i \mathbf{X}_i \qquad (5.1)$$

where X_i = a vector of demand and supply variables influencing choice

A_i = a vector of parameters that represent the effect of each variable

It is common to think of the choice function in a positive way as a utility function, so that an alternative with a higher value of $V(\cdot)$ has a higher chance of being chosen. This can always be done by adjusting the signs of the parameters A. With this definition of the choice function, the decision rule for deterministic choice is quite simple.

Choose j if

$$V(j) = \max_{i \in I} [V(i)] \qquad (5.2)$$

which says that the traveler will choose the alternative with the highest utility, as measured by the choice function $V(\cdot)$. A simple example of this is the choice of route. If an individual is faced with a number of alternative routes for a journey and if these routes are identical in every respect except the travel time they consume (i.e., they have the same cost, capacity, etc.), then it is a fairly good assumption that the individual will choose the one with the shortest travel time and that a deterministic choice model is appropriate. In this case, there is only one variable in the vector X_i, namely, the travel time t_i, of alternative i. The value of A_i is the same for all alternatives and is equal to -1. Equation (5.2) ensures that the individual will choose the route with the shortest time. To illustrate what combination of demand and supply variables might be included in the X vector, we suppose further that the routes differ by their travel cost as well. If the traveler's response to the differences in travel cost between different alternatives is related to his or her income, then we have two additional variables in the choice function: travel cost and income. Let us suppose the following $V(i)$ function:

$$V(i) = -0.20t_i - \frac{1.0c_i}{B}$$

where t_i, c_i = the travel time in hours and travel cost in dollars of alternative i, respectively

B = annual income of the individual in thousands of dollars

Such a choice function would have an interesting interpretation. By holding $V(\cdot)$ fixed, the function shows the following marginal rate of substitution between cost and time:

$$\frac{dc}{dt} = -0.2B$$

which indicates that the rate at which the individual is willing to exchange money for time is proportional to income. In this case, this "value of time" per hour is equal to 20 percent of the annual income measured in thousands of dollars. In other words, a person with an annual income of $20,000 would value time at $4/h and a person with an income of $50,000 would value time at $10/h, and so forth.

When the same decision rule is applied to a market with a population of individuals all facing the same set of choices I, then it is possible to simply extend this disaggregate choice model into an aggregated market model by adding up for each alternative i the number of times it is chosen and then converting these into proportions of the total number. Note that in order to extend the choice model to the market level, the definition of the choice function must be modified and related to each individual in the market. Thus each individual k in a market of K people will have a specific choice function $V_k(i)$ for each alternative i. This extension is necessary not only because the demand variables, such as income, will vary from one individual to another, but also because the supply variables such as time and cost might be perceived differently by different people, even for the same alternative. There are different methods for aggregating individual choice functions into market functions. The aggregation problem in choice modeling is discussed in a later section in this chapter.

Not all deterministic choices need follow the simple rule of Eq. (5.2). Indeed, the assumptions made in the two examples used to illustrate deterministic choice are quite limiting and unrealistic. In many cases, the alternatives available differ by many attributes, and it is not realistic to expect that even the simple rule of Eq. (5.2) can be easily applied in a traveler's mind. This is often referred to as the *all-or-nothing rule* because it assigns all traffic to the "best" alternative, because is not suitable in situations where capacity constraints limit the amount of traffic any particular alternative can handle, or when the attributes of a particular choice are not independent of the number of people making that choice. In these cases, it is more appropriate to revise the choices and equilibrate them with variable choice functions much in the same way in which demand and supply functions are equilibrated. We shall see some of these methods in Chap. 7 which deals with mode and route choice in urban travel.

Stochastic Choice

Experience with travel behavior analysis suggests that the deterministic model of choice may be limited in its replication of real life situations. Three primary reasons suggest that a *stochastic* model of choice may be preferable. One is that the behavior of individuals may not always follow the rational rules of choice exactly and that the idiosyncrasies of traveler behavior cannot be anticipated in a deterministic model. The second is that it is usually not possible to include in the choice function $V(\cdot)$ all the variables that can possibly influence choice. If such a function were possible, it would no doubt be so complicated as to render it impractical. The third reason is that the typical potential traveler is not likely to have perfect information about the transportation system and the alternatives it offers. Thus the set of alternatives I, identified by the analyst, may be larger than that encountered in fact by the traveler, or the function $V(\cdot)$ may contain variables about which the information as perceived by the traveler may be absent or incomplete.

These reasons suggest that a good model of choice might be one in which the choice function is considered a random function that takes on different values with certain probabilities. This random function reflects the possibility that given values of the choice function $V(\,\cdot\,)$ or of any of its attributes are perceived differently by different individuals or by the same individual on different occasions. The perceived utility, call it $U(\,\cdot\,)$, is then a random function. This results in a stochastic choice process, the outcome of which depends on the specific values taken by the random components of $U(\,\cdot\,)$. This postulation is referred to as the *random utility model*. It is expressed as follows:

$$U(i) = V(i) + e(i) \qquad\qquad (5.3)$$

where $U(i)$ = choice function for alternative i
$\quad\quad V(i)$ = deterministic function of the attributes of (i)
$\quad\quad e(i)$ = a stochastic component, a random variable that follows some distribution

From empirical investigation, and from behavioral postulates, it is possible to specify the form of the $V(i)$ function and to select the variables to include in it. The empirical observation of the random component of the choice function is less practical, for it requires the observation of an individual on repeated occasions, under experimentally controlled conditions, in order to observe the variability of perception and behavior in the face of a choice function. Therefore, statistical assumptions are made regarding the distributional nature of the $e(i)$.

The development of the choice model on the basis of $U(i)$ follows from the basic principle that the individual will choose an alternative (i) if the perceived $U(i)$ of alternative (i) is the largest of all such values. Therefore, the probability that (i) is chosen can be given by

$$p(i) = p[U(i) > U(j) \quad, \quad \text{for all } j \neq i] \qquad\qquad (5.4)$$

This can be further developed as follows:

$$p(i) = [V(i) + e(i) > V(j) + e(j) \quad, \quad \text{for all } j \neq i]$$
$$= p[e(j) < V(i) - V(j) + e(i) \,, \quad \text{for all } j = i]$$
$$= \int_{e(i)} F[V(i) - V(j) + e(i) \quad, \quad \text{for all } j \neq i] f_i(\phi)\, d\phi \qquad (5.5)$$

where $F[\,\cdot\,]$ is the joint distribution function of the $[e(i), e(j), \ldots]$ terms for all the alternatives and $f_i(\phi)$ is the marginal density function of $e(i)$. Distributional assumptions and simplifications can now be made in order to turn Eq. (5.5) into a useful choice model.

Note that the postulate of random utility is just one of many that can be made in order to reflect stochastic choice behavior. It is perhaps the most general and has therefore come to underlie the derivation of most stochastic choice models. In the following two sections, we introduce the two most commonly used models: the *probit* and the *logit* models.

5.2 THE PROBIT MODEL

This model is obtained by assuming that the random utilities $[U(i), U(j), \ldots]$ have a multivariate normal distribution (MVN)

$$\begin{pmatrix} U_1 \\ U_2 \\ \vdots \\ U_n \end{pmatrix} \sim \text{MVN} \left[\begin{pmatrix} V_1 \\ V_2 \\ \vdots \\ V_n \end{pmatrix} ; \begin{pmatrix} \sigma_1^2 & \sigma_{12} & & \sigma_{1n} \\ \sigma_{12} & \sigma_2^2 & & \vdots \\ \vdots & & \ddots & \\ \sigma_{1n} & \cdots & & \sigma_n^2 \end{pmatrix} \right] \qquad (5.6)$$

where n is the number of alternatives and σ_{ij} is a variance-covariance matrix. This is equivalent to saying that the random components of the utility function, the e_i's, follow a multivariate normal distribution with a zero mean and a finite variance-covariance matrix:

$$e_i \sim \text{MVN}(\mathbf{0}, \Sigma) \qquad (5.7)$$

The probit model of choice is obtained by combining Eq. (5.6) or (5.7) with Eq. (5.5). The closed-form solution is very cumbersome and the probit model cannot be used in the multivariate case without making some simplifying assumptions. Two types of approximation can be utilized. One is to use a Monte Carlo simulation applied directly to Eq. (5.5) as suggested by Lerman and Manski (1977). This can be extensive and expensive. Another is an approximate closed-form solution based on some findings of Clark (1961), who approximated the distribution of the maximum of n normally distributed variables by a normal distribution:

$$\max [U(1), U(2), \ldots, U(n)] \sim N(V_{\max}, \sigma_{\max}^2) \qquad (5.8)$$

where $U(i)$ are multivariate normal variables with means $V(i)$ and covariance σ_{ij}. Defining for any two normally distributed variables U_1 and U_2,

$$E(U_1) = V_1 \qquad E(U_2) = V_2$$

$$\text{var}(U_1) = \sigma_1^2 \qquad \text{var}(U_2) = \sigma_2^2 \qquad \text{var}(U_1 + U_2) = \sigma_1^2 + \sigma_2^2 - 2\rho_{12}\sigma_1\sigma_2$$

$$\text{cov}(U_1, U_2) = \sigma_1\sigma_2\rho_{12}$$

where ρ_{12} is the correlation coefficient; Clark showed that

$$\mu_{12} = E[\max(U_1, U_2)] = V_1\Phi(\alpha_{12}) + V_2\Phi(-\alpha_{12})$$
$$+ \sqrt{\text{var}(U_1 + U_2)}\,\phi(\alpha_{12}) \qquad (5.9)$$

where $\alpha = (V_1 - V_2)/\sqrt{\text{var}(U_1 + U_2)}$ and Φ and ϕ, respectively, are the standard normal distribution and density functions. Clark also showed that

$$\omega_{12} = E[\max(U_1, U_2)]^2 = (V_1^2 + \sigma_1^2)\Phi(\alpha_{12}) + (V_2^2 + \sigma_2^2)\Phi(-\alpha_{12})$$
$$+ (V_1 + V_2)\sqrt{\text{var}(U_1 + U_2)}\,\phi(\alpha_{12}) \qquad (5.10)$$

and finally that the correlation between any third normally distributed variable U_3 and the maximum of U_1 and U_2 is given by

$$\rho_3' = \rho[U_3, \max(U_1, U_2)] = \frac{[\sigma_1\rho_{13}\Phi(\alpha_{12}) + \sigma_2\rho_{23}\Phi(-\alpha_{12})]}{\sqrt{\omega_{12} - \mu_{12}^2}} \quad (5.11)$$

Equations (5.9) to (5.11) can be used to derive directly the probit model of choice when there are three alternatives. The choice probability of each, for example, $p(3)$ is given by

$$p(3) = p[U_3 > \max(U_1, U_2)]$$

$$= \Phi\left(\frac{V_3 - \mu_{12}}{\sqrt{\sigma_3^2 + \sigma_m^2 - 2\rho_3'\sigma_3\sigma_m}}\right) \quad (5.12)$$

where $V_3 = E(U_3)$; μ_{12} and ρ_3' are as given by Eqs. (5.9) and (5.11); and $\sigma_m^2 = \text{var}[\max(U_1, U_2)]$. σ_m^2 can be obtained from Eq. (5.10):

$$\sigma_m^2 = (\omega_{12} - \mu_{12}^2) \quad (5.13)$$

For any number of alternatives larger than 3, the choice problem can be reduced to a trinomial case recursively by considering that for n alternatives

$$\max(U_1, U_2, \cdots, U_n) = \max\{\max \cdots \max$$
$$[\max(U_1, U_2), U_3] \cdots U_n\} \quad (5.14)$$

For the simpler case of two alternatives, the so-called binary case, the probit model can be derived directly from Eq. (5.5):

$$p(1) = p[U(1) > U(2)]$$

$$= p[U(2) - U(1) \leq 0]$$

$$p(1) = \Phi\left[\frac{V(2) - V(1)}{\sqrt{\sigma_1^2 + \sigma_2^2 - 2\rho_{12}\sigma_1\sigma_2}}\right] \quad (5.15)$$

Note that once the probit choice model is written in a form such as in Eqs. (5.12) or (5.15), its use becomes straightforward since $\Phi(\cdot)$ and $\phi(\cdot)$ are functions that are readily available in table form. Rather efficient algorithms have been developed now for the estimation and use of the probit model [see Daganzo, Bouthelier, and Sheffi (1977) and Daganzo and Bouthelier (1979)].

Example To illustrate the use of the probit model and of Eqs. (5.9) to (5.12), we consider a numerical example as follows. Consider a situation with three choices, say three modes, which have random choice functions following a multivariate normal distribution:

$$\begin{pmatrix} U_1 \\ U_2 \\ U_3 \end{pmatrix} \sim \left[\begin{pmatrix} -12 \\ -10 \\ -15 \end{pmatrix}; \begin{pmatrix} 4 & 2 & 0 \\ 2 & 4 & 0 \\ 0 & 0 & 4 \end{pmatrix}\right]$$

This implies a vector $\mathbf{V} = [-12, -10, -15]$ where the numbers represent negative utilities such as costs or travel times. The attributes of alternatives 1 and 2 are correlated with $\rho_{12} = 0.5$ so that $\sigma_{12} = \rho\sigma_1\sigma_2 = 0.5 \times 2 \times 2 = 2$. In order to compute $p(1)$, we apply Eqs. (5.9) to (5.11) to find that since $\rho_{23} = 0$,

$$\text{var } (U_2 + U_3) = 4 + 4 = 8$$

$$\alpha_{23} = \frac{-10 + 15}{\sqrt{8}} = 1.77$$

$$\mu_{23} = E[\max (U_2, U_3)] = -10\Phi(1.77) - 15\Phi(-1.77) + (\sqrt{8})\phi(1.77)$$

$$= -10 \times 0.9616 - 15 \times 0.0384 + 2.82$$

$$\times \, 0.0833$$

$$= -9.956$$

$$\omega_{23} = E[\max (U_2, U_3)]^2 = (100 + 4)\Phi(1.77) + (225 + 4)\Phi(-1.77)$$

$$+ (-25)(\sqrt{8})\phi(1.77)$$

$$= 102.9$$

and using Eq. (5.11)

$$\rho_1' = \rho[U_1, \max (U_2, U_3)] = \frac{\sigma_2 \rho_{12} \Phi(1.77)}{\sqrt{102.9 - (-9.956)^2}}$$

$$= \frac{2 \times 0.5 \times 0.9616}{\sqrt{3.78}}$$

$$= 0.495$$

Equation (5.12) now gives

$$p(1) = \frac{-12 + 9.956}{\sqrt{4 + 3.77 - 2 \times 0.495 \times 2 \times 1.94}}$$

$$= \Phi(-1.0311)$$

$$= 0.15$$

$p(2)$ can be calculated in a similar manner:

$$\text{var } (U_{-1} + U_{-3}) = 4 + 4 = 8$$

$$\alpha_{13} = \frac{-12 + 15}{\sqrt{8} = 1.06}$$

$$\mu_{13} = E[\max (U_1, U_3)] = -12\Phi(-1.06) - 15\Phi(1.06) + \sqrt{8}\Phi(1.06)$$

$$= -12 \times 0.855 - 15 \times 0.1446 + 2.83 \times 0.2275$$

$$= -11.785$$

$$\omega_{13} = E[\max (U_1, U_3)]^2 = (144 + 4)\Phi(1.06) + (225 + 4)\Phi(-1.06)$$

$$-(27)(\sqrt{8})\phi(1.06)$$

$$= 142.28$$

$$p_2' = \rho[\max(U_1, U_3), U_2] = \frac{\sigma_1\rho_{12}\Phi(1.06)}{\sqrt{142.28 - (11.785)^2}}$$

$$= 2 \times 0.5 \times \frac{0.855}{\sqrt{3.39}}$$

$$= 0.464$$

and using Eq. (5.12)

$$p(2) = \Phi\left(\frac{-10 + 11.785}{\sqrt{4 + 3.39 - 2 \times 0.464 \times 2 \times 1.84}}\right)$$

$$= \Phi(0.895)$$

$$= 0.81$$

Now calculating $p(3)$,

$$\text{var}(U_1 + U_2) = 4 + 4 + 2 \times 0.5 \times 2 \times 2$$
$$= 12$$

$$\alpha_{12} = \frac{-12 + 10}{\sqrt{12}} \ -0.577$$

$$\mu_{12} = E[\max(U_1, U_2)] = -12\Phi(-05.77) - 10\Phi(0.577) + \sqrt{12}\phi(-0.577)$$

$$= -12 \times 0.718 - 10 \times 0.282 + 3.464 \times 0.3377$$

$$= -10.266$$

$$\omega_{12} = E[\max(U_1, U_2)]^2 = (144 + 4)\Phi(-0.577) + (100 + 4)\phi(0.577)$$

$$-22\sqrt{12}\phi(-0.577)$$

$$= 148 \times 0.718 + 104 \times 0.282 - 76.2 \times 0.3377$$

$$= 109.85$$

$$\rho_3' = p[U_3, \max(U_1, U_2)] = 0 \qquad \text{since } \rho_{13} = \rho_{23} = 0$$

$$\sigma_m^2 = 109.85 - (10.266)^2 = 4.46$$

$$p(3) = \Phi\left(\frac{-15 + 10.266}{\sqrt{4 + 4.46 - 0}}\right)$$

$$= \Phi(-1.627)$$

$$= 0.050$$

We can now add $p(1) + p(2) + p(3) = 0.15 + 0.81 + 0.05 = 1.01$, which is sufficiently close to 1.0 due to rounding errors.

A special case of the binary probit model is obtained when $U(1)$ and $U(2)$ are assumed independent and identically distributed with a normal distribution:

$$
\begin{bmatrix} U(1) \\ U(2) \end{bmatrix} \sim N \begin{bmatrix} V(1) & \sigma_1^2 \\ V(2) & , & \sigma_2^2 \end{bmatrix} \tag{5.16}
$$

In this case, using Eq. (5.12) yields

$$
p(1) = \Phi \left\{ \frac{1}{\sigma} \left[V(2) - V(1) \right] \right\} \tag{5.17}
$$

$$
p(2) = 1 - p(1) \tag{5.18}
$$

This simple binary model can be illustrated graphically as in Fig. 5.1. The rectangular curve represents a deterministic all-or-nothing choice where the pro-

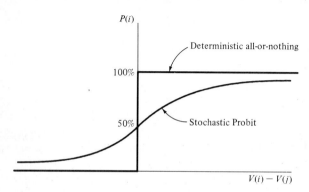

Figure 5.1 Binary choice.

portional choice of alternative 1 is 100 percent whenever $V(1) > V(2)$ and 0 percent otherwise. The S-shaped curve corresponding to Eq. (5.17) illustrates the stochastic choice where even with $V(1) < V(2)$ there is a nonzero probability of choice of alternative 1, either due to the randomness in the behavior of the individuals or because the V functions are perceived in a random way so that even when $V(1) < V(2)$, the opposite is sometimes perceived to be the case. Note that $V(\cdot)$ is specified as a utility function so that the larger its value for an alternative, the larger is the probability of choice of that alternative.

While the assumption of independence does lead to a simplification of the probit model, there is no reason why it should be made. One of the strengths of the probit model is that it permits an application of the stochastic choice model when the alternatives have attributes that are perceived correlated. Therefore, to make the independence assumption robs this model of one of its strongest features. There are simpler models such as the logit, which can be more easily applied when independence is a good assumption. This point is elaborated on further after the introduction of the logit model.

5.3 THE LOGIT MODEL

This model is obtained by assuming that the random components $c(i)$ of the choice utility function are all independent and identically distributed with a Gumbel (double exponential) distribution function:

$$F_e(x) = e^{-\theta e^{-x}} \quad ; \quad \theta > 0; \ -\infty < x < \infty \tag{5.19}$$

This distribution is similar to the normal and gives similar results to the probit model when the independence assumption is made. By combining Eqs. (5.5) and (5.19), we obtain

$$p(i) = \int_{-\infty}^{+\infty} \prod_{j \neq i} \exp\left[-\theta e^{-[V(j) - V(i) + x]}\right] \theta e^{-\theta} e^{-\theta \exp - x} \, dx$$

$$= \int_{-\infty}^{+\infty} \prod_{j} \exp\left[-\theta e^{-[V(j) - V(i) + x]}\right] \theta e^{-x} \, dx$$

$$= \int_{-\infty}^{+\infty} \exp\left[-\theta e^{-x} \sum_{j} e^{V(j) - V(i)}\right] \theta e^{-x} \, dx$$

$$= \frac{1}{\sum_{j} e^{V(j) - V(i)}}$$

$$= \frac{e^{V(i)}}{\sum_{j} e^{V(j)}} \tag{5.20}$$

which is a well-known form of the logit model referred to as the *multinomial logit* (MNL). The logit model has numerous advantages stemming for its amenability to mathematical manipulation. Its parameter estimation as well as its application and interpretation is easier than those of the multinomial probit. Its major disadvantage is its restriction to situations where alternatives have independent choice function, a limitation which can be quite disadvantageous in some applications such as route choice over complex networks.

Example We can illustrate the use of the logit model with the same trinomial choice example used to illustrate the probit model. Recall the choice vector $\mathbf{V} = [-12, -10, -15]$. Direct application of Eq. (5.20) gives

$$p(1) = \frac{e^{-12}}{e^{-12} + e^{-10} + e^{-15}} = 0.12$$

$$p(2) = \frac{e^{-10}}{e^{-12} + e^{-10} + e^{-15}} = 0.875$$

$$p(3) = \frac{e^{-15}}{e^{-12} + e^{-10} + e^{-15}} = 0.005$$

$$\sum_{i} p(i) = 1.0$$

These numbers are approximately similar to those obtained from the probit model in the previous section. The differences between them illustrate a feature common when comparing the results of these models. The resulting logit model has the tendency to reduce the choice for the relatively low $V(\cdot)$ as with $p(3)$ and increase it with the relatively high $V(\cdot)$ as with $p(2)$, when compared with the probit model. In numerous applications, it is found that when the independence of the utilities is assumed, then there is not much difference between the results. An example of the comparative results is shown in Fig. 5.2 when binary probit and

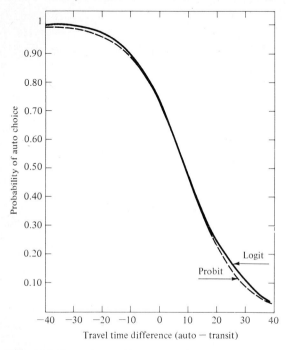

Figure 5.2 Comparison of binary logit and probit models of mode choice.

logit results are shown for the same data set [see DeDonnea (1971)]. The choice between these two models should always be made on the basis of whether the independence assumption can be made or not. This, in general, is related to the nature of the choice process on hand. If there are alternatives with similar attributes, or with overlapping components, such as when alternative routes overlap on some links, then independence cannot be assumed and the probit might be a better model of choice. When, on the other hand, the alternatives can be considered mutually exclusive such as in intercity travel mode choice or in urban destination choice analysis, then a logit model would be appropriate.

To illustrate the importance of overlap between alternatives and the effects of the independence assumption, the following common example is given.

Consider the network shown in Fig. 5.3*a*. This could be a road network offering three different routes between points *A* and *B*, or a representation of any other

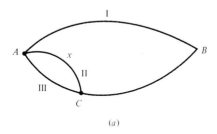

(*a*)

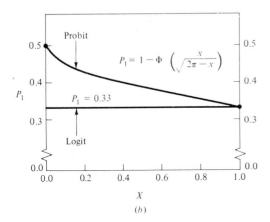

$$P_1 = 1 - \Phi \left(\sqrt{\frac{x}{2\pi - x}} \right)$$

$P_1 = 0.33$

X

(*b*)

Figure 5.3 Choice model error caused by the assumption of independent alternatives. (*a*) Network with overlapping routes; (*b*) difference between probit and logit estimates of route choice.

types of transportation alternatives such as modes where, for example, I could represent a highway mode, II a bus mode with walking access, and III a bus mode with automobile access. If trip makers perceive the attributes of these three choices in a random fashion so that $e(i)$ represents the differences between the actual and the perceived attributes of each alternative, then it is hardly likely that the differences between perceived and actual values for alternatives II and III would be independent. This is because these two alternatives are for the most part overlapping.

To illustrate the extent of the error that can be obtained from the independence assumption, let the extent of the overlap between II and III be measured by x, where x measures the length of AC in comparison to AB, so that at $x = 0$, there is total overlap between II and III and there are, in principle, only two alternatives: I and III; and at $x = 1.0$, there are three mutually independent alternatives I, II, and III. Assume that the true $V(\cdot)$ for all alternatives are identical. In this case, one would expect that at $x = 0$, $p(\text{I}) = p(\text{III}) = 0.50$, and at $x = 1.0$, $p(\text{I}) = p(\text{II}) = p(\text{III}) = 0.33$. It is easy to see that applying a choice model without a dependence between $e(\text{II})$ and $e(\text{III})$, such as the logit model, will always predict $p(\text{I}) = 0.33$. On the other hand, applying a model with a dependence term would predict a more realistic result that $p(\text{I}) = 0.33$ only when $x = 1.0$. Daganzo and Sheffi (1977) have demonstrated this by simply applying a probit model where the covariance between $e(\text{II})$ and $e(\text{III})$ is proportional to x and obtained the results shown in Fig. 5.3b.

This does not mean that a choice model that is simplified by the independence assumption, such as the logit model, cannot be applied. Indeed, there is considerable flexibility in applying choice models to deal with special cases such as the one illustrated in Fig. 5.3a in the above example. When x is low, for instance, one may consider not specifying II and III as distinct alternatives. When x is large, a good approximation would be to nest the choices and first consider the choice between close alternatives such as II and III and then proceed to consider the choice between I on the one hand and II or III on the other. This approach is used in mode choice analysis where similar alternatives often arise when public modes use different access modes but overlap on the line-haul portion. The approach results in models that are variously referred to as the *nested choice model* or the *cascading choice model*. Nesting, or sequencing, choices with stochastic models is discussed in a later section in this chapter. In route choice applications, the overlap is likely to be extensive and substantial since many routes connecting points in an urban transportation network are likely to share links. In such applications, a multinomial probit choice model with dependence between the choice functions is a more suitable model of choice.

The Independence of Irrelevant Alternatives

Consider the logit model of Eq. (5.20) and look at the relative odds of choosing one alternative over another, say i over j:

$$\frac{p(i)}{p(j)} = \frac{e^{V(j)}}{e^{V(j)}} \tag{5.21}$$

This indicates that the relative odds between any two alternatives are only a function of the attributes of these two and are independent of any other alternatives that may be available. This property of choice models is referred to as the *independence of irrelevant alternatives* and is considered a weakness of models that have it, such as the logit model. For example, if one is dealing with urban mode choices, then this property might imply that the relative odds of taking an automobile over taking a bus is independent of whether there is train service to the same destination. This is not likely since the presence of a train as a third alternative is likely to affect the probability of choosing the bus more so than that of choosing the automobile and hence likely to change their relative odds. It is interesting to note that this property was originally postulated as a general rule of multinomial choice by Luce (1959). The binary logit model (then referred to as the logistic diversion curve) was derived as a deterministic choice model. It is also interesting to note that this property leads to a simplification that makes the logit model quite straightforward and intrinsically linear. By taking logarithms, Eq. (5.21) can be transformed to

$$\ln \frac{p(i)}{p(j)} = V(i) - V(j) \qquad (5.22)$$

Given that most $V(\cdot)$ functions are specified as linear function, it is clear that Eq. (5.22) represents a great simplification. For example, the parameters of the logit model when transformed into Eq. (5.22) can be estimated using linear regression, although the estimates thus obtained may not be efficient.

Modifications in the formulation of the logit model are possible in order to overcome this weakness. But, whenever there are similar alternatives so that the independence of irrelevant alternative is limiting, then the probit model, which does not have this property, should be used. Indeed, in such cases, independence between the choice functions cannot be assumed anyway.

Elasticities of Choice

In some policy analyses utilizing choice models, one might be interested in assessing the sensitivity of the choice of a particular alternative to changes in some of the attributes in the $V(\cdot)$ function of the alternative itself or of some of the other alternatives. To do this one can calculate the choice elasticities and cross-elasticities using the definition of Eqs. (2.20) to (2.22). The elasticity of choice in this case will give the relative change in the choice probabilities as a function of the relative change in any of the variables in the choice model. Thus, if the choice model is given by

$$p(i) = g_i \, [V(i) \quad, \quad \text{for all } i] \qquad (5.23)$$

and if $V(\cdot)$ is a function of d demand and s supply variables $D_{i1}, D_{i2}, \ldots, D_{id}$ and $S_{i1}, S_{i2}, \ldots, S_{is}$, then the direct choice elasticity with respect to any variable, say S_{ik}, is defined as

$$ec_i(S_{ik}) = \frac{\partial p(i)/p(i)}{\partial S_{ik}/S_{ik}} \qquad (5.24)$$

and the choice cross-elasticity with respect to, say, S_{jk} is defined as

$$ec_i(S_{jk}) = \frac{\partial p(i)/p(i)}{\partial S_{jk}/S_{jk}} \qquad (5.25)$$

The computation of the point elasticities can be quite cumbersome for models such as the probit. In such cases, Eq. (2.51) or (2.52) can be used to calculate approximate arc elasticities. For the logit model, it is possible to compute point elasticities as follows:

$$ec_i(S_{ik}) = \frac{S_{ik}}{p(i)} \cdot \frac{\partial p(i)}{\partial S_{ik}}$$

$$= \frac{S_{ik} \sum_j e^{V(j)}}{E^{V(i)}} \cdot \frac{\partial}{\partial S_{ik}} \left[\frac{e^{V(i)}}{\sum_j e^{V(j)}} \right]$$

$$= S_{ik}\theta_{ik}[1 - p(i)] \tag{5.26}$$

where $\theta_{ik} = \partial V(i)/\partial S_{ik}$, which in the case of a linear $V(\cdot)$ function is the value of the parameter of the kth variable. Note that the elasticity has the same sign as $\theta_{ik} S_{ik}$, which is the contribution of variable S_{ik} to the choice function $V(i)$. Also note that the choice elasticity according to the logit model is not constant but is proportional to θ and inversely proportional to $p(i)$. This means that the more likely a particular choice is, the less sensitive it is to changes in the value of $V(i)$. Using the same principle

$$ec_i[V(i)] = \frac{\partial p(i)/p(i)}{\partial V(i)/V(i)} = V(i)[1 - p(i)] \tag{5.27}$$

gives the elasticity of choice with respect to the whole $V(i)$ function.

To illustrate the choice elasticity, consider the numerical example of the previous section in which mode choice was given by a logit model with a choice function $V(i) = -0.2t_i - 0.1c_i$. The conditional probabilities of mode choice $P(m|j)$ were computed as

$$p(m|j) = \begin{bmatrix} 0.62 & 0.11 & 0.80 \\ 0.38 & 0.89 & 0.20 \end{bmatrix}$$

Using Eq. (5.2), we can compute $ec_m(t_m)$ as follows:

$$ec_{m|j}(t_m) = \theta_t t_m[1 - p(m|j)] \tag{5.28}$$

where $\theta = -0.20$, and t_m is given by the values calculated in the example as

$$t_{mj} = \begin{bmatrix} 20 & 30 & 40 \\ 25 & 20 & 50 \end{bmatrix}$$

The elasticities of the conditional choice are then, by Eq. (5.28),

$$ec_{m|j}(t_m) = \begin{bmatrix} -1.52 & -5.34 & -1.6 \\ -3.1 & -0.44 & -8.0 \end{bmatrix}$$

These elasticities clearly indicate the larger sensitivity of choice of the modes for which the choice probabilities are small such as $p(2|3)$ or $p(1|2)$.

5.4 SEQUENCING STOCHASTIC CHOICE

In many applications, it is necessary to consider choice made according to some sequence. This happens in urban transportation when a sequence is postulated in which mode, destination, and route choices are assumed to follow some sequence. It also happens when a choice is made between groups of alternatives and then followed by a choice within the chosen group. For example, a hierarchy of mode choices can be postulated where a trip maker may decide between public and private transportation and in the event that the former is chosen, a choice is made between the public modes that may be available. In such a case, the choice of public transport would depend on the expected value of the utility of its modes, as perceived by the traveler. Likewise, if mode choice occurs after destination choice in a sequenced process, then the choice of each destination is likely to be based on the expected supply attributes of all modes serving the destination, again as perceived by the user.

It may be recalled from the previous chapter that sequenced choice in the deterministic case was based on the weighted average of the supply attributes at each level in the choice hierarchy. This weighted average is analogous to the expected value of the actual attributes as represented by the $V(\cdot)$ functions in a stochastic choice function. In other words, suppose that there are n alternatives with stochastic choice functions $U(i) = V(i) + e(i)$, $i = 1, 2, \ldots, n$. Suppose also that a choice model gives for each set of values $V(i)$ choice probabilities $p(i)$, $i = 1, 2, \ldots, n$. The expected value of the choice function is given by

$$\hat{V} = \sum_i p(i)V(i) \quad , \quad \text{for all } i \tag{5.29}$$

Strictly, however, this is not the correct measure of the expected utilities to be used in predicting choice at the next hierarchy of choice. It is only correct in the case of deterministic choice, and only an approximation in the case of stochastic choice. In this latter case, it is the expected value of the perceived attributes that is relevant. This can be calculated by finding the expected value $\tilde{V}$ of the utility U of the alternative chosen:

$$\tilde{V} = E[\max_i U_i]$$

$$= \int_1 \int_2 \cdots \int_n [\max_i U_i] f(U_1, U_2, \ldots, U_n)\, dU_1, dU_2, \ldots, dU_n \tag{5.30}$$

Replacing $U(i)$ by $[V(i) + e(i)]$ we obtain

$$\tilde{V} = \int_1 \int_2 \cdots \int_n \max_i [V(i) + e(i)] f(e_1, e_2, \ldots, e_n)\, de_1, de_2, \ldots, de_n \tag{5.31}$$

where $f(\cdot)$ is the joint density function of the random utility components $e(i)$. By making the assumption that the values of $e(i)$ are not related to the values of $V(i)$, Eq. (5.31) can be reduced to show that

$$\frac{\partial \tilde{V}}{\partial V(i)} = p(i) \tag{5.32}$$

as has been demonstrated by Daganzo and Sheffi (1977). This relationship is a fundamental property from which follow a number of interesting interpretations of stochastic choice models. For choice models where a solution of Eq. (5.32) can be obtained, one can derive the exact value of $\tilde{V}$. For the logit model, this is possible and can be done as follows:

$$\frac{\partial \tilde{V}}{\partial V(i)} = \frac{e^{V(i)}}{\sum_j e^{V(j)}} \tag{5.33}$$

$$\tilde{V} = \int_{V(i)} \frac{e^{V(i)}}{\sum_j e^{V(j)}} \, dV(i)$$

$$= \ln \sum_j e^{V(j)} \tag{5.34}$$

In a similar manner, the expected perceived value of any attribute of a linear $V(\cdot)$ function, say X_k, can be obtained as

$$\tilde{X}_k = \frac{1}{\theta_k} \ln \sum_j e^{V(j)} \tag{5.35}$$

where θ_k is $\partial V(i)/\partial X_k$ or the parameter of variable X_k in the choice function when it is linear. The difference between $\tilde{V}$ and $\hat{V}$ is that the first is the expected value of the maximum of a set of random variables, whereas the second is a weighted average of the expected values of these random variables. Even using $V_{\max}$ as a measure of the utility of a choice is not correct for it will reflect the maximum of the expected values, which is not the same as the expected value of the maximum. Using $\hat{V}$ or $V_{\max}$ for sequencing choice should be recognized as an approximation which should not be done when the logit model is used since Eq. (5.34) is quite easy to use.

Example In order to illustrate the difference between deterministic and stochastic sequencing of choice we recall parts of the example used in the previous chapter to sequence route, mode, and destination choice. Simplifying the example, we let the following t_{mj} matrix describe travel times by two modes m to two destinations j:

$$t_{mj} = \begin{array}{c} \\ m \end{array} \begin{array}{c} \\ 1 \\ 2 \end{array} \begin{array}{cc} j=1 & j=2 \\ \left[\begin{array}{cc} 20 & 30 \\ 25 & 40 \end{array} \right] \end{array}$$

We assume that mode choice conditional on destinations choice is given by

$$p(m|j) = \frac{e^{-0.2t_{mj}}}{\sum_r e^{-0.2t_{rj}}} \qquad j = 1, 2$$

$$p(m|j) = \begin{cases} m=1 \\ m=2 \end{cases} \begin{matrix} j=1 & j=2 \\ \begin{bmatrix} 0.73 & 0.88 \\ 0.27 & 0.12 \end{bmatrix} \end{matrix}$$

We can calculate the expected actual values V_j or t_j for each destination using the averages weighted by the conditional choice probabilities. Since $V = -0.2t$, we can limit our comparisons to $\hat{t}_j$ and compare it with $\tilde{t}_j$ as obtained from Eq. (5.35):

$$\hat{t}_j = t_{1j}p(1|j) + t_{2j}p(2|j)$$

$$= (20 \times 0.73 + 25 \times 0.27, \ 30 \times 0.88 + 40 \times 0.12)$$

$$= (21.35, 31.2)$$

These are the expected values of the actual times to each destination after the choices of mode are made. The expected *perceived* times $\tilde{t}_j$ are given by Eq. (5.34):

$$\tilde{t}_j = \frac{1}{-0.2} \left[\ln(e^{-0.2\tilde{t}_j 11} + e^{-0.2\tilde{t}_j 21}), \ \ln(e^{-0.2\tilde{t}_j 21} + e^{-0.2\tilde{t}_j 22}) \right]$$

$$= (18.4, 29.4)$$

The values of $\tilde{t}_j$ are more appropriate for inclusion in the destination choice model than $\hat{t}_j$ since they represent the perceived values on the basis of which choices are presumably made. It should not be surprising that the values of $\tilde{t}_j$ are lower than the minimum values of t_{mj} for each j, since they represent the outcome of a stochastic perception process. The difference between the two results will impact the results of the destination choice model. To illustrate this impact, we assume that destination choice is inversely proportional to t_j^2 (as in the gravity model of trip distribution); then using $\hat{t}_j$ will give a destination choice $p_j = (0.68, 0.32)$ and using $\tilde{t}_j$ will give $p_j = (0.72, 0.28)$.

When postulating a sequenced choice process and using a stochastic choice approach, it is advisable to use a logit model and compute $\tilde{V}$'s for sequencing. When postulating a deterministic model of choice, then $\hat{V}$ is valid for sequencing. When sequencing is necessitated by grouped alternatives due to overlapping attributes, then it is best to use a probit model with a dependence between the utility functions and to avoid sequencing altogether.

5.5 CHOICE FUNCTIONS AND DEMAND FUNCTIONS

In most cases it is not sufficient to know the choice probabilities; one needs to estimate the volume of users on any transportation system. For this, the relationship between choice models and demand models must be explored. In general, if it is known that N people are making a trip and that certain proportions of them are choosing certain modes or routes or destinations, then it is possible to estimate the specific traffic volumes involved. In the deterministic case, this is done simply by multiplying N with the proportions of choice, however defined. For example, let $P(m, j, r)$ be the proportion of all users of a particular mode, destination, and route combination (m, j, r), then the traffic volume X_{mjr} can be predicted from

$$X_{mjr} = Np(m, j, r) \qquad (5.36)$$

This traffic will occur during a period over which the N trips are supposed to be made. In a sequenced choice approach in urban travel demand, when a trip generation predicts the total number of trips N that are made during, say, an average weekday, X_{mjr} would then be daily flows of traffic. Equation (5.36) will then be a demand function for daily trips with attributes mjr.

When the choice model used is stochastic, then the number of trips will be a random variable with a multinomial distribution and with an expected value

$$E(X_{mjr}) = Np(m, j, r) \qquad (5.37)$$

and a variance

$$\text{Var}(X_{mjr}) = Np(m, j, r)[1 - p(m, j, r)] \qquad (5.38)$$

Taking the example of the previous section for an illustration, we recall the three-mode situation where the logit model predicted $P(m) = [0.12, 0.875, 0.005]$. If there are 1000 trips distributed among the three modes, then the expected values of traffic by each mode X_m will be

$$X_m = 1000\, p(m)$$
$$= [120, 875, 5]$$

and the variance of the number of trips will be

$$\text{Var}[X_m] = 1000[0.12 \times 0.88, 8.875 \times 0.125, 0.005 \times 0.995]$$
$$= [105.6, 109.4, 4.975]$$

Note that the values of the variances relative to the means are lower for the higher traffic volumes.

The relation between demand and choice can also be illustrated by reference to Eq. (5.32): $\partial \tilde{V}/\partial V(i) = p(i)$, which shows that the expected marginal utility of choice with respect to one alternative equals the probability of choice of that alternative. This is analogous to the definition of demand in terms of marginal benefits as discussed in Chap. 2. With a population of N trips to be divided among alternatives I, the expected demand for each alternative is given by the expected marginal utility

$$E[X(i)] = N\frac{\partial \tilde{V}}{V(i)} = Np(i) \qquad (5.39)$$

5.6 CALIBRATION OF CHOICE MODELS

As with other types of travel demand models, the calibration process of choice models consists of estimating the parameter values, evaluating the statistical significance of the estimates, and then validating the model by comparing its prediction with observed behavior. The first two steps are usually carried out simultaneously as a statistical process of estimation. The third requires that model predictions be compared with actual data, preferably other than those used to estimate the parameters.

Since most choice models are nonlinear, their estimation is usually more complex than that of simple demand models which can be linearized. Regression techniques and least-squares estimation methods have rather limited applications here, since these techniques are not suitable for nonlinear models. The single exception is when a binary logit model is used, with aggregate market choice data. In such a case, a simple linear form can be obtained, as in Eq. (5.22), provided the choice functions $V(\cdot)$ are linear, which nearly always is the case. This linear function can be estimation with regression analysis.

To illustrate this, consider a survey taken of travelers between two cities A and B. Suppose that of 10 respondents, 4 chose a bus mode, and 6 chose an auto mode. Suppose further that the travel times for these two modes are $t_B = 47$ and $t_A = 38$ for the bus and the auto, respectively. These are times that are measured and assumed to be true for all 10 respondents. Suppose the mode choice is modeled by a binary logit of the form

$$p(A) = \frac{e^{\alpha t_A}}{e^{\alpha t_A} + e^{\alpha t_B}} \qquad p(B) = \frac{e^{\alpha t_B}}{e^{\alpha t_A} + e^{\alpha t_B}}$$

It is possible to estimate the value of α from this data rather easily. By applying Eq. (5.22) to the above data, we obtain

$$\frac{p(A)}{p(B)} = \frac{e^{38\alpha}}{e^{47\alpha}} = e^{-9\alpha}$$

$$\frac{0.6}{0.4} = e^{-9\alpha}$$

$$\alpha = \frac{\ln 6/4}{-9} = -0.045$$

Had the $V(\cdot)$ function contained more variables than in this case, then a simple regression might be used to estimate the parameters. Note that in this simple case, only one parameter could be estimated since there is effectively one piece of information, namely $p(A) = 0.6$ and $p(B) = 1 - p(A)$. To estimate a larger number of parameters would require a larger number of observations in the form of probabilities of choice for other groups facing different values of t_A and t_B.

In general, the estimation of choice model parameters is done using the maximum likelihood method. We discuss this method in the following paragraphs for the general case of multinomial choice, at the disaggregate and aggregate levels. We return after that to the binary case as a special instance and illustrate some of its features.

Multinomial Disaggregate Models

At the disaggregate level, the choice function includes demand and supply variables that are measured specifically for each individual. Given a sample of N individuals, $n = 1, 2, \ldots, N,$ and given K choices $k = 1, 2, \ldots, K,$ a choice function $V(n, k)$ is constructed for each individual and alternative. This function includes demand and supply variables represented by a vector $\mathbf{X}_{nk}$.

A choice model is then postulated to give the choice probability p_{nk} of each alternative for each of the individuals. Assuming without loss of generality that the choice function is linear, we can write $V(n, k) = \mathbf{AX}_{nk}$, where $\mathbf{A}$ is a vector of parameters to be estimated. In other words

$$V(n, k) = \sum_k a_{ik} x_{ink} \tag{5.40}$$

where x_{ink} is the value of the ith variable for alternative k as measured for individual n. The choice model is now written as

$$p_{nk} = f_k[V(n, k)] = g_k\left[\sum_i a_{ik} x_{ink}\right] \tag{5.41}$$

In estimating the model parameters a_{ik}, we observe a number of individuals N and we note the choice of each individual. At the same time, we observe the values of x_{ink}. To construct the likelihood function of the observed choices, we define the following random variable:

$$Y_{ik} = \begin{cases} 1 & \text{if individual } n \text{ chooses alternative } k \\ 0 & \text{otherwise} \end{cases} \tag{5.42}$$

and we define

$$N_k = \sum_{n=1}^{N} Y_{nk} \tag{5.43}$$

N_k becomes the number of individuals who choose alternative k in the observed sample. We now partition the sample N into K subsets S_k, each of which contains the N_k individuals who select alternative k. Assuming that the values of Y_{nk} represent the outcomes of independent Bernoulli trials, i.e., assuming that the choices of different individuals are independent, then the probability of N_k individuals in each subset S_k is given by the multinomial distribution. Hence the likelihood of the observed sample is given by

$$\Lambda = p(N_1, N_2, \cdots, N_k | A)$$
$$= \frac{N!}{N_1! N_2! \cdots N_k!} \prod_k \prod_{n \in S_k} (p_{nk}) \tag{5.44}$$

In order to find the maximum likelihood estimates of the parameters A, we can rewrite Eq. (5.44) by taking logarithms to simplify the maximization and dropping the constant multiplier $(N!N_1!N_2! \cdots N_k!)$ to give

$$\Lambda^* = \sum_k \sum_{n \in S_k} \ln p_{kn} \tag{5.45}$$

The maximum likelihood estimates of the parameters A can be obtained by computing for each

$$\frac{\partial \Lambda^*}{\partial a_{ik}} = 0 \quad \text{for all } i \tag{5.46}$$

The maximum likelihood estimators $\hat{a}_{ik}$ thus estimated are asymptotically efficient, consistent, and normally distributed. The confidence intervals for $\hat{a}_i$ can be estimated from their variance-covariance matrix:

$$\hat{\Omega} = -\left\{ \frac{\partial^2 \Lambda^*}{\partial a_{ik} \partial a_{jk}} \right\}^{-1} \bigg|_{a = \hat{a}} \tag{5.47}$$

The significance of the estimated vector $\hat{\mathbf{A}}$ can also be tested using the likelihood ratio test, as we shall demonstrate with an illustration. The facility in applying Eq. (5.45) to (5.47) to estimate and evaluate parameter values of a choice depends on the form of the model itself. The logit model, for example, lends itself to relatively straightforward estimation. The probit model on the other hand requires computational procedures that are rather complex and for which computer codes have only recently become available [see, for example, Daganzo (1979)].

It should be noted that the specification of the model in Eq. (5.40) implies through the a_{ik} parameters that choice is alternative-specific rather than attribute-specific. This is because the a_{ik} parameters are allowed to differ for any given variable i from one alternative to another. A special case of this is when $a_{ik} = a_i$, meaning that the attributes have the same effect on choice regardless of which alternative they described. The alternative-specific model obviously contains a larger number of parameters and requires more data for its calibration. It has the potential advantage of capturing effects of factors that are specific to alternatives. Its disadvantage is in that it is not as amenable to policy analysis as the attribute-specific option because it cannot predict the choice probabilities for novel alternatives since no parameter values will exist for them. The alternative is to make the parameters attribute-specific, or equivalently choice abstract. This permits the prediction of the shares of any alternatives once the values of their attributes are specified. However, the assumption of abstractiveness does cause a loss of explanatory power. We shall see some of these models in later chapters.

When the choice model used is a multinomial logit, then it is possible to write down the explicit solutions to the estimation problem using Eqs. (5.43) to (5.45). For the MNL model, Eq. (5.44) can be written as

$$\Lambda = \frac{N!}{N_1!N_2! \cdots N_k!} \prod_k \prod_{n \in S_k} \frac{e^{V(n,k)}}{\sum_k e^{V(n,k)}} \tag{5.48}$$

Taking logarithms and dropping the constant multiplier gives

$$\Lambda^* = \sum_k \sum_{n \in S_k} V(n, k) - \ln \sum_k e^{(Vn,k)} \qquad (5.49)$$

By replacing $V(n,k)$ with $\sum_i a_{ik}x_{ink}$ and maximizing Λ^*, we obtain the equations

$$\frac{\partial \Lambda^*}{\partial a_{ik}} = \sum_k \sum_{n \in N_k} x_{ink} - \sum_k \sum_n x_{ink}\frac{e^{V(n,k)}}{\sum_k e^{V(n,k)}} = 0 \qquad (5.50)$$

Solution of these equations for each a_{ik} value can be obtained by using iterative procedures such as the Newton-Raphson algorithm. Computer codes are available for doing this [see, for example, Gosling (1977)].

Binomial Disaggregate Models

The binomial (or binary) disaggregate choice is a special case with two alternatives. In this case, the likelihood function Eq. (5.43) can be simplified:

$$\Lambda = \frac{N!}{N_1!N_2!} \prod_{n \in S_1} (p_{n1}) \prod_{n \in S_2} (p_{n2}) \qquad (5.51)$$

which for the logit model can be simplified upon taking logarithms to

$$\Lambda^* = \sum_{n \in S_1} V(n, 1) + \sum_{n \in S_2} V(n, 2) - \sum_n \ln \left[e^{V(n,1)} + e^{V(n,2)} \right] \qquad (5.52)$$

to which Eq. (5.49) can be applied to obtain the estimates of the parameters A.

Note that in the case of disaggregate calibration it is not possible to take the advantages of the simplifying property of the logit model that is shown in Eq. (5.22). The relative odds of alternative 1 and 2 in the disaggregate case are given by

$$\frac{p(1)}{p(2)} = \frac{e^{V(n,1)}}{e^{V(n,2)}} \qquad (5.53)$$

The right-hand side is individual-specific, and hence it is not possible to obtain different observations for $p(1)/p(2)$ in order to calibrate its parameters. The linearization of Eq. (5.52) and the use of regression for the estimation of the parameters can only be done in the aggregate case.

It is rather cumbersome to illustrate the disaggregate model estimation with a numerical example, for the number of probabilities one needs to calculate is rather large and equal to the product of the number of the individuals in the sample by the number of alternatives. We can, however, illustrate the construction of the likelihood function, for example, with a small sample size and a very simple choice model.

Suppose that the data given in Table 5.1 give the travel times measured for five individuals, for each of two modes. Suppose that of these people the first two were observed to select the first mode and the other three the second mode.

Suppose that a simple choice model is used to explain this choice process as follows:

Table 5.1

	n	x_{n1}	x_{n2}
S_1	1	5	7
	2	4	6
S_2	3	6	4
	4	6	4
	5	4	5

$$p(nk) = \frac{e^{b_k t_{nk}}}{\sum_k e^{b_k t_{nk}}}$$

where t is the travel time given in Table 5.1 and b_k is a choice-specific parameter that needs to be estimated. Applying Eq. (5.48), we can directly write the likelihood function

$$\Lambda^* = \frac{e^{5b_1}}{e^{5b_1} + e^{7b_2}} \cdot \frac{e^{4b_1}}{e^{4b_1} + e^{6b_2}} \cdot \frac{e^{4b_2}}{e^{4b_2} + e^{6b_1}} \cdot \frac{e^{4b_2}}{e^{4b_2} + e^{6b_1}} \cdot \frac{e^{5b_2}}{e^{5b_2} + e^{4b_1}}$$

and the log-likelihood function

$$\Lambda^* = (9b_1 + 13b_2) - [\ln(e^{5b_1} + e^{7b_2}) + \ln(e^{4b_1} + e^{6b_2}) + 2\ln(e^{4b_2} + e^{6b_1}) + \ln(e^{5b_2} + e^{4b_1})]$$

The parameter estimates $\hat{b}_1$ and $\hat{b}_2$ can be obtained by solving

$$\frac{\partial \Lambda^*}{\partial b_1} = 0 \quad \text{and} \quad \frac{\partial \Lambda^*}{\partial b_2} = 0$$

Multinomial Aggregate Models

In the aggregate choice model, it is assumed that the variables in the choice function are the same for all individuals in a sample, i.e., $x_{ikn} = x_{ik}$. This means that there is a single value of the measured choice function for each alternative and that the probabilities of choice are also the same for individuals in each subset S_k, i.e., $p_{nk} = p_k$. In this case, the likelihood function given in Eq. (5.44) becomes

$$\Lambda = \frac{N!}{N_1! N_2! \ldots N_k!} \prod_k (p_k)^{N_k} \tag{5.54}$$

and the simplified log-likelihood function becomes

$$\Lambda^* = \sum_k N_k \, p_k \tag{5.55}$$

The rest of the estimation proceeds, as before, by maximizing Λ^*.

Example We can illustrate the estimation of the parameters of a multinomial aggregate choice model using an example with three alternatives. Suppose that three modes exist for travel between two cities. Suppose that the travel time and travel costs of these modes are as given by Table 5.2.

Table 5.2

	t_k	c_k
$k = 1$	15	3
$k = 2$	10	4
$k = 3$	20	7

Suppose that of 100 people surveyed, it was found that 50 used the first 1,6 mode, 40 used the second, and 10 used the third. In other words, $p_k = (0.5, 0.4, 0.10)$. A logit model of the following form is postulated for this problem:

$$p_k = \frac{e^{at_k + bc_k}}{\sum_k e^{at_k + bc_k}}$$

where a and b are attribute-specific parameters to be estimated by the maximum likelihood method.

We construct the likelihood function using Eq. (5.54) as follows:

$$\Lambda = \frac{100!}{50!40!10!} (p_1)^{50}(p_2)^{40}(p_3)^{10}$$

and simplified log-likelihood function as follows:

$$\Lambda^* = 50(15a + 3b) + 40(10a + 4b) + 10(20a + 7b) - 100 \ln Y$$

where $Y = e^{15a + 3b} + e^{10a + 4b} + e^{20a + 7b}$.

$$\frac{\partial \Lambda^*}{\partial a} = 1350 - 100\left(\frac{15e^{15a + 3b} + 10e^{10a + 4b} + 20e^{20a + 7b}}{Y}\right) = 0$$

$$\frac{\partial \Lambda^*}{\partial b} = 380 - 100\left(\frac{3e^{15a + 3b} + 4e^{10a + 4b} + 7e^{20a + 7b}}{Y}\right) = 0$$

This can be solved manually in this simple case. The above two equations can be resolved to

$$-150e^{15a + 3b} + 350e^{10a + 4b} + 1350e^{20a + 7b} = 0$$

and

$$80e^{15a + 3b} - 20e^{10a + 4b} - 320e^{20a + 7b} = 0$$

Solved simultaneously, these equations give

$$a = -0.02868 \qquad b = -0.36640$$

which can be checked by recomputing the observed probabilities of choice:

$$e^{15a + 3b} = 0.2166$$

$$e^{10a + 7b} = 0.1733$$

$$e^{20a + 7b} = \underline{0.0433}$$
$$0.4332$$

$$p_1 = \frac{0.2166}{0.4332} = 0.50 \qquad p_2 = \frac{0.1733}{0.4332} = 0.40 \qquad p_3 = \frac{0.0433}{0.4332} = 0.10$$

With the estimated parameters, it is possible to predict the market share of a hypothetical new mode. For example, if a fast, expensive alternative is introduced as the fourth mode with time and cost $t_4 = 5$, $c_4 = 12$, then the new choice probabilities can be estimated as follows:

$$e^{15a + 3b} = 0.2166$$

$$e^{10a + 4b} = 0.1733$$

$$e^{20a + 7b} = 0.0433$$

$$e^{5a + 12b} = \underline{0.0107}$$
$$0.4439$$

for which

$$p_1 = \frac{0.2166}{0.4439} = 0.488 \qquad p_2 = \frac{0.1733}{0.4139} = 0.390 \qquad p_3 = \frac{0.0433}{0.4439} = 0.09$$

and

$$p_4 = \frac{0.0107}{0.4439} = 0.024$$

Notice that if the model had included choice-specific parameters a_1, b_1, a_2, b_2, etc., then this type of prediction would not be possible since values for a_4, b_4 would not be available. Additional choice data would also be necessary to estimate the model with choice-specific parameters. In this example, three observed choices would allow the estimation of only two parameters since $p_1 + p_2 + p_3 = 1$. The parameter estimates obtained in this numerical example cannot be considered significant since all the information available is used to obtain them and no degrees of freedom are left. The estimation in this example is analogous to fitting a straight line through two given points, rather than by regression or a larger sample of points. Had other groups of trip makers with different time and cost vectors been surveyed and their choice proportions recorded, then it would be possible to obtain parameter estimates using the same method. If the choice model is a good model of the behavior of all the various groups surveyed, then such estimates will have finite variances that will reflect on the significance of the estimates. (The smaller the variances, the higher the significance level.)

The example discussed here represents an extreme situation where all the surveyed population is aggregated into one group. The other extreme is the totally disaggregated model wherein each individual is considered separately with an individual probability on the basis of individually measured values of time and cost. It is virtually certain that in reality the totally aggregated model is not accurate, for it is unlikely that all individuals in the survey population will experience precisely the same values of t_k and c_k. Given the data availability, it is always preferable to use a disaggregate model when estimating the parameters. When disaggregate data are not available, then the analyst should exercise care in aggregating data in order to avoid biases in parameter estimation. The effect of different levels of aggregation on the results will of course depend on how model variables do vary from one individual to another or from one segment of the survey population to another. In general, the aggregation method shown by Eq. (2.47) can be used, but its application in practice is limited severely by data availability. The reader interested in choice model aggregation can refer to any of a number of illustrated studies including Daganzo (1978) and Westin (1974).

Binomial Aggregate Models

In this case, aggregate data on choice are available for a survey population in a binary choice situation. Equations (5.54) and (5.55) become

$$\Lambda = \frac{N!}{N_1! N_2!} (p_1)^{N_1} (p_2)^{N_2} \tag{5.56}$$

and
$$\Lambda^* = N_1 \ln p_1 + N_2 \ln p_2 \tag{5.57}$$

The rest of the estimation proceeds as in the previous cases. In the case of the logit model, it is now possible to use the simplified procedure, taking advantage of the linear form of Eq. (5.22). The aggregate model is commonly used in intercity travel analysis where disaggregate information is not readily obtainable. We illustrate such an application with the following numerical example.

Example In a survey of air travelers, it was found that volumes were split between two types of services: first-class and economy, according to the data given in Table 5.3. The data cover a 5-year period and include for each year the fares charged for each class of air service.

Table 5.3

Year	Traffic 1	Traffic 2	Fares 1	Fares 2
1	330	1000	90	60
2	330	1100	110	70
3	350	1200	130	80
4	350	1400	140	80
5	340	1800	160	90

The following logit choice model is postulated:

$$p(1) = \frac{e^{a_1 + bF_1}}{e^{a_1 + bF_1} + e^{bF_2}}$$

$$p(2) = \frac{e^{bF_2}}{e^{a_1 + bF_1} + e^{bF_2}}$$

where a_1 and b are parameters to be estimated and F_1 and F_2 are the air fares for first-class and economy service, respectively. Note that a_1 is a choice-specific parameter and reflects the attributes of first-class service relative to economy service. One would expect $a_1 > 0$ since with equal fares more than half the people are likely to fly first class.

To calibrate this model, we use Eq. (5.22) to obtain

$$\frac{p(1)}{p(2)} = e^{a_1 + b(F_1 - F_2)} \qquad \text{and} \qquad \ln \frac{p(1)}{p(2)} = a_1 + b(F_1 - F_2)$$

Using the data in Table 5.3, we obtain the corresponding values of $\ln[p(1)/p(2)]$ and $(F_1 - F_2)$ as shown in Table 5.4.

Table 5.4

Year	T_1/T_2	ln $[p_1/p_2]$	$F_1 - F_2$
1	0.33	−1.11	30
2	0.30	−1.20	40
3	0.29	−1.24	50
4	0.25	−1.39	60
5	0.19	−1.66	70

Table 5.5

Year	$F_1 - F_2$	p_1 observed	p_1 estimated
1	30	0.25	0.25
2	40	0.23	0.23
3	50	0.21	0.22
4	60	0.19	0.20
5	71	0.17	0.16

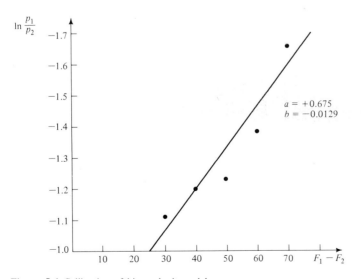

Figure 5.4 Calibration of binary logit model.

These values are regressed against each other to obtain $a_1 = 0.675$ and $b = -0.0129$. The results are shown graphically in Fig. 5.4. Using the estimated parameters, the choices for each year can be predicted and compared to the observed values as shown in Table 5.5 for p_1.

PROBLEMS

5.1 A typical travel demand problem with a predetermined activity pattern is work trip mode choice. Let us assume that we have m workers residing at zone A and working in zone B.

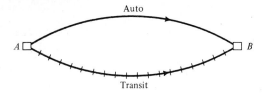

Each worker has a choice of auto (A) or transit (B). We know that workers seek to maximize their utility in making travel choices and that an individual's utility is affected by travel time and travel cost in the following way:

$$U_{ij} = \alpha_t t_{ij} + \alpha_c \left(\frac{c_{ij}}{Y_i} \right)$$

where U_{ij} = utility to individual i of mode j

$\quad t_{ij}$ = time for individual i on mode j

$\quad c_{ij}$ = cost for individual i on mode j

$\quad Y_i$ = income of individual i

$\quad \alpha_t, \alpha_c$ = coefficients of time and cost, respectively

$$j = \begin{cases} A \text{ for auto} \\ T \text{ for transit} \end{cases}$$

(a) What signs would you expect for α_t and α_c?

(b) There is no analogue to the budget constraint in travel choice analysis. Assume for the moment that times are invariant and that auto cost is a constant $\overline{C_A}$. For what values of C_T would a utility-maximizing individual choose transit? If all m individuals have the same income $\overline{Y}$, what is the aggregate demand function for transit?

(c) The result of question b shows that pure utility maximization based on quantifiable attributes is an insufficient explanation for travel behavior. One alternative is to assume that individuals react in a probabilistic manner to perceived (dis)utility. (This is equivalent to the assumption that individual choice is a random variable whose distribution is a function of the utilities.) The ratio of exponential utilities is often used to compute these probabilities:

$$P_A^i = \frac{e^{V_{iA}}}{e^{V_{iA}} + e^{V_{iT}}}$$

$$P_T^i = \frac{e^{V_{iT}}}{e^{V_{iA}} + e^{V_{iT}}} = 1 - P_A^i$$

Using these equations and the assumptions of question b, what is the new aggregate demand function for transit? Does this seem more reasonable than your result in part b?

(*d*) Suppose $\overline{Y}$ now represents the mean of an income distribution. Do the same aggregation issues discussed in your answer to the first problem apply to this travel demand problem as well? Would they still apply if income was not a factor in the utility equation?

5.2 A survey is taken of travelers from city A to city B. Of the 10 respondents, it is known that 4 chose bus and 6 chose auto. But travel time data are unavailable. Computer analysis of the highway and bus networks has provided the following time data:

From \ To	A	B
A	5	25
B	25	8

Auto times

From \ To	A	B
A	10	30
B	30	7

Bus times

(*a*) Compute the total travel time by each mode, counting intercity times and intracity times for both ends of the trip.

Given these data, it is possible to estimate the coefficients of the utility function using the maximum likelihood technique.

(*b*) How many coefficients must be estimated? How many data points do you have? Why can't the maximum likelihood problem be solved under these conditions?

(*c*) Assume that $a = 0$, and compute the maximum likelihood estimate of b.

5.3 Given a logit mode choice mode for two modes—auto and bus—with utilities

$$U_A = a_A + bt_A$$
$$U_B = bt_B$$

where t_k = travel time by mode k
A = auto
B = bus
a_A = auto-specific constant
b = time coefficient

(*a*) Why would it be meaningless to add a_B, a bus = specific constant term, to U_B?

(*b*) Can you think of a theoretical justification for including a constant term in the utility equation?

(*c*) If you had reason to believe that age is a factor in mode choice—specifically, that older people are less likely to ride the bus—how would you incorporate it into the utility equations? Would it appear in both equations, or just in one?

(*d*) Suppose a new mode, say rail, is introduced and is assumed to have the utility

$$U_R = b \cdot t_R$$

What happens to P_A and P_B after the introduction of the third mode? What happens to the ratio P_A/P_B?

5.4 In most economic derivations of mode choice models it is found that the choice between two modes is expressed as a function:

$$\frac{T^k}{T^m} = \frac{g_k{}^{(C_k)}}{g_m{}^{(C_m)}} \tag{1}$$

where T^k and T^m represent the traffic quantities on modes k and m, respectively, and $g(c)$ is a function of the cost of travel C by the different modes. However, it is often assumed that travelers' behavior in mode choice is that they perceive of the difference in costs between modes rather than of ratios. Thus it is necessary to modify the model to

$$\frac{T^k}{T^m} = \phi_{km}(C_k - C_m) \tag{2}$$

Show how this can be done, by assuming the Eq. (1) is given and deriving the form of the function ϕ in Eq. (2).

REFERENCES

Clark, C. E.: The Greatest of a Finite Set of Random Variables, *Oper. Res.*, vol. 9, pp. 145–162, 1961.

Daganzo, C. F.: *CHOMP User's Manual*, Research supported by NSF Grant Eng, 77-05701 and Faculty Research Grant 617, Institute of Transportation Studies, Research Report, Berkeley, Calif., 1978.

————, and F. Bouthelier: Aggregation with Multinomial Probit and Estimation of Disaggregate Models with Aggregate Data: A New Methodological Approach, *Transp. Res.*, vol. 13B, no. 2, pp. 133–146, 1979.

————, F. Bouthelier, and Y. Sheffi,: Multinomial Probit and Qualitative Choice: A Computationally Efficient Algorithm, *Transp. Sci.*, vol. 11, no. 4, pp. 338–358, 1977.

————, and Y. Sheffi: On Stochastic Modes of Traffic Assignment, *Transp. Sci.*, vol. 11, no. 3, pp. 253–274, 1977.

DeDonnea, F. X.: *The Determinants of Transport Mode Choice in Dutch Cities,* Rotterdam University Press, 1971.

Finney, D. J.: *Probit Analysis,* Cambridge University Press, Cambridge, 1962.

Gosling, G. D.: MLESTIM II, A Program for the Estimation of the Choice Model, Institute of Transportation Studies Memorandum, Berkeley, Calif., 1977.

Lerman, S. R., and Manski, C. F.: "An Estimator for the Generalized Multinomial Probit Model," Transportation Research Board Meeting, 1977.

Luce, H.: *Individual Choice Behaviour,* John Wiley & Sons, Inc., New York, 1959.

Westin, R.: "Prediction From Binary Choice Models," *J. Econometr.*, vol. 2, pp. 1–16, 1974.

TRIP DISTRIBUTION ANALYSIS

Trip distribution analysis is concerned with the flow of traffic between trip origins and destinations. The question of distribution arises mostly in urban passenger transportation demand analysis but is common in other demand analysis including intercity transportation, commodity distribution, and other situations where a choice of destination is to be made, such as the distribution of central business district parkers among parking facilities or the distribution of national park visitors among camping facilities. Trip distribution models have been constructed and applied to all these situations. But most of the developments in trip distribution analysis have been made in the study of urban passenger transportation demands.

This chapter deals with trip distribution in the context of urban transportation demand analysis, although the general structure of the models discussed is applicable to many of the other processes such as intercity transportation and commodity transportation.

6.1 TRIP DISTRIBUTION IN URBAN TRAVEL DEMAND ANALYSIS

As discussed in Chap. 4, trip distribution represents the step in the sequential approach to urban traffic estimation that deals in the destination choice. When it is performed right after trip generation analysis, its purpose is to synthesize origin-destination flows by all available modes and to estimate interzonal flows for mode choice analysis. When, on the other hand, it is performed after mode choice analysis, its purpose is to synthesize origin-destination flows by particular modes and to estimate flows for assignment to specific modal network routes. The importance of trip distribution derives from the fact that it provides the spatial dimension to traffic demand estimates and thereby permits policy analyses with respect to the planning of transportation networks. This importance has perhaps been exaggerated in the urban transportation studies of the 1950s and 1960s, and a disproportionate attention has been given to trip distribution modeling vis-à-vis other aspects of traffic estimation. In contrast, less attention was given to the problem of how to use traffic flow estimates in the planning process. The result is that there exists today a large number of trip distribution models with little coherent theory, constituting a rather limited contribution to the planning problem.

Almost all the trip distribution models that have been developed and used are related, and although many appear to be derived from different behavioral postulates, in the end they do not differ much. Further modeling in such a case may be counterproductive, and the transportation analyst should concentrate on improving the use of the models in the planning process.

6.2 FUNDAMENTALS OF TRIP DISTRIBUTION ANALYSIS

Purpose of the Analysis

The question of trip distribution arises because trip makers in an urban area normally have a number of destinations for trips of different purposes. If it were evident that every traveler selected the closest, or largest, of the possible destinations, and did that consistently, then the trip distribution process would be completely understood, and a simple calculating scheme rather than a complicated trip distribution model would suffice to estimate traffic flows. However, such is not the case. Indeed, it is found in urban traffic studies that the trip distribution process is complex and requires analysis. Not all travelers select the closest destination, and a typical traveler may not consistently select the same destination, except, naturally, for the trip to work. The purpose of trip distribution analysis is to identify the determinants of this process and to adopt demand and supply variables that can consistently predict the manner by which trips are distributed from origins to destinations.

There are two types of trip distribution processes in urban areas. One may be called a long-term process, such as the distribution of home-to-work trips, and the other, a short-term process, such as the distribution of convenience shopping trips. The first is a process that is stable and changes only in the long run, either by the change of residential location or of employment. But from day to day, the trip maker will always select the same destination, that of place of work. The second process is more random in its nature, for it is possible that a trip maker may change the destination of even a regular shopping trip, from day to day. This process is more subject to the idiosyncrasies of the trip maker and depends more directly on trade-offs between the attributes of the different choices available at any time. Essentially, different behavioral constructs should be postulated for each of these processes. To use the same distribution model, but stratified by trip purposes, may not be sufficient. Different variables, and possibly a different structure, may be required.

Approaches to Trip Distribution Modeling

Trip distribution models can be classified into three categories according to the basic modeling approach. These categories are introduced here and discussed in detail in subsequent sections.

1. *Origin-destination demand models.* The number of trips between an origin and a destination is derived from a travel demand model that is based on the utility maximization priciple. The demand model is normally multiplicative in the socioeconomic and supply system variables. The basic feature of this approach is that it generates total traffic flows, rather than choice probabilities. In addition, it does not force a given number of origins and destinations through the network as other approaches do. The so-called utility model of trip distribution and the generation-distribution models belong to this category. It is shown later that when the demand model is in a multiplicative form, it is also referred to as an *unconstrained gravity model*.
2. *Choice models.* Trip distribution is viewed as a destination choice process. A traveler originating from a particular location is faced with a number of alternative destinations that satisfy a specific trip purpose. The choice of destination is made on the basis of a comparison of the attributes of all the available alternatives and may be also a function of the socioeconomic characteristics of the traveler. The model structure used in this approach is that of the basic choice model discussed in Chaps. 4 and 5. The dependent variable is a choice probability that is either unconditional, $p_i(d_j)$, or conditional on a previously made choice of mode, $p_i(d_j|m)$. Some of the well-known trip distribution models, such as the intervening opportunity model and the gravity model, can be formulated as choice models.
3. *Physical models of spatial interaction.* These models are not based on the economic principle of utility maximization. Instead, they are derived from postulates regarding spatial interaction, most of which are inspired by analogies to physical systems. Most of the original formulations of trip distribution models belong to this category, including Lille's (1891) law of travel, which is based on analogy with the gravitational attraction between potentials, and Stouffer's (1940) postulate concerning intervening opportunities. This category also includes families of models derived from concepts of statistical likelihood and entropy and models of optimal network distributions such as the Hitchcock transportation problem.

Nomenclature

Trip distribution is described by a matrix $\mathbf{T} = \{t_{ij}\}$ of the number of trips during a given time period between origin location i and destination location j. This matrix is referred to as a *trip table*, or a distribution matrix. It is of dimension $m \times n$, where m is the number of origin locations and n the number of destination locations. In most urban study cases $m = n$ since the same zones serve as origins and destinations. Such a matrix is shown in Fig. 6.1.

Destinations

	1	2	3	$\cdots$	n
1	t_{11}	t_{12}	t_{13}		t_{1n}
2	t_{21}	t_{22}	t_{23}		t_{2n}
3	t_{31}	t_{32}	t_{33}		t_{3n}
$\vdots$					
m	t_{m1}	t_{m2}	t_{m3}		t_{mn}

Origins

Figure 6.1 Typical trip matrix.

The row sum of $\{t_j\}$, a_i represents the total number of trips originating from i:

$$a_i = \sum_j t_{ij} \qquad (6.1)$$

and is referred to as the *trip production* of i. The column sum b_j is the total number of trips destined to j:

$$b_j = \sum_i t_{ij} \qquad (6.2)$$

and is referred to as the *trip attraction* of j. The grand total D of the matrix represents the total number of trips in the system:

$$D = \sum_j a_i = \sum_j b_j = \sum_{ij} t_{ij} \qquad (6.3)$$

and is referred to as the *total trip demand*.

The trip table can be conveniently normalized by dividing all cells by D so that each cell contains the proportion of the total system demand that is between a particular origin-destination pair as shown in Fig. 6.1. The following notation is then used:

$$\rho_{ij} = \frac{t_{ij}}{D} \tag{6.4}$$

$$u_i = \frac{\bar{a}_i}{D} = \sum_j \rho_{ij} \tag{6.5}$$

$$v_j = \frac{\bar{b}_j}{D} = \sum_j \rho_{ij} \tag{6.6}$$

$$1 = \sum_i u_i = \sum_j v_j = \sum_{ij} \rho_{ij} \tag{6.7}$$

Another notation that is useful in trip distribution analysis, particularly when using choice models, is to represent the trip table so that each cell contains the proportion π_{ij} of the total originations in i that are destined to j:

$$\pi_{ij} = \frac{t_{ij}}{a_i} \tag{6.8}$$

Note that in this case the row sum of a π_{ij} matrix is unity. The column sum is not interesting.

Transportation supply in the system is represented by a matrix $\mathbf{C} = \{C_{ij}\}$ where C_{ij} is a composite cost function for travel between i and j and may include travel time, money travel cost, and other attributes of the transportation system. In other words, $\mathbf{C}$ is a matrix of those transportation system attributes that are likely to affect destination choice.

Basic Properties of Trip Distribution Models

In order to be useful for traffic estimation, any trip distribution model should satisfy a set of internal consistency rules in addition to being behaviorally logical and empirically significant. These rules are

1. *Conservation*. The traffic estimates must satisfy the basic conservation Equations (6.1) to (6.3). The conservation rule should be imposed on a distribution model when the model itself estimates the flows t_{ij}, or π_{ij}, as well as the row and column sums a_i and b_j. However, when a_i and b_j are exogenously input from other models, such as in the case of trip generation analysis, then it is not necessary that the equations be satisfied, for there is no reason why the estimates from two separate models should be exactly equal.

In this regard, it should be mentioned that in most urban transportation studies, considerable effort has been spent on iterating the solution of trip distribution models in order to ensure exact equality between row and column sums and previously estimated trip productions and attractions. A simple statistical reasoning should show that such efforts are not necessary.

2. *Nonnegativity.* This is a simple rule which states that all values of t_{ij}, estimated by a model, should be nonnegative. On the surface, this may seem a superfluous rule. However, it often happens in calibrating distribution models that, if not constrained, some calculating schemes yield negative estimates.
3. *Divisibility and compressibility.* This rule applies to aggregated models in which origin and destination locations are made up of zones. Divisibility requires that if a zone is redefined by dividing it into two zones, then the model estimates for the two new zones should add up to the estimates for the original zone. For example, if a destination zone j is divided into two zones j' and j'' such that $j' + j'' = j$, then the divisibility rule states that the model-estimated traffic values should satisfy the following:

$$t_{ij'} + t_{ij''} = t_{ij} \qquad \text{for all } i \qquad (6.9)$$

which in turn ensures that the row and column sums also satisfy this constraint. Compressibility is the opposite and requires that if two zones are compressed together into one, the model-estimated traffic flows for the new zone should be the sum of the values for the original two zones. It should be noted that this property is not satisfied exactly except in the simplest models, which are mathematically separable functions of their variables. Most useful trip distribution models are nonlinear functions and do not satisfy the property exactly. In practice, it should be sufficient, however, for a model to yield results that approximately satisfy the divisibility and separability conditions.

General Structure of Trip Distribution Models

The general structure of a trip distribution model can be written as follows:

$$T_{ij} = f(A_i B_j C_{ij}) \qquad (6.10)$$

where T_{ij} represents the traffic flow between locations i and j, measured by either t_{ij}, ρ_{ij}, or π_{ij}; A_i and B_j are functions of the socioeconomic characteristics of locations i and j, respectively, representing their potentials as trip origins and destinations; and C_{ij} is a general function representing the impedence to travel between i and j.

Nearly all trip distribution models can be reduced to this general structure. The detailed specifications of the functions A, B, or C depend on the available information and on the nature and purpose of the model at hand. For example, in most physical models of spatial interaction, A_i and B_j are simply trip productions and attractions determined by trip generation analysis. On the other hand, in demand models of trip distribution, they are functions of socioeconomic variables that are specified according to behavioral constructs and empirically validated in the calibration process.

6.3 DEMAND MODELS OF TRIP DISTRIBUTION

The most basic approach to modeling trip distribution is to construct a demand model for trips between an origin and a destination. This model, usually stratified by trip purpose, can be an individual or an aggregate function, depending on the information available for calibration. However, as with other demand models, it is derived as an individual function by using the utility maximization principle.

It is assumed that an individual originating from a location i has a utility function associated with the satisfaction of a particular trip purpose. This function depends on the trips taken by the individual to each of the available destinations that can satisfy the trip purpose. In other words, the utility function is

$$U = U(X_{i1}, X_{i2}, \ldots, X_{in}) \tag{6.11}$$

when X_{ij} is the number of trips taken by the individual from the origin i to destination j in a system where there are in mutually exclusive alternative destinations ($j = 1, n$). Associated with these trips are travel costs given by

$$C = C(X_{i1}, X_{i2}, \ldots, X_{in}) \tag{6.12}$$

If it is assumed that the trips to the different destinations are made independently and that for each unit of X_{ij} the traveler incurs a travel cost c_{ij}, then Eq. (6.12) can be written as

$$C = \sum_j c_{ij}X_{ij} \tag{6.13}$$

The utility maximization principle states that the individual will select the values of X_i in order to maximize U without exceeding an upper limit on total travel costs. As seen in Chap. 2, this leads to the general result

$$\frac{\partial U}{\partial X_{ij}} = \frac{\partial C}{\partial X_{ij}} \quad \text{for all } j \tag{6.14}$$

In other words, the marginal utility and marginal cost of additional trips to a particular destination j should be equal. This equality represents the most basic demand model of trip distribution. In order to utilize it, assumptions have to be made regarding the form of the utility function U.

Beckmann and Golob (1970) have derived distribution models for a number of different assumptions regarding U. One such assumption is that U is a constant elasticity function

$$U = \sum_j \alpha_j X_j^\rho \quad 0 < \rho \le 1 \tag{6.15}$$

where α and ρ are parameters.

By substituting this into Eq. (6.14), the following result for X_j is obtained:

$$X_j = \left(\frac{\alpha_j \rho}{c_{ij}}\right)^{1/1-\rho} \tag{6.16}$$

and letting $B_j = (\alpha_j \rho)^{1/1-\rho}$ and $\gamma = (1/1-\rho)$ gives

$$X_j = B_j c_{ij}^{-\gamma} \tag{6.17}$$

With γ clearly positive, this demand function shows that the number of trips made to destination j decreases with the cost of travel to j and increases with B_j, which is analogous to the attraction of location j for the trip purpose in question.

If the total number of individuals in location i with similar utility functions as in Eq. (6.15) is denoted by A_i, then the aggregate demand function is obtained by adding up all the individual functions:

$$\begin{aligned} t_{ij} &= A_i X_j \\ &= A_i B_j c_{ij}^{-\gamma} \end{aligned} \tag{6.18}$$

which follows the general structure of distribution models given by Eq. (6.10) and which can be recognized as a simple gravity model.

In general, demand models of trip distributions are specified according to Eq. (6.18) directly and without explicit assumptions regarding the form of the utility function. Socioeconomic variables for both i and j are specified directly as proxies for the production and the attraction of trips, and the model is calibrated directly using data on t_{ij}.

These models are generally referred to as *generation-distribution models* because they combine both these steps of the sequential modeling approach. This combination has the advantage that, unlike the case when trip generation and distribution are analyzed separately, it allows for an elasticity of total trip generation with respect to travel cost and does not require a distribution model to "force" a given number of trip productions and attractions through a transportation network regardless of its level of service. It is an approach that is clearly much more responsive to transportation policy and thus more useful in planning. Generation-distribution models are normally constructed for total person-trips by purpose and not on a mode-by-mode basis and are not therefore as complete demand models as the ones described in Chap. 4.

Generation-distribution models are most commonly of the multiplicative form given in Eq. (6.18). They are usually calibrated using maximum likelihood estimation or linearized by a logarithmic transformation and calibrated with multiple regression analysis.

Some of the earliest work on generation-distribution models is due to Osofsky, who constructed models of trip distribution among destination zones and calibrated them for a number of cities in California. Osofsky's models were calibrated separately for each origin zone and contained only socioeconomic variables for destination zones. They were very simple linear functions and indeed of limited use in forecasting trip patterns. However, they do represent an early attempt to include the effect of travel cost on trip generation as well as trip distribution.

Another early attempt to model generation and distribution simultaneously was made by Wardrop (1961). Their model recognizes the cross-elasticities of the demand for travel to alternative destinations. However, it had a rather limited specification including population as the only socioeconomic variable:

$$t_{ij} = \frac{P_i P_j e^{-\beta D_{ij}}}{\sum\limits_{k} P_k e^{-\beta D_{ik}}} \tag{6.19}$$

where P is population and D_{ij} is the distance between zones i and j. An interesting feature of this model is the denominator which indicates a cross-elasticity of the demand to a particular destination with respect to the population and travel cost of other destinations. Another feature is the modification of the travel cost function from a constant elasticity $C_{ij}^{-\gamma}$ to the exponential form which implies a travel cost elasticity that decreases with cost. This exponential form is very common in trip distribution models and, as is discussed later in this chapter, has some advantages over the simple polytropic function. It should also be noted that this model can be looked upon as a choice model when the quantity multiplied by P_i on the right-hand side of Eq. (6.19) is viewed as a proportion of all trips generated in i that are destined to j.

In general, it is advantageous to distinguish between the socioeconomic variables of the origin and of the destination and not to force all variables to have the same elasticity. Different socioeconomic variables should be selected depending on the trip purpose. As an example, the following model from home-based trips was calibrated with traffic distribution data for the county of Alameda, California:

$$T_{ij} = 0.45 e^{-0.165 c_{ij}} P_i^{0.719} E_j^{1.128}$$

where T_{ij} = total home-based daily trips between zones i and j
    c_{ij} = travel time between the zone centroids
    P_i = population of the origin zone
    E_j = total employment in the destination zone

There were 727 origin-destination pairs in this calibration, the coefficient of multiple determination was 0.71, and the F value was 1013. Note that the exponential travel time function implies a variable elasticity of $-0.165 c_{ij}$. In principle, a model of this type should preferably be stratified by trip purpose if data permit.

6.4 CHOICE MODELS OF TRIP DISTRIBUTION

The second approach to the analysis of trip distribution is to view it as a destination choice process. The fundamental difference between this and the demand model approach is that it postulates a sequential, separable trip-making decision process and treats the choice of destination independently from the other steps of the process. It is concerned with the percentage distribution of trips from a given origin to the available destinations and not directly with the flow of traffic between them. This latter is obtained by applying to the percentage distributions exogenously determined total numbers of trip originations.

There are two basic types of choice models of trip distribution. The first follows the general structure of the transportation choice model discussed in Chap. 5 and is based on the principle of individual utility maximization. The second is based on the principle of choice among competitive opportunities for trip purpose satisfaction and is not directly related to utility maximization. The second type includes the well-known intervening opportunities model and related opportunity models for trip distribution.

General Transportation Choice Model

The general destination choice model follows the structure of the transportation choice model of Chap. 5 and is derived from the principle of utility-maximizing choice. For an individual or a homogenous group of individual trip makers i, J destinations are available for a particular trip purpose. The choice probability is given by

$$\pi_{ij} = P_i(j|J) = f(\mathbf{A}_{ij}; \mathbf{A}_{ik} \qquad \text{for all } k \in J) \tag{6.20}$$

where $p_i(j|J)$ is the probability of choice of destination j from among the available J destinations; $\mathbf{A}_{ij}$ is a vector of attributes of destination j for traveler i and can include the attractiveness of j for the particular trip purpose in question, the travel cost between i and j, and relevant socioeconomic attributes of the individual or the group i. The specific functional form most commonly used is the multinomial logit, where

$$\pi_{ij} = P_i(j|J) = \frac{e^{V_i(j)}}{\sum_k e^{V_i(k)}} \tag{6.21}$$

The choice function $V_i(j)$ usually includes a generalized travel cost component C_{ij} and some measures of attractiveness of j as a destination for the trip purpose in question.

The trip distribution $\{t_{ij}\}$ is obtained by multiplying π_{ij} by the number of trip makers aggregated for the analysis:

$$t_{ij} = a_i \pi_{ij} \tag{6.22}$$

Opportunity Models of Trip Distribution

Opportunity models are a family of trip distribution models derived from postulates regarding destination choice that are different from those of the general transportation choice model. The most commonly known opportunity model is the *intervening opportunity model*. The main postulate of this model, from Stouffer (1940), is that the probability of choice of a particular destination is proportional to the opportunities for trip purpose satisfaction at that destination and inversely proportional to all such opportunities that are closer to the trip maker's origin, which are called the intervening opportunities.

In deriving a trip distribution model from this basic postulate, a probability structure is defined and related to the spatial distribution of opportunities with respect to the trip maker's origin. The distribution of opportunities is given by a function $V(j)$ which is the cumulative function of all trip destination opportunities from the origin up to an including the jth destination away. If there are J such destinations ordered so that $j = 1$ represents the closest opportunity and $j = J$ the farthest, then $V(0) = 0$, and $V(J) =$ the total destination opportunities in the system. The opportunities at the jth destination are $[V(j) - V(j - 1)]$. The probability structure is defined by the cumulative probability $P[V(j)]$ which is the probability that the trip maker chooses a destination within the $V(j)$ accumulation of opportunities or by the time the jth destination has been reached. The destination choice model is given by

$$dP[V(j)] = L\{1 - P[V(j)]\}\, dV(j) \tag{6.23}$$

where L is a proportionality constant.

This model states that the probability of choice of the jth destination $dP[V(j)]$ is proportional to the opportunities in that destination $dV(j)$ and to the probability that the destination choice has not yet been made by the time the jth destination is reached, $1 - P[V(j)]$. The solution of Eq. (6.23) together with the condition $P[V(0)] = 0$ yields the following:

$$P[V(j)] = 1 - e^{-LV(j)} \tag{6.24}$$

In other words, if the spatial distribution of opportunities $V(j)$ is known and if the value of the proportionality constant L is obtained from a calibration, then it is possible to obtain the trip choice probability function $P[V(j)]$. Resorting to discrete notation and calling the probability of choice of the jth destination π_{ij}, it can be seen that

$$\pi_{ij} = P[V(j)] - P[V(j - 1)] \tag{6.25}$$

$$= e^{-LV(j - 1)} - e^{-LV(j)}$$

This form of the opportunity model was first proposed by Schneider (1960) and applied in the Chicago Area Transportation Study (1956). It should be noted that Eq. (6.25) does not satisfy the basic properties of a probability model $\{\Sigma_i p(i) = 1$, or that $P[V(j)] = 1\}$ since it states that $P[V(J)]$ approaches infinity. In order to correct this, the probability structure of the model is altered so that the destination choice model is $P[V(j)|V(J)]$, which is the probability that a destination choice will occur by the time the jth destination is reached, given that it is made by the time the Jth destination is reached. Using Baye's theorem, Ruiter (1967) derived the following correction:

$$P[V(j)|V(J)] = \frac{1 - e^{-LV(j)}}{1 - e^{-LV(j)}} \tag{6.26}$$

Combining Eqs. (6.26), (6.24), and (6.25) the following choice model is obtained:

$$\pi_{ij} = \frac{e^{-LV(j-1)} - e^{-LV(j)}}{1 - e^{-LV(J)}} \tag{6.27}$$

This revised model satisfies the essential property that $\sum_j \pi_{ij} = 1$. The model is sometimes referred to as the *forced interchange opportunity model*. It has also been applied in the Chicago Area Transportation Study.

As before, the trip distribution $\{t_{ij}\}$ is obtained by multiplying the probability function in Eq. (6.27) by the number of trip makers in location i who can be aggregated for the analysis. Using earlier notation.

$$t_{ij} = a_{ij}\pi_{ij} = a_i \frac{e^{-LV(J-1)}e^{-LV(J)}}{1 - a^{-LV(J)}} \tag{6.28}$$

This trip distribution model differs from the general structure of Eq. (6.10). The probability function $P(j)$ is not explicity a function of the characteristics of location j and of the transportation cost between i and j. This results from the structure of the opportunity model which bases destination choice on the spatial ordering of opportunities rather than on the cost of travel to particular destinations. It is shown in the next section that when the spatial distribution of opportunities is known and can be formulated in terms of distance (or travel cost), then the opportunity model can be explicitly written in the form of Eq. (6.10).

Other opportunity models of trip distribution include the competing opportunities model, which considers the competition between destination opportunities within the same travel time or cost from the origin, and the impedence-dependent opportunity model, which modifies the destination choice probability depending on the distance to the next available destination.

6.5 PHYSICAL MODELS OF SPATIAL INTERACTION

The earliest attempts to model trip distribution were not based on microeconomic demand theory or on utility-maximizing choice models. They were based on postulates regarding spatial interaction, which were mostly based on analogies with observable physical distribution phenomena. For this reason, the models derived with this approach are referred to as *physical models of spatial interaction*. This approach is aggregate in nature and is not based on behavioral assumptions regarding individual destination choice. It is concerned with the behavior of a totality of trip makers in a system of origins and destinations connected by a transportation network. Three approaches have been used to derive trip distribution models that belong to this category. The first is the *gravity approach*, based on the analogy with Newton's law of the gravitational pull between two masses. The second is the *entropy approach*, based on the analogy with the laws of statistical mechanics concerning the behavior of particles in a system and also related to the entropy concepts of information theory. The third is a *network theoretic approach*, based on the analogy with electrical systems theory and optimal network flows.

The absence of an explicit microeconomic behavioral construct in these models does not mean that they have no behavioral content. Indeed, all these models postulate that trip makers are attracted to larger destinations for the satisfaction of their trip purposes and that they will resist, to the extent possible, more costly trips. These have been shown to be related to those of microeconomic demand theory and of consumer choice behavior, and, indeed, the models resulting from this approach are strikingly similar to those of the other two approaches.

Gravity Models of Trip Distribution

Most of the earlier applications of the gravity concepts were for intercity transportation. The idea that the magnitude of population movements between cities is similar to the gravitational pull between masses was first suggested by Ravenstein (1885), who in studying the flow of migrants between Europe and North America observed that the number of people moving between any city pair seems to be proportional to the sizes of the cities and inversely proportional to the distance between them. This same idea formed the basis of Lille's model of intercity travel on the German railroad network in 1891. This concept of gravitation inspired by analogy to the gravitational attraction between two potentials, which, according to Newton's law, is proportional to the product of the masses and inversely proportional to the square of the distance between them, was extensively applied to the analysis of spatial interaction and provided the main vehicle for modeling phenomena such as intercity migration and retail activity location. The model was again proposed for urban trip distribution analysis in the early 1950s after it became evident that the growth factor methods then in use were not adequate for forecasting traffic flows.

The simplest statement of the gravity model as applied in urban traffic distribution analysis is

$$t_{ij} = k_i A_i B_j d_{ij}^{\theta} \tag{6.29}$$

where k is a proportionality factor, and d_{ij} is the distance between locations i and j. The use of θ rather than -2.0 as the exponent of distance represents the first departure from the simple gravity formula of Newton. The value of θ was to be determined in the calibration process. The latter modifications of this simple form included the replacement of d_{ij}^{θ} with a more general function C_{ij} of travel cost. The resulting model $t_{ij} = kA_iB_jC_{ij}$ is the general trip distribution model of Eq. (6.10), where the proportionality factor k is embodied as one of the functions A, B, or C. When socioeconomic variables for trip production and attraction are used for A and B, this model is also similar to the general trip distribution demand model of Eq. (6.18).

One of the most commonly used forms of the gravity model and one that is employed in the sequential traffic estimation process is the form $A_i = a_i$, which is the number of trips originating in location i as determined by trip generation. In this case, it is common to require that the model satisfy the conservation equation property of Eq. (6.1). The constraint is satisfied by specifying the appropriate value of the proportionality constant k as follows:

$$
\begin{aligned}
a_i &= \sum_j t_{ij} \\
&= \sum_j ka_iB_jC_{ij}
\end{aligned}
\tag{6.1}
$$

which gives

$$
k = \frac{1}{\sum\limits_j B_jC_{ij}}
\tag{6.30}
$$

Substituting Eq. (6.30) into Eq. (6.29) gives the following distribution model:

$$
t_{ij} = a_i \frac{B_jC_{ij}}{\sum\limits_j B_jC_{ij}}
\tag{6.31}
$$

This model is often referred to as the *origin-constrained gravity model*, because it satisfies the conservation constraint with respect to the row sums. Note the similarity between this model and the choice model of Eq. (6.22). It should also be noted from Eq. (6.30) that k is an origin-specified factor.

Another form of the gravity model that has been commonly used is one where $A_i = a_i$ and $B_j = b_j$ are both trip originations and destinations, respectively, and determined exogenously by trip generation analysis. The model, now required to satisfy both conservation constraints Eq. (6.1) and Eq. (6.2), is specified with two proportionality factors, one row-specific, k_i, and one column-specific, k_j.

The values result in the following model formulation:

$$
t_{ij} = k_ia_ik_jb_jC_{ij}
\tag{6.32}
$$

with the values of k_i and k_j required to satisfy conservation given by

$$
k_i = \frac{1}{\sum\limits_j k_jb_jC_{ij}}
\tag{6.33}
$$

and
$$k_j = \frac{1}{\sum_i k_i a_i C_{ij}} \tag{6.34}$$

which clearly requires an iterative solution technique. This model is often referred to as the *origin-* and *destination-constrained gravity model*, and is sometimes called the interactance model.

It should be noted as mentioned earlier that there is no obvious need for the model to satisfy an exogenously specified conservation requirement. While the required iterative solutions have been shown to converge in general, it is hardly likely that the extra effort spent on such artificial calibration techniques is warranted. The model of Eq. (6.32) does not possess any behavioral advantage over the simple gravity model. When a sequential modeling approach is adopted and the values of a_i and b_j are exogenously specified from trip generation analysis, they should be used as explanatory variables in the distribution model without requiring the model to reproduce them exactly.

Entropy Models of Trip Distribution

Another approach to trip distribution modeling that is based on physical analogy is the entropy model approach of Wilson (1970). In this approach, a system of origins and destinations is considered and the distribution of a total of D trips is sought. The analogy is made between such a system and a physical system such as a gas composed of a large number of particles. A particular distribution given by a matrix $\mathbf{T} = \{t_{ij}\}$ is defined as a state of the system. Such a matrix is determined for flows between origins and destinations and is not specific to particular trips in any one (i, j) cell. It is therefore a description of the aggregate behavior of the system. The number of ways in which D trips can be arranged to give rise to a distribution $\mathbf{T} = \{t_{ij}\}$ is given by the combinatorial equation

$$W(\mathbf{T} = \{t_{ij}\}) = \frac{D!}{\prod_{ij} t_{ij}!} \tag{6.35}$$

It is assumed that the probability of a particular distribution $\{t_{ij}\}$ is proportional to the W value. W can be shown to have a sharp maximum, and consequently the most likely trip distribution is defined as the one with the maximum W value of all the possible distributions.

As an example, consider the following two distributions:

Distribution 1: All trips in the system D are between one origin-destination pair (i, j). In other words

$$\left. \begin{array}{l} t_{ij} = D \\ t_{pq} = 0 \end{array} \right\} \quad \text{for all } (p, q) \neq (i, j) \tag{6.36}$$

Distribution 2: The trip interchanges between all origin-destination pairs are equal. In other words

$$t_{ij} = \frac{D}{mn} \quad \text{for all } (i, j) \tag{6.37}$$

Clearly, there is only one way by which distribution 1 can arise, namely when all trip makers are going between i and j. This can be seen by computing the W value W_1 of this distribution:

$$W_1 = \frac{D!}{0!0! \cdots D! \cdots 0!0!} \tag{6.38}$$
$$= 1$$

On the other hand, there are many more arrangements of the trips which result in distribution 2. Namely, it is possible to switch individual trips between cells in the distribution matrix in such a way as to maintain the equality $t_{ij} = D/mn$. The W value for this distribution is

$$W_2 = \frac{D!}{\left(\dfrac{D}{mn}!\right)^{mn}} \tag{6.39}$$

which can be shown to be much larger than $W_1 = 1$. This means that the second distribution is much more likely than the first. In fact, it can be shown by differentiation that distribution 2 maximizes W subject to the following constraint:

$$\sum_{ij} t_{ij} = D$$

This differentiation is the method used to derive particular trip distribution models following the entropy analogy. $W(T)$ of Eq. (6.35) is maximized subject to constraints describing a priori known or required characteristics of the distribution model. This process has been shown to be analogous to maximizing the likelihood of trip distribution. The entropy maximization method has also been shown to have similarities to information theory [see, for example, Wilson (1970)].

As an example of this method, the following constraints are specified in deriving a trip distribution model:

$$\sum_{j} t_{ij} = a_i \tag{6.1}$$

$$\sum_{j} t_{ij} = b_j \tag{6.2}$$

$$\sum_{ij} t_{ij} c_{ij} = TC \tag{6.40}$$

Equations (6.1) and (6.2) are the conventional conservation constraints, and Eq. (6.40) is an assumption that the total transportation cost expended in the system must be limited to an upper-bound TC.

In maximizing W subject to these constraints, a lagrangian is formulated in terms of log W, which is easier to differentiate. This lagrangian is

$$M = \log W - \lambda_i(\sum_j t_{ij} - a_i) - \lambda_j(\sum_i t_{ij} - b_j) - \gamma(\sum_{ij} t_{ij}c_{ij} - TC) \quad (6.41)$$

where λ_i, λ_j, and γ are Lagrange multipliers. The values of $\{t_{ij}\}$ are obtained by solving the first-order conditions:

$$\frac{\partial M}{\partial t_{ij}} = 0 \quad \text{for all } t_{ij} \quad (6.42)$$

which give

$$t_{ij} = e^{-\lambda_i - \lambda_j - \gamma C_{ij}} \quad (6.43)$$

setting

$$\frac{e^{-\lambda_i}}{a_i} = A_i \quad \text{and} \quad \frac{e^{-\lambda_j}}{b_j} = B_j \quad (6.44)$$

which results in

$$t_{ij} = A_i a_i B_j b_j e^{-\gamma C_{ij}} \quad (6.45)$$

which follows the general structure of Eq. (6.10) and is similar to trip distribution models derived in an earlier section. It should be noted that the constraint equations need not be specified as shown if exact conservation is not required. These equations can be modified by requiring that the row and column sums of the resulting matrix $\{t_{ij}\}$ be proportional to the known a_i and b_j values. This will not change the model structure because the constants of proportionately will be imbedded in A_i and B_j. An interesting result in Eq. (6.45) is the exponential form of the cost function resulting from the constraint on the total transport cost expenditure in the system. With a given total number of trips D, this constraint is equivalent to specifying the average trip cost. As is shown in the subsequent section, this property is often used in model calibration, where an average trip length observed in a traffic survey is used to find the appropriate value of the parameter γ.

The entropy maximization approach can be used to derive other types of trip distribution models. By varying the assumptions and requirements specifed as constraints on the maximization of W, different model forms result. Wilson (1970) has shown how the intervening opportunity model can be derived using this approach.

The entropy approach to modeling trip distribution is responsive to a variety of assumptions and requirements. However, its behavioral content can always be questioned, for it is now based on an explicit statement of individual, or group, behavior in a process of destination choice. The widespread interest in and use of this approach can perhaps be attributed to the fact that the models it produces are not different from those derived from economic utility principles or from behavioral choice postulates.

Other Models of Spatial Interaction

Other approaches to modeling trip distribution include the application of spatial interaction models used commonly in other fields. For example, the minimum cost transportation problem used in the optimization of distribution systems has been proposed for urban trip distribution modeling. This method assumes that the trip distribution matrix $\{t_{ij}\}$ is obtained by minimizing the total transport cost

$$\sum_{ij} t_{ij} c_{ij}$$

subject to the conservation constraints j, ij, i of Eqs. (6.1) to (6.3). This implies that individual trip makers behave in such a manner as to minimize not their own transport cost but that of the total system. This is not a behavioral assumption, and the approach is only valid under the special cases where sufficient control can be exercised over traffic movements to ensure an optimal pattern. It is interesting to note, however, that when the C_{ij} function is made to decay extremely fast with c_{ij}, such as when the value of θ in $c_{ij}^{-\theta}$ is very large, then the solution of any of the distribution models discussed so far will be very close to that of the cost minimization problem.

Another model that has limited application in trip distribution analysis is the so-called proportional model. This model ignores the effect of c_{ij} on trip distribution and postulates that

$$t_{ij} = kA_iB_j \tag{6.46}$$

where k is a proportionality factor. It can also be written in the production- and attraction-constrained version:

$$t_{ij} = \frac{a_ib_j}{T} \tag{6.47}$$

in which case it satisfies all the constraints of Eqs. (6.1) to (6.3). Clearly a very approximate and aggregate model, the proportional model is not without its uses. It can be used in situations where transportation costs are negligible. It may also prove adequate in situations where the distribution process is thought of as long-term and involving the choice of origins as well as the choice of destination, such as in industrial areas where blue collar workers have little locational choice with respect to residence and place of work. This model can be looked upon as a special case of the general trip distribution model with $C_{ij} = 1$.

A variation on the proportional model that has been proposed is the *trip potential model* [see Loubal (1967)]. This model postulates that $\{t_{ij}\}$ can be given as an additive function of two matrices:

$$\{t_{ij}\} = \{P_{ij}\} + \{G_{ij}\} \tag{6.48}$$

where $\{P_{ij}\}$ is the trip distribution according to the proportional model and $\{G_{ij}\}$ is a vector of corrections that can be related to the travel cost matrix $\{C_{ij}\}$. The advantage claimed for this model is that it permits the separation of the effects of demand growth and supply changes, when forecasting trip distribution, by separately forecasting $\{P_{ij}\}$ and $\{G_{ij}\}$.

Continuum Approximations in Trip Distribution Analysis

Urban areas that are densely built up, where the land-use pattern does not have abrupt changes, lend themselves well to continuum approximations in trip distribution analysis. In this approach, the area of study is no longer looked at in terms of discrete origin and destination locations such as zones but is described by means of continuous functions of trip production and attraction. These functions describe the number of trip origins or destinations, or opportunities per unit area, during a given time period. Often, a further simplification is made by making the model one-dimensional. This simplification is useful when the analysis deals with a linear city, a traffic corridor, or a narrow area adjacent to a high-volume facility such as a freeway.

The continuum model for trip distribution does not differ much in its structure from the discrete model. Trip production and attraction are represented by functions $A(x, y)$ and $B(x, y)$ of the location (x, y) measured on an appropriately selected two-dimensional cartesian. The travel cost c between two locations (x_1, y_1) and (x_2, y_2) is usually made a function of the distance $[(x_1 - x_2)^2 - (y_1 - y_2)^2]^{1/2}$. A and B are usually single-variable functions measuring production and attraction by variables appropriate for the trip purpose in question. The distribution model in continuous form is generally

$$T[(x_1, y_1), (x_2, y_2)] = A(x_1, y_1) \, B(x_2, x_2) \, C[(x_1, y_1), (x_2, y_2)] \quad (6.49)$$

Examples of specific articulations of this general continuous model are discussed by Angel and Hyman (1972). The continuous model has the advantage that it permits the analyst to obtain important insights into the process of trip distribution using only simple mathematics. At least qualitative inferences can be made without having to calibrate a model in the conventional sense.

As an illustration, a continuous model is constructed and used to show that when the spatial distribution of trip destination opportunities is known, then the intervening opportunity model and the gravity model are equivalent. To do this, a large urban area is assumed to have a uniform density of trip destination opportunities of μ per unit area. The distribution of trips originating from a location in the center of the area is sought, and the hypothesis of intervening opportunities is to be used. As illustrated in Fig. 6.2, the incremental opportunities dV at a distance c from the origin of the trips is proportional to the area of the ring of width dc:

$$dV = 2\pi\mu c \, dc \quad (6.50)$$

where μ is the density of trip destinations. The intervening opportunities IV_j

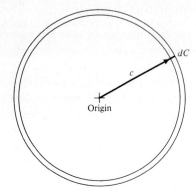

Figure 6.2 Continuum model of intervening opportunities.

between the origin and the jth destination, or the destination that is c_j away from the origin, are obtained by integration

$$IV_J = \int_0^{c_j} dV = \int_0^{c_j} k\mu c \, dc \qquad (6.51)$$

$$= kc_j^2$$

Thus is is possible to translate intervening opportunities into a function of distance (or equivalent travel costs). The intervening opportunities model postulates that the distribution of trips to a destination is proportional to opportunities at that destination and inversely proportional to intervening opportunities:

$$\pi_{ij} = \frac{k' V_j}{IV_j} \qquad (6.52)$$

Combining Eqs. (6.52) and (6.51) yields

$$\pi_{ij} = \frac{KV_j}{c_{ij}^2} \qquad (6.53)$$

which can be seen as a simple gravity model where k' and K are proportionality constants. Equation (6.53) clearly shows a gravity-type model.

Other assumptions concerning dV will result in other model forms, but the gravity structure will always appear. In other words, if the distribution of V is known and can be translated into a function of distance, then the gravity and opportunity models are fundamentally the same.

6.6 CHOICE OF SOCIOECONOMIC VARIABLES

Socioeconomic variables are included in trip distribution models in order to account for the trip-making potential of individuals, or the trip production potential of origins, and the trip attraction potential of destinations. In general, the same variables that are used in trip generation analysis for both production and attraction models should be considered for trip distribution models. The most important requirement is that trip purpose be taken into consideration when selecting these variables. The specification of socioeconomic variables will naturally differ depending on the type of trip distribution model used. This specification is discussed briefly for each of the three types. The choice of socioeconomic variables will be different for each is made differently depending on which of the three types of distribution models is being used.

Demand Models of Trip Distribution

Because these models are general generation-distribution models, they should include both trip production and trip attraction variables.

Choice Models

Here the important socioeconomic variables are those of trip attraction. Since choice models are usually constructed for homogenous groups of trip makers, socioeconomic characteristics of the trip makers themselves may or may not be explicit in the model but may be used to stratify trip makers into homogenous groups. Traffic flows between origins and destinations are obtained by multiplying the choice probabilities with total trip originations either obtained from the available data base (traffic survey) or estimated in trip generation analysis using an appropriate aggregation procedure.

Physical Models of Spatial Interaction

In these models, trip productions and attractions obtained from survey data or estimated from trip generation analysis are normally used in place of the socioeconomic variables. However, as mentioned earlier, there should be no need to force these values as conservation constraints on the models being constructed.

6.7 CHOICE OF TRANSPORT SUPPLY VARIABLES

The attributes of the transportation system relevant to demand analysis are normally represented by the generalized cost function, which in the case of origin-destination flows is c_{ij}. This function is constructed either as a single variable, e.g., travel time or distance, or as a combined multiattribute function that includes all the relevant attributes. The construction of c_{ij} functions is discussed in detail in Chap. 3, where various aggregate and disaggregate forms are presented.

In applying the generalized transportation cost function c_{ij} to models of trip distribution and of destination choice, a further transformation $C_{ij} = f(c_{ij})$ is made. The purpose of this transformation is to take into account transportation supply impacts that are specific to the process of destination choice. Typically, a simple c_{ij} containing either travel time or distance is used, and then a transformation leading to C_{ij} is applied using a function referred to as the *travel time* function. More complex formulations of c_{ij} are sometimes used in trip distribution modeling; however, it is probably more advisable to construct a transformation into C_{ij} which is appropriate to the distribution problem at hand than to construct an elaborate generalized cost function.

Different forms of the $C_{ij} = f(c_{ij})$ transformation are possible, and the choice should depend on the knowledge of the spatial distribution of trip destination opportunities available in a study area. Some of the more commonly used forms are discussed below.

Common Forms of the C_{ij} Function

C_{ij} is a function of the generalized trip cost c_{ij} introduced into the trip distribution model in order to reflect the impedance to travel. In some practical applications, a direct relationship is assumed between the observed trip cost distribution and the assumed C_{ij} function. This is not strictly correct, because the observed distribution is not only the result of an impedance function C_{ij}, but also of the actual spatial distribution of trip production and attraction.

C_{ij} is normally a decaying function, the simplest form of which is the hyperbolic function $C = c^{-\theta}$ (where $\theta = 2$ represents the original gravity hypothesis). This function has the tendency to lead to the overestimation of shorter trips, because it increases quickly as c decreases and approaches infinity when c approaches zero. To correct this, another decaying function $C = \theta_1 e^{-\theta_2 c}$, which is the exponential function, is often used. This function has the advantage of being bounded, since it approaches θ_1 when c approaches zero. The two functions are clearly related, for by transforming c logarithmically, one function can be translated into the other. It is interesting to note that the exponential function has been derived by assuming an upper bound on total travel cost in the entropy approach. In other words, θ_1 and θ_2 are related to the total (or average) trip cost in a system, although this relationship is usually not expressed explicitly.

Both the hyperbolic and the exponential functions are monotonically decreasing functions of c. This may not always be desirable. When trip distribution is applied to vehicular trips only, that is, not including walking trips, then it is found that very short trips are not common. Also, for trip purposes such as work trips and specialty shopping trips, very short trips are not common, when the land-use pattern is such that residential land use is not mixed with commercial and employment land use. In these cases, it is advantageous to postulate a C function that is unimodal but that approaches zero as c does. The most commonly used function with these characteristics is a gamma function $C = \theta_1 c e^{-\theta_2 c}$.

In practice, an empirical C function is sometimes calibrated by studying the distribution of $C_{ij} = t_{ij}/A_i B_j$ as a function of c_{ij}.

More complex functions have been calibrated on the basis of empirical

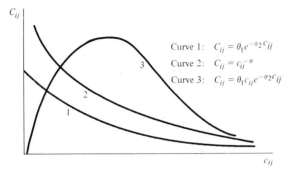

Curve 1: $C_{ij} = \theta_1 e^{-\theta_2 c_{ij}}$

Curve 2: $C_{ij} = c_{ij}^{-\theta}$

Curve 3: $C_{ij} = \theta_1 c_{ij} e^{-\theta_2 c_{ij}}$

Figure 6.3 Typical trip distribution cost functions.

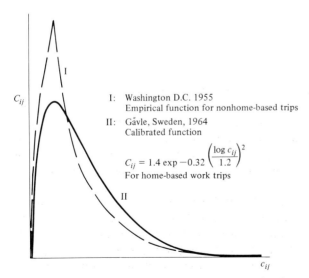

I: Washington D.C. 1955
Empirical function for nonhome-based trips

II: Gåvle, Sweden, 1964
Calibrated function

$$C_{ij} = 1.4 \exp -0.32 \left(\frac{\log c_{ij}}{1.2} \right)^2$$

For home-based work trips

Figure 6.4 Examples of calibrated trip distribution cost functions.

distribution of C. Figures 6.3 and 6.4 show some of the functions that have been calibrated empirically for different trip purposes.

6.8 CALIBRATION OF TRIP DISTRIBUTION MODELS

Model calibration has been discussed in earlier chapters. In the context of transportation demand analysis, calibration is taken to mean the specification of a model structure, the statistical estimation of its parameters, and the evaluation of the parameter estimates. In this section, the calibration of trip distribution models is presented within the same framework.

The approach to model calibration is based on the principle of empirical validation in the statistical rather than the numerical sense. In other words, a statistical probability framework is set up that is consistent with the structure of the model calibrated. Observations on trips are made within this framework, and statistical estimation techniques are used to estimate the parameters of the model and to derive evaluation statistics. This approach is distinct from one that has been commonly applied in urban transportation studies, where trip distribution models are calibrated numerically by applying adjustment factors and iterative algorithms aimed at "fine tuning" a model in such a way as to provide the best fit with observed trip data. There are two main reasons for preferring statistical rather than numerical calibration. First, numerical model calibration and fine tuning leaves a model that is not obviously amenable to behavioral interpretation and consequently is of little value in planning and forecasting. Second, a model can always be sufficiently manipulated to yield required answers, and to force a model to reproduce observed trip interchanges, totals, or trip length frequency distribution is to defeat the initial purpose of the model, which is to provide an estimation within a theoretical construct of trip making or of traffic. Second, behavioral modeling recognizes the stochastic nature of transportation demand in all its aspects, and consequently the calibration of models of trip making should be done within the framework of statistical inference.

Trip distribution model calibration starts by selecting the socioeconomic variables and the transportation cost function to be used. Model specification is then adopted, depending on the modeling approach taken. With sufficient data and modeling resources, alternative model specifications can always be postulated and empirically tested.

The next step is the estimation of the values of the model parameters. The choice of estimation technique depends on the structure of the model at hand. For the purpose of statistical estimation, the types of models discussed in the previous sections can be regrouped into the following four groups depending on their structure and the appropriate statistical framework required for estimation: (1) the trip distribution demand model, (2) the gravity model, (3) the trip destination choice model, and (4) the intervening opportunity model.

The Trip Distribution Demand Model

The structure of this model is as shown in Eq. (6.10):

$$t_{ij} = A_i B_j C_{ij} \tag{6.10}$$

where A_i and B_j are functions of socioeconomic variables for the origin and the destination, respectively. In most applications, it is found that simple model specifications, with one or at most two variables in each of A and B, are superior to complex multivariables models. They are not superior because they have more explanatory power, but because they are usually statistically more significant with sufficient explanatory power. Simpler models also have the advantage of avoiding some of the statistical difficulties of complex models, such as multi-collinearity. As discussed in the previous section, population, income, and employment are the most commonly used variables, and C_{ij} is the transport cost function, usually either $c_{ij}^{-\theta}$ or $e^{-\theta c_{ij}}$.

Because the demand model is usually an aggregate of individual functions for aggregated trip makers in i, then the socioeconomic variables in A_i usually include measures of the magnitude of the origin i, such as population or the number of households. Stratifications by income are often made.

The empirical structure for the estimation of this model consists of observing a sample of origin-destination flows n_{ij}. The corresponding t_{ij} values are estimated by the model and the estimation procedure attempts to seek the closest agreement between t_{ij} and n_{ij}. Two estimation techniques are suitable for this situation. The first is least-squares estimation where it is necessary to minimize the sum of squares:

$$S^2 = \sum_{ij} (n_{ij} - t_{ij})^2 \tag{6.54}$$

When t_{ij} is given by a model with k parameters $\theta_1, \ldots, \theta_k$, then the minimization process yields k normal equations of the form

$$\sum_{ij} (n_{ij} - t_{ij}) \frac{\partial t_{ij}}{\partial \theta_r} = 0 \qquad r = 1, \ldots, k \tag{6.55}$$

The solution of these normal equations is usually an iterative process because t_{ij} is usually a nonlinear function of the θ's. A number of iterative procedures exist for this problem [see *Transportation Research*, vol. 4, no.1 (1970)], and fast solution routines are usually available in packaged computer programs.

When the demand model is intrinsically linear, which means that it can be linearized by a transformation, then multiple linear regression analysis can be used to estimate the parameters for the linearized model. For example, when the model has the common multiplicative form, then it can be linearized by a logarithmic transformation. The only advantage of this is that it permits the use of a simple estimation procedure and avails the analyst of a number of linear statistics that can be used for evaluating the significance of the model parameter estimates. However, the logarithmic transformation may cause distortions when there are large variations in the values of n_{ij}. Therefore, it is preferable to estimate the untransformed model directly in order to avoid any such distortions. The parameter estimates obtained from linear regression on the transformed model are usually good initial solutions for the iterative process required for the estimation from the untransformed model.

The Gravity Model

As seen in earlier discussions, the gravity model can be formulated in a number of ways, some totally unconstrained resembling the general demand model and some constrained to satisfy certain conservation conditions. The simplest gravity model is one where no constraints are imposed, but where exogenously determined trip productions and attractions are specified with unit elasticities

$$t_{ij} = ka_ib_je^{-\theta c_{ij}} \tag{6.56}$$

where k is a proportionality factor and where the exponential cost function is taken as an illustration. With the model so specified, the empirical framework is similar to that of the demand model in that observations on origin-destination flows n_{ij} are made. The difference is that the only explanatory variable with a parameter to be estimated is c_{ij} since both a_i and b_j are introduced with their fixed unity parameters.

This model is instrinsically linear, and with a logarithmic transformation it can be calibrated using simple linear regression, the regression model being

$$\ln \frac{t_{ij}}{a_ib_j} = k' - \theta c_{ij} \tag{6.57}$$

where $k' = \ln k$.

Alternatively, and to avoid any possible distortion in the estimate of θ, if there are large variations in the magnitudes of the c_{ij} values, a least-squares function similar to Eq. (6.54) can be used for the estimation.

When the gravity model is written in probability terms, then it lends itself to maximum likelihood estimation, which normally is to be preferred to the least-squares method. As an example, consider the following model:

$$\rho_{ij} = A_iB_jc_{ij}^{-\theta} \tag{6.58}$$

where A_i and B_j are socioeconomic variables normalized and measured in percentage of the system totals. When observations n_{ij} are made of origin-destination flows, these are used directly to estimate the model parameters. Using the maximum likelihood function

$$L = K \prod_{ij} (\rho_{ij})^{n_{ij}} \tag{6.59}$$

the best estimates of the model parameters can be obtained by maximizing L (or equivalently its logarithm). However, when the model is specified in probability terms, then a constraint

$$\sum_{ij} \rho_{ij} = 1.0$$

should be imposed for consistency. This can be added to the maximum likelihood function by constructing a lagrangian:

$$L' = \log L - \lambda\left(\sum_{ij} \rho_{ij} - 1\right) \tag{6.60}$$

$$= \sum_{ij} n_{ij} \ln n_{ij} - \lambda\left(\sum_{ij} \rho_{ij} - 1\right)$$

Parameter estimates can now be obtained by solving the lagrangians. The method is quite efficient for estimating parameters of gravity models. By use of the lagrangian, any constraint imposed on the model can be included in the likelihood functions.

The Trip Destination Choice Model

The general multinomial model of destination choice is calibrated in the same manner as the general transportation choice model discussed in Chap. 5 using maximum likelihood estimation. The general empirical framework is such that observations are made for each origin of the trips to each destination $n_{ij}|i$. The likelihood function is then formulated in terms of the postulated model for the choice probabilities $p_{ij}|i$:

$$L = \prod_{j} (\pi_{ij}|j)^{n_{ij}|i} \tag{6.61}$$

Given a sufficient number of destinations, this function can be maximized separately for each i, thus permitting the choice model to exhibit different parameter values for the different origins, or, alternatively, if the same choice model is postulated to hold for all origins, such as when the model specification includes variables describing the origin characteristics, then the likelihood function can be constructed for all observations in the system:

$$L = \prod_{i} \prod_{j} (\pi_{ij}|i)^{n_{ij}|i} \tag{6.62}$$

Note that it is not necessary to impose any consistency constraints on this likelihood function, because the choice model structure itself ensures that $\sum_{j} \pi_{ij} = 1.0$, for all i.

The Intervening Opportunity Model

This model has a basically different structure from those of the models described earlier, although as has been demonstrated, it is related to them. The calibration of the intervening opportunity model is slightly more complicated than the calibration of the gravity type and the other choice models.

Calibration begins by adopting a measure of destination opportunities. This is usually taken as a single socioeconomic variable chosen according to the trip purpose in question, such as retail employment for shopping trips and total employment for work trips. Alternatively, it can be a trip attraction model such as the ones discussed in the previous chapter. Such multivariable models have not shown significantly higher explanatory power, and consequently the use of simple one-variable measures of opportunity is to be preferred.

For each origin location (usually a zone), the destination opportunities are ordered according to their distance, travel time, or the generalized cost c_{ij}. From this ordering, the function $V(j)$ is constructed showing the cumulated opportunities up to and including the jth destination. This process is repeated for each origin. Next, the observations of destination choice proportions π_{ij} are made from trip data. From these observations, the empirical probability distribution function of trip attenuation $P[V(j)]$ is constructed showing the cumulative proportion of all trips originating from the origins that are destined to zones up to and including the jth destination.

With this information, the simple model form of Eq. (6.24) can be calibrated using simple linear regression. Recalling Eq. (6.24),

$$P[V(j)] = 1 - e^{-LV(j)} \tag{6.24}$$

this can be transformed logarithmically to yield the regression equation

$$\ln\{1 - P[V(j)]\} = -LV(j) \tag{6.63}$$

In this case, the calibration of the model consists of estimating the value of the parameter L. It has been found advantageous to postulate different L values for trips of different length (or cost) ranges, and consequently the data on $P[V(j)]$ and $V(j)$ may be accordingly stratified.

The P and V values for all origins and destinations are usually pooled together in the regression. With that, the value for end zones $V(J)$ cannot be used because the corresponding $1 - P[V(J)] = 0$, for which the logarithmic transformation is not feasible.

The calibration of the corrected model is not as straightforward, because as can be seen from Eq. (6.26)

$$P[V(j)|V(J)] = \frac{1 - e^{-LV(j)}}{1 - e^{-LV(J)}} \tag{6.26}$$

it is not intrinsically linear. Consequently, an iterative estimation procedure using either least-squares or maximum likelihood techniques has to be applied.

Other Estimation Approaches

Estimation approaches using methods other than the statistical least-squares or maximum likelihood methods have been extensively used in the calibration of trip distribution models. The most popular among these is to attempt to calibrate the model on the basis of an observed trip length frequency distribution or simply an average systemwide trip length (length may be measured in units of generalized cost c_{ij}, or simply by travel time). Model calibration that is guided by average trip cost has been shown to be related to statistical estimation for the simple gravity models. On the other hand, calibration that attempts to reproduce the whole empirical trip length frequency with the model requires extensive iterative procedures and model adjustments, particularly by trying alternative cost functions C_{ij}.

The intervening opportunity model has also been calibrated on the basis of observed average trip lengths. For example, Ruiter (1967) has shown that L is related to the mean of the V distribution function. By assuming uniform opportunity distribution over space, Ruiter has also shown that L can be assumed to be inversely proportional to the density of opportunities and to the square of average trip length. These findings, approximate as they are, are useful guidelines in model calibration.

Examples This section includes an illustration of some of the calibration techniques discussed earlier, using a simple two-origin three-destination system. Figure 6.5 shows the system schematically, indicating for each of the origin zones the population p, and for each of the destination zones, the

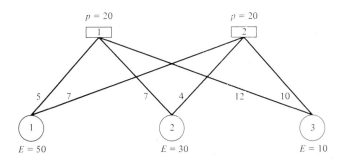

Figure 6.5 Origins and destinations for numerical example.

employment E. It also indicates the travel cost c_{ij} between the origins and the destinations. It is assumed that the models to be calibrated will use only these three variables P, E, and c_{ij}. The observed origin-destination trips by a specific purpose, e.g., shopping, are shown in the trip tables of Fig. 6.6, which include n_{ij}, π_{ij}, and ρ_{ij}.

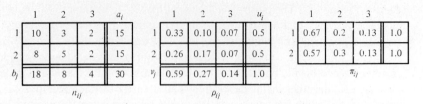

	1	2	3	a_i
1	10	3	2	15
2	8	5	2	15
b_j	18	8	4	30

n_{ij}

	1	2	3	u_i
1	0.33	0.10	0.07	0.5
2	0.26	0.17	0.07	0.5
v_j	0.59	0.27	0.14	1.0

p_{ij}

	1	2	3
1	0.67	0.2	0.13	1.0
2	0.57	0.3	0.13	1.0

π_{ij}

Figure 6.6 Trip tables for numerical example.

The first model to be calibrated is the simple gravity model of Eq. (6.29), where trip productions a_i and trip attractions b_j are specified with unit elasticities and an exponential cost function C_{ij} is assumed:

$$t_{ij} = Ka_ib_je^{\theta c_{ij}} \qquad (6.64)$$

a simple regression on the linearized model

$$\ln \frac{t_{ij}}{a_ib_j} = \ln K + \theta c_{ij} \qquad (6.57)$$

is performed. The calculations for this regression are shown in Table 6.1 and Fig. 6.7. The regressions yield the following values

$$\ln K = -2.94 \rightarrow K = 0.053$$
$$\theta = -0.069$$

which result in the following estimated trip distribution:

$$t_{ij} = 0.053a_ib_je^{0.069\theta C_{ij}}$$

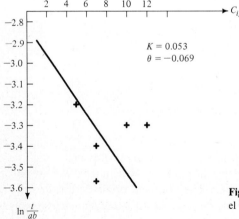

$K = 0.053$
$\theta = -0.069$

Figure 6.7 Estimation of gravity model parameters.

Table 6.1

$i-j$	n_{ij}	$a_i b_j$	$\dfrac{n_{ij}}{a_i b_j}$	$\ln \dfrac{n_{ij}}{a_i b_j}$	c_{ij}	θc_{ij}	$e^{\theta c_{ij}}$	t_{ij}	Proportional model $\dfrac{a_i b_j}{T}$
1–1	10	270	0.0371	−3.296	5	−0.345	0.708	10.1	9
1–2	3	120	0.0250	−3.687	7	−0.483	0.617	4.0	4
1–3	2	60	0.0333	−3.40	12	−0.828	0.437	1.3	2
2–1	8	270	0.0296	−3.51	7	−0.483	0.617	9	9
2–2	5	120	0.0416	−3.1179	4	−0.276	0.759	5	4
2–3	2	60	0.0333	−3.40	10	−0.69	0.501	1.5	2

The model-estimated trip table is shown in Table 6.1, and a comparison

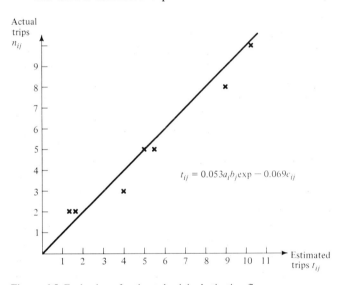

$$t_{ij} = 0.053 a_i b_j \exp - 0.069 c_{ij}$$

Figure 6.8 Evaluation of estimated origin-destination flows.

between t_{ij} and n_{ij} is shown in Fig. 6.8. The average trip cost estimated by the model $\hat{c} = 6.122$ compared to the average of the observed trips $c_{ij} = 6.37$.

Intervening opportunity model The next model calibrated with the same data is the simple intervening opportunity model of Eq. (6.25),

$$\pi_{ij} = e^{-LV(j-1)} - e^{-LV(j)} \qquad (6.25)$$

in which the value of L is estimated using the simple regression model of Eq. (6.63). Using employment as the measure of opportunities, the $V(j)$ functions for

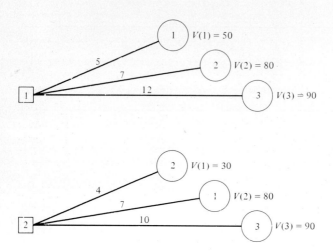

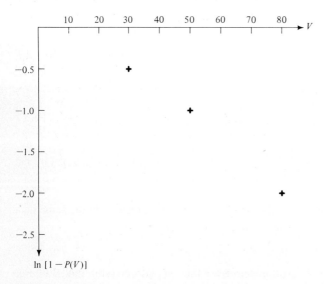

Figure 6.9 Arrangement of origins and destinations for the intervening opportunities model.

each of the two origins are calculated as shown diagrammatically in Fig. 6.9. Likewise, the π_{ij} table is transformed into the $P[V(j)]$ functions by accumulating the trip distribution proportions according to the destinations ordered as in Fig. 6.9.

The resulting values of $V(j)$ and $\ln \{1 - P[V(j)]\}$ are shown in Table 6.2 and are plotted in Fig. 6.10. The regression yields a value for $L = 0.0214$.

Figure 6.10 Estimation of intervening opportunities model parameter L.

Table 6.2

i	j	c_{ij}	Ordered j	E	$V(j)$	π_{ij}	$P[V(j)]$	$1 - P[V_j]$	$\ln\{1 - P[V_j]\}$	$e^{-LV(j)}$	$\hat{\pi}_{ij}$
	1	5	1	50	50	0.67	0.67	0.33	-1.11	0.343	0.66
1	2	7	2	30	80	0.20	0.87	0.13	-2.04	0.180^5	0.162
	3	12	3	10	90	0.13	1.00	—	—	0.146	0.034
	1	7	2	50	80	0.53	0.87	0.13	-2.04	0.180^5	0.345
2	2	4	1	30	30	$0.3\overset{.}{3}$	0.33	0.67	-0.40^5	0.526	0.474
	3	10	3	10	90	0.13	1.00	—	—	0.146	0.034

Using this value of L in Eq. (6.25) yields the estimates $\hat{\pi}_{ij}$ of the trip distribution according to the intervening opportunity model. These are compared in Table 6.2 and Fig. 6.11 with the actual values of π_{ij}.

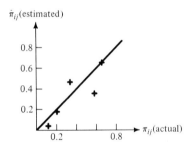

Figure 6.11 Evaluation of estimated destination choice probabilities.

It is interesting to note that in this uncorrected model, only 0.895 of the trips from each origin are distributed to the available destinations. The corrected model of Eq. (6.26) will, of course, ameliorate this deficiency but would require an iterative parameter estimation process. Figure 6.10 also confirms the notion that a constant L value may not be an accurate assumption. Clearly, the curve of $\ln(1 - P)$ cannot be linear, since this quantity approaches infinity as P approaches unity, which should occur when $V(j) = V(J)$. A practical approach to this problem has been to postulate a stepwise linear L function with L decreasing as V (or equivalently c_{ij}) increases.

PROBLEMS

6.1 The "interactance" model is a commonly used form of a gravity distribution model:

$$T_{ij} = A_i \, B_j \, a_i b_j \, f(c_{ij})$$

where A and B have the interpretation of accessibility measures, a and b are the productions and attractions, and $f(c)$ is a function describing the resistance to travel.

Is it possible to state this model as a probability statement? If so, what would be the interpretation of the various terms?

6.2 An intervening opportunities model is formulated as follows: The trips between an area i and an area j will be directly proportional to the destinations available in j and inversely proportional to the destinations lying between i to j.

Consider a plane where trip destinations are uniformly distributed over an area. Using the model stated above, derive the formula for the distribution of trips originating from a zone i. What does the result tell about the relationship between opportunity models and gravity models of the trip distributions?

6.3 Show whether the following distribution models do or do not satisfy the separability and compressibility characteristics of a trip distribution matrix:

(a)
$$t_{ij} = \frac{a_i b_j \, f(c_{ij})}{\sum\limits_k b_k f(c_{ik})}$$

(b)
$$t_{ij} = \frac{a_i b_j}{T}$$

where t_{ij} = trips from i to j
a_i = trip origins at i
b_j = trip destinations at j
$f(c_{ij})$ = travel cost function
T = total trips in the system

6.4 An area with three zones has a present trip distribution pattern as shown:

5	6	5	16
7	4	3	14
4	2	9	15
16	12	17	

It is expected that during a planning period the three zones will grow by the growth factors shown:

$$G_1 = 2 \qquad G_2 = 1.5 \qquad G_3 = 2.5$$

How would the trip distribution pattern change when the growth has taken place?

6.5 Given the following trip time matrix and total productions and attractions, obtain the maximum entropy distribution such that the mean travel time is 5.50.

Travel time matrix c_{ij}:

	1	2	3	4
1	5	4	3	2
2	10	8	4	7
3	9	9	8	4

Productions $a_i = \{5, \ 5, \ 5\}$
Attractions $b_j = \{1, \ 6, \ 2, \ 6\}$

REFERENCES

Adler, T. J., and M. Ben-Akiva: Joint Choice Model For Frequency, Destination, and Travel Mode for Shopping Trips, *Trans. Res. Rec.*, no. 569, pp. 136–150, 1976.

Angen, S., and H. Hyman: Urban Spatial Interaction, *Environment and Planning*, vol. 4, pp. 99–118, 1972.

Ansah, J. A.: Destination Choice Modelling and Disaggregate Analysis of Urban Travel Behavior, *Purdue Joint Highway Res. Proj.*, Report 75-74, 1974.

Beckmann, M. J., and T. F. Golob: A Utility Model for Travel Forecasting, *Trans. Sci.*, vol. 4, no. 4, pp. 365–382, 1970.

Chicago Area Transportation Study: Final Reports, 1956.

Burnett, P.: A Bernoulli Model of Destination Choice, *Trans. Res. Rec.*, no. 527, pp. 33–44, 1974.

Heanue, K. E., and C. E. Pyers: A Comparative Evaluation of Trip Distribution Procedures, *Highway Res. Rec.*, no. 114, pp. 20–37, 1966.

Lille, E.: *Das Resisegesetz und Seine Anwendung auf den Eisenbahnberkehr*, Vienna, 1891.

Loubal, P.: A New Model For Trip Distribution, Institute of Transportation Studies, Dissertation Series, Berkeley, 1969.

Osofsky, S.: The Multiple Regression Method of Forecasting Traffic Volumes, *Traff. Quart.*, pp. 423–445, July, 1959.

Ravenstein, E. G.: The Laws of Migration, *J. Stat. Soc.*, vol. 48, pt. 11, pp. 167–227, 1885.

Ruiter, E. R.: Towards a Better Understanding of the Intervening Opportunities Model, *Transp. Res.*, vol. 1, no. 1, 1967.

Schneider, M.: Appendix to Panel Discussion on Inter-Area Travel Formulas, *Highway Res. Board Bull.*, no. 253, pp. 136–138, 1960.

Stouffer, S.A.: Intervening Opportunities: A Theory Relating Mobility and Distance, *Am. Soc. Rev.*, vol. 5, no. 6, pp. 845–867, 1940.

SEVEN

MODE AND ROUTE CHOICE

Mode and route choices are major steps in the trip-making decision process. These choices occur in urban and in intercity transportation. However, most mode and route choice analyses have evolved within the context of urban transportation. A major concern in urban travel analysis is the prediction of link flows on specific transportation facilities, particularly during periods of potential congestion. This concern with peak flows has necessitated that mode and route choice analyses be quite microscopic in detail in order to permit demand models to address a variety of policy issues dealing with transportation systems management. In mode choice analysis, one is interested in assessing the impact of policies such as exclusive lanes for high-occupancy vehicles or increased parking taxes for private automobiles on the distribution of urban trips among modes available, particularly during daily peak-flow periods. In route choice anlaysis one is often concerned with the impacts of such policies as tolls, metering on freeway ramps, or joint fare systems on the routes chosen by the traffic using any given mode of transportation. It is common in urban travel demand analysis to associate mode and route choice together, and, indeed, in many applications it is useful to consider a simultaneous mode and route choice as an appropriate model of the trip-making decision process.

The hierarchy, or sequence, of choices is generally agreed to be the mode followed by the route choice, although it is quite common to consider both simultaneously. If the scope of the problem at hand is manageable, it may be desirable to model each mode and route combination as a separate alternative. This can, however, lead to excessive numbers of alternatives in large-scale networks. In such cases it is preferable to analyze mode choice first and then follow this by route choice or by what is referred to often as the *assignment* of traffic to links of the modal network.

Mode and route choice analysis follows in a relatively straightforward manner the procedures described in Chaps. 4 and 5. In most cases the transportation choice models are applied directly to these choice problems. However, some considerations apply specifically to mode and to route choice. These are discussed in this chapter together with some examples of applications.

7.1 MODE CHOICE

Early developments in urban travel mode choice analysis resulted in rather primitive aggregate diversion models where traffic flows were split between modes on the basis of some simple formulation of their relative attributes. Indeed, *mode split* is the term often used to refer to this type of analysis. Most early applications were limited to the binary choice case because traffic was split between the automobile and the transit modes. In sequencing mode choice analysis with the rest of analyses of urban travel, it was common to perform trip distribution analysis first, and then to split origin-destination flows among modes. Trip end mode split was also done in which trips generated in zones or by households would be split among modes on the basis of some aggregate modal accessibility measure and then distributed among the destinations reachable by these modes. Rapid developments have occurred recently, encouraged by the developments in general transportation choice modeling, most of which were in fact aimed at improving mode choice analysis. With multinomial choice models it is possible now to analyze large numbers of alternatives rather efficiently. This allows the specification of transportation mode in much more detail than in the past. For example, while the simple diversion curves of the 1950s could be used to split traffic between two modes only, automobile and transit, it is possible now to consider specific choices such as bus with automobile access, car pool, or rail transit with walk access.

Binary Diversion Analysis

This approach is based on comparing the attributes of private and public transportation (automobile and transit) and then breaking the traffic down between them in some fashion such that the percentage use of either is correlated with some measure of their relative attributes. The diversion method has been used both for trip and modal split (before trip distribution analysis) and for trip interchanges determined from a distribution model. Numerous examples of diversion analysis have been documented by the Bureau of Public Roads (1966).

In the case of trip end diversion, an accessibility measure is usually computed for each of a number of zones in a study area, for each of the two modes, automobile and transit. This accessibility measure could be a weighted average of the travel time or travel cost from the zone in question to all other zones in a study area, with the weights determined by some measure of attraction such as zone population. The difference or the ratio of the accessibility by automobile and transit is then correlated against mode split information obtained from a traffic survey. Figure 7.1 shows an example of such a diversion curve developed on the

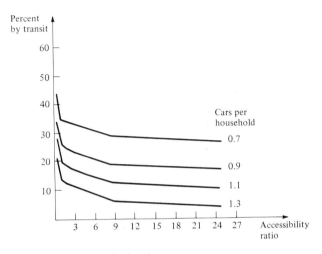

Figure 7.1 Auto-transit diversion curves.

basis of accessibility ratios. Sometimes the diversion curves would be stratified on the basis of some socioeconomic characteristics such as average car ownership or household size. Note, however, that the diversion curves based on zonal accessibility can only be applied at a rather aggregate level.

In the case of trip interchange diversion, origin-destination flows measured in person-trips are distributed among the two modes using a similar diversion procedure. The difference here is that the attributes used for the diversion are specific to origin-destination pairs and can therefore include more than a single measure of accessibility. Diversion curves can then be developed on the basis of travel time ratios and travel cost ratios, and so forth. Examples of this are the diversion curves developed for the Toronto, Ontario, Transportation Study, as reported in Hutchinson (1974). These diversion curves were based on travel-time ratio, travel-cost ratio, and a service ratio defined as the ratio of the times spent in access to each of the two modes.

Diversion curves of mode choice are simple tools for analysis, but their limitations are too many and too serious to make them of much use in the types of policy analyses for which demand studies are done. The diversion curve method is too aggregate in nature and hence does not lend itself to prediction of the impacts of transportation policies that might affect different groups of urban travelers differently. That, together with the absence of specific socioeconomic variables in the choice function, precludes the differentiation between captive and noncaptive choice makers. Households without automobiles, for example, are captive public transportation users and have little or no mode choice, as are households in areas that are not easily accessible to points of public transportation service: they are captive automobile users. Another serious deficiency in diversion analysis is its limitation to binary choice situations. This precludes its use in most applications of demand analysis, since it is generally agreed that multiple choices are available in most transportation systems. Even when the choices are limited to two general categories of modes such as automobile and bus, multiple choices are possible since bus transport can be combined with several access modes including auto access, walking access, and so forth. Automobile transportation can also be identified as more than a single mode as when car pooling is an option.

Behavioral Models of Mode Choice

Mode choice models that follow the general structure of choice analysis described in Chaps. 4 and 5 are referred to as *behavioral models*. They are usually based on the usual underlying postulates of utility maximization. Models in this category differ in the specifications of their utility of choice functions and in their model forms. Most comonly used are the logit and probit models, although other statistical models have also been applied to mode choice including discriminant functions and linear probability functions.

Variables That Describe Mode Choice

The variables used to explain mode choice belong to two categories: socio-economic demand variables and level of service or supply variables. As we shall see in the examples presented in the next section, many variables have been used to explain observed mode choices. As with other demand analyses, a model can always be fitted to observed data if a sufficiently large number of variables is used. The challenge in good mode choice analysis is not only to select the variables that are significant but those that can be used to reflect the type of policy analysis or planning for which mode choice modeling is intended in the first place. It is important to note that the assumptions regarding the underlying utility maximization process are just that. The selection and continued use of modes of travel is largely a social behavioral phenomenon. The attempts to characterize it as an economic process can only be partly successful. Therefore, there is little reason to take the highly complex model of mode choice too seriously. It is always desirable to keep the models simple.

The following are some of the socioeconomic demand variables used to explain mode choice behavior:

1. *Income*. This is by far the most commonly used demand variable. The choice between modes can often be characterized as a trade-off between expensive, convenient, and inexpensive but less convenient modes. Income is often seen as a determinant of such a trade-off. In addition, notwithstanding the influence of income on the valuation of travel time, it is also a proxy for other less quantifiable variables that reflect some of the social aspects of mode choice. For example, it can be noted that in many urban travel situations, the wealthy will prefer automobile to bus transportation, even when it is both more expensive and slower and not obviously more convenient.

2. *Age and role in household*. This variable is used to express the different modal preferences of individuals at different stages in their life. The very young and the very old (e.g., under 20 and over 70) are less likely to drive and will depend more on collective modes of travel than individuals in the professionally active years of their life. The head of a household may have a different mode choice pattern from other members of the household. In a single-automobile household the head is more likely to use the automobile for work trips, leaving the other members of the household as captive users of public transportation. For large households, particularly with children, this tendency might be reversed.

3. *Car ownership*. The number of autos available to a household has repeatedly been found to explain much of their mode choice behavior. Clearly, the more cars that are available, the less likely are members of a household to use public transportation. However, the likelihood of using such modes as car pools for trips to work is not explained by car ownership. Mode choice models usually assume car ownership to be an exogenous variable and hence do not reflect the possible mutual interaction between mode choice and car acquisition decisions. Some attempts have been made to model these two choices simultaneously.

4. *Household size*. This variable is included in mode choice models in a variety of ways. The total number of persons in a household can often be a proxy for the number of cars in the household and would reflect the impact of that factor on mode choice. The number of persons in the household who can drive has also been used, because it reflects more directly the likelihood that automobile modes will be chosen, but it too is likely to be well correlated with household car ownership. The difficulty with household characterization in mode choice models is that it tends to reflect the socioeconomic attributes of a household as a whole. Oftentimes, one might find that different members of a household would have different mode choice behavior. The majority of disaggregate mode choice models deal with households as the unit of analysis and do not attempt to reflect the differences in behavior between members of the same household. If it is possible to obtain disaggregate data at the individual level, then it would always be preferable to consider the mode choice behavior of each individual separately, and hence the variables describing the household as a whole might be less relevant.

5. *Residential location.* Some of the earlier models of mode choice have included variables that describe the residential location of a household as a determinant of mode choice. Households residing within the central part of a city are more likely to use public transportation than those located in the suburbs. It is possible to obtain a better resolution on the effect of this factor by considering the supply characteristics rather than simply the residential location. If the central areas of a city have better accessibility to public transportation than the suburbs, then one would expect people in the central area to choose public transportation more frequently.

6. *Profession.* It has been observed that trip makers who are engaged in white collar professions are more likely to use private transportation than those engaged in blue collar activities. This of course might be due to other social and income characteristics that are correlated with the nature of a person's profession. In modern mode choice analysis it cannot be postulated a priori whether white collar workers are less likely to use public or collective means of transportation. Indeed, we find now that relatively high income, professionally employed urban residents use public transportation and car-pool modes increasingly for travel to central work locations. On the other hand with factories located in outlying urban locations it is not surprising that blue collar workers will use private transportation as the mode for work trips quite often.

As mentioned earlier, it is likely that one or two socioeconomic variables, say income and age, would explain as much of mode choice behavior as can be expected on the basis of quantifiable demand variables. The rest is probably to be found in unquantifiable social factors and, of course, in the supply characteristics of the modes available. The following are some of the more important supply variables used to explain mode choice behavior:

1. *In-vehicle travel time.* The line-haul travel time needed is a major component of the total travel time of the journey. In situations where a change of vehicle in midstream is necessary, such as when transferring between bus or train lines, it is customary to separate out the transfer and the waiting times and to identify them as different components of total journey time. The reason for this is because the effects of the different components of travel time might be perceived differently by travelers.

2. *Access, waiting, and transfer times.* These components of travel include the time required to get to the starting point of service of the mode used and to get to the final destination from the end point of service. This component is more relevant in the case of public modes where it would be the time required to get to and from the stations or stops used. In private automobile transportation, the corresponding travel time component would be the parking and unparking times required especially at the nonhome ends of a journey. Waiting

time is a component relevant to scheduled mode where the traveler must wait for the arrival of the vehicle. It is sometimes possible to represent that component of travel time by including the frequency of service of the schedule mode in question, the reason being that frequency is a variable about which information is readily available, whereas waiting time has to be calculated on the basis of assumptions regarding the pattern of arrival at the stations and the headway between vehicles. If information about waiting times is obtained from interviews with the system users, then, of course, it would be preferred to either frequency or calculated waiting times. The third component of travel time included in this category is the transfer time which would be spent in cases where a transfer of vehicle occurs.

Depending on the resolution with which trip data are obtained from a traffic survey, it may be necessary to aggregate all these components of travel time into one variable, referred to as *out-of-vehicle time* as opposed to the in-vehicle time. This distinction between the two is important, for it is often found in mode choice studies that the mode choice is more sensitive to out-of-vehicle time than to in-vehicle time. This indicates that policy options which would affect out-of-vehicle time may have more impact on mode choices than options which would result in similar effects but on line-haul times.

3. *Travel cost.* This factor is usually also broken down into two components. One is in-vehicle cost, and the other out-of-vehicle cost. The first would be the fare paid on a public transportation mode and the perceived vehicle operating cost for private automobile transportation. The second would include costs associated with access to the mode used, such as parking for automobiles when they are used as primary mode, or as a mode of access to public transportation service. It is also customary to identify separately costs that can be considered out-of-pocket. This refers to monies actually spent during the journey and paid directly then as opposed to costs that may be perceived but not paid directly during the journey. The out-of-pocket costs would include any tolls, parking fees, or fares paid directly, while private vehicle operating costs and taxes are not considered out-of-pocket. The reason for this is that it is considered that the out-of-pocket costs are perceived differently by trip makers.

4. *Qualitative and attitudinal variables.* There are a number of supply factors that can affect mode choice but that cannot be captured by the variables mentioned above. Such things as comfort, reliability, and safety are known to affect mode choice. Recent attitudinal surveys seem to indicate that people who perceive such factors differently are likely to have different mode choice behavior. [See, for example, Levin et al. (1976).] If traffic survey information includes people's perceptions of some of these factors, then it is possible to stratify the samples on that basis and to calibrate separate choice models on the basis of expressed attitudes.

Mode-Specific and Mode-Abstract Models

In constructing behavioral models of mode choice it is possible to adopt either of two postulates regarding the way by which the alternatives are perceived. The first is the *mode-abstract postulate* which states that the person making the choice perceives the attributes themselves rather than the mode being considered and that two distinct modes which have the same level of service attributes would be treated as one. This postulation is derived from Lancaster's (1966) theory of abstract commodities which proposes that consumers decide on the basis of characteristics of goods and services rather than the goods themselves. The attractiveness of this idea for mode choice analysis, as indeed for all transportation choices, is that it permits one to predict with a mode-abstract model the likelihood of choosing alternatives under hypothetical situations, such as when predicting the market share of a mode that does not yet exist. The abstract mode models of travel demand have been applied in intercity transportation, as we shall see in the next chapter, and have been used to estimate the demand potential for novel technologies such as high-speed ground transportation or short takeoff and landing aircraft systems. In urban mode choice analysis the mode-abstract assumption implies that all modes will be described by the same choice function and that the parameters of this function will be the same for all alternatives.

The second postulate is the mode-specific, where the assumption is that choices are influenced by the level of service attributes, but these influences will vary from one alternative to another. In quantitative terms the difference between a mode-abstract and a mode-specific model is in the specification of the choice function used. In the first case the choice function parameters will not have any relation to specific modes and only the values of the variables would vary according to the alternative in question. On the other hand, in the mode-specific case the parameters would also vary depending on the alternative in question and would thus represent the mode-specific influences of the variables they relate to. The use of mode-specific dummy variables in choice functions is an attempt to capture mode effects that are not captured by the variables common to all alternatives. As an illustration consider the choice function of a choice model in the case of two modes: auto A and bus B. Suppose that the variables in the function are travel time T_A and T_B and travel cost C_A and C_B. The mode-abstract specification of the choice model would result in the following choice function:

$$V(i) = \alpha T_i + \beta C_i \qquad (7.1)$$

where α and β are constant parameters, and $i = A$ or B. In the mode-specific formulation the choice function would be

$$V(i) = \alpha_i T_i + \beta_i C_i \qquad (7.2)$$

and in addition, the mode-specific choice function may include dummy variables or constant terms that are specific to each alternative:

$$V(i) = \alpha_i T_i + \beta_i C_i + \gamma_i \qquad (7.3)$$

where γ_i is a mode-specific constant term that will have different values for A and B.

The mode-abstract postulate has an intellectual appeal in mode choice modeling, because it attempts to quantify mode characteristics that affect their likelihood of being chosen and, consistent with other transportation demand analyses, build on the framework of modern microeconomic theory. It also has the pragmatic advantage of requiring a lower number of model parameters than the alternative approach. Of course in order for the mode-abstract model to capture all the factors that can influence mode choice it may need to include a large number of models and thereby lose its pragmatic advantages. The experience in mode choice modeling, in both urban an nonurban travel, has, however, pointed to the inability of mode-abstract models to account adequately for mode choice behavior and to reproduce observed travel patterns with statistical significance. Mode choice studies repeatedly find that a certain amount of "unabstractness" exists in people's mode choice behavior. Indeed, the unquantifiable social factors that influence people's choice among modes may be a major cause for this. A situation that is not so hypothetical can be used to illustrate this point. Consider two modes, a private automobile and a public bus. Suppose that these two modes have exactly the same values of the attributes included in a mode choice model. Suppose further that the model has a sufficiently complete specification that it includes most of the variables that are considered to influence mode choice and that can be quantified. Observation of travel behavior might well indicate that the split of traffic between the two modes is not equal and that more than 50 percent of the traffic uses the automobile. This suggests that in addition to all the mode-abstract effects there are one or more mode-specific effects that must be included in the model. In most cases, this has been done by the introduction of mode-specific constants (or dummy variables). Of course this might improve the statistical fit of the model, but it does not contribute to its logical content, explanatory power, or predictive capability. Another vivid example of mode-specific attributes of choice is the fear of flying which influences intercity mode choice. This effect, which causes certain people to choose surface transportation modes regardless of the quantifiable attribute values, can realistically be introduced only as a variable specific to the air mode.

Examples of Urban Mode Choice Models

Applications of behavioral models to urban mode choice abound in the transportation literature. The transportation choice models discussed in Chaps. 4 and 5 have a great flexibility that permits their use in a variety of situations and in many different environments. Although the transferability of models calibrated in one urban area for use in another has not yet been demonstrated effectively, similar model structures and similar calibration procedures are emerging as almost universal tools for mode choice analysis. Atherton and Ben Akiva (1978) have shown how similar models of mode choice could be calibrated for different cities, albeit with different parameter values.

The recent interest in transportation system management (TSM) methods and in low capital policies for improving the efficiency of urban transportation systems has focused attention on public transportation and other high-occupancy vehicle (HOV) modes such as car and van pools. Many of the TSM methods may be associated with control strategies that are intended to encourage shifts in mode choice. Such strategies include increasing gasoline prices, raising parking taxes, or ramp metering and control on congested freeways. They also include more positive measures such as car- and van-pooling information services, exclusive lanes for public and high-occupancy vehicles, and parking and toll incentives for the latter. While these strategies will have impacts on many aspects of urban travel demand, they will in all probability have a most profound impact on mode choices. It is for this reason perhaps that we find considerable research being conducted in mode choice analysis. Most advances, however, are being made in the empirical methods and in the expansion of the scope of mode choice modeling to a wider variety of situations. Theoretical developments on the other hand are much slower, and the fundamental structure of models in use currently is only marginally different from models developed nearly two decades ago.

The following is a selection of examples of mode choice models intended to illustrate the variety of situations in which they have been applied.

A stochastic binary model Most of the earlier applications of stochastic choice models were in cases of binary choice [see, for example, Warner (1962), Lisco (1967), and Quarmby (1967)]. The reason for this was simply pragmatic and due to the absence of efficient, computer-based estimation techniques for multinomial models.

In one of the earlier applications De Donnea (1970) constructed a model to describe the choice between auto and bus transit in Rotterdam, the Netherlands. De Donnea calibrated both a logit and probit model to the same data with a rather insignificant difference in the results. De Donnea's model is a mode-specific model with choice functions of the following form:

$$V(1) = a_1 + a_2 Y t_i + a_3 H \tag{7.4}$$

and
$$V(2) = a_2 Y t_2 \tag{7.5}$$

where $V(1)$ is the choice function for the auto mode, and $V(2)$ the choice function for the transit mode. Y is the individual's income, t the travel time, and H a dummy variable with $H = 1$, if the individual is the head of a household, and $H = 0$ if not, and a_1, a_2, a_3 are parameters.

Using the simplified binary choice function

$$L = V(1) - V(2)$$
$$= a_1 + a_2 Y(t_1 - t_2) + a_3 H$$

De Donnea estimated the parameters of the two models:

$$P(1) = \frac{e^L}{1 + e^L} \qquad P(2) = \frac{1}{1 + e^L}$$

and the probit model

$$P(1) = \Phi(L) \qquad P(2) = 1 - \Phi(L)$$

and obtained the following results:

	Logit model	Probit model
a_1	0.0226	0.0117
a_2	−0.0024	−0.0014
a_3	1.0800	0.6600

In both calibrations the values of all three parameters were found to be significant, and the model as a whole was also found to explain the observed mode choice patterns significantly. The presence of two mode-specific parameters in the model (a_1 and a_3) supports the argument that a certain amount of mode unabstractness seems to underlie mode choice behavior.

A trinomial model There have been a number of applications in the trinomial case, the case where there are three alternatives in the choice set. A recent example of the trinomial mode choice analysis is a model calibrated on data for the Pittsburgh, Pennsylvania, region by Ganek and Saulino (1976). In addition to automobile and transit modes, the car-pool alternative was identified as the third choice. The car pool in this case represents a mode that is intermediate between the alternative to drive alone and the public transportation mode. It is interesting to note that in Ganek and Saulino's model some of the socioeconomic and the transport supply variables are mode-specific in addition to the specification of mode-specific constant terms. The variables used in the model are the following:

In-vehicle time
Access time and egress times
Total cost
Relative comfort and convenience
Flexibility
Mode reliability
Car availability
Location of work place
Household income
Sex
Mode constants

It is also interesting to note the presence of qualitative comfort and convenience variables in the model. These variables were based on individual survey responses coded for each person included in the disaggregate sample used to calibrate the model. The *comfort* and *convenience* variables were based on subjective scales varying from − 2 to + 2; the *flexibility* variable was based on whether the person indicated that he or she valued that attribute or not and was specified only for the car-pool alternative. *Mode reliability* was measured by the number of days in each week that mode was available to the user. The *car availability* variable, measured in number of cars in the household per driver, was specified separately for the drive-alone and for the car-pool modes. The *workplace location* variable was a dummy variable indicating whether the location of the workplace was the central business district or not, and was specified separately for each mode. The *household income* and *sex* variables were also mode-specific, with the latter being a binary variable.

With these specifications the model contained a total of 18 variables and, calibrated on work trips, it was used to draw some conclusions about the underlying mode choice behavior. Some of the conclusions drawn include the fact that CBD (central business district) and non-CBD workers have basically different work trip mode choice behavior. The former are more sensitive to in-vehicle time, and the latter more sensitive to access time. Non-CBD commuters seem to be more likely to car-pool than CBD workers, possibly due to the greater and more frequent availability of transit as an alternative mode to the CBD.

A multimodal model for auto and transit choice It is possible perhaps to obtain a better resolution on mode choice behavior if the automobile and transit modes are differentiated into more alternatives depending on the possbile combinations that can be made for particular journeys. In a study of San Francisco Bay Area households Train (1976) estimated the parameters of a multinomial logit choice mode for four alternatives consisting of auto alone, bus with walking access, bus with automobile access and car pool. Again, the choice function used was predominantly mode-specific and contained a rather large number of variables. An interesting feature of this model is that the cost variables are measured in relation to the posttax wage. By using the marginal rate of substitution between cost thus measured and the various travel time variables in the model, it was possible to estimate the revealed valuation of travel time as a percentage of wage. The variables used in the model were

Cost divided by posttax wage, in cents per cent per minute
On-vehicle time in minutes
Walk time in minutes
Transfer time in minutes
Number of transfers
Bus headways in minutes stratified below and above 8 minutes

Family income stratified in income classes
Length of residence in the community
Number of persons in the household who can drive
Mode dummy variables

Using samples of households stratified on the basis of household characteristics (married couples, with and without children, etc.) different sets of parameters were estimated for each household group. The values of time revealed by the choice were computed using the marginal rates of substitution between cost and time using the procedure described in Chap. 4. The interesting result is that transfer and waiting time were always found to be valued as more expensive than in-vehicle time or access time. For example, for households with married couples and without children the values obtained were as follows: the value of time saved as a percentage of wage for on-vehicle time was 30 percent, for access time was 86 percent, and for transfer and wait time 118 percent. Of course the exact percentages do not mean much in general, but their relative values are revealing. It is obvious that these particular numbers are slightly exaggerated, for it is unlikely that a traveler would value any component of travel time at 118 percent of the wage rate. These results do, however, suggest typical relative values of the various components of travel time, at least insofar as they affect mode choice behavior.

A multimodal choice model Another example that illustrates the variety in scope of mode choice modeling is a multimodal model calibrated by Ben Akiva and Richards (1976) on data obtained for some Dutch cities. The interesting feature of this model, which otherwise is a straightforward application of multinomial logit modeling, is that six alternatives were identified including both motorized and nonmotorized modes. These are walking, bicycle, moped, automobile, bus, and train. It is indeed an interesting hypothesis that a multinomial logit model can explain the choice from among such a wide variety of transport modes. The model used in this study was also mode-specific, as it would have to be, and contained seven demand and supply variables in addition to the mode-specific dummy variables. The variables used in this model are

In-vehicle time
Out-of-vehicle time
Out-of-pocket cost
Household income
Car availability
Occupation
Mode-specific dummy variables

It is interesting to note that significant estimates were obtained for nearly all model variables. Many of these variables were, however, specified separately for each mode. This suggests that the pure mode effects prevail and, when combined with socioeconomic variables, account for most of the variations of mode choices. Indeed the authors of the model concluded that mode choice is determined largely by factors other than the level of service attributes of the mode. The fact that there may be hierarchies of choice, first between motorized and non-motorized transport, then between public and private transport, and finally between modes, suggests that a multinomial probit model might be a more suitable approach to a problem of this nature. One might also suspect that such a wide variety of modes cannot be adequately analyzed by a conventional transportation choice model.

Some Limitations of Urban Mode Choice Models

The examples presented in the previous section are meant to illustrate the power and versatility of behavioral choice models to the study of urban mode choices. They do, however, at the same time demonstrate the fundamental limitations and weaknesses of a mode choice modeling. The models shown, as most models that exist in the literature and in practice, consist of formulations that have been made to fit observed choices by the inclusion of the necessary number of variables. As such, these models can be used to evaluate the effects of minor and gradual changes in the choice environment on mode choices, though only in the area where they have been calibrated. The transferability of model forms from place to place does not guarantee that models calibrated in one place can be used to predict in another. Indeed, choice theory might be taken to support the use of similar model forms, but it says nothing about the universality of parameter values. Hence the temptation to generalize the results of mode choice modeling exercises is a dangerous one and should be resisted. Applications in modeling should not go farther than can be supported by the theory from whence they originate.

Another source of weakness in mode choice modeling is the fact that most models that can be considered successful in predicting behavior are mode-specific rather than mode-abstract models. Indeed, in most models available in the literature one can find that the mode-specific dummy variables together with some socioeconomic variables (particularly income car ownership) explain most of the variations of mode choice behavior among individuals or households. This means that apart from the socioeconomic indicators of demand, there remains considerable ignorance about mode choice behavior in general. This suggests perhaps that the social factors that probably influence mode choice are indeed dominating. The net result of this is that policy analysis in urban transportation planning, particularly where it affects mode choice behavior, will have to depend on social analysis in addition to the quantitative methods of demand analysis. Advances in mode choice modeling alone will not necessarily make policy analysis and planning any easier. The quantitative models can contribute to the planning process only if they are coupled with perceptive assessments and analyses of the social factors that influence the behavior of urban travelers.

7.2 ROUTE CHOICE

While the behavioral process of route choice does not differ fundamentally from other urban travel choice processes, it does have a number of particular features that make its modeling somewhat different. In the route choice problem a person traveling between a point of origin and a point of destination is faced with a number of routes that connect these two points. The selection of route occurs on the basis of route attributes, and it also depends on the socioeconomic characteristics of the trip maker. Hence, the route choice model is basically the same in its logical structure as other transportation choice models. However, since the concern in route choice analysis is with the prediction of flows on specific links of a transportation network, and since route choice is often assumed to occur at the end of a sequence of choices regarding trip characteristics, it follows that a more microscopic look is usually taken at the transportation system in this case. Attributes such as travel time and travel costs have to be identified for specific links of the network and cannot be aggregated over large segments, as might be the case in mode or destination choice analysis. Furthermore, when looking at the specific attributes of transportation links, the effects of traffic flows on these attributes cannot be ignored. Thus, while in destination and mode choice it is customary to assume that the system attributes (cost, time, etc.) are fixed, in route choice analysis this assumption cannot often be made, and a feedback between flow and supply characteristics must be taken into account. This leads to a modification in the structure of many of the choice models used. It also limits the extent to which conventional choice models that measure response in probability or proportion terms can be used. It is not sufficient to know the probability of choice for a particular route in order to estimate the travel time on the links in that route; what is necessary is knowledge of the absolute value of the traffic flow.

An additional feature of urban route choice analysis is that in urban networks, which are typically dense, routes between different pairs of origins and destinations, or routes that can be considered alternative connections between any given pair of points will often share links. This means that the characteristics of alternative routes will often not be independent. This can be illustrated in a simple example. Suppose points A and B are joined by the transportation network shown in Fig. 7.2. A trip maker between A and B has a choice between three possible routes that connect these two points. These routes are identified by the numbers of the nodes they pass through and are 1-2-4, 1-2-3-4, and 1-3-4. It is easy to see that the first two routes share link 1-2 and that the second and third routes share

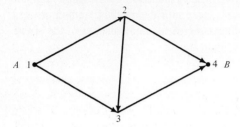

Figure 7.2 Network with three overlapping routes.

link 3-4 among them. Thus if each of these routes is considered an alternative, it is clear that the attributes of the alternatives will be correlated, for if anything happens to change the characteristics of links 1-2, for example, then it would influence the attributes of the two routes that share this link. In addition to that, it is typical in dense urban networks to find that any of the links shown in Fig. 7.2 may also be a part of other routes that connect points other than *A* and *B*. This feature of the network problem will influence the way in which choice models can be constructed to deal with the route choice problem. Recall from Chap. 5 that not all models of choice have the capability of dealing with alternatives which have correlated attributes. It is for these reasons that we find that the application of stochastic choice models to this problem is still at an early stage and that many simplifying assumptions are usually made in order to make the route choice problem in urban networks manageable. Early techniques of analysis (referred to as *traffic assignment techniques*) were based on heuristic iterative methods where traffic was allocated to the links of a network on the basis of some rule.

Approaches to Route Choice Analysis

The different approaches available for route choice analysis stem from the assumptions made regarding two aspects of the process: (1) the manner by which link characteristics are influenced by traffic flow and (2) the manner by which trip makers choose between routes. As to the first there are two possible approaches. The first is to assume that link characteristics are constant and unaffected by traffic flow. The second is to introduce some functional relationship between traffic flow and link attributes (usually travel time), using supply analysis as described in Chap. 3. Concerning the second feature there are more assumptions that can be made. One is that a trip maker will always take the shortest route available; another is that trip makers will be distributed among the few shorter routes, but not necessarily all take the single shortest one. This assumption results directly in postulating the route choice process as a random one in applying a stochastic choice model to the problem. In addition to these postulations, there are two classes of route choice models that differ fundamentally according to the assignment rule used. The first is referred to as the *user equilibrium approach*, which postulates that trip makers choose their routes in order to minimize their own individual travel costs. The second is the optimal route choice which assigns traffic to a network in such a way as to minimize the total cost expended on the system. These two approaches are referred to, respectively, as *Wardrop's first and second principles of traffic assignment*, since they were first explicitly stated by Wardrop (1952). The optimal assignment methods are not behavioral in the sense that they do not pretend to represent people's behavior in the system. They are useful, however, as analysis tools in situations where some means of traffic controls are contemplated that would move the distribution of trips among routes from the user equilibrium toward system optimal.

Notation

We adopt the following notation for discussing the route choice problem. Let V_{ij} be the traffic flow between points i and j in a transportation system. Let i and j belong to sets I and J, respectively, where I and J could be the same or over-lapping sets representing all the points of origin and destination of trips in the system. Let V_l be the flow on link l in the network. The cost attributes of the link that are relevant to route choice are represented by a function $S_l(V_l)$ where S represents an average cost or a supply function. It is customary in route choice analysis to use simple supply functions consisting of travel time only. Let V_{ij}^r be the part of the flow between i and j that takes place on route r where r belongs to a set R_{ij} which is the set of all routes that can be reasonably assumed to connect points i and j. We assume that flows V_{ij} are given and that the supply functions $S_l(V_l)$ are known for all links in the network.

In the case where the link costs are independent of traffic flow, then $S_l(V_l) = S_l$. When the link costs depend on traffic volume, then supply functions similar to those shown in Figs. 3.3 and 3.4 can be used.

The conservation of flows V_{ij} between origins and destinations requires that

$$\sum_{r \in R_{ij}} V_{ij}^r = V_{ij} \qquad \text{for all } i, j \tag{7.6}$$

Furthermore, if we define δ_r^l as a binary variable that takes on a value of 1 if link l is a part of route r and 0 otherwise, then the link and route conservation properties require that

$$\sum_{i \in I} \sum_{j \in J} V_{ij}^r \delta_r^l = 0 \tag{7.7}$$

which states that the flow on any link is the sum of the flows on all routes of which the link is a part. With this notation it is possible now to state formally the postulates for the various route choice models.

Optimal Traffic Assignment

This assignment process allocates the traffic flows V_{ij} to the links and routes of the network in such a way as to minimize total system cost, subject to the constraints of Eqs. (7.6) and (7.7). The problem is formulated as a mathematical programming problem which seeks to find the value V_{ij}^r in such a way as to minimize

$$\text{Total cost} = \sum_l V_l \, S_l(V_l) \tag{7.8}$$

subject to Eqs. (7.6) and (7.7) and to $V_{ij}^r \geq 0$. If the supply functions $S_l(\cdot)$ are invariant to flow, then the objective function in Eq. (7.8) becomes a linear function, and since the constraints of Eqs. (7.6) and (7.7) are also linear, the problem resolves to a linear programming problem. Note that the optimal assignment model is a deterministic model in that it seeks the single solution by which the total system cost is minimized.

Deterministic User Equilibrium

In this model it is assumed that the users will choose routes in such a way that no individual trip maker can improve the choice by unilaterally changing routes. In other words the equilibrium occurs when all trip makers are each on their individual minimum-cost path. This occurs when the travel times on all routes connecting any origin-destination pair are equal. To see this we illustrate the model with a simple example where there is one single origin-destination pair and two alternative routes connecting them. Let the network connecting two points A and B be as shown in Fig. 7.3a with two routes identified as routes 1 and 2. Each of these two routes is described by a supply function $S_r(V_r)$, where for the sake of simplicity of the example, each route is assumed to contain only one link. The supply functions are illustrated in Fig. 7.3b. Suppose that a fixed amount of traffic V is to be allocated between these two routes. The user equilibrium postulate states that the resulting allocation will be such that no user can improve the situation by changing routes unilaterally. To show that this equilibrium solution occurs when the values of the cost are equal, we modify the supply graphs as shown in Fig. 7.3c, where on the horizontal axis we measure flow V_1 from left to right and flow V_2 from right to left, and where we plot the corresponding supply functions in the same manner. We fix the dimension of the horizontal axis to the given amount of total traffic V. Any point on that axis (V_1, V_2) will represent a particular allocation of the flow to the two routes such that $V_1 + V_2 = V$. If the allocation is any point other than $(V_1, V_2)^*$ where the values of the two cost functions are equal, such as point (V_1, V_2) in Fig. 7.3c, then it will pay for users of route 2 to switch to route 1, thereby reducing their average cost even though the average cost on route 1 will increase due to this switch. As long as the value $S_2(V_2) > S_1(V_1)$, additional users will continue to switch routes.

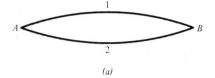

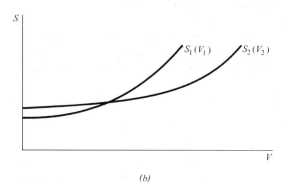

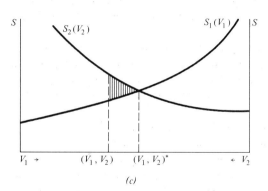

Figure 7.3 Equilibrium assignment to network with two routes. (*a*) Net work structure; (*b*) link supply functions; (*c*) equilibrium assignment.

However, when the allocation reaches point $(V_1, V_2)^*$, then any additional switch of route by any user (of either facility) will result in an increase in the travel cost. Hence if each individual user sought to minimize the travel cost, then the resulting equilibrium would occur at $(V_1, V_2)^*$, or at the point where travel costs on both alternative routes are equal. In order to formulate this equilibrium postulate using the notation adopted earlier, we note again by reference to Fig. 7.3c that assignment $(V_1, V_2)^*$ is the one that minimizes the total area under the average cost curves $S_1(V_1)$ and $S_2(V_2)$. To see this, note that at any assignment such as (V_1, V_2) the area under the cost curves equals that for $(V_1, V_2)^*$ plus the amount shown in the cross-hatched area. That amount is always positive as long as the functions $S_1(\cdot)$ and $S_2(\cdot)$ are increasing functions of volume. Consequently traffic assignment $(V_1, V_2)^*$ will minimize the area under the cost curves. Extending this property to a general route choice model, we can state the deterministic user equilibrium route choice problem as a mathematical program as follows:

$$\text{Minimize} \quad \sum_l \int_0^{V_l} S_l(x)\, dx \qquad (7.9)$$

subject to Eqs. (7.6) and (7.7) and to $V_{ij}^r \geq 0$. Note that since the supply (or average cost) function for each route is the series aggregation of the supply function for links that form a part of the route, the formulation of Eq. (7.9), which minimizes the total area under the supply curves of all links, will also minimize that area for all the routes. Also note the similarity between the optimal and the user equilibrium solutions in that in the first case minimizing the total costs is equivalent to minimizing the integrals of the marginal costs and results in a solution at which the marginal costs on all routes are equal. In the second case, the solution is obtained by minimizing the integrals of the average costs and occurs when the average costs are equal. The comparisons of the two solutions can be illustrated then by looking at the assignments with equal average and equal marginal costs as shown in Fig. 7.4 where $(V_1, V_2)'$ corresponds to the optimal

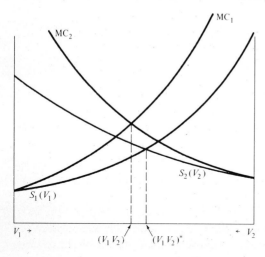

Figure 7.4 Optimal and equilibrium assignments to two routes.

assignment with equal marginal costs, and $(V_1, V_2)^*$ corresponds to the equilibrium assignment with equal average costs. In general the two solutions are not synonymous, and some sort of traffic control measure would be needed if it is desired to move from $(V_1, V_2)^*$ to $(V_1, V_2)'$.

The deterministic user equilibrium method of route choice analysis has emerged as a powerful tool for analyzing large-scale urban transportation networks. Due to many algorithms, notably the one developed by Le Blanc et al. (1975), it has become possible to seek equilibrium efficiently in large-scale networks using computer programs of manageable size. The network equilibrium algorithm can be described in five steps as follows:

1. Starting with an initial feasible solution V_l compute the average cost $S_l(V_l)$ on each link in the system.
2. Using the costs computed in step 1, find the minimum cost path route for each origin-destination pair.
3. Assign all trips V_{ij} between every origin-destination pair to the route r which has the minimum cost as computed in the previous two steps; call the new flows V_l'.
4. Combine the initial solution with the solution obtained in step 4 as follows:

$$V_1'' = \lambda V_1 + (1 - \lambda)V_1'$$

   where λ is a parameter whose value is found heuristically in such a way as to minimize the objective function in Eq. (7.9).
5. Repeat by replacing V_1 with V'' until convergence occurs when the objective function of Eq. (7.9) is minimized.

The algorithm has been shown to converge as long as the supply functions $S_l(\cdot)$ are convex functions. The algorithm has been incorporated in computerized urban travel analysis packages that are readily available in practice. [See, for example, U.S. Department of Transportation (1977).] A later improvement to the algorithm was introduced by Daganzo (1977) who suggested a modification whereby the interpolation parameter λ can be chosen in such a way as to avoid any link in the system operating over its capacity, thus extending the scope of the algorithm to capacitated networks.

Stochastic Route Choice Models

The application of stochastic choice models to the problem of route choice is a recent advance in urban travel analysis methodology. The postulate is that there is no reason why all users who are faced with a set of routes will invariably choose the one with the lowest cost. In the stochastic model the cost perceived by any trip maker is assumed to be a random variable, and the choice follows a utility maximization (cost minimization) principle resulting in a distribution of users among the routes that is caused by the distribution of the manner by which each user perceives of the route cost. The stochastic user equilibrium principle is similar to the deterministic but differs in that it assumes that equilibrium occurs when no trip makers believe that they can improve their situation by unilaterally changing routes.

The earlier stochastic route choice models assumed that link costs were invariant to flow. This permitted the use of stochastic choice models of the type described in Chap. 5 by using choice probabilities that are functions of the attributes. Since the cost on each route is fixed, probabilities of choice would be a meaningful measure regardless of the value of the absolute number of trips to be assigned. Later on, attempts were made to incorporate congestion effects and more realistic link supply functions in stochastic route choice models.

Stochastic models with fixed link costs The earliest attempt at stochastic choice modeling is perhaps that of Dial (1971), who postulated that traffic will not all flow on the minimum cost route but will be distributed among the few reasonable routes connecting an origin and a destination. A reasonable or efficient route was defined as one where all links place the trip maker closer to the destination and farther from the origin. Dial then devised an algorithm in which flows between origins and destinations are distributed according to a multinomial logit choice model of the following form:

$$p(r) = \frac{e^{\theta(S_o - S_r)}}{\sum\limits_{j \in R} e^{\theta(S_o - S_j)}} \qquad (7.10)$$

where $p(r)$ is the probability of choice of route r, S_r is the cost on route r, S_o is the cost on the minimum cost route between the origin and the destination, R is the set of all reasonable (or efficient) routes for the given origin-destination pair, and θ is a constant parameter. In order to ensure that flows from a large number of origin-destination pairs will all be distributed according to the logit model, and since there will in general be many routes that share links, an algorithm rather than a closed-form solution was necessary. Dial's method is well known and also available in computer programs that are widely used in practice. [See again, U.S. Department of Transportation (1977).] It does have a fundamental weakness that stems from the properties of the multinomial logit model. As demonstrated in Chap. 5 the logit model is not suitable in situations where alternatives are perceived to have overlapping attributes. The example shown in Fig. 5.3*a* and *b* illustrates the potential errors that can be made in applying the logit model to this route choice problem.

An alternative to the logit model for route choice analysis was proposed by Daganzo and Sheffi (1977). With fixed link costs still an underlying assumption, Daganzo and Sheffi assumed that the perceived travel cost S_l' on a link of measured cost S_l would be a normally distributed random variable when measured across a population or across repeated trip-making decisions of the same individual. The variable would have a mean S_l and a variance that is proportional to the value of S_l. In other words, for any link l

$$S_l' \sim N(S_l, \alpha S) \qquad (7.11)$$

where α is a parameter that represents the accuracy with which people perceive link travel costs. The travel cost for a route is obtained by series aggregation over all links in that route:

$$S_r' = \sum_l S_l' \delta_l^r \tag{7.12}$$

Since Eq. (7.12) is a linear transformation, it results in route costs that follow a multivariate normal distribution where the route costs have a covariance that is proportional to the values of costs over the links where they overlap. In other words,

$$\text{var } (S_r') = \alpha S_r \tag{7.13}$$

$$\text{cov } (S_r', S_k') = \alpha S_{rk} \tag{7.14}$$

where S_{rk} is the costs over the segments where routes r and k overlap. As an example of this we refer back to the network in Fig. 7.2 where there are three routes connecting points A and B. Route 1-2-4 overlaps with route 1-2-3-4 over link 1-2; and route 1-2-3-4 overlaps with route 1-3-4 over link 3-4. If the values of the cost on each of the links were equal to, say, s then the covariances of the costs perceived on the three routes would be

$$\text{cov } (S_{1\text{-}2\text{-}4}, S_{1\text{-}2\text{-}3\text{-}4}) = \text{cov } (S_{1\text{-}2\text{-}3\text{-}4}, S_{1\text{-}3\text{-}4}) = \alpha s$$

and
$$\text{cov } (S_{1\text{-}2\text{-}3}, S_{1\text{-}3\text{-}4}) = 0$$

$$\text{var } (S_{1\text{-}2\text{-}3}) = \text{var } (S_{1\text{-}3\text{-}4}) = \alpha(2s)$$

and
$$\text{var } (S_{1\text{-}2\text{-}3\text{-}4}) = \alpha(3s)$$

Using this formulation the application of the multinomial probit model to the route choice problem follows directly Eqs. (5.6) to (5.13) in Chap. 5.

The advantage of the probit formulation of the route choice problem is that it yields a model that is sensitive to the topology of the network, because it takes into account explicitly any overlaps between routes. As mentioned before, such overlaps are likely to be very common, at least in dense urban networks. Again, refer to the comparison shown in Fig. 5.3a and b which illustrates the difference between a logit and a probit formulation for the problem of overlapping routes.

Stochastic Assignment with Variable Link Costs

The modification of the stochastic choice model to account for variable link costs is relatively recent. The procedure is to follow an iterative algorithm similar to that of the deterministic user equilibrium, but to apply the stochastic choice model at every stage when allocating traffic to routes. The connection between choice probabilities and route flows, which is necessary in order to introduce the flow-dependent cost functions, is provided by reference to the weak law of large numbers which implies that if there is a sufficiently large number of trip makers following the same decision rules, then

$$V_{ij}^r = P_{ij}(r)V_{ij} \qquad \text{for all } i, j, r \tag{7.15}$$

where $p_{ij}(r)$ is the choice probability of route r for trip makers between i and j. The actual travel costs on each link S_l are calculated on the basis of the flows; the perceived costs S_l' are related to the actual costs in the same way as when the travel costs are constant. The actual travel cost on any route r is given by

$$S_r = \sum_l S_l(V_l)\delta_1^r \tag{7.16}$$

The perceived route costs are derived from the actual values depending on which choice model is used. In the case of the probit model the perceived costs S_r' are multivariate normal variables with means

$$E(S_r') = \alpha S_r \tag{7.17}$$

and covariances

$$\text{cov}(S_r', S_k') = \alpha S_{rk} \tag{7.18}$$

where S_r is as defined in Eq. (7.16) and S_{rk} is the sum of the flow-dependent costs on the link where routes r and k overlap. With this formulation Eqs. (5.6) to (5.13) can be applied to compute

$$P(r) = p(S_r' > S_k' \qquad \text{for all } r, k \in R) \tag{7.19}$$

where the i, j subscripts have been dropped for simplicity. In a recent study by Sheffi and Powell (1980) a deterministic equilibrium algorithm was modified to apply the stochastic probit model for route choice. Sheffi and Powell demonstrated the similarity between stochastic and deterministic model results when the network is congested. As congestion is approached, the differences between alternative routes become more accurately perceived by users, and the route choice tends to approach the deterministic equilibrium solution. The implication of this is that with overcongested networks, it may be sufficient to use deterministic equilibrium methods, particularly since those are readily available in practical computer packages. In a situation where congestion is not an issue, then it may be sufficient to use the stochastic choice model with fixed link costs. In situations where congestion will occur but not on all routes and links, it may be desirable to use a stochastic choice model with flow-dependent link costs. This approach is, however, relatively new, and considerable additional research is perhaps needed before it becomes readily applicable and available to the practitioner.

SUMMARY

Mode and route choice analysis has come a long way since the early days of diversion curves. We have attempted to summarize the important aspects of this methodology in this chapter. We have focused on the recent development perhaps best characterized by the use of choice models reflecting a utility-based choice process and accommodating the assumptions of randomness in the behavior of choice makers.

Considerable development continues in this field which has attracted considerable interest among transportation researchers. Most of the recent and current developments seem to focus on improving models that reflect the current paradigm of choice analysis: the choice maker is a rational person, behaving in such a way as to maximize utility, albeit in a random fashion, and the determinants of choice among modes and routes can by and large be represented by quantifiable variables. Improved model estimation techniques, as well as efficient methods of solving complex problems that arise in choice analysis, such as stochastic network equilibrium, are continually being developed. What most of these developments have largely excluded are the less quantifiable and the less understandable social determinants of mode and route choice. This is rather difficult to deal with in choice models, for no amount of socioeconomic stratification is likely to capture the complex and subtle social influences that affect the choice process. Predicted and observed choice patterns in complex urban transportation situations have been and will likely always be different. There is no danger in this as long as the transportation planners using demand analysis recognize the limitations of these models and incorporate the social aspects of transportation demand in their planning activities.

PROBLEMS

7-1 A simple road network connects two cities:
The demand for travel from city A to city B is given by

$$V_{AB} = 5000 - 125t_{AB}$$

where V_{AB} = volume of travel from A to B
t_{AB} = travel time (in minutes) between A and B

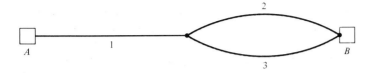

The travel times on links 1, 2, and 3 depend on traffic volume. They are given by

$$t_1 = \begin{cases} 5 & V_1 \le 2000 \\ \dfrac{V_1}{400} & V_1 > 2000 \end{cases}$$

$$t_2 = \begin{cases} 5 & V_2 \le 2000 \\ \dfrac{V_2}{400} & V_2 > 2000 \end{cases}$$

$$t_3 = \begin{cases} 5 & V_3 \le 1000 \\ \dfrac{V_3}{400} & V_3 > 1000 \end{cases}$$

Determine the equilibrium values for V_{AB}, t_{AB}, V_1, V_2, V_3, t_1, t_2, and t_3.

7-2 During a peak hour period, the following traffic demands (inelastic) are observed as shown in the following table:

	A	B	C
A	—	—	500
B	—	—	3000
C	—	—	—

Areas A, B, and C, are connected by the following network:

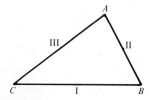

The attached graphs show the travel time functions for each of the links I, II, and III.

(a) What will be the route choice at equilibrium and without any traffic control?

(b) Is it desirable to close link II in order to improve the operation of the system?

Road I

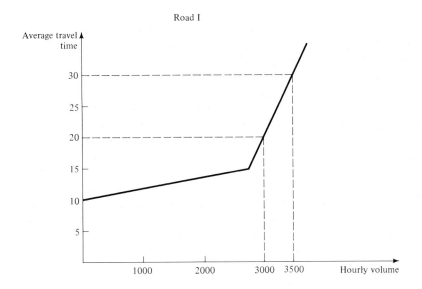

Road II

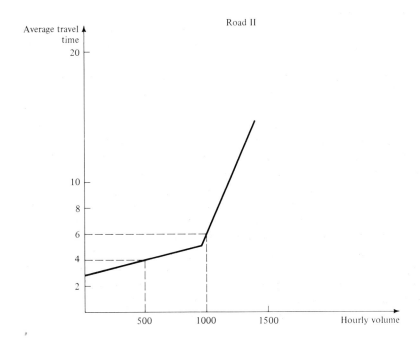

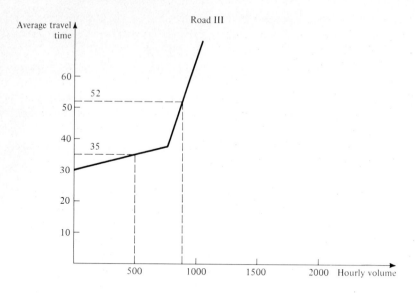

REFERENCES

Atherton, T., and M. Ben Akiva: Transferability and Updating of Disaggregate Travel Demand Models, *Transp. Res. Rec.,* no. 610, pp. 12–18, 1976.

Ben Akiva, M., and M. G. Richards: Disaggregate Multimodal Model for Work Trips in the Netherlands, *Transp. Res. Rec.,* no. 569, pp. 107–123, 1976.

Daganzo, C. F.: On the Traffic Assignment Problem with Flow Dependent Costs, *Transp. Res.,* vol. 11, no. 6, pp. 433–438, 1977.

Daganzo, C. F., and Y. Sheffi: On Stochastic Models of Traffic Assignment, *Transp. Sci.,* vol. 11, no. 3, pp. 253–274, 1977.

De Donnea, F. X.: *The Determinant of Transport Mode Choice in Dutch Cities,* Rotterdam University Press, Holland, 1971.

Dial, R.: A Probabilistic Traffic Assignment Model which Obviates Path Enumeration, *Transp. Res.,* vol. 5, no. 2, pp. 83–222, 1971.

Hutchinson, B. G.: *Principles of Urban Transport System Planning,* McGraw-Hill, New York, 1974.

Lancaster, K. J.: A New Approach to Consumer Theory, *J. Pol. Econ.,* vol. 64, pp. 132–157, 1966.

Le Blanc, L. J., E. K. Morlok, and W. P. Pierskalla: An Efficient Approach to Solving the Road Network Equilibrium Traffic Assignment Problem, *Transp. Res.,* vol. 9, no. 5, pp. 309–318, 1975.

Levin, I. R., et al.: Measurement of Psychological Factors and Their Role in Transportation Behavior. Iowa Univ. Inst. of Urban & Regional Research. TR-82-, 1976, 17 pp.

Lisco, T. E.: "The Value of Commuter Travel Time: A Study in Urban Transportation," University of Chicago, unpublished Ph.D. dissertation, 1967.

McFadden, D.: The Measurement of Urban Travel Demand, *J. Pub. Econ.*, vol. 3, pp. 303–323, 1974.

Quarmby, D. A.: Choice of Travel Mode for the Journey to Work, *J. Transp. Econ. Pol.*, vol. 1, no. 3, pp. 273–314, 1967.

Sheffi, Y., and W. Powell: A Comparison of Stochastic and Deterministic Traffic Assignment over Congested Networks, *Transp. Res.*, vol. 15B, no. 1, pp. 53–64, 1980.

Train, K.: "Work Trip Mode Split Models: An Empirical Exploration of Estimate Sensitivity to Model and Data Specification," Berkeley Urban Travel Demand Forecasting Project, working paper no. 7602, 1976.

U.S. Federal Highway Administration: Computer Program for Urban Transportation Planning: PLANPAC/BACKPAC, General Information Manual, GPO Stock No. 050-011-00125-0, 1977.

U.S. Urban Mass Transit Administration: UT PS Reference Manual, 1977.

Wardrop, J. G.: Some Theoretical Aspects of Road Traffic Research, *Proceedings,* Institution of Civil Engineers (Part II) no. 1, pp. 325–378, 1952.

Warner, S. L.: *Stochastic Choice of Mode in Urban Travel, A Study in Binary Choice,* Northwestern University Press, Evanston, 1962.

EIGHT

INTERCITY PASSENGER TRAVEL DEMAND

As in the urban case, intercity passenger travel demand analysis is aimed at relating intercity traffic to the socioeconomic characteristics of the travelers and to the technical and level of service characteristics of the transportation system. The motivation for this stems mainly from the need to perform feasibility analyses of transportation projects. Unlike urban transportation planning, the design of transportation facilities is not as closely related to the results of demand analysis, because except in some special cases intercity transportation systems are normally not capacity-constrained. The crucial question in intercity transportation planning is often the feasibility of transportation system links, rather than their specific capacity and design characteristics.

The fundamentals of intercity transportation demand analysis rest on the observation of the regularities in the spatial distribution of socioeconomic activities, as indicated by the location of cities. Indeed, as in the case of urban transportation, these regularities permit the development of a consistent methodology and the construction of demand models. Due to the scale of intercity systems and to the large distances that separate cities, idealizations such as the ones made in urban transportation analysis are no longer feasible. For example, the analytical advantages that can be obtained from assuming relatively high, uniform densities of socioeconomic activities in urban areas cannot be achieved in the case of intercity analysis. On the other hand, the basic characteristic of the spatial distribution of cities, for example, that the distance between cities seems to increase with city size, provides a very important underlying basis for intercity transportation models. Distance or generalized transportation cost enters into almost all intercity transportation models. It not only stands for the cost of travel

219

in the conventional sense required by demand theory but also stands as a proxy for many other qualitative aspects of the interaction among cities of different sizes, aspects that would indeed be very hard to model analytically. As is described later, the stratification of intercity transportation analysis by distance is desirable and, in many cases, essential.

This chapter is concerned with the developments in intercity passenger transportation demand analysis. The next section contains a brief discussion of the characteristics of intercity transport demand. This is followed by a discussion of the major approaches to the analysis: the general multimodal intercity models and the mode-specific models. These are discussed in subsequent sections.

8.1 CHARACTERISTICS OF INTERCITY TRAVEL DEMAND

Intercity travel characteristics differ in many of their aspects from those of urban travel. These differences necessitate that intercity models be structured differently in terms of their trip purpose stratifications, temporal patterns, and even their behavioral postulates. The following aspects of intercity travel are important considerations for demand analysis.

Trip Purpose

Intercity travel is normally not undertaken for the same trip purposes common in urban travel: work and convenience shopping. The most common trip purposes in intercity travel are business, recreation, and personal business. Business travel has a purpose usually related to the traveler's work, but it is not work travel in the sense known in urban areas. Sales representatives' everyday travel, travel to business meetings, to company head offices, and on government business are the common purposes that are normally classified under business travel. Recreation travel is usually related to the traveler's vacation, although it could also be intended for other specific recreational activities such as sports events or political and religious rallies. The most common purpose under personal business travel is visiting friends and relatives, which is usually referred to as *vfr*.

The distinction among these three trip purposes is important in intercity demand analysis. At the least, the distinction between business and nonbusiness is essential, because the demands for these different trip purposes have different basic characteristics. Business travel can be expected to be cost inelastic because the trip cost is usually not paid out of a personal budget but out of a corporate budget of which it is usually a miniscule proportion. However, it can be expected to be travel time elastic and elastic with respect to other convenience-related attributes such as schedule frequency and reliability of service. Business travel can be expected to have a temporal pattern that is fairly uniform year round, except during major holidays and in situations where institutionalized vacations cause a drastic decrease in business activities during a specific period of the year, as is the case in France, for example, where little business traffic can be expected during the month of August.

Recreation travel can be expected to exhibit elasticity characteristics that are the reverse of those of business travel, i.e., to have higher cost elasticities and lower time and convenience elasticities. The reason for this is that the cost of a recreation trip is normally taken out of the personal budget of the traveler. This type of travel usually exhibits strongly peaked temporal patterns with peaks during vacation seasons and special recreational events. Similar characteristics can be expected of *vfr* travel. However, these two types of nonbusiness travel do have a distinguishing factor with regard to their elasticities. The transportation cost is normally only a proportion of the total cost of the recreational trip, but almost the total cost of a *vfr* business trip. Consequently, *vfr* travel can be expected to have higher transportation cost elasticities than recreation travel. On the other hand, where a choice of destination is available, a vacation traveler can conceivably change destinations if the transportation cost to one increases, a flexibility that the *vfr* traveler does not have. This would have the opposite effect on elasticities. The extent to which these two effects cancel out depends on the availability and practicality of destination choice and determines whether the combination of the two trip purposes into one nonbusiness travel is desirable.

Trip Length

The demands for intercity travel over different trip lengths exhibit fundamentally different characteristics. They have different elasticities to their various determinants and follow different temporal patterns. Consequently, the stratification by trip length is an essential disaggregation in intercity demand analysis.

In most intercity transportation demand analyses, it is customary to distinguish between two types of travel, long-haul and short-haul. One thousand kilometers is commonly taken as the boundary between them, although this number should not be considered a fixed threshold. The distinction is based on travel behavior and depends on the characteristics of the transportation system available.

Long-haul travel demand is usually less elastic with respect to the attributes of the transportation system than short-haul travel. One reason for this is the limited extent of choice in long-haul travel, for as the trip length increases, the number of alternatives (modes, routes, etc.) with comparable levels of service decreases. The extent to which this phenomenon occurs, of course, depends on the availability of transportation systems and on the geographic nature of the region in consideration.

In general, it is safe to assume that the demands for long-haul travel by the different modes are not related and can be handled separately. The reason for this is not only that separate markets may exist for each mode, which is hard to verify empirically anyway, but also that in long-haul analysis, the magnitude of the system at hand becomes very large, and the application of multimodal transport models is not practical.

Long-haul travel is not as sensitive to transportation attributes such as schedule frequency and modal access and egress times as is travel in the shorter haul. The reason for this is that the travel time is usually so large that the variations brought about by changes in these attributes are not very consequential. When dealing with long-haul traffic, it is usually sufficient to treat business travel on an annual basis and nonbusiness traffic on a seasonal basis.

Demand analysis for short-haul travel is normally more complex than for the longer hauls. In the short haul, there is often a choice of mode and a choice of route available to the traveler. In addition, the travel time is usually sufficiently small so that attributes such as frequency and access characteristics become important determinants. The analysis of short-haul travel demand approaches in its complexity that of urban travel. Indeed, when the distances between cities are as small as, say, 100 km, then travel behavior becomes similar to the urban case. There are many intercity corridors where commuting work trips are made or where multimodal transportation networks are so ubiquitous that a mode choice situation arises that is similar to the urban case and is analyzed using urban models.

Short-haul trips are made with larger frequencies than long-haul trips and exhibit weekly, and sometimes even daily, temporal patterns, so that analysis on an annual basis may not be sufficient.

Intercity Travel Behavior

Disaggregate studies of individual intercity trip makers are expensive and difficult to conduct. Consequently, not many such studies have been conducted, and intercity travel behavior remains not nearly as well understood as urban travel behavior. As mentioned earlier, the magnitude of the intercity system precludes the conduct of detailed investigations of trip behavior. As a result, most of the behavioral postulates used in constructing demand models are conjectural in nature and are validated empirically only in an aggregate fashion. The studies conducted by Lansing and Suits (1961) can perhaps be considered unique in that they provide individual trip-making information on intercity travelers. They have been extensively used in the development of intercity demand models.

As in urban transportation, the potential intercity traveler faces a series of choices concerning the various attributes of the trip (destination, route, time, etc.). In the demand analysis, it is implicitly assumed that this choice process is simultaneous and consequently most intercity models, whether they are mode-specific or multimodal, are simultaneous demand models.

8.2 APPROACHES TO INTERCITY DEMAND ANALYSIS

Two approaches have evolved for the analysis of intercity transport demand. One approach is multimodal in nature and recognizes that the demands for travel by different modes are related and should be analyzed simultaneously. The other is a mode-specific approach that is based on the proposition that the demands for travel by different modes are independent, or can be so assumed, and therefore analyzed separately. These two approaches are not alternatives but should be considered complementary. In general, long-distance travel is handled with the mode-specific approach, and short-haul travel, including urban corridor travel, with the multimodal approach. Even with this distinction in mind, the choice of approach should depend on the transportation system in question and be guided by the extent to which demands for different modes may be related. Naturally, the mode-specific approach has the advantages of simplicity and economy, but its adoption should be based on an assessment of the validity of the assumption of independent demands.

The general structures of the transport models used in both approaches are quite similar, differing only in the presence of the modal dimension in one and its absence in the other. The postulates behind the models are also similar: travel between two cities is considered in the aggregate to depend on the magnitude of the traffic-generating characteristics of the cities and on the characteristics of the transportation systems between them. Most intercity models treat two-way traffic between a pair of cities, but some do consider the differences between the trip-attracting and the trip-producing characteristics of cities and treat one-way traffic between city pairs.

The choice of socioeconomic variables in intercity models is also quite similar in both approaches. What differs, of course, is the vector of transportation variables. Not only is the difference in the vector mode-specific in one and multimodal in the other, but also the level of detail of the specification of the transportation system vector is considerably higher in the multimodal approach. This is because the multimodal approach is used in short-haul analysis where, as mentioned before, many more attributes of the transportation system need to be considered.

Multimodal Models of Intercity Travel

As discussed in an earlier section, there is a need to consider the cross-elasticities of the demand for travel by various modes when dealing with short-haul intercity travel or with other situations where it is believed that the demands for different modes are related. Consequently, the multimodal models of intercity travel postulate that the demand for travel between a pair of cities by a particular mode is a function of the socioeconomic characteristics of the cities and of the supply attributes of that mode plus those of all other modes available. As such, the multimodal model is a combined destination and mode choice model with an implicit assumption that these two choices are made simultaneously.

Mode-specific and mode-abstract models Intercity models can be either mode-specific or mode-abstract. In the first case, they would contain parameters or dummy variables that are specific to modes, whereas in the second case, their parameters would have no mode subscripts and they would not contain any mode-specific dummy variables. The advantage of the mode-specific models is that they can explain observed trip behavior better and allow for qualitative idiosyncrasies concerning mode choice that are otherwise unaccounted for in model variables. On the other hand, the mode-specific models cannot be used to forecast travel on novel modes and technologies not available at the time of their calibration, a disadvantage that the mode-abstract models circumvent.

Most of the intercity demand models used in short-haul travel demand analyses have been developed as variants of mode-abstract models, although the recent trend appears to be toward the realization that "unabstractness" is an important aspect of mode choice behavior and one that cannot be ignored in intercity travel modeling. The early and mid-sixties saw most of the developments in short-haul intercity models. These were times when considerable expectations existed for the development of novel transportation technologies that would necessitate the use of mode-abstract models for forecasting. The recent realizations that no drastically novel technologies appear forthcoming have reversed this trend and permitted the relaxation of the assumptions of mode abstractness in intercity models.

With regard to destination choice, most models are choice-abstract in the sense that they do not include mode- (or city-) specific parameters or dummy variables. However, calibrations of similar models in different intercity corridors show different parameter values, so that intercity travel behavior cannot be said to be choice-abstract in the general sense. Of course, this leads to the unfortunate result that models calibrated in one region cannot be used to forecast traffic in others, and the calibration exercises have to be repeated.

General model structure The general structure of most models is usually of the gravity or related type, where traffic is proportional to a product form of the demand variables for the city pair in question and of the supply variables of the transport system between them. In general, the model structure is as follows:

$$T_{ijm} = f(\mathbf{D}_i, \ \mathbf{D}_j, \ \mathbf{S}_m, \ \mathbf{S}_k \qquad \text{for all } k \neq m) \tag{8.1}$$

where T_{ijm} is the traffic between cities i and j using mode m, and $\mathbf{D}$ and $\mathbf{S}$ are vectors of demand and supply variables. The distinction between $\mathbf{S}_m$ and $\mathbf{S}_k$ is introduced to permit the flexibility of specifying the supply vectors differently for the mode chosen and for the competing modes.

The application of the general multimodal transport model in the form specified in Eq. (8.1) has been quite limited. The reason for this is that a model that includes the supply attributes of all modes available between city pairs invariably exhibits severe multicollinearity, which precludes the estimation of its parameters. Clearly, different as they may be, attributes such as travel time and travel cost will vary similarly from one city pair to another, and the variables will therefore be collinear. For this reason, simplified versions of the general model are specified where most of the cross-elasticities are assumed away and only one or two important ones are left. For example, a model for short-haul air travel demand would include only the cost of travel by an alternative mode such as rail, if available, or bus.

The most common version of the multimodal transport model used in short-haul intercity analysis is one where the demand for travel by a mode is assumed to be related only to one other mode, usually the one offering the best supply characteristics. This model, having been developed initially as a mode-abstract model aimed at forecasting traffic for novel technologies, is normally referred to as the *abstract mode model* and is discussed next.

The abstract mode model The *abstract mode model* developed by Quandt and Baumol (1966) represents the earliest attempt to apply a choice-abstract approach to modeling intercity transportation. Originally, the model was intended for use in the northeast corridor, a short-haul intercity corridor served by a number of transport modes, all with relatively dense networks. The model was later applied to other corridors, including the California corridor, and used in studies aimed at forecasting demand for novel technologies such as the short takeoff and landing aircraft (STOL) (see Chap. 9).

The abstract mode model simplifies the general multimodal transport model by specifying a demand function where for each of the supply variables, the values of only two modes are present: the mode in question and the mode offering the best value of the attribute in question.

The specification of the abstract mode model is one where the values of the supply attributes of each mode are defined in a relative manner according to the following transformation:

$$S^r_{km} = \frac{S_{km}}{S_{kb}} \qquad \text{for all } k, m \qquad (8.2)$$

where S^r_{km} is the value of supply variable k for mode m measured in relative terms, and S_{kb} is the best value of supply variable k among all available modes and is usually the maximum value when the attribute is measured on a utility scale (e.g., departure frequency) and the minimum value when it is measured on a disutility scale (e.g., travel time, cost).

In the earlier versions of the abstract mode model, the S_{kb} values were selected across modes. In other words, the base modes for different attributes could be different. This is illustrated by the following example. Consider three modes with the travel times and travel costs as given in Table 8.1. Mode 1 has the best (minimum) travel time, while mode 2 has the best travel cost. In constructing the relative values of the two variables, mode 1 is used as the base for travel time and mode 2 as the base for travel cost, giving the relative attribute values shown in the table.

Table 8.1

	Absolute values Mode			Relative values Mode		
	1	2	3	1	2	3
Time	2	4	5	1	2	2.5
Cost	4	2	5	2	1	2.5

This early version of the model was applied with alternative specifications of the demand and the supply variables. One form used in the analysis of California intercity traffic is given as an example:

$$T_{ijm} = \alpha_o P_i^{\alpha_1} P_j^{\alpha_2} Y_i^{\alpha_3} Y_j^{\alpha_4} M_i^{\alpha_5} M_j^{\alpha_6} (H_{ijm}^r)^{\beta_1} (H_{ijb})^{\beta_2} (C_{ijm}^r)^{\beta_3} (C_{ijm})^{\beta_4} \qquad (8.3)$$

where P = city population

Y = per capita income

M = percentage of total employment that is in manufacturing

H_{ijm}^r = travel time by mode, m relative to best travel time

H_{ijb} = best (shortest) travel time between i and j

C_{ijm}^r = travel cost by mode m relative to best cost

C_{ijb} = best travel cost between i and j

α, β = parameters

The population, income, and manufacturing employment variables are conventional demand variables for intercity models. It is expected a priori that the first two will have positive parameters and the third a negative parameter, since it is the nonmanufacturing employment activities that are likely to generate intercity travel.

The parameter estimates and their associated t values are given below:

	Constant	P_i	P_j	Y_i	Y_j	M_i	M_j	H^r	H_b	C^r	C_b
Parameter	−38.0	0.92	1.14	4.59	3.11	−0.73	−0.96	−2.01	−0.92	−3.15	−0.61
t Value	−1.1	4.4	6.2	1.3	1.0	−0.5	−0.1	−5.5	−0.6	−11.5	−0.7

Not all the parameter estimates are significant. It seems from such a calibration that population, relative time, and relative cost alone may account for most of the variations in the T_{ijm} values. It is interesting to note that the parameter values of the relative attribute variables are higher than those of the best attribute variables. Quandt and Baumol have shown this to be a requirement for the internal consistency of the model. It is also interesting to note the similarity between the parameter values for P_i and P_j. Most later modifications of the model incorporated these two variables into one population product variable P_iP_j. This combination is also justified by the observation that the amount of interaction, and consequently traffic, is proportional to the number of pairs of people in i and j, and therefore proportional to the population product.

Many other interesting variations of the abstract mode model have been attempted to test various hypotheses regarding the demand elasticities. Young (1969) and Quandt and Young (1969) compared various model specifications and concluded that the mode competition variables can be generalized so that not only the best attributes are included in the model, but that a weighted average of all attributes that are better than the one in question should be included. Another related generalization is to use a consistent mode as the base for computing the relative modal attributes. This is based on the hypothesis that it is unlikely that a potential traveler will compare the different attributes for different modes when making a modal choice decision, and therefore one base mode is used for the transformation of all attributes. Lave (1971) showed how this improves the quality of the model by applying this generalization and using scheduled air as the base for transforming the supply attributes. It has also been shown that "unabstractness" should be allowed for in the model by including dummy variables for modes. An example of this is the following model where it is postulated that the income elasticities of the demands for different modes are different:

$$T_{ijm} = \alpha_o(P_iP_j)^{\alpha_1}(H_{ijm}^r)^{\beta_1}(H_{ijb})^{\beta_2}(C_{ijm}^r)^{\beta_3}(C_{ijb})^{\beta_4}(F_{ijm}^r)^{\beta_5}Y_{ij}^{\alpha_2 + \alpha_3A_m + \alpha_4B_m} \quad (8.4)$$

where Y_{ij} = the weighted average per capita income in cities i and j

A_m = a dummy variable that takes on a value of 1 if mode m is an automobile, and 0 otherwise

B_m = a dummy variable that takes on a value of 1 if mode m is a bus, and 0 otherwise

and all other variables are as defined before. Note that in this specification, the income elasticity is $(\alpha_2 + \alpha_3)$ for automobile travel and $(\alpha_2 + \alpha_4)$ for bus travel. The income elasticity for any other mode is α_2. This will also be the elasticity for any new mode for which the model may be used to predict traffic. Thus, it can be seen that, while such a generalization may improve the model's capability as a demand analysis tool, it does limit its applicability as a forecasting tool.

Another aspect of "unabstractness" that appears to be important for intercity demand analysis is to account for the social and economic character of the intrinsic city characteristics that cannot be represented easily with conventional model variables.

The theory of intrinsic characteristics The basic hypothesis behind the theory of intrinsic characteristics is that the effects of the conventional demand variables on intercity travel vary with the economic and social characteristics of the city. These intrinsic characteristics cannot be represented adequately by quantitative variables.

This observation was first made by Lansing et al. (1961), who calibrated two simple gravity models, one for New York and one for Chicago, relating total traffic between each of these two cities and a selected number of cities. The two models were

For New York: $$T_j = P_j^{1.66} I_j^{1.23} D_j^{-0.21}$$

For Chicago: $$T_j = P_j^{1.38} I_j^{1.25} D_j^{-0.79}$$

where P_j is the population, I the per capita income, and D_j the distance.

The differences between most of the parameter values of the two models were significant. Lansing and Suits sought to explain these differences from a qualitative knowledge of the characteristics of the two cities. Most importantly was the difference in the distance D_j elasticity, showing travel to decline faster with distance from Chicago than from New York. This may be partly due to the relative geographic locations of the cities and to the fact that Chicago is more of a regional market center whereas New York is more of a national and international center. The same reasoning can be given for the fact that New York generates more trips per capita than Chicago. The income elasticities for both cities do not appear to be significantly different.

Similar observations were made in later studies of intercity travel. It appeared impossible to specify a general intercity demand model with quantitative variables that can account for all the differences in the trip production and attraction characteristics of cities.

To incorporate the notion of intrinsic city characteristics in the model estimation process, Quandt and Young (1969) suggested a modification to the conventional regression model by decomposing the error term into two additive components, one for intrinsic characteristics and one for random errors. Assuming the intrinsic components to be the same for all modes but different for each city pair, they developed a generalized least-squares estimation procedure. This procedure, as well as ordinary least squares, was applied to a model similar to that of Eq. (8.4).

The results showed that the generalized least-squares method produced parameter estimates that were vastly superior to those produced by the ordinary least-squares method. A number of interesting "intrinsic characteristics" values were derived for city pairs. Some of these values are shown in Table 8.2. Since the model used was multiplicative, a value of greater than 1 indicates that the city pair generates more traffic than would be expected from the demand and supply variables alone, and a value less than 1 indicates the opposite.

Table 8.2 Intrinsic characteristics of city pairs

Washington–New Haven	1.801
Washington–Boston	3.293
Washington–Trenton	1.741
Washington–Baltimore	3.919
Baltimore–Trenton	0.516
New Haven–New York	0.578

Source: Quandt and Young (1969).

Interesting observations can be made from figures such as these. For example, it is clear that Washington generates more traffic and Trenton and New Haven generate less traffic than would be estimated by a model that is applied indiscriminately to all city pairs.

The application of this generalized least-squares method to derive city pair–specific characteristics is interesting and reflects an intuitively appealing hypothesis. However, such a model modification, while improving the statistical fit significantly, does have two drawbacks. The first is that the model can no longer be used as it is for any city pairs other than those for which it was calibrated, and the second is that even for those city pairs, the model can be used for forecasting only if it can be assumed that the "intrinsic characteristics" of the cities involved will remain unchanged over the forecasting period.

Mode-Specific Analysis of Intercity Travel

The mode-specific approach to intercity travel demand analysis is based on the assumption that the demands for travel by different modes are independent and can be analyzed separately using mode-specific models. This assumption is quite a limiting one: the mode-specific approach is usually only valid in long-haul travel analysis and even there only when the characteristics of the transportation system are such that no significant competition is likely to exist between modes.

The most important developments in mode-specific intercity analysis are those in the demand for air travel. Not only does this stem from the importance of this mode in intercity travel, but also because the assumption of independence is best justified in the case of air travel. Particularly in long-haul travel and in terms of travel time, air is so far superior to other modes that it caters to a segment of the population for whom travel time is the most important supply attribute, and for whom other attributes such as cost, for which the air mode has no advantages, are less important relatively. On the other hand, the demand for travel by long-haul intercity bus is so much cheaper than the air mode that it caters to a segment of the population where cost is the most important supply attribute and for whom travel time can be sacrificed for this economy. It is customary to assume these two segments to be independent and to analyze their travel demands separately.

The independence assumption is only valid in the short run, and the mode-specific models cannot be used to analyze long-range time series travel data, nor can they be used for long-range forecasting. It is evident from the study of the histories of modal evolutions that even in long-haul travel shifts have occurred between modes and that there are long-run cross-elasticities. Figure 8.1 shows a trend in intercity travel in the United States which clearly indicates the shifts between the rail and air modes.

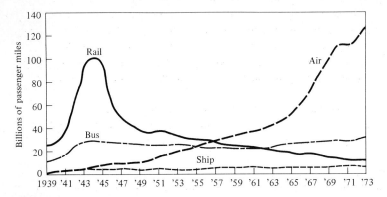

Figure 8.1 Historic development of intercity travel in the United States.

General form of the mode-specific model Mode-specific travel demand models are generally of the gravity type. The travel between a given city pair is a function of a product form of socioeconomic variables and supply variables. The mode-specific model is generally calibrated with cross-sectional traffic data where traffic flows between city pairs are taken as observations assumed to follow the same model and to estimate its parameters. The choice of socioeconomic and supply variables is usually quite simple for the mode-specific models, due to their approximate nature and limits, and does not warrant sophisticated specifications.

As mentioned earlier in this section, the mode-specific analysis is not suitable for the analysis of time series data. Lave (1971) has shown this by calibrating a number of mode-specific models for automobile, rail, and bus travel and by showing the weaknesses of these calibrations.

Intercity mode choice analysis It often arises in transportation planning that one is interested in the distribution of traffic within a given intercity corridor among available modes of transport. In short-haul corridors the choice is often binary, between highway and railroad transportation, while in longer distance corridors, the choice is between air, rail, and to a lesser degree highway transportation. In such situations it is customary to apply mode choice analyses much in the same way as they are applied in urban transportation, except for the changes in the specific demand and supply variables chosen.

Supply variables are commonly specified in a simple aggregate fashion using travel cost and travel time. In disaggregate analysis, socioeconomic characteristics of sampled households can be used as demand variables, and detailed supply characteristics such as access times and costs to the intercity modes can be used in the choice models. An interesting example of the use of disaggregate analysis in intercity mode choice is found in the work of Watson and Westin (1975), who calibrated a number of binary logit models on data for the Edinburgh-Glasgow corridor. The models were specified with four variables: travel time difference; travel cost difference; the difference between the number of segments (walking, waiting, etc.) associated with each mode; and the access walking time associated with the train mode. The models were used to estimate the choice between auto and rail travel in the corridor and were calibrated on disaggregate data stratified on the basis of residential location within the cities. Disaggregate models were shown to provide better predictive capabilities with at most as much data as aggregate models.

In another example of intercity mode choice analysis, Leake and Underwood (1978) compared a number of model formulations calibrated on data from two intercity corridors: London-Manchester and London-Glasgow. The models were used to predict choice between air and rail travel. From among the various specifications tested, including logit models, discrimination functions, and linear choice functions, they found that the linear choice functions provided at least equally good statistical results. Interestingly, in the choice between air and rail travel, time appeared to be the most significant variable.

8.3 SUMMARY

Intercity travel demand analysis can be conducted at two levels, mode-specific and multimodal. The former is suitable for long-haul transportation but can be quite limited in short-haul corridors where modes do interact and compete for traffic. The structure of models for multimodal intercity analysis is quite similar to that of the urban models: a series of choices of modes, destinations, and routes are identified. Usually these are modeled simultaneously, although it is common to focus on mode choice analysis of given corridors. Trip distribution analysis in intercity transportation runs into the limitation of the intrinsic characteristics of cities. This suggests that individual city pairs are to be treated separately.

Research in intercity passenger transportation demand analysis is not as advanced as in the urban case or as for commodity transportation. The only exception is perhaps the analysis of air travel demand. As an illustration of the trends in methodology and analysis of intercity transportation, we shall focus attention in the next chapter on air transport demand analysis.

REFERENCES

Baumol, W., and R. Quandt: The Demand for Abstract Modes: Theory and Measurement, *Journal of Regional Science,* vol. 6, no. 2, pp. 13–26, 1966.

Lancaster, K. J.: A New Approach to Consumer Theory, *J. Polit. Econ.,* vol. 14, pp. 132–157, 1966.

Lansing, J. B., et al.: An Analysis of Interurban Air Travel, *Quart. J. Econ.,* vol. 75, no. 1, pp. 87–95, 1961.

Lave, L.: The Demand for Intercity Passenger Transportation, *J. Region. Sci.,* vol. 12, no. 1, pp. 71–84, 1971.

Leake, G. R., and J. R. Underwood: Comparison of Inter-city Bi-modal Split Models, *Transp. Plan. Tech.,* vol. 5, pp. 55–69, 1979.

Mathematica, Inc.: *Studies in Travel Demand,* vols. 1–4, Princeton, N. J., 1965.

Quandt, R., and K. H. Young: Cross-sectional Travel Demand Models: Estimates and Tests, *J. Region, Sci.,* vol. 9, pp. 201–214, 1969.

Watson, P. L., and R. B. Westin: Transferability of Disaggregate Mode Choice Models, *Region. Sci. Econ.,* vol. 5, 1975.

Young, K. H.: An Abstract Mode Approach to the Demand for Travel, *Transp. Res.,* vol. 3, pp. 443–461, 1969.

NINE

THE DEMAND FOR AIR TRANSPORTATION

Demand analysis for air transportation need not always be performed within the multimodal intercity context discussed in the previous chapter. The technical and economic characteristics of the air transportation system in many ways make air transportation a special mode. Indeed, some of these characteristics have led to the advancement of air transportation demand analysis beyond the level achieved for intercity transportation in general.

Air transportation attracts considerable attention in transportation and economic planning, despite its relatively minor role in the total transportation sector, for by its nature, air transportation is mostly a system that is interstate and international. This leads to considerable involvement of governmental agencies in its operation and regulation. It is often the subject of political negotiations among nations and is sometimes an instrument of a nation's foreign policy.

The regulation of air transportation has contributed to the advancement of demand analysis in two ways: first, because the development and implementation of regulatory policies require elaborate demand analyses in order to assess the social and economic impacts of these policies; and, second, because the implementation of regulation necessitates that the regulatory agencies monitor the operation of the air transportation system very closely and require its operators to supply data on their operation. This means that data normally available on air transportation exceed in scope and quality those that can be obtained for other modes. This in turn encourages and facilitates the conduct of demand analysis and leads to the advancement of its methodology.

There are long-distance transport situations where the multimodal context becomes irrelevant and where the aircraft becomes the only feasible mode of transport. The specific trip length at which this occurs varies depending on the nature of the system at hand and on the extent to which other modes of transportation can compete in terms of level of service with the air mode. For example, for a 200-km trip across a body of water, there would be little serious competition from other modes; on the other hand, it would take up to 600 or 700 km over land before such a competition could be assumed away.

Air transportation requires large infrastructures in the form of airport and aircraft systems and depends on a technology with a rather long lead time for development and implementation. Consequently, the forecasting of air transportation requirements has become a relatively important activity in economic planning, and hence the need to focus attention on this mode.

This chapter deals with the methodology for air transportation demand analysis. It begins with a brief discussion of the more important characteristics of air transportation and with the measures used to describe air transportation activity. This is followed by a discussion of the two approaches used to analyze air travel demand: the macro approach and the micro approach. The modeling of air travel demand using these two approaches is then discussed in the subsequent sections.

9.1 MEASURE OF AIR TRAVEL ACTIVITY

A measure of air travel activity is the dependent variable in air travel demand model, which is normally the variable of interest in forecasting. There are three important measures that can be used to describe the level and nature of air travel activity. These measures can be stratified according to many characteristics depending on the purpose of the analysis and on the nature of the forecasting problem at hand. The three are as follows:

1. *Passenger volume* is the total number of passenger trips in the system in question during a given period of time. When used as a systemwide level indicator of traffic, passenger volume is often measured in terms of enplanements. For airport planning, on the other hand, total volume consisting of enplanements and deplanements is used as the indicator of the passenger traffic handled by an airport system.
2. *Aircraft operations* are the total number of aircraft departures on revenue-generating flights, often referred to as *revenue departures*. It should be noted that aircraft operations can serve as an indicator of supply as well as traffic, for when combined with a description of the aircraft fleet, the number of aircraft departures can be converted to a number of available seat departures.
3. *Passenger-kilometers (or passenger-miles)* are the number of passenger trips, each multiplied by its length. This is the most general measure of travel activities and of the output of the air transport system, for it not only indicates the passenger volume but the distances traveled, and thus the total amount of

transportation performed. This measure is normally compiled only for fare-paying passengers and is referred to as *revenue passenger-kilometers* (RPK) or *revenue passenger-miles* (RPM).

These three measures of air travel activity can be compiled and stratified in a variety of ways, depending on the nature of the analysis for which they are used. The more important stratifiers used in air travel demand analysis are the following:

1. *Trip purpose.* As with other transportation demand analyses, trip purpose is perhaps the most important characteristic of passenger traffic volume, since as discussed earlier, the demand for travel is derived from the demand for the activity at the destination, represented by trip purpose. The distinction between business and nonbusiness traffic is the most common classification for demand analysis. Nonbusiness traffic is sometimes further stratified into vacation, and visiting friends and relatives (vfr) traffic. The importance of this further stratification stems from the fact that the cost of air travel constitutes only a portion of a vacation trip, whereas it may be the major component of the cost of a trip with a vfr purpose.

    Despite its importance, trip purpose is often not taken into consideration in air travel demand analysis. The reason for this is the unavailability of trip purpose information in the data normally compiled for air transportation. As with other modes, trip purpose information can only be obtained by passenger interviews, which are costly and not easily conducted. Whenever trip purpose information is available, even approximately, it should be taken into consideration and used to stratify demand analyses.

2. *Temporal stratifications.* Air travel statistics can be stratified temporally in many ways depending on the purpose of the analysis. Thus for long-range forecasting and for systemwide analyses, it may be sufficient to consider annual traffic. Seasonal or monthly traffic stratifications are sometimes important considerations, particularly in markets where significant variations in demand exist, such as vacation travel markets where the demand is significantly higher during the summer than other seasons of the year. Daily and hourly stratifications are important when the interest is in airport planning. Demand analyses on a daily or hourly basis are normally not performed because they would require large amounts of data and would be too complex in nature. Consequently, daily and hourly variation factors are usually applied to the results of seasonal or annual models.

3. *Origin-destination stratification.* Analysis of the demand for air travel by origin and destination is often required for the planning of the air transport network and for airport planning. Therefore, the stratification of air travel statistics by origin and destination is important. Trip tables similar to those used in urban passenger transportation are usually constructed. These are used in calibrating distribution-type demand models applied to air transportation.

An important distinction when stratifying travel statistics in this fashion should be made between origin-destination volumes and link volumes. Often, available statistics relate to the latter. The two are generally not the same, because flow on any link may include traffic that is transferring from other parts of the network. Demand analysis is more appropriately performed on the basis of origin-destination traffic.

4. *Length of haul stratifications.* Because air travel over differing lengths of haul exhibits differing demand characteristics, it is useful to stratify air travel statistics on the basis of length of haul. Long and short haul are the two most commonly used stratifications, in which short haul is defined by trip lengths under 700 to 1000 km. The importance of this distinction in air travel demand analysis is that, in the short haul, multimodal analysis may be required, whereas, for long-haul traffic, models dealing only with air travel are sufficient.

5. *Stratification by type of service.* This stratification is useful for airport planning studies. The most commonly used classes in this stratification are air carrier, charter, third level (or commuter), general aviation, and military traffic. Clearly, different demand models may be suitable for each of these categories.

6. *Other stratificiations.* It is sometimes useful to stratify air travel statistics further according to characteristics that are relevant for special analyses. In some airport planning situations, for example, an important distinction is made between international and domestic traffic, with separate demand models used for each of these categories. Another stratification that is useful for demand analyses in some markets is by fare type. This is useful in designing fare structures and forecasting the traffic that would result from various fare packages.

9.2 APPROACHES TO DEMAND ANALYSIS

The analysis of air transportation demand follows in general the approach used for intercity transportation. In this, models of air travel demand usually have the same structure consisting of a vector of socioeconomic variables and a vector of system supply, or level of service variables. Microeconomic demand theory and the theory of consumer behavior underlie air transportation demand analysis in the same way they do other transportation demand analyses. However, the special characteristics of the air mode impose further limitations on the application of these theories. For instance, the air traveler does not have as wide a choice as in urban transportation, for the air mode is clearly not as ubiquitous as the ground modes and not as amenable to the continuous variable modeling as they are. Furthermore, the air mode is not as amenable to abstract mode characterization as other ground transport modes are, which places a further limitation on the applicability of choice models.

Most air transportation demand analysis can be classified into either of two groups, macroanalysis and microanalysis. Macroanalysis is concerned with systemwide air transportation activities and deals with traffic models that are not highly stratified. Microanalysis is concerned with more specific origin-destination flow and with highly stratified measures of traffic activities. These two types of analysis have different structures and are conducted for different purposes; they are discussed separately in the following sections.

9.3 MACROANALYSIS OF AIR TRAVEL DEMAND

Macroanalysis of air travel demand is intended for forecasting overall activity levels in air transportation. It deals with systemwide measures of air travel and is not normally concerned with specific airport analyses or with origin-destination flows. It is usually performed on an annual or seasonal basis and is not concerned with daily or hourly variations or peaking characteristics.

It is aggregate in nature in that it does not take into consideration the characteristics of particular links or modes in a network, or of a particular traveler or group of travelers. Consequently, only aggregate measures of socioeconomic activity and of the air transportation service can be used in macromodels. Examples of aggregate macromodels of air travel demand are those used by the U.S. Civil Aeronautics Board (CAB), for analyzing total U.S. domestic RPMs, or by the International Air Transport Association (IATA) for analyzing total RPK in markets such as the North Atlantic or the Pacific. Examples of these models are shown later in this section.

Macromodels of Demand

The general structure of a macromodel of air travel demand is based on economic demand theory and on the theory of consumer behavior. It consists of two sets of variables: a vector of socioeconomic activity levels for the area of concern and a vector of air transport system attributes. A typical model would then have the following general formulation:

$$T = T(\mathbf{D}, \mathbf{S}) \tag{9.1}$$

where T = the measure of traffic
   $\mathbf{D}$ = a vector of socioeconomic activity levels that determine the demand for air travel
   $\mathbf{S}$ = a vector of transport supply variables

In macromodels, only general systemwide indicators are normally used. Typically T would be represented by the RPK or RPM of travel, total enplanements, or total operations. It can be measured either on a per capita basis or as a total number for the whole population. In the latter case, care should be taken to include in the vector of socioeconomic activity levels **D**, a variable representing the magnitude of the total potential market, such as population. The normal time period for which these models are typically constructed is a year. Due to their general nature, these macromodels are not suitable for analysis of highly stratified measures of traffic. There are situations, however, where analysis of seasonal traffic using macromodels is desirable. In many air travel markets, different air traffic service characteristics (fares, capacities) are offered during different seasons of the year (e.g., peak and off-peak seasons). These differing levels of service evolve as a response to different seasonal demand levels. Clearly, demand analysis on a seasonal basis is desirable in such markets. An alternative way of dealing with seasonal variations in demand is to consider the different seasons as alternatives, from among which a potential traveler chooses one, and to apply a choice model [see Kanafani et al. (1974)]. Although they are aggregate in nature, macromodels should be stratified by trip purpose whenever data permit. This will considerably improve the logical and statistical strengths of the models and will facilitate the choice of appropriate socioeconomic variables.

Choice of socioeconomic variables The purpose of vector **D** of socioeconomic variables is to include in the model a set of descriptors of the nature and level of the socioeconomic activities that are likely to generate the demand for air travel. As discussed in Chap. 2, if it were possible to measure *demand,* then it would suffice to include that variable in the model. The socioeconomic variables included in **D** are used as proxies for demand, and their choice should be based on their logical relations to it.

A large number of socioeconomic variables suggest themselves for inclusion in macromodels of air travel demand. The general rules for choice of variables that are discussed in earlier chapters do apply in this case. Logical content and the availability of suitable data are the major considerations. Macromodels are general in nature and normally do not warrant sophisticated articulations of socioeconomic variables for demand. The variables most suitable for inclusion in macromodels of air travel demand are discussed below:

1. *Population.* This variable is usually included in order to account for the size of the potential market for air travel. In most cases, population is a variable that changes slowly; consequently, it is not always necessary to include it in the model. This is particularly the case when a macromodel is to be used for forecasting traffic in the same region, in which case the population effect can be subsumed in the model constants. Alternatively, per capita traffic can be modeled directly, thus eliminating the need for the direct inclusion of the population variable.

   When included in a macromodel of air travel, population would be expected to have a positive elasticity in the neighborhood of $+2$. However, because population varies smoothly with time in most regions, it often happens that due to collinearity problems, a distortion is obtained. This is demonstrated in the next section where models with various specifications of the population variables are discussed.

2. *Income.* According to demand theory, income is an essential variable in any demand function, because it represents the consumer's purchasing power and habits. In transportation demand models, income is not only an indicator of a traveler's ability to purchase air transportation, but also of the level of economic activity that in turn generates a demand for air travel. This is particularly true in aggregate macromodels where individual travelers are not treated separately.

There are many forms in which income can be included in a macromodel of air travel demand. All the measures are aggregate in nature although some of them do attempt to account for income distribution among the population of interest. The appropriate specification of the income variable should in principle be based on the trip purpose considered. The reason for this is that while for nonbusiness travel income can be considered a measure of the ability of potential travelers to purchase air transportation, for business travel income is used as an indicator of the level of economic activities that generate demand for air travel, because the price of a business trip is often not paid by the traveler (but by the employer) and does not figure into the traveler's personal budget.

The following are the different variables that can be used to measure income for macromodels:

Total income This is the crudest measure and consists of the total of all the personal incomes within the region of interest. It should not be confused with regional or national income, which is discussed separately later on.

Disposable income Based on the argument that income after taxes is a better measure of the demand for travel, disposable income is often a better variable than total income. As with total income, disposable income when used on a total regional basis will result in confounding the effects of population and of income changes, and to use population and income in the same model is likely to result in a collinearity problem. Consequently, it is best to use an average figure, such as the per capita disposable income or the median disposable income. Disposable income typically has a stronger influence on the demand for air travel than population does. Consequently, the elasticity associated with this variable is usually larger than that associated with total income and is typically in the range 2.0 to 3.0, not including long-term effects.

Discretionary income Nonbusiness air travel is mostly associated with a recreational trip purpose and is not an essential consumption item. This means that the demand for nonbusiness travel is likely to be dependent on a traveler's discretionary, rather than disposable, income. The only difficulty in using per capita discretionary income is that data on this variable are not as commonly available from conventional data sources.

Permanent income The permanent income hypothesis argues that consumption of air travel in a particular year is not only dependent on income in that year but also on past incomes. The basis for this argument is that a person's expectation of income changes will affect that person's demands. Permanent income is then defined at any point in time t by

$$I_t' = \sum_x \lambda_x (1 - \lambda_x)^x I_{t-x} \qquad 0 \le \lambda < 1 \qquad (9.2)$$

where I' is permanent income, I_x is income in year x, and λ_x is referred to as the *expectation coefficient*. λ may be assumed constant or may vary in a decaying fashion over time. Many air travel macromodels have a permanent income variable included in them which has the effect of improving explanatory power. The elasticity of demand with respect to permanent income is referred to as the *long-term income elasticity*, because it indicates the total effect over a number of years of an income change. It is normally higher than the short-term elasticity. It should be noted that in some macromodels the permanent income effect is incorporated in variables other than income but is related to it. For example, many models include consumption variables instead of income variables. In these models, it is possible to apply the permanent income formulation using Eq. (9.2) formulated in terms of a consumption variable.

Income distribution The use of aggregate income averages in demand models results in models that are unable to respond to changes in income distribution which may leave the average unchanged. Ideally, it would be desirable to characterize the income distribution in a transportation demand model. As seen earlier, however, this is not easy, particularly when dealing with aggregate macromodels.

There is no sample measure that can satisfactorily account for income distribution. One variable that has been commonly used is the proportion of the population with income above a particular level. However, this single variable cannot account for all the characteristics of the income distribution. Another specification is to construct an index based on a weighting of trip-making rates for different population classes stratified by income and other demographic characteristics, much in the same manner in which trip generation cross-classification analysis is done in urban transportation. Such indexes are complex and certainly hard, if not impossible, to forecast, which greatly limits their usefulness in macroanalysis. Again, since macromodels are general in nature, it does not seem to be worthwhile to spend much effort on articulating complex income distribution variables for them. What can be done instead is to monitor the calibrations of these models over long periods of time and to watch for any changes in income elasticities that may be attributed to observed changes in income distributions.

Personal consumption It is often found that variables which describe personal consumption are statistically more significant in macromodels than income variables. This may be an indication that decisions to purchase air travel, at least for nonbusiness purposes, are made after savings decisions are made. Consequently, the demand for air travel will be determined by personal disposable income less savings, which is equivalent to personal consumption expenditures.

This variable is most suitable for macromodels of nonbusiness travel demand, where having an elasticity larger than that of income would be expected. If it is possible to isolate recreation expenditures or travel expenditures from personal consumption statistics, then these would be expected to be even more significant variables in nonbusiness travel models.

Regional product Whereas personal income and consumption are suitable explanatory variables for nonbusiness air travel demand, they do not represent the levels of economic activity that generate demand for business travel. This demand depends on the total wealth of the region and on the amounts of business activities.These can be measured by a variety of monetary variables, the most important of which is the total regional product. When the analysis deals with the air transport system of a nation, then the gross national product (GNP) may be used as an explanatory variable, and when it deals with only a part of a nation, then the gross regional product (GRP) may be more appropriate.

Other monetary variables When using a variable such as GNP in an analysis involving time series data, it is essential to deflate it into real terms. However, even when that is done, it may still be necessary to include other variables in the model that will account for short-term fluctuations in interest rates and in the availability of money for business activities. One such variable is called the *velocity of money* and is defined by $V = GNP/M$, where GNP is measured in current dollars and M is the total money supply. This variable has been found to improve goodness of fit in some macromodels [see Aureille (1975)]. Another variable can be constructed as the ratio of long and short term interest rates. This variable may be used to account for an effect similar to that of permanent income, namely the effects of expectations on business travel demand.

Business indexes Business travel demand has also been shown to depend on indexes of business activity that are normally derived from economic planning. In the United States, the *composite business index* is a measure of the confidence of the business community in economic development and has been shown to explain significantly the development of business traffic [Kanafani et al. (1974)]. The difficulty with using complex indexes of economic activity as explanatory variables in macromodels of business traffic is that these indexes are not easily forecast. Consequently, they may be of value in constructing demand analysis models and used to explain historic traffic developments but are of little value in forecasting models.

Investment and trade These two variables can be used to measure the level of business activities taking place between two regions. Therefore, they are useful for macromodels that are used to analyze business travel demand in specific markets. For example, in a model of business travel across the North Atlantic, annual investment between the United States and western Europe was found to be a significant explanatory variable [see Kanafani et al. (1974)].

Choice of transport supply variables The purpose of the vector of transport supply variables is to represent in the traffic model those attributes of the transportation system that will affect the extent to which air travel demand materializes into traffic volumes. For macromodels of air travel demand, no detailed articulations of level of service variables are usually needed, because they are not warranted due to the aggregate nature of these models. This aggregate nature makes the specification of appropriate supply variables difficult. Consider, for example, a macromodel dealing with the total passenger-kilometers in domestic traffic in the United States. The air transportation system in question is the total network of the country and includes thousands of links and modes. How should the price of air travel be represented in such a model, what other supply characteristics are relevant, and what variables should be used to represent them?

What is needed in a macromodel is a set of supply variables including only those that are likely to affect the evolution of the overall level of travel in the system and that are likely to undergo sufficient change to warrant their consideration as independent variables. Naturally, the most important variable is one describing the price of air transportation in the system. Others may be included to account for the effect of the price of travel by competitive modes, when appropriate, and of the speed of air travel. How some of the more important supply variables are constructed for macromodels is discussed in the following paragraphs.

Price of travel An aggregate measure of the price of air travel is required for a macromodel. The variable that directly suggests itself, and the one used most commonly in macroanalysis, is the average price. This average is usually constructed by weighing the traffic on the various routes in the system by the fares (per passenger or per passenger-kilometer) on these routes. When each route in the system has a number of different fares, as is normally the case with first-class, economy, and promotional fares, then the weighted average fare on each route is used in the construction of the system average. For example, consider a system with n routes, with each route having k fare types with fare levels F_{ik}. Let T_{ik} be the traffic on route i using fare type k, and T_i the total traffic on route i. Then the average fare per passenger on route i will be

$$F_{i.} = \frac{\sum_k T_{ik} F_{ik}}{T_i} \tag{9.3}$$

and the average fare in the system will be

$$F_{..} = \frac{\sum_i T_i F_{i.}}{\sum_i T_i} \tag{9.4}$$

A variable that is commonly used in this regard is the yield which measures the net revenue to the airline, such as in cents per passenger-kilometer. The yield represents a weighted average of the fares paid on all sectors served by an airline. It does differ from the average fare in two ways. First, it is net of the commissions, normally about 10 percent paid to travel agents. Second, it does include the effect of prorating ticket revenues between carriers which together share segments of an air trip from origin to destination.

Clearly, it is necessary to consider fares on a per mile basis in order to make the averaging valid over a number of links with different lengths. Consequently, $F_{..}$ is usually measured as average fare per passenger-kilometer or passenger-mile.

The use of systemwide average fare as a surrogate for the price of travel normally prevents the strict interpretation of the macromodel as a true demand model for travel and may result in a biased estimate of the price elasticity of demand. Links with different lengths will normally have different per kilometer fares, the longer links having the relatively lower fares. To see this, consider, for example, two links of different lengths with the longer one having a lower per kilometer fare. If the demand on the longer route is more income-elastic, for instance, than the demand on the shorter route link, then an increase in income will result in an increase in traffic that is larger on the longer link than on the shorter. This will consequently cause a decrease in the average per-kilometer price. In estimating the parameters of the macromodel, biased price and income parameters will result, since a part of the increase in traffic will be attributed to the average price change, even though no air fares have changed. Strictly, the average price is valid only when the demand functions on all the links are identical and when the per-kilometer fares on all links are the same. Neither of these two conditions is met in practice.

Because of such problems one finds a wide range (-0.5 to -4.0) in price elasticities derived from macromodels. Consequently, the price elasticity should be used only to assess the traffic impact of air fare changes if it can be assumed that changes in trip lengths, or shifts in demand functions in parts of the network, do not occur.

Attempts to overcome the shortcomings of average fare for use in macro-models have included the construction of price indices based on fares on important links in the system. One such index used by Verleger (1972) is described in a subsequent section. Clearly, while indexes may not suffer the shortcomings of average fare, they rarely can be constructed to be truly representative of the price of air travel in the aggregate. Average fares are consequently more common in macromodels.

Speed of air travel For macromodels that deal with a number of air travel links, the speed is normally used as a proxy for travel time. This variable has been useful in explaining the evolution of systemwide air travel over periods of time, during which significant changes in speed did occur.

Other supply variables that have been used in macromodels include the index for accident rate to account for the safety of air travel. However, because air safety changes very slowly over time, it would require a model calibration period that is very long in order to detect the impact of such a variable on demand. In one example, Lave (1971) estimated significant accident elasticities of -0.1014, but using as a model calibration period the years 1929–1966. It is hard to believe that one macromodel of air travel demand can be valid over such a long period.

Calibration of Macromodels

As with other demand analyses, the calibration of a macromodel for air travel demand consists of three steps: (1) the specification of a model structure, (2) the selection of a data base, and (3) the estimation and evaluation of parameters. Macromodels deal with a total air transportation system, not with particular city pairs. Consequently, it is not possible to obtain cross-sectional data upon which to base these models, because such data would require the partitioning of a system into components, each of which is to constitute an observation. Therefore, macromodels are based on time series data and are constructed and calibrated to explain the historic evolution of air traffic.

A macromodel is calibrated on the basis of correlation analysis of the historic development of a number of factors associated with traffic and of traffic itself. However, a logical construct should always underlie such analysis, and a conceptual model of demand and of supply should precede the specific selection and specification of variables for the vectors **D** and **S** to be included in the model. Although correlation analysis permits investigating many variables and combinations of variables in constructing a model, the adoption of a logical structure will greatly facilitate this process. Careful choice of variables for inclusion in the vectors **D** and **S** should be exercised, particularly taking into consideration trip purpose when data permit this stratification.

As with other demand analyses, particularly for intercity travel, most macro-models of air travel demand have a multiplicative constant elasticity specification. While this specification possesses conceptual and statistical advantages, it does have an inherent weakness that should be carefully considered. This weakness results from the constant elasticity structure, which implies that the effect of the growth in demand on traffic growth has always been and will remain the same. The constant elasticity model cannot be used to forecast for more than a very limited number of years at a time. When applied to forecasting, most constant elasticity models result in such traffic volumes that are simply unrealistic given the expected population and the potential of intercity travel by all modes. Figure 9.1 shows the actual trend of air traffic volume in the California corridor

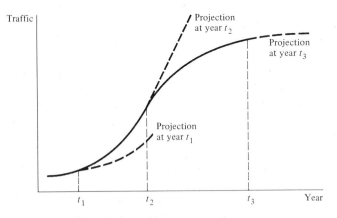

Figure 9.1 Traffic projections with constant growth rates.

compared with a constant elasticity prediction. The results are clear: if the model is estimated during a high growth rate period, then future traffic will be overestimated and vice versa. If one has to use a macromodel with constant elasticities, then such a model should be recalibrated as often as practicable in order to ensure that a correction in the growth rates of air traffic is made, especially as air travel takes on a larger and larger share of total intercity travel. Alternatively, model specifications can be altered to permit variable elasticities and to allow for a leveling off of air traffic growth as related to the growth in the demand variables. Such alternative model structures are not yet commonly used and still require considerable research.

In addition to the choice of demand and supply variables for a macromodel, there are many basic structural forms that can be selected. These include (1) the simple time series model, (2) the partial adjustment model, (3) the permanent income model, and (4) other time-lagged effects models. The forms of these models and examples of them are discussed in the next section.

The next step in the calibration of the macromodel is the selection of an appropriate data base. This includes the specification of the geographic limits of the system to be modeled and the selection of the number of years of time series data to be used. Naturally, both of these choices depend on data availability. In the choice of the geographic system limits, it is important to ensure that the resulting system constitutes a coherent set in terms of traffic rather than in other political or geographic terms. For example, in considering domestic air traffic in the United States, it makes as much sense to include traffic between the United States and points such as Montreal and Toronto as it does to include traffic between continental United States and Alaska.

In time series analysis for macromodel calibration, the statistical observation is usually taken as 1 year of traffic. Because it is essential that the socioeconomic variables included in the model do undergo change from one observation to another, it is not practical to be a macromodel on any smaller time period. Furthermore, most socioeconomic variable statistics are available on an annual basis. The important decision that the analyst has to make is with regard to the choice of the number of years to be needed for the calibration. Clearly, statistical resolution can be increased by increasing the number of years of observations. On the other hand, as the time period of the analysis extends, it becomes doubtful whether one model, especially a constant elasticity model, can be valid for the whole period. Models are commonly used that are based on calibration periods extending over 30 years. In general, it is not desirable to construct one single model to cover such a long period. Nor is the use of dummy variables for periods within a long calibration based recommended, for it forces the same model structure over the total period anyway. Of course, the length of the calibration data period is governed by the number of variables included in a model. In general, choosing a period in such a way that about 10 degrees of freedom remain for parameter estimation should be sufficient.

Time series models In order to discuss the time series models and their calibration, the following notation is adopted:

T_t = the traffic volume in year t
D_{kt} = the value of the kth demand variable in year t
S_{mt} = the value of the mth supply variable in year t
K = the total number of demand variables; $k = 1, 2, \ldots, K$
M = the total number of supply variables; $m = 1, 2, \ldots, M$
α_k = the parameter for the kth demand variable
β_m = the parameter for the mth supply variable

A simple time series model This model relates traffic in year t to the demand and supply variables for that year and does not take into consideration any lagged time effects of changes in the variables or in the demand itself. In its most general form, the multiplicative constant elasticity form, the model is as follows:

$$T_t = C \prod_k D_{kt}^{\alpha_k} \prod_m S_{mt}^{\beta_m} \qquad (9.5)$$

where C is a constant term. The parameters are estimated using the maximum likelihood estimation technique which is suitable due to the nonlinear form of the model. Alternatively, and in order to permit the use of multiple linear regression techniques, the model can be linearized by the logarithm transformation. Thus, if the variables are denoted by their logarithms, then the model will be as follows:

$$T_t' = C' + \sum_k \alpha_k D_{kt}' + \sum_m \beta_m S_{mt}' \qquad (9.6)$$

In this model, the parameter values α_k and β_m represent the elasticities of demand to the respective variables, and the (') indicates a logarithm.

Due to its simplicity, this model is most commonly used in macroanalysis of air travel demand. It is, however, a weak model because it does not account for the dynamic nature of the evolution of demand as the other models do.

An example of the simple time series model is one that has been calibrated by Lave (1971) for total domestic U.S. travel measured in revenue passenger miles (RPM). Lave used data over the period 1929–1966 and calibrated the following multiplicative model, shown here in linearized form:

$$RPM_t = -2.34 + 3.03\text{pop} + 1.90DI - 3.22F - 0.01\text{Acc}$$

where RPM_t stands for the domestic U.S. revenue passenger miles in year t; pop is total U.S. population; DI is disposable income; F is average fare per passenger mile; and Acc is the fatality rate of aircraft accidents, all variables measured for year t. The model has a high coefficient of multiple determination, $R^2 = 0.99$, and all the parameter estimates are significant. The model shows a fare elasticity of -3.22 which is slightly on the high side. However, because fare is measured by the aggregate average fare per passenger-mile in all U.S. domestic air travel, its absolute value should not be taken very seriously, especially since the calibration period extends over a long span of time during which significant changes in the structure of the air network have taken place.

The population and disposable income variables deserve some discussion. The indicated elasticities of $+3.03$ and $+1.90$ for population and disposable income, respectively, indicate that a growth in population would have a larger impact on demand than an equal growth in income. Whether the two variables are kept separate, as they are in this model, or combined into one per capita disposable income variable is an important difference and would result in two distinct model specifications. In the first case, as with this model the two variables are allowed to have two different impacts on demand. If the population elasticity is larger than the income elasticity, as is the case in this example, then this would imply that an increase in population concomitant with a similar decrease in income would still result in an increase in demand despite the resulting drop in per capita income. When the two variables are combined by dividing income by population, then the resulting positive elasticity of the per capita variable implies that income and population have equal but opposite elasticities, which in turn implies that an increase in population would result in an increase in demand only if there is a concomitant increase in income that is at least equal to it. Therefore, these two specifications are fundamentally different and should not be used exchangeably. It is hard to determine which is more suitable for this particular model. The data base extending over the period 1929–1966 suggests the possibility that air travel underwent phenomenal growth not necessarily due to the increase in disposable income. However, whether population growth is truly responsible for this or whether it was simply a trend best related to time remains a question. Some light can be cast on this question by including time as a variable in the model and studying the effect of this on the elasticity estimates. The use of linear time in a logarithmic model is purely due to the inability to explain the meaning of logarithmic time variable. Lave's calibration with linear time included resulted in the following model:

$$\text{RPM}'_t = -10.9 - 5.01\text{pop}' + 1.23\text{DI}' - 2.00F' - 0.04\text{Acc}' + 0.07t$$

Note that the fact that time is introduced in its linear form means that 0.07 coefficient of this variable cannot be interpreted as an elasticity. What it means is that when everything else is constant, traffic grows at 7 percent annually. Symbol t stands for all factors that vary with time, that affect growth in air traffic, and that are not included in other model variables. The most notable effect of the introduction of t is the change in population elasticity from $+3.03$ to -5.01. The constant term also increased from -2.34 to $+10.9$, indicating that a linear function of time dwarfs the effects of the other variables on the growth of air traffic. This casts some doubt on the validity of the remaining parameter values, especially when one considers the potentially high multicollinearity with the time variables. Nonetheless, the population and income parameters in this model mean that a 10 percent increase in population would have to be associated with approximately a 40 percent increase in income in order to cause an increase in demand, which is rather unlikely.

These results point to the weakness of the simple time series model, especially calibrated over such a long period of time. It does not take into consideration the long-term versus short-term effects of changes in variables, nor the dynamic nature of demand growth. The inclusion of a time variable obfuscates the interpretation of the model as a demand model. It is tantamount to projection by extrapolation over time and has no behavioral meaning and should consequently be avoided.

A simple time series model calibrated over a shorter period of time, say 10 years, should preferably include the per capita income variable rather than the two separate population and income variables because it is more likely that per capita income changes will cause a change in air travel demand than simply the change in population and income. Furthermore, over such a short calibration period population may not change significantly to add much resolution to the demand model, and the effect of the total size of the market can then be taken up in the constant term.

Another example of simple time series modeling is the application of such a model to international air travel demand. Behbehani and Kanafani (1980) obtained the following models using data for 1970–1976. International markets were identified using fairly common geographic groupings and the following models were obtained:

Europe–Central America:

$$T_t = e^{-4.92}(\text{income})_t^{1.05}(\text{trade})_t^{0.755}e^{-0.373(\text{yield})_t}$$

North America–South Pacific:

$$T_t = e^{-12.6}(\text{income})_t^{2.99}(\text{trade})_t^{0.2}e^{-0.005(\text{fare})_t}$$

where income is a weighted average of the per capita income in selected countries in the market, trade is the total flow of trade in dollars between countries on both ends of the market, and yield is the overall market average yield.

Note the mixed multiplicative and exponential specification of these models. In the first, yield is specified exponentially and the same is true of the fare in the second. This specification, reminiscent of the supply variable specifications in trip distribution models, implies a variable elasticity that is proportional to the value of the variable. In the first model, yield was selected as a price variable because it was not possible to find a representative fare for the market. Europe–Central America is a market where there is good proportion of non-business traffic and many types of promotional fares. On the other hand, the North America–South Pacific market (dominated by the United States–Australia flows) is more homogeneous and a representative fare (in this case Los Angeles–Sydney) was found to be a suitable price variable.

The partial adjustment model This model is based on the hypothesis that the complete adjustment of the level of traffic which takes place due to changes in factors influencing the demand and supply of travel requires more than one time period to materialize. Consequently, the level of traffic materializing in a year t represents only a portion of the potential demand for that year. When formulated in terms of the "desired demand" or "desired level of traffic" T_t^*, the partial adjustment model will look exactly like the simple time series model:

$$T_t^* = C \prod_k D_{kt}^{\alpha_k} \prod_m S_{mt}^{\beta_m} \tag{9.7}$$

T_t^* is the desired traffic level, and the partial adjustment hypothesis states that not all of this quantity will in fact materialize in year t. The hypothesis is stated as follows:

$$\frac{T_t}{T_{t-1}} = \left(\frac{T_t^*}{T_{t-1}}\right)^\mu, \qquad 0 < \mu \le 1 \tag{9.8}$$

where μ is a coefficient that measures the proportion of the total adjustment in demand that actually materializes in the observed traffic level T_t in year t. By combining the two formulas the partial adjustment model can be written in terms of observed traffic linearized with the logarithmic transformations as follows:

$$T_t' = \mu C' + \sum_k \mu \alpha_k D_{kt}' + \sum_m \mu \beta_m S_{mt}' + (1 - \mu)T_{t-1}' \qquad (9.9)$$

The important difference between the two formulations is that α and β represent long-run elasticities, whereas $\mu \alpha$ and $\mu \beta$ represent the smaller short-run elasticities. In its form given in Eq. (9.9), the partial adjustment model is calibrated in the same manner as the simple time series model, the only difference being the inclusion of the additional variable T_{t-1}.

The partial adjustment model has a behavioral appeal, for it is quite likely that the potential change in demand which is due to a change in the socioeconomic environment takes more that 1 year to materialize. The positive value of $(1 - \mu)$ indicates that a "healthy" market will respond faster to such changes than a weaker one, which is appealing and corroborated by the history of traffic evolution. Care should be exercised when using a partial adjustment model in that the value of μ is likely to vary considerably over time, particularly if the economic environment oscillates between periods of strong growth and others of stagnation or depression.

Due to its advantages, the partial adjustment model is commonly used in macroanalysis of air travel demand. An example of its application is the following model calibrated by the U.S. CAB for the purpose of forecasting total U.S. domestic passenger-miles:

$$\text{RPM}_t' = -2.12 - 0.81F_t' + 1.07\left(\frac{\text{DI}}{\text{pop}}\right)_t' + 0.67\text{RPM}_{t-1}' \qquad (9.10)$$

The parameter estimates were based on a data base covering the period 1946–1966. The short-run and long-run income elasticities are $+1.07$ and $+3.24$, respectively. The short-run and long-run price elasticities are $–0.81$ and $–2.45$, respectively. It is interesting to note that while the demand appears to be price-inelastic in the short run, the long-run effect of a continuous change in price indicates an elasticity of demand. There is little correspondence between the parameters of this model and those of the simple time series model discussed earlier. Given the choice between the two model forms, it should be clear that this one is to be preferred.

Another example of a partial adjustment model is one that was calibrated by Young (1972) on the basis of data from 1937 to 1966 on the total number of air passenger trips per capita in the United States:

$$T_t' = -1.98 + 1.04I_t' - 1.59F_t' - 0.52H_t' + 0.67T_{t-1}$$

where T is the per capita air trips in year t, I is the per capita disposable income, F is the average fare *per trip*, and H is the average travel time per trip. The last two variables are rather aggregate. Fare is constructed by dividing the total airline revenues by the total number of passengers, and T by dividing the average trip length by air travel speed. It is interesting, however, to note the similar value of μ of 0.33 to that of the CAB model as well as the similar values of the income parameters. The difference in fare elasticity is probably due to the way in which the F is constructed in this model and to the possible existence of multicollinearity between it and H.

The permanent income model This model is based on the hypothesis that permanent income rather than current income is a more appropriate factor in the demand model. The argument is that a person's consumption in year t is not only a function of income in that year, but depends on past income and expected future income. The most common formulation of permanent income is the following:

$$I_t^* = \sum_\theta \omega_\theta I_{t-\theta} \qquad (9.11)$$

where I_t^* is the permanent income in year t, and ω_θ is a coefficient applied to the lagged income value $I_{t-\theta}$. A simple formulation of ω_θ is

$$\omega_\theta = \lambda (1 - \lambda)^\theta \qquad 0 < \lambda \le 1 \qquad (9.12)$$

where $<$ is assumed constant and referred to as an expectation coefficient. More elaborate formulations assume that ω_θ decreases according to some specified decay function in such a way that it vanishes after a specified number of time periods.

The specification of the permanent income model is the same as the simple time series model, except that I_t^* is used instead of current income I_t. In the most commonly used log-linear form, the permanent income model is specified as follows:

$$T_t' = C' + \sum_{k \ne I} \alpha_k D_{kt}' + \alpha_I I_t'^* + \sum_m \beta_m S_m' \qquad (9.13)$$

where
$\qquad I$ = the income variable
$\qquad D_{kt}$ for all $k \ne I$ = all other demand variables in year t
$\qquad I^*$ = permanent income defined according to a transformation such as in Eq. (9.11)

and all other variables are as previously defined, with the (') indicating logarithms.

It should be noted that the coefficient of the permanent income variable is a permanent income elasticity. It is sometimes referred to as a long-term income elasticity because it describes the effect of an income change over a period of time extending over a number of years. This should not be confused with the long-run elasticity as obtained in the partial adjustment model due to the time-lagged effect of demand changes. The current income elasticity depends on the form of the coefficient ω_θ. In the special case where ω_θ is according to Eq. (9.12), the current income elasticity is given by $\lambda \alpha_I$.

Since the values of the parameters of ω, e.g., λ, are not known, it is necessary to try alternative values in the estimation of model parameters. Consequently, the estimation of a permanent income model requires an iterative process.

An example of such a model applied to air transportation demand is the one calibrated by Young (1972) with the same data base and the same basic model specification as his partial adjustment model. Using the specification of ω_θ that is given in Eq. (9.12), Young obtained the following result:

$$T_t' = -25.89 + 4.42I_t'^* - 2.90F_t' - 0.86H_t'$$

where the variables are as defined earlier. The value of λ that was found to produce the best model fit was 0.30. This means that while the permanent, or long-term, income elasticity is $+4.42$, the current, or short-term, income elasticity is only $+1.33$. It is interesting to note that the current income elasticity is similar in magnitude to the one obtained in the current income, partial adjustment model.

Another formulation of a permanent income model is one where the hypothesis is applied to an income-related variable rather than to income itself, e.g., personal consumption expenditures. As discussed earlier, the specification in terms of a consumption, rather than income, variable is based on the argument that savings decisions precede trip-making decisions, at least for nonbusiness travel. One such model was used by the Douglas Aircraft Company [see Aureille (1975)] to study total domestic U.S. revenue passenger-miles, using a data base extending over the period 1946–1968. The Douglas model had a log-linear form as follows:

$$\text{RPM}_t' = -2.16 + 2.04\text{PCE}_t'^* - 1.35F_t' + 1.06\text{VEL}_t' + 0.09\text{INT}_t' + 0.82\text{TL}_t'$$

where PCE* is a time-lagged per capita personal consumption expenditures variable defined according to the permanent income hypothesis; F is the average fare defined by constant 1958 yields in cents per mile; VEL is a velocity of money variable defined by the ratio of the GNP to the money supply in year t; INT is the ratio between long-term and short-term interest rates; and TL is the average trip length. Note that this model has two types of demand variables: personal consumption expenditures presumably stands for nonbusiness travel demand, and the monetary variables VEL and INT stand for business travel demand. The addition of TL is an attempt to overcome some of the deficiencies in F_t as an aggregate measure of the price of travel. Its positive coefficient is as expected since an increase in average trip length will lead to an increase in RPM even if nothing else, including the number of trips, changed.

In this model, the PCE_t^* variable is constructed using a ω_θ coefficient that is assumed to decay according to a truncated geometric progression and to vanish in 5 years:

$$\omega_\theta = k\rho^\theta \qquad 0 < \rho < 1 \tag{9.14}$$

where k is defined such that

$$\sum_{\theta=0}^{5} \omega_\theta = 1 \tag{9.15}$$

Using an iterative solution technique, an optimal value of $\rho = 0.4$ was arrived at, resulting in the following:

$$\text{PCE}_t^* = 0.60\text{PCE}_t + 0.24\text{PCE}_{t-1} + 0.10\text{PCE}_{t-2} + 0.04\text{PCE}_{t-3}$$
$$+ 0.014\text{PCE}_{t-4} + 0.006\text{PCE}_{t-5}$$

This result indicates that the permanent income elasticity is 2.04, which is the PCE_t^* parameter in the model; that an income change will have an effect spread over a 5-year period; and that during the first year only, 60 percent of that effect materializes. The current, or short-term, income elasticity according to this model is then $0.60 \times 2.04 = 1.22$.

A general time series model This model combines both the permanent income and the partial adjustment hypotheses, and thereby attempts to account for the dynamic aspects of demand changes fully. The model includes the T_{t-1} variable as well as an income, or related, variable constructed according to the permanent income hypothesis. In log-linear form, the general time series model is as follows:

$$T_t' = \mu C + \mu \sum_{k \neq I} \alpha_k D_{kt}' + \mu \alpha_I I_t'^* + \mu \sum_m \beta_m S_m' + (1 - \mu)T_{t-1}' \tag{9.16}$$

Note that since this model has a permanent income variable, its estimation requires an iterative procedure and that the resulting parameter estimates represent short-run elasticities.

An example of the general time series model is the one calibrated by Young (1972) using the same data base as the two previous models:

$$T_t' = -9.79 + 2.01 I_t'^* - 1.71 F_t' - 0.59 H_t' + 0.49 T_{t-1}'$$

With an optimal value of $\lambda = 0.30$ and an estimated value of $\mu = 0.51$, these parameter estimates imply a short-run price elasticity of -1.71 and a short-run current income elasticity of 0.6. The long-run elasticities are -3.35 for price and 3.94 for permanent income.

In most statistical comparisons, it is normally found that the general time series model is superior to the other three. However, the advantage of this model over the partial adjustment model may not warrant the added complexity in estimation resulting from the need for an iterative solution. Consequently, the partial adjustment model is more commonly used for time series analysis.

In a recent study of nonbusiness air travel demands in the United States, Kanafani (1980) estimated four models using data from 1967 to 1974. The data were in the form of annual nonbusiness revenue passenger-miles. The four models estimated are

I. $\text{RPM}_t = \text{RE}_t^{2.296} P_t^{-0.405}$

II. $\text{RPM}_t = \text{RE}_t^{1.062} P_t^{-0.09} \text{RPM}_{t-1}^{0.396}$

III. $\text{RPM}_t = \overline{\text{RE}}_t^{2.032} P_t^{-0.899}$

IV. $\text{RPM}_t = \overline{\text{RE}}_t^{1.554} P_t^{-0.579} \text{RPM}_{t-1}^{0.170}$

where RE_t = per capita recreation expenditures in year t

$\quad P_t$ = average per mile domestic fare in constant 1967 dollars

$\quad \overline{\text{RE}}_t$ = permanent measure of per capita recreation expenditures.

These results illustrate the possible differences between long-run and short-run elasticities of demand. The reader can check the following:

1. *Short-run.* Price elasticity = -0.579; current recreation expenditure elasticity = 0.466; permanent recreation expenditure elasticity = 1.554
2. *Long-run.* Price elasticity = -0.697; recreation expenditure elasticity = 1.872.

The long-run elasticities of demand are larger than the short-run and indicate that a lagged time series model may indeed be a better forecasting tool. The F statistics given for the four models also illustrate how the fit is improved with the assumption of lagged effects.

It should be noted that these models represent only a sample of the types of time series models that can be used to analyze air traffic data. There are many methods of specifying lagged effects in a demand model. Box and Jenkins (1970) have illustrated the power of time series analysis as a tool for describing and projecting trends such as traffic. It is important to remember, however, that time series analysis alone is not adequate for explaining demand. The logical structure of the models used should always be the primary guide in building demand models.

Variable elasticity models In order to adapt the macromodel for traffic forecasting, it is necessary to consider model specifications where elasticities are not constant. As mentioned earlier, models with variable elasticities are not very common yet but are the subject of research. In one attempt to calibrate a variable elasticity model, Kanafani et al. (1974) postulated that the price-elasticity of demand varies with the price itself. In other words, if the average price of travel decreases substantially, then it may be expected that the demand will become less price-elastic, since the price will become a smaller percentage of a traveler's total expenditures. Observations in many markets seem to bear this postulate out. The model claibrated on the basis of this hypothesis was a macromodel for nonbusiness air trips across the North Atlantic. The model used is

$$\frac{T_t}{T_b} = k \left(\frac{\text{RE}_t}{\text{RE}_b}\right)^\alpha \left(\frac{e^{F_t}}{e^{F_b}}\right)^\beta \qquad (9.17)$$

where T_t is the total nonbusiness air trips in year t; T_b is the trip during a selected base year; RE is per capita recreation expenditures in constant dollars; F is the average fare paid by nonbusiness travelers. The reason for dividing by the traffic and variables of a base year is simply to allow a straightforward interpretation of the constant term k which is now dimensionless and represents the proportion of the base year's traffic that is estimated by the model. This specification also normalizes the model for the size of the potential market, although it does not allow for a change in that size. This is not critical since the calibration period 1964–1973 is not very long. The estimated model is

$$\frac{T_t}{T_b} = 0.938 \left(\frac{\text{RE}_t}{\text{RE}_b}\right)^{2.205} \left(\frac{e^{F_t}}{e^{F_b}}\right)^{-0.00434}$$

with all the estimates having t values upward of 10. This result indicates that with an average fare of \$230 the price elasticity will be unity (0.00434×230); and with an average fare of \$300, it will be -1.30. The actual average fares were \$241 in 1970 and \$215 in 1973.

The variable elasticity model has the appealing characteristics of being a more useful policy tool than the constant elasticity model. The implications of a model such as this one, for example, are that below an average fare of \$230 the demand is relatively inelastic, and above it, it is elastic. This can be of use in developing a pricing policy.

9.4 MICROANALYSIS OF AIR TRAVEL DEMAND

While macromodels of air travel demand can be useful in explaining the historic evolution of traffic volumes, they have shortcomings that stem primarily from their highly aggregate nature and that preclude their effective use as policy tools. For example, the common U.S. domestic RPM model can hardly be used to develop a pricing policy unless it is known that the demand functions underlying the traffic in all parts of the system are all identical. In fact, it is known that they are not. Furthermore, macromodels can only be calibrated with time series data that are usually not easily available. Microanalysis of air travel demand, performed on a more finely stratified basis, is necessary as a planning and policy analysis tool.

The most common stratification in microanalysis is by origin and destination. The resulting models are called *city-pair models*. Other types of microanalyses include the airport-specific demand models and the application of choice models to the study of air traveler route choice, choice of airline, fare type, and airport choice in urban areas served by multiple airport systems.

City-Pair Models of Air Travel Demand

The general structure of most city pair models is of the gravity type. The demand model for traffic between two cities takes on the form of a product of the socioeconomic variables of the two cities and of the level of service characteristics of the air transport system connecting them:

$$T_{ij} = T(\mathbf{D}_i, \mathbf{D}_j, \mathbf{S}_{ij}) \tag{9.18}$$

where T_{ij} is the air traffic between cities i and j, $\mathbf{D}$ is a city-specific vector of socioeconomic activity levels, and $\mathbf{S}$ is a vector transport supply characteristic.

When T_{ij} is measured by the total two-way traffic between the cities i and j, then the two vectors $\mathbf{D}_i$ and $\mathbf{D}_j$ are identical and no distinction is made between an origin city and a destination city. Alternatively, T_{ij} can be measured by traffic originating in i and destined to j, in which case separate socioeconomic variables may be included in $\mathbf{D}_i$ and $\mathbf{D}_j$ on the grounds that the determinants of the generation and the attraction of travel demand may be different. This distinction is sometimes made only by allowing the variables to have different parameter values for the origin and the destination city while using the same socioeconomic variables for both.

Socioeconomic characteristics of the two cities involved are usually sufficient, and it is not normally necessary to include, as one does in urban trip distribution models, characteritics of all cities in the system. The argument for this is that in air transportation there is little destination competition and it can be assumed that the traffic between any two cities depends only on their characteristics. However, it is important to remember when using city-pair models of this type for forecasting or for policy analysis that this is simply an assumption. The analyst using such models should always watch for structural changes in the system which may affect the city-pair travel demand and give rise to a destination choice situation, in which case a destination choice distribution model rather than a simple city-pair model may be more appropriate. For example, consider the air traffic between San Francisco and New York, a considerable amount of which is traffic transferring to international flights out of New York. Now, if international services were increased significantly out of, say, Boston, then the travelers from San Francisco could choose between the two destinations. Clearly in a situation such as this, the traffic between a city pair, San Francisco–New York, is not independent of the system characteristics of a third city, Boston. In other words, there is a cross-elasticity of the San Francisco–New York demand with respect to the supply characteristics of San Francisco–Boston air service.

Choice of socioeconomic variables The choice of socioeconomic variables for city-pair models is substantially more straightforward than for general macromodels. Although still aggregate in nature in that they do not consider individual demand functions, city-pair models have a level of aggregation much smaller than macromodels, and their variables are defined on a city basis.

1. *Population.* The population of the total metropolitan area served by an airport, rather than just the city, in question should be used.

2. *Employment.* The total employment in a metropolitan area is a measure of the level of economic activities that generate travel or attract travel. In some cases, employment is stratified by manufacturing and nonmanufacturing for better resolution in the demand model.
3. *Disposable income.* This variable is usually measured on a per capita basis. When income distribution information is available, this is often combined into a weighted population-income index and used as a measure of "potential" in the gravity model.

Choice of supply variables Supply variables can also be specified for city-pair models without much aggregation. Since the characteristics of the air transport system connecting any two cities are well known, it is possible to specify supply variables with greater detail and thereby to permit in the city-pair model a thorough treatment of the effects of level of service characteristics on demand. The supply variables commonly used in city-pair models are the following:

1. *Air fare.* This is usually an average for all the fare types available between any two cities. It is based on the fare for the most direct routing.
2. *Travel time.* Here again, this is measured on the most direct route available. Travel time will permit the separation between money and time costs of air travel.
3. *Distance.* Air travel distance is often used as a proxy for travel time or for fares if these latter are proportional to distance. Distance should preferably not be used together with the other two variables as this will lead to serious multicollinearity problems.
4. *Frequency of service.* Here is a variable that describes the convenience of travel between the two cities in question. The larger the number of flights the more convenient are the departure and arrival times likely to be. This variable is measured by nonstop, or direct, flights only. In using time series to calibrate city-pair models the danger of simultaneous equation bias is present and should be tested for. This is because schedule frequency is likely to depend on the factors that affect demand and cannot be treated strictly as an exogenous variable.
5. *Other level of service attributes.* These include flight schedules, routings, and equipment types.

Calibration of city-pair models City-pair models can be calibrated with both cross-sectional and time series data. In cross-sectional calibration, the same model is assumed to hold for a number of different city pairs, and the data for these city pairs during one time period are used for parameter estimation. While this estimation method avoids the difficulties of time series analysis, it does imply the strong assumption that the same model can be used for all the city pairs in the sample. Different city pairs have different demand functions and the aggregation of city pairs for cross-sectional analysis should be done very carefully.

For use of cross-sectional data in model calibration, two ways of aggregating city pairs have been done in practice. One is to aggregate on the basis of distance, thus keeping the long-haul, medium-haul, and short-haul city pairs separate. Another is on the basis of the sizes of the market, keeping major city pairs and low volume city pairs separate. It is clear from the discussions of the previous chapters that travel demand between city pairs of different economic size and character may well be different. The stratification on the basis of the magnitude of the traffic volume is an attempt to construct different demand functions for these possibly different demands. Furthermore, the stratification on the basis of distance is important on more than one count. First, it is known that short-haul demand for air travel may have cross-elasticities to the characteristics of other modes of travel. Second, it is not likely that the price elasticities of demand will be the same regardless of the length of the trip. When the fare is about $25 such as between Los Angeles and San Francisco, one would expect the fare elasticity to be much smaller than with a $200 fare such as between Los Angeles and New York, as indeed has been demonstrated in many studies. To demonstrate the impact of this type of aggregation on model estimates, a simple gravity model calibrated by the U.S. CAB and recalibrated by Verleger (1972) is used as an example.

The model, originally calibrated by the CAB in 1966, is of the simple gravity type:

$$T_{ij} = M_{ij}^{\alpha_1} \; C_{ij}^{\alpha_2} \; P_{ij}^{\beta_1} \; E_{ij}^{\beta_2} \; D_{ij}^{\beta_3} \qquad (9.19)$$

where T_{ij} = total air traffic between cities i and j
M_{ij} = product of aggregate income in i and j
C_{ij} = number of phone calls between the two cities
P_{ij} = price averaged over first class and coach
E_{ij} = elapsed flying time
D_{ij} = distance between the cities

The use of distance, flying time, and air fare all in the same model probably causes some multicollinearity and should not be common practice in calibrating this sort of model. Also, the use of phone calls as a socioeconomic variable to measure the interaction between two cities cannot be easily justified. Both phone calls and airline traffic may be considered endogenous variables depending on the same or similar socioeconomic variables. Nonetheless, this particular model is chosen because it has been calibrated with different levels of city-pair aggregation and it presents a chance to study the effect of these aggregations on parameter estimates.

The first calibration performed by the CAB was on the basis of 441 city pairs ranging in distance from approximately 100 miles to nearly 2700 miles, and including markets with annual traffic ranging from under 10,000 to over 150,000 passengers. The model was then recalibrated by Verleger (1972) for city pairs in successive 500-mile distance intervals. The results from these calibrations are shown in Table 9.1.

Table 9.1 Verleger's cross-sectional results listed by distance

Distance (miles)	Constant	Price	Income	Calls	Distance	Time	R^2	OBS	SSR*
All city pairs	8.92	− 0.92	0.14	0.52	− 0.32	− 0.40	0.72	441	101.15
	(4.21)	(3.42)	(4.62)	(15.44)	(3.96)	(3.45)			
0 to 500	5.64	− 1.03	0.12	0.54	0.03	0.21	0.65	100	18.01
	(1.84)	(2.84)	(2.92)	(8.88)	(0.15)	(0.79)			
500 to 1000	9.32	− 0.91	0.18	0.47	− 0.20	− 0.79	0.70	129	19.74
	(1.90)	(1.55)	(3.59)	(8.60)	(0.81)	(3.71)			
1000 to 1500	11.17	− 2.08	− 0.32	0.99	0.35	− 0.80	0.67	91	22.29
	(1.67)	(2.59)	(2.53)	(7.98)	(0.69)	(0.44)			
1500 to 2000	7.33	1.03	0.35	0.18	− 1.24	− 1.60	0.64	61	13.66
	(0.73)	(0.99)	(3.22)	(1.76)	(1.57)	(3.26)			
Over 2000	23.09	− 1.62	− 0.02	0.70	1.31	− 3.77	0.83	60	10.16
	(2.80)	(2.20)	(0.14)	(6.21)	(1.24)	(6.01)			

* Sum of squared residuals.
Note: t statistics in parentheses.
Source: Verleger (1972).

Table 9.1 shows that the model parameters are subject to wide variations. The price elasticity varies from − 0.91 to − 2.08, income elasticities vary from 0.12 to 0.35, and there are even some negative income elasticities probably due to the multicollinearity present in the model. A Chow F test has been used to determine that these differences are significant. This demonstrates that the demand functions are not identical for all city pairs in all distance categories. This would be expected a priori on the argument that for the short-haul city pairs closer than, say 300 miles, the demand function for air travel cannot be assumed independent from the characteristics of potentially competing ground transport modes.

The second stratification applied to the basic model of Eq. (9.19) was on the basis of traffic volume. The 441 city pairs were grouped into two groups, one including the full sample and the other including only those city pairs with traffic levels above 50,000 annual passengers. The results of this stratification are shown in Table 9.2. Here again, it is clear that the two models are significantly different, indicating that major and minor city pairs cannot be modeled with the same cross-sectional demand models.

Table 9.2

	All city pairs	Major city pairs
Constant	8.94	12.93
Price	− 0.92	− 1.74
Income	0.14	0.04
Calls	0.52	0.52
Distance	− 0.32	− 0.15
Time	− 0.4	2.074
R^2	0.72	0.65

These results should not be used to conclude that time series analysis is the only means of calibrating valid city-pair demand models. Indeed, when properly stratified and when not applied indiscriminately to all city pairs in a system, cross-sectional models probably provide the strongest tool for this type of demand analysis.

However, cross-sectional models of air travel demand for city pairs in a short-haul market may have to take into account other modes of transportation. The demand for air travel between city pairs in the short haul may have to be analyzed with the general intercity models of the previous chapter, because substantial intermodal cross-elasticities may exist. What modeling approach is best suited for a particular set of city pairs should be decided according to the basis of the characteristics of the total transportation system. Thus, in the northeast corridor of the United States, considerable modal interaction exists and the corridor is best analyzed with the multimodal intercity models. On the other hand, other corridors with similar geographic character but with a different transportation system do not require multimodal analysis. An example of this is the San Francisco–Los Angeles corridor in California, where air travel demand models have been successfully applied with no cross-elasticity components [see Kanafani and Fan (1974)].

City-pair models can also be calibrated using time series data. In this case, a demand model is calibrated for a particular city pair using data extending over a time period. This type of analysis has two advantages. One is that it permits the construction of a demand function specific to one city pair and eliminates the aggregation necessary for cross-sectional analysis. The other is that time series analysis provides models that are more suitable for forecasting.

Disaggregated Models of Air Travel Demand

A model calibrated on the basis of individual trip data is referred to as a *disaggregated model*. The advantage of such a model is that when calibrated with cross-sectional data, it permits the study of contemporaneous interdependencies that may exist between the demands of different individuals, or groups, within the same environment. Most disaggregate demand models are constructed in a manner similar manner to urban passenger trip generation models, in the sense that the variable of interest is the number of air trips made regardless of the destination. This is due to the type of survey data available. The construction of a disaggregated origin-destination model for air travel requires a rather large amount of interview information and is consequently not normally practiced. The trip generation type of demand model implies, as it does in the urban case, that the transport supply variables have to be system aggregate variables because not all the characteristics of the trip (destination, route, etc.) are known.

The general form of the disaggregated travel demand model is as follows:

$$T_i' = C' + \sum_k \alpha_k D_{ik}' + \sum_m \beta_m S_m' \qquad (9.20)$$

where T_i is the number of air trips undertaken by individual i, D_{ik} is the value of the kth socioeconomic variable for individual i, and the rest of the variables are as defined earlier. Note the absence of the i subscript for the supply variable S_m.

One important hypothesis that this type of model can be used to test is the so-called demonstration effect hypothesis, which states that the demand of a particular income group may depend on the demands of other income groups, especially those close to it. It is tested by defining the following quantity:

$$T^{**} = \frac{1}{2}(T_{i+1} + T_{i-1}) \qquad (9.21)$$

as the *reference demand*, where $i + 1$ and $i - 1$ refer to the income groups immediately above and below i. The reference demand variable is then added to the model of Eq. (9.20), so that

$$T_i' = C' + \sum_k \alpha_k D_{ik}' + \sum_m \beta_m S_m' + \delta T_i'^{**} \qquad (9.22)$$

where δ is expected to have a positive value indicating the encouraging influence of the demonstration effect on demand. The test of the hypothesis is then performed by testing for the significance of δ and by evaluating the demonstration effect model relative to the simple model of Eq. (9.20).

An example of this test is the one performed by Young (1972) using data from a travel survey conducted by Lansing (1961) (See Chap. 8). Young used the following model:

$$T_k' = a + bI_k' + cT_k'^{**} \qquad (9.23)$$

where k refers to income groups rather than individuals, an aggregation made necessary by the data available for the test; a, b, and c are parameters; and the variables are taken in logarithmic form. Young calibrated the model with and without the T^{**} variable and obtained the following results:

The simple model: $T_k' = -13.26 + 1.62\,I_k'$

$$R^2 = 0.89$$

The demonstration effect model:

$$T_k' = -10.18 + 1.26I_k' + 0.38T_k'**$$

$$R^2 = 0.94$$

The estimate of c had a t statistic of 4.8 indicating its significance. The demonstration effect model appears to be slightly superior to the simple model because it explains a larger proportion of the variations, indicating that the hypothesis may be a valid one. It is interesting to note that the introduction of the reference demand variable causes an expected reduction in the income elasticity.

Airport-Specific Demand Analysis

In airport planning, a need often arises for forecasting the traffic volume to be handled by the airport in question. In the early stages of planning and feasibility analysis, only forecasts of total traffic, without much stratification by trip characteristics, are normally used. To provide the capability for forecasting airport-specific demand analysis, airport-specific demand models can be quite useful in providing these types of forecasts.

Two types of airport traffic demand models are common in practice. The first is aggregate in nature and is concerned with the total traffic volume, and the second is more detailed and is concerned with traffic distribution among destinations. Clearly the second model provides for a better forecasting capability and, unlike the first, can account for changes that may occur at other locations in the system and that may affect the traffic at the airport in question.

The general form of the aggregate airport demand model is quite similar to the systemwide macromodel discussed earlier in this chapter. Socioeconomic variables are introduced in the same fashion as in the macromodel, only here they refer to the metropolitan area served by the airport in question. The transportation supply variables, mostly the air fare, are also averaged over all the links emanating from the airport. An example of this model is one that was constructed for St. Louis, Missouri, and subsequently used in preparing a traffic forecast for that region [Haney (1975)]:

$$T_t' = -0.177 + 2.46P_t' + 1.63E_t' + 0.87I_t' - 0.80F_t'$$

where T is the total annual traffic measured in enplanements, P is the population of the region, E is the total employment, I is the per capita income, and F is the average fare per mile for all services to the airport, and where all variables are taken in their logarithmic form. It should be clear that such a model can only be calibrated with time series data. Calibrated over a period of 20 years, the model shows a high explanatory power with an $R^2 = 0.99$. Most airport forecasts used in airport planning are based on models of this type, although there are other techniques currently. This type of model is very common and is used in most airport planning studies.

The destination-stratified model takes on a gravity form in most applications. However, since the model always deals with one particular airport, the gravity structure is slightly modified in that one of its two components, that of the airport in question, is constant. Otherwise, this model does not differ much from the usual city-pair model. A typical origin-destination model applied to a single airport is one that was constructed by Howry (1969) for the Cleveland Hopkins Airport:

$$T'_{ij} = a + b(P'_i P'_j) + c S'_{ij} \tag{9.24}$$

where T_{ij} represents the annual air traffic between i (in this case Cleveland) and j; P is population; and S is the supply variable, which Howry varied in three separate calibrations using distance in the first, travel time in the second, and air fare in the third; and where all variables are in logarithmic form. The use of the population product as a variable with one parameter, rather than allowing P_i and P_j to have separate parameters, is a simplification, but one that is based on experience with earlier models showing both population figures to have similar parameter values. It is certainly valid in this case since two-way traffic is used and no distinction is made between production and attraction of trips.

Howry used this model for two purposes, the first was to study the stability of the parameters over the period 1960–1965. The second was to compare this simple gravity formulation with a multimodal abstract mode model using the same data base, plus information on other modes. Howry showed in that comparison that it was not possible to improve on the simple gravity model and that the abstract mode model, while statistically significant, did not exhibit a higher explanatory power.

Air Travel Choice Models

Choice models are applicable in air travel demand analysis when the situation involves a passenger choosing from among alternative services. The situations that arise most commonly and that lend themselves to choice analysis include route choice, airport choice, airline choice, and fare-type choice.

Route choice occurs when the air network is not highly connected so that there are not direct links connecting all city pairs. In this case, different routings may exist between a given city pair. A choice may be made if, for example, one routing offers a higher schedule frequency and the other a shorter travel time.

Airport choice occurs in metropolitan areas that are served by more than one airport. In such areas, it may happen that a traveler can choose between a closer airport with access travel advantages and a farther airport with schedule frequency advantages. Obviously different airports at the origin or at the destination may result in different routes, in which case the airport and the route choice problem are combined.

An example of the application of a choice model to the problem of airport route choice is the study of the California corridor conducted by Kanafani et al. (1977) between the San Francisco and Los Angeles metropolitan areas. Both of these areas are served by multiple airport systems: the San Francisco area is served by three air carrier airports, and the Los Angeles area by five. Twelve direct links were available in the corridor during the study period (1970). The situation is diagrammatically shown in Fig. 9.2, which indicates that a traveler

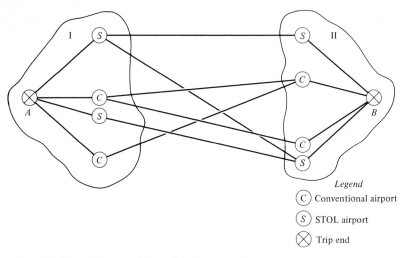

Figure 9.2 Schematic representation of air travel corridor.

between the two regions can choose from among 12 different services. These services differ in their travel times, access and egress times, schedule frequency, and air fare, although this latter does not change much from one route to another.

Using travel survey data for both regions to obtain origin-destination and airport choice information, it was possible to calibrate two separate multinomial choice models of the logit form, one for business and another for nonbusiness traffic.

The model used has the same form in both cases, but the estimation resulted in different parameter values for each of the trip purposes. The following model was used:

$$P_{ijk} = \frac{e^{V_{ijk}}}{\sum_r e^{V_{ijr}}} \tag{9.25}$$

where P_{ijk} is the proportion of the traffic between origin zone i and destination zone j that uses the kth route, and V_{ijk} is the choice function of the attributes of route k for travelers between i and j. The zonal system was set up by dividing the San Francisco and the Los Angeles areas into 7 and 8 zones, respectively, giving 56 origin-destination pairs on which to calibrate the choice model. The choice function V was constructed as a linear additive function of three attributes of the choice:

$$V_{ijk} = \alpha H_{ijk} + \beta F_k + \alpha C_k \tag{9.26}$$

where H_{ijk} is the total travel time between i and j using route k, and including the access and egress times from zones i and j to the respective airports constituting route k; F_k is the schedule frequency on route k measured in total weekly flights; and C_k is the coach air fare on route k.

Table 9.3 California corridor route choice model parameters

	Time	Frequency	Fare
Business	−0.10	0.003	−0.04
Nonbusiness	−0.10	0.002	−0.06

The separate calibrations for business and nonbusiness traffic gave the parameter estimates shown in Table 9.3. These results are displayed in Fig. 9.3,

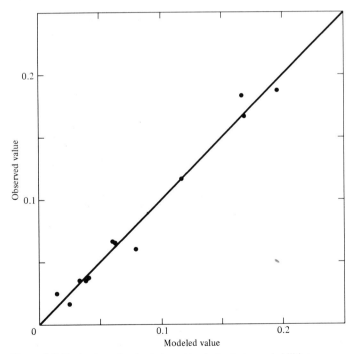

Figure 9.3 Evaluation of estimated corridor route choice probabilities.

which shows the comparison of observed and estimated business traffic proportions on each of the 12 routes. The results shown in this table suggest that business travel is more sensitive to schedule frequency and less sensitive to fares than nonbusiness traffic. This type of choice model can be a useful tool in evaluating the impact of adding or removing direct service links in the corridor of interest. A similar model has been used by Kanafani et al. (1974) to study the demand potential for STOL routes operating out of small "downtown" airports in the San Francisco and Los Angeles metropolitan areas.

Another useful application of choice models in air travel demand analysis is to the problem of traffic distribution among available fare types. This is an important consideration in markets where there are complex fare packages including first-class, economy, excursions, charters, etc. In such markets, the distribution of traffic among the fare types available is an important determinant of the total revenue received by the airlines and knowledge of it is an important factor in pricing analysis.

Kanafani et al. (1974) used a multinomial logit model to study the distribution of traffic among fare types and seasons in the North Atlantic market (North America–Europe, predominantly). In any typical year with three travel seasons, peak (June, July, August), low (December, January, February), and shoulder (all other months), there would be about seven or eight types of fares available. The following model was calibrated on data from 1967 to 1972:

$$P(i, s, t) = \frac{e^{V(i, s, t)}}{\sum_{i,s} e^{V(i, s, t)}} \qquad \text{for all } t \qquad (9.27)$$

The logit choice function calibrated for the North Atlantic market for the study period was as follows:

$$V(i, s, t) = a(i) = b(i, s) + c(i, t) + dp(i, s, t) + \sum_{k \in k_i} e(i, k)\left(\frac{\Delta p}{p}\right)_k \quad (9.28)$$

where $V(i, s, t)$ = choice function for fare type i in season s and year t

$a(i)$ = fare type–specific parameter, which attempts to reflect the effect of service attributes such as any restrictions on the use of a

$b(i, s)$ = a fare type–and season-specific parameter that represents the effects of the "natural" distribution of the traffic by fare type i among the three seasons of the year

$c(i, t)$ = parameter that attempts to capture any special effects for fare type i during a specific year t; this includes effects such as the introduction of a new fare type by allowing the first year or two to have a different market share from later years

d = price parameter

$p(i, s, t)$ = fare level for fare type i in season s and year t

$e(i, k)$ = parameter that attempts to capture the effects of the relative difference between the fare level s of fare types that have otherwise similar attributes

$(\Delta p/p)_k$ = relative fare difference between fare types i and k

ki = set of fare types that have similar service attributes but different prices to fare type i

Notice that the introduction of the $\Delta p/p$ variable in the $V(i, s, t)$ function eliminates the independence of irrelevant alternative property of the choice model. Such property could not be assumed to exist among the various fare types available.

During the years of study, the following fare types were available in the market:

First class: no associated restrictions

Economy normal: no associated restrictions

Short excursions: length of stay restriction to 14–21 days

Long excursions: length of stay restriction to 42–45 days

Group-inclusive tour: travel in a group and purchase of accommodations at the destination as a part of the travel package

Charter: specified group travel requirements and preset travel dates, special airport handling procedures

Youth: upper limit on the age of the traveler

These fare types are listed in decreasing order of price level. The calibration results obtained for one segment of the market, vacation travelers, are shown in Table 9.4. Figure 9.4 shows a comparison of the actual traffic on each fare type with traffic estimated by multiplying the total traffic by the choice probability. It is easy to see that a good fit can be obtained with this type of analysis. One should not forget, however, that with such a large number of variables in the model, one is bound to have a good fit. The abundance of data available for this study is not common in demand analysis, and the challenge is to try to model travel behavior accurately with less data and simpler models. The choice model developed in this case was later used to estimate elasticities and cross-elasticities between the demand for travel by the various fares. This provided a pricing policy analysis tool useful in relating pricing schemes to specific traffic predictions [see Kanafani et al. (1979)].

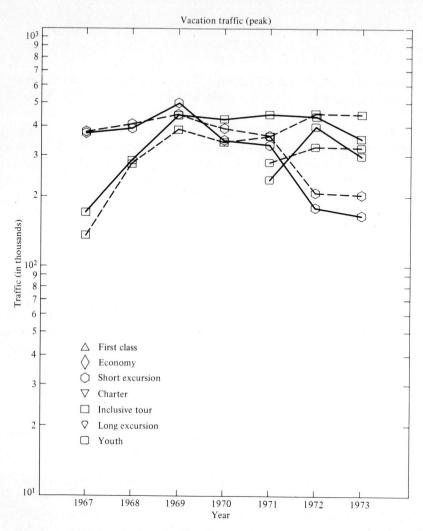

Figure 9.4a Evaluation of estimated traffic volumes by fare type for North Atlantic vacation traffic during peak season.

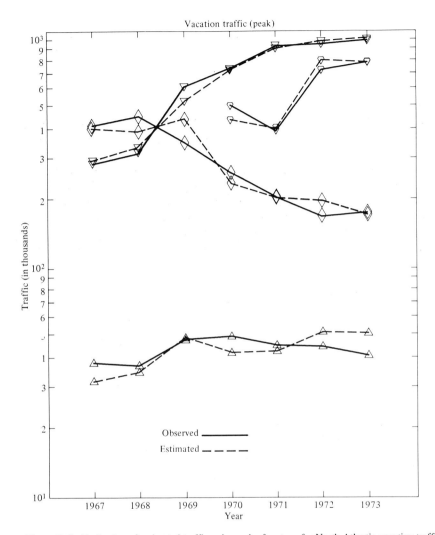

Figure 9.4b Evaluation of estimated traffic volumes by fare type for North Atlantic vacation traffic during peak season.

Table 9.4 Fare type choice model parameters—North Atlantic vacation air traffic

Variable	Parameter value	Standard error
Fare type dummy parameters (a)		
Economy, first class	0.0	—
Long excur., short excur.	− 1.19	0.17
GIT, charter	− 1.75	0.21
Youth	− 2.34	0.19
Seasonal parameters (b)		
Peak (first class)	0.79	0.12
Peak (economy)	1.13	0.07
Peak (charter)	1.04	0.04
Peak (long excur.)	1.58	0.07
Peak (youth)	1.75	0.10
Peak (short excur., GIT)	1.41	0.04
Shoulder (first class, youth)	0.51	—
Shoulder (economy)	0.58	0.08
Shoulder (charter)	0.60	0.05
Shoulder (long excur.)	0.85	0.08
Shoulder (short excur., GIT)	0.90	0.05
Winter—all fares	0.0	—
Fare type year parameters (c)		
GIT 1967	− 0.56	0.11
Youth 1971	0.0	—
Short excur. 1967–1971	0.65	0.08
Long excur. 1970–1971	− 0.38	0.07
Price variable (d)	− 0.007	0.0004
Relative fare difference (e)		
Economy charter	− 0.24	0.07
Economy long excur.	− 0.36	0.09
Short excur. charter	− 0.24	0.07
Short excur. GIT	− 0.63	0.16
Charter long excur.	− 0.77	0.18

9.5 SIMULTANEOUS MODELS OF DEMAND AND SUPPLY

So far, the discussion has focused on models in which the supply characteristics are implicitly assumed exogenous and fixed, and hence models that are specified in single equations. This limitation can be relaxed if it is believed that one or more of the supply variables is not in fact exogenous, but depends on the endogenous variable representing traffic volume. In such a case, a multiequation model would be necessary in order to properly estimate the parameters of the demand model. The simultaneity between demand and supply has so far been assumed away in the estimation of traffic demand models, particularly in urban transportation. This is justified on the grounds that supply models can be estimated independently from engineering type analyses, and that for any demand model, the values of the supply variables given at each traffic level are fixed and exogenous, having previously been estimated. This assumption is relaxed in some of the route choice models whereby equilibrium between demand and supply are sought directly.

The use of time series analysis in modeling air travel demand opens up the issue of simultaneity since it often cannot be assumed that observed trends in traffic and in supply variables such as price and capacity are independent. This two-way causality can result in model systems that are rather difficult to calibrate. One of these difficulties results from what is referred to as the *identification problem* in econometrics.

The Identification Problem

This problem arises when a model system (more than one equation) contains two-way causality, so that there is a sort of imbalance between the endogenous and the exogenous variables. Since the exogenous variables are the source of information on which to base the estimation of model parameters, an insufficient number of them might preclude the estimation of the parameters of all the endogenous variables. Equations that do not contain the sufficient number of exogenous variables, and whose parameters cannot be estimated, are referred to as *unidentified equations*. The identification problem can be illustrated by a simple example. Suppose a demand and supply model system is given by

$$T = a_0 + a_1 P \qquad (9.29)$$

$$P = b_0 + b_1 T \qquad (9.30)$$

where T is the traffic volume; P is the unit price; and a_0, a_1, b_0, and b_1 are parameters to be estimated from observation. Both equations of this model are said to be unidentified since it is not possible to estimate their parameter value from empirical observations. Referring to Fig. 9.5, it can be seen that the two

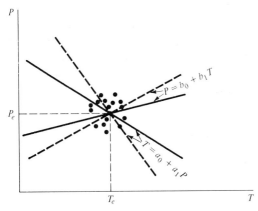

Figure 9.5 Unidentified demand and supply functions.

equations will result in equilibrium, if at all, at only one point (T_e, P_e). Hence, observations on traffic volume and price cannot be used to estimate parameters of either equation, since they will all refer to only one point on each curve. Observations thus obtained will result in an average of the location of the equilibrium point, and a rather poor average at that, as indicated by the possible scatter in the data illustrated in Fig. 9.5. In order to estimate either the demand equation or the supply equation, it is necessary in this model to identify an additional exogenous variable. As illustrated in Fig. 9.6, an additional exogenous

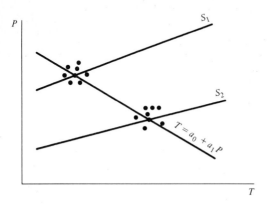

Figure 9.6 Additional supply variable S permits estimation of demand function.

variable, say S which has an impact on the location of the supply function but not that of the demand function, will permit making observations of traffic and price at different levels of S. These observations made on different supply curves will permit the estimation of the demand curve. This is analogous to adding an exogenous variable in the model which will change it to

$$T = a_0 + a_1P + a_2S \tag{9.31}$$

$$P = a_0 + b_1T + b_2S \tag{9.32}$$

$$S = S$$

When S does not influence the demand, i.e., when $a_2 = 0$, it becomes possible to make observations of T and P at different values of S, which means observations of the equilibrium points at different supply curves, but on the same demand curve. Such observations will permit the identification of the demand function, as illustrated in Fig. 9.6. Similarly, in order to estimate the supply function, it would be necessary to have an additional exogenous variable, say Q, which affects the demand without affecting the supply. The model then becomes

$$T = a_0 + a_1P + a_2S + a_3Q \tag{9.33}$$

$$P = b_0 + b_1P + b_2S + b_3Q \tag{9.34}$$

with both $a_2 = 0$ and $b_3 = 0$. It is now possible to obtain observations of the equilibrium point at different values of Q, which means at different levels of demand but with the same supply (without varying S). This will permit the estimation of the supply equation, as illustrated in Fig. 9.7.

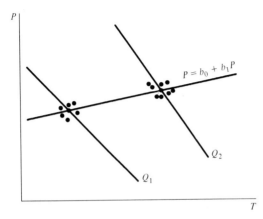

Figure 9.7 Additional demand variable Q permits estimation of supply function.

    This example illustrates the fact that in order for an equation to be identifiable, it is necessary that a certain relation exist between the endogenous and the exogenous variables included in it. In general, it is sufficient to have the vector of parameters for the model equations be all independent and orthogonal. In practice, it often suffices that the following relationship between the number of variables in an equation be met: Let EX be the number of exogenous variables in the whole model, EN be the number of endogenous variables in the whole model, ex be the number of exogenous variables left in any model equation, and en be the number of endogenous variables left in any equation; then for any model equation to be identifiable, the following relationship must hold:

$$(EX - ex) + (EN - en) \geq EN - 1 \qquad (9.35)$$

When the equality is strict, then the equation is said to be identified, and when the inequality holds, then the equation is said to be overidentified. An unidentified equation is one for which the inequality in the equation is reversed. It is possible to estimate parameters for identified and overidentified equations, but not for equations that are unidentified. In the example used earlier in this section, the following relationships hold.

    For Eqs. (9.29) and (9.30), EX = 0, ex = 0, EN = 2, en = 2, for both equations. Applying Eq. (9.35) yields

$$(0 - 0) + (2 - 2) < (2 - 1)$$

which is the same for both equations and which indicates that neither is identifiable.

For Eqs. (9.33) and (9.34), EX = 2, ex = 1, EN = 2, en = 2, for both equations. Again, applying Eq. (9.35) yields

$$(2 - 1) + (2 - 2) = (2 - 1)$$

which indicates that both equations are identified.

Estimation of Simultaneous Equations

Ordinary least squares is not a suitable technique for estimating the parameters of multiequation model systems. It usually results in biased parameter estimates. For such a situation other techniques of regression analysis have been developed, including the indirect least squares and the two-stage least squares [see Taneja (1979)]. The first is used only when the model equations are exactly identified, but the second can be applied for identified and overidentified equations. In order to illustrate the two-stage technique, consider the following model system:

$$T = a_0 + a_1P + a_3Q \tag{9.36}$$

$$P = b_0 + b_1T + b_2S \tag{9.37}$$

These two equations can be reduced to forms where each includes only one endogenous variable. This can be done by combining the two to yield

$$T = a_0' + a_2'S + a_3'Q \tag{9.38}$$

$$P = b_0' + b_2'S + b_3'Q \tag{9.39}$$

It is easy to see that, for example,

$$a_0' = \frac{a_0}{(1 - a_1b_1)} \quad \text{and} \quad a_2' = \frac{a_2}{(1 - a_1b_1)}$$

and so forth. Equations (9.38) and (9.39) are referred to as the *reduced form* of the structural equations (9.36) and (9.37). Two-stage least squares consists of using the reduced forms to estimate $\hat{T}$ and $\hat{P}$, and then reestimating the structural model as two independent equations

$$T = a_0 + a_1\hat{P} + a_3Q \tag{9.40}$$

$$P = b_0 + b_1\hat{T} + b_2S \tag{9.41}$$

Note that Eqs. (9.40) and (9.41) are no longer simultaneous since $\hat{P}$ and $\hat{T}$ are not the same as P and T but are exogenous variables already known during the second stage.

An example of the simultaneous model is the following two-equation model estimated by Eriksen (1978) using two-stage least squares:

$$T_t' = -6.35 - 0.52F_t' + 2.00SE_t' - 0.0179LS_t'$$

$$LS_t' = -3.02 + 0.345F_t' - 0.038COMP_t' + 0.105T_t'$$

This model was calibrated using data from 1973 and 1974 for a sample of 14 city pairs in the United States. T is traffic, F is the fare level, SE is a population product of the two regions, LS is a level of service variable represented by the ratio of the nonstop jet flight time to the average actual travel time, and COMP is a variable that describes the competition in the market which is computed by summing the squares of the market shares of the airlines serving the market. The model was calibrated using 1973 and 1974 data for a sample of 14 region pairs.

Note that the specification of simultaneous demand and supply models is not always necessary. In the case of cross-sectional analysis, it can be assumed that a static equilibrium exists and that the supply variables are not influenced by demand. This is not as good an assumption in time series modeling where the data will reflect adjustments of supply conditions from time period to time period that are possibly influenced by demand. In the specification of time series models with time-lagged effects, such as the partial adjustment model, it is possible to avoid simultaneous equation estimation by using the proxy variable method. In this method, the supply variable in the demand equation may be lagged, or vice versa. When estimating either of these models, the lagged variable becomes an exogenous variable, already known from the previous time period. This will avoid the need to estimate both models simultaneously. This specification is often necessary when data limitations preclude the application of two-stage least squares or other simultaneous estimation techniques [see, for example, Behbehani and Kanafani (1980)].

PROBLEMS

9.1 Given the following time series models of traffic *expressed in logarithms:*

$$T_t = 0.4 + 0.5P + 1.2I + 1.8A + 0.4T_{t-1}$$

where T_t = log of traffic in year t
P = log of population
I = log of income
A = log of accessibility

It is forecasted that between year t and $t + 1$ the population will increase by 1 percent and income will increase by 0.5 percent. The accessibility will remain constant. What will be the resulting percentage change in traffic between year t and $t + 1$?

9.2 The following is a time series model calibrated for total revenue passenger miles of air travel in the U.S.:

$$\text{RPM}_t = 2.16 + 2.04C_t' - 1.35F_t$$

where RPM_t = total revenue passenger-miles in year t
F_t = average air fare during the year t

C_t' = measure of "permanent" per capita personal consumption in real terms, defined according to the formula

$$C_t' = 0.6C_t + 0.3C_{t-1} + 0.1C_{t-2}$$

(a) What is the permanent consumption elasticity?

(b) What is the short-run consumption elasticity?

(c) How many years will it take for the effect of a one-time increase in personal consumption to materialize fully?

9.3 The following data show the split in air traffic across the North Atlantic between regular economy class and excursion fare class over a period of 10 years.

Annual passenger traffic by fare type

	Economy	Excursion
1963	500,000	72,000
1964	682,000	156,000
1965	902,000	211,000
1966	1,042,000	275,000
1967	1,097,000	277,000
1968	1,064,000	235,000
1969	1,039,000	346,000
1970	974,000	245,000
1971	1,001,000	255,000
1972	924,000	192,000

Fares in constant dollars by fare type

	Economy	Excursion
1963	499.7	350.
1964	395.05	297.03
1965	387.38	291.26
1966	376.42	283.02
1967	366.06	275.23
1968	350.	263.16
1969	350.	250.00
1970	330.71	236.22
1971	342.42	243.94
1972	350.72	252.9

Suggest, construct, and calibrate a choice model to describe the process by which travelers seem to be choosing between these two alternative transportation services. Constant dollar fares for the two services are given for the 10-year period.

Explain the calibration procedure used, and discuss the model in view of the calibration results.

REFERENCES

Aureille, Yves G.: The Outlook for the U.S. Airline Industry: An Econometric Approach, *Proceedings:* Workshop on Air Transportation Demand and Systems Analysis, MIT report R75-8, pp. 386-439, 1975.

Behbehani, R., and A. Kanafani: "Demand and Supply Models of Air Traffic in International Markets," Berkeley, Institute of Transportation Studies, research report ITS-WP-80-5, 1980.

Box, G., and G. Jenkins: "Time Series Analysis, Forecasting and Control," Holden-Day, San Francisco, 1970.

Brown, S., and W. S. Watkins: The Demand for Air Travel: A Regression of Times Series and Cross-Sectional Data in the U.S. Domestic Market, *Highway Res. Rec.*, vol. 213, pp. 21–34, 1968.

Eriksen, S.: "Demand Models for U.S. Domestic Air Passenger Markets," MIT, Flight Transportation Lab, report FTL-R78-2, 1978.

Gronau, R.: The Value of Time in Passenger Transportation: The Demand for Air Travel, *Natl. Bur. Econ. Res.*, Occasional Paper 109, Columbia University Press, New York, 1970.

Haney, D. G.: "Review of Aviation Forecasting Methodology," U.S. DOT, Report DOT-40176-6, 1975.

Howry, E .P.: On the Choice of Forecasting Models for Air Travel, *J. Region. Sci.*, vol. 9, pp. 215–224, 1969.

Kanafani, A., E. Sadoulet, and E. C. Sullivan: "Demand Analysis for North Atlantic Air Travel," Institute of Transportation Studies, Berkeley, research report, vol. 1, 1974.

———, and S. L. Fan: Estimating the Demand for Short Haul Air Transportation, *Transp. Res. Rec.*, no. 526, pp. 1–15, 1974.

———, G. Gosling, and S. Taghavi: "Studies in the Demand for Short Haul Air Transportation," Institute of Transportation Studies, Berkeley, special report, 1977.

———, and E. Sadoulet: The Partitioning of Long Haul Air Traffic, A Study in Multinomial Choice, *Transp. Res.*, vol. 11, no. 1, pp. 1–8, 1977.

———, H. S. Yuan, and R. Behbehani: "Integrated Forecasting Process for International Air Transportation," Institute of Transportation Studies, Berkeley, research report UCB-ITS-RR-79-1, p. 182, 1979.

———: Price Elasticities of Nonbusiness Air Travel Demand, *Transp. Eng. J. ASCE*, vol. 106, no. TE2, pp. 217–225, 1980.

Lave, Lester B.: The Demand for Intercity Passenger Transportation, *J. Region. Sci.*, vol. 12, no. 1, pp. 71–84, 1972.

Mathematica, Inc.: *Studies in Travel Demand*, vols. 1–4, Princeton, N.J., 1967–1969.

Taneja, N. K.: Airline Traffic Forecasting, D. C. Heath, Lexington, Mass., 1979.

Verleger, P. K.: Models of the Demand for Air Transportation, *Bell J. Econ. Mgmt. Sci.*, vol. 3, no. 2, 1972.

Young, Kan Hua: A Synthesis of Time-Series and Cross-Section Analysis: Demand for Air Transportation Service, *J. Am. Stat. Assoc.*, vol. 67, no. 339, pp. 560–566, September 1972.

COMMODITY TRANSPORT DEMAND

The application of demand theory to commodity transportation is more recent and possibly less extensive than in the case of passenger transportation. This is not so much due to any difficulties in the application—although until recently detailed commodity flow data were not typically readily available—but it is due primarily to the fact that attention to commodity transportation and to the important policy and planning issues associated with it came at a much later date than similar concerns with passenger transportation. However, because of the amenability of commodity transportation demand to formal analysis, rapid developments have occurred in recent years, and it can be said today that the state of the art in both commodity and passenger demand analysis is essentially on a par. Indeed, most fundamental models of transportation demand, such as route choice and mode choice models, are applied to both types of analysis.

The motivation for the transportation of commodities can be said to be purely economic. As such it may be said that commodity travel demand lends itself better to formal analysis using economic demand theory. The idiosyncrasies and unexplainable variabilities observed in passenger trip-making behavior are much less pronounced in commodity shipping decisions, although they are by no means absent. Three fundamental aspects of commodity transportation demand go to make it more amenable to analysis. First, it can be assumed that some sort of economic optimization process underlies commodity transportation decisions. In particular, there is no reason why the decision maker in this case will not seek to minimize the total cost associated with the movement of commodities or with the economic activities of which this movement is a part. The challenge to the analyst of commodity transportation is then not to postulate what the decision process might be, but to construct representative models that include all the costs of commodity transportation. Second, the demand for commodity transportation is totally derived from the demands for the commodities themselves at points of consumption that are spatially separated from the points of production. This is true regardless of whether the commodity is used as an input into a production process or directly as a consumable good. This means that the nature of the transportation demand function is related to and can be found by understanding the nature of the production, consumption, or marketing process that gives rise to commodity transport demand. Third, commodity flows are likely to be subject to fewer fluctuations and peaking since it is possible for most commodities to use warehousing in order to ensure uninterrupted supply to absorb fluctuations in demand. This means that observations of commodity flow can be taken as more representative of expected flows and can be readily used in calibrating the appropriate models.

10.1 APPROACHES TO DEMAND ANALYSIS

There are three basic approaches to the analysis of commodity transportation demand. The first is the microeconomic approach, in which the basic decision unit of analysis is the firm which is the potential user of transportation. In this approach the demand for commodity transportation is derived by considering transportation as one of the inputs into the production or the marketing process of the firm. In order to produce its output of goods or services, the firm may require the transportation of certain commodities and hence become itself a consumer of transportation.

The second approach is that of spatial interaction modeling. In this approach, which is aggregate in nature, surpluses and deficits of commodities are located at various points in space, and a process is then postulated whereby flows of commodities will occur from points of excess supply to points of excess demand. Gravity models of spatial interaction and optimization models of trip distribution are often used in this approach.

The third approach is the macroeconomic approach in which the inter-relations between sectors of an economy are analyzed, usually with the help of an input-output model. With transportation identified as one of the sectors it becomes possible to analyze transportation requirements of the other sectors and then to translate those into flows of commodities. Multiregional input-output modeling is a method that is suitable for this sort of analysis. The macroeconomic approach to commodity demand modeling will also result in aggregate demand functions and will not permit the sort of policy analysis that can be made with the help of, say, a microeconomic commodity mode choice model that is calibrated with disaggregate data.

10.2 MICROECONOMIC ANALYSIS OF COMMODITY FLOW

The basic assumption of the microeconomic approach to commodity transportation demand analysis is that the decision unit is a single firm or individual who is engaged in some economic activity. This firm could be a producer of some product for which inputs have to be obtained from different points in space or to which the product itself has to be shipped to different points as a part of a marketing process. The firm could also represent a retailer of goods and services who requires the transportation of commodities from the locations where they are produced to the retail location. In such a case it is possible to estimate the retailer's demand for commodities from a consumption function describing the consumer demands in the area served by the retailer; such a consumption function could be derived using conventional microeconomic demand theory as described in Chap. 2.

The approach to analyzing the commodity transportation demand of a firm is to first consider the firm's demand for the commodity itself and then *derive* the transportation demand function from that. In order to do this one needs to consider the process by which the firm produces its output, the production process, and the process by which it determines its level of output, the marketing process.

Production and Cost Functions

Consider a firm which produces outputs that can be described by an output vector $\mathbf{Z}$, using a set of inputs that can be described by an input vector $\mathbf{X}$. The production processes available to the firm can be described by a series of functional relationships between $\mathbf{Z}$ and $\mathbf{X}$. In general these processes can be described by a family of functions of the form:

$$P(\mathbf{Z}, \mathbf{X}) = 0 \qquad (10.1)$$

where P represents a production function. The choice of a specific production process is normally assumed to result from an optimization process in which the firm tries to find the minimum cost process given the prices of the various inputs $\mathbf{X}$; Let the prices of the inputs $\mathbf{X}$ be given by a prices vector $\mathbf{W}$, the selection of a production process will then follow an optimization in which the total production cost $C(\mathbf{Z}, \mathbf{W})$ is minimized subject to the constraint that the combination of inputs follows the production function.

Minimize $\qquad\qquad C(\mathbf{Z}, \mathbf{W}) = \mathbf{WX} \qquad\qquad (10.2)$

subject to $\qquad\qquad P(\mathbf{Z}, \mathbf{X}) = 0$

The result of this optimization is a set of values representing the quantities of each of the inputs used to produce any given level of outputs $\mathbf{Z}$ and the associated cost of this production as given by the cost function $C(\mathbf{Z}, \mathbf{W})$. A simple example will serve to illustrate this. Let us assume that the production function is separable; that is, it is possible to separate the inputs and the outputs so that Eq. (10.1) can be written in the following form:

$$\mathbf{Z} = Z(\mathbf{X}) \tag{10.3}$$

Let us assume further that there is a single output Z and two inputs X_1 and X_2 with unit prices W_1 and W_2, respectively, and that the production function has the following form:

$$Z = \alpha_0 X_1^{\alpha_1} X_2^{\alpha_2} \tag{10.4}$$

where α_0, α_1, and α_2 are constant nonnegative parameters. Equation (10.4) is a well-known function called in production theory the Cobb-Douglas function. The total cost of the inputs X_1 and X_2 is

$$C(\mathbf{X}) = W_1 X_1 + W_2 X_2 \tag{10.5}$$

The optimal production process can be derived by minimizing Eq. (10.5) subject to Eq. (10.4). This can be done using a lagrangian as follows:

$$L = W_1 X_1 + W_2 X_2 - \lambda(Z - \alpha_0 X_1^{\alpha_1} X_2^{\alpha_2}) \tag{10.6}$$

where λ is a constant multiplier. The optimal values of X_1 and X_2 can be found by solving the first-order conditions

$$\frac{\partial L}{\partial X_1} = 0 \qquad \frac{\partial L}{\partial X_2} = 0 \tag{10.7}$$

which yield

$$X_1 = \alpha_0^{\theta}\left(\frac{W_2 \alpha_1}{W_1 \alpha_2}\right)^{\theta} Z^{\theta} \tag{10.8}$$

and

$$X_2 = \alpha_0^{\theta}\left(\frac{W_1 \alpha_2}{W_2 \alpha_1}\right)^{\theta} Z^{\theta} \tag{10.9}$$

where $\theta = 1/(\alpha_1 + \alpha_2)$.

The total cost function $C(Z, \mathbf{W})$ can be derived by substituting Eqs. (10.4), (10.8), and (10.9) into Eq. (10.5) to give

$$C(Z, \mathbf{W}) = \theta \alpha_0^{-\theta} \alpha_1^{-\alpha_1 \theta} \alpha_2^{-\alpha_2 \theta} Z^{\theta} W_1^{\alpha_1 \theta} W_2^{\alpha_2 \theta} \tag{10.10}$$

If the prices W_1 and W_2 are assumed fixed and independent of the quantities X_1 and X_2, then the firm's demand functions for inputs X_1 and X_2 can be obtained by using the relationship referred to as *Shephard's lemma* [see Shephard (1953)]:

$$\frac{\partial C(Z, \mathbf{W})}{\partial W_i} = X_i(Z, \mathbf{W}) \tag{10.11}$$

which is a conditional demand function giving the relationship between the quantity X_i and the price W_i for a given level of output 2. In this case the demand functions are

$$\frac{\partial C(Z, \mathbf{W})}{\partial W_1} = X_1(Z, \mathbf{W}) = \theta^2 \alpha_0^{-\theta} \alpha_1^{1-\alpha_1\theta} \alpha_2^{-\alpha_2\theta} Z^\theta W_1^{-\alpha_2\theta} W_2^{\alpha_2\theta} \quad (10.12)$$

$$= KZ^\theta \left(\frac{W_2}{W_1}\right)^{\alpha_2\theta}$$

and similarly

$$X_2(Z, \mathbf{W}) = K'Z^\theta \left(\frac{W_1}{W_2}\right)^{\alpha_1\theta} \quad (10.13)$$

where K and K' are constants combining α_0, α_1, and α_2.

If a rule for determining the output level is known, then it can be applied to derive the value of Z. The demand functions (10.12) and (10.13) can be converted into unconditional functions of the form $X_i = X_i(W_i)$. For example, if the output level Z is determined by maximizing a profit function such as

$$\pi = rZ - C(Z, \mathbf{W}) \quad (10.14)$$

in which r is the unit revenue from the sale of the product, then the optimal level Z^* can be derived from

$$\frac{\partial \pi}{\partial Z} = 0 \quad \rightarrow \quad Z = Z^* \quad (10.15)$$

and the demand functions $X_1(Z^*, W)$ and $X_2(Z^*, W)$ are constructed accordingly. The same can be done for any other production strategy or market structure.

Note that the application of Shephard's lemma to derive the input demand function is based on the assumption that the supply function for the inputs is horizontal (their prices are fixed). The separable production is another assumption that is necessitated by the need to make the derivation of the demand functions mathematically tractable, although it is not required by the theory. A commonly used production function is the Cobb-Douglas function used in Eq. (10.4). However, the derivation of demand functions is often done directly from the cost functions since it is usually easier to obtain data and to calibrate cost functions than production functions.

Transportation Demand Function

The firm's demand for transportation can now be derived from its demands for the various inputs. This can be done by directly considering the cost function and by respecifying the unit price of each input to include its cost of transportation. In the simplest case where it is assumed that an input i will be transported and that the transport cost is known and fixed, the unit price for i becomes

$$W_i' = W_i + T_i \quad (10.16)$$

where T_i is the unit transport cost of input i. In this case the demand function for transportation of commodity i can be given by

$$V_i = \frac{\partial C(Z_1, W_i')}{\partial T_i} \tag{10.17}$$

where V_i is the transportation volume of commodity i demanded by the firm.

This simple case is too idealized to allow disaggregate demand analysis. In reality the decision of whether a particular input is to be transported results from a sequence of choices, much in the same way as in urban passenger transportation, in which origins of the commodity, mode of transport, and shipment size are determined in such a way as to minimize the total cost of acquiring the required quantity of that input. The demand functions given by Eq. (10.17) are analogous to trip generation models in urban passenger travel and share some of their conceptual limitations. An attempt to introduce the choice of mode into this type of model has recently been made by Friedlaender and Spady (1981) who constructed aggregated demand models for groups of commodities by constructing production cost functions in which both truck and rail transportation were specified explicitly.

The Friedlaender and Spady cost function has the following form:

$$C = C(T_r, T_t, q_r, q_t, \mathbf{X}, Z) \tag{10.18}$$

where T_r, T_t = unit transport costs by rail and truck, respectively

q_r, q_t = shipment and transportation characteristics of the two modes; examples of these characteristics are average length of haul and shipment size

$\mathbf{X}$ = a vector of inputs other than transportation, such as capital and labor

Z = level of output

By applying Eq. (10.11), demand functions for transportation by each mode are derived. The following is an example of the models derived and the demand functions for transportation of durable manufactures by rail and truck, respectively:

$$V_r = SS_r^{-0.184} LH_r^{-0.356} SS_t^{0.531} LH_t^{0.05} VAL^{-0.167} T_r^{-0.84} T_t^{0.167}$$

and

$$V_t = SS_t^{-0.5} LH_t^{-0.05} SS_r^{0.25} LH_r^{0.25} VAL^{0.158} T_t^{-0.82} T_r^{0.16}$$

where V_r, V_t = volumes of the commodities transported by rail and truck, respectively, measured in annual tons

SS = average shipment size

LH = average length of haul

VAL = average value of the commodity

T = unit transportation cost (rate)

As mentioned earlier, a number of restrictive assumptions underlie the derivation of demand models such as these. The underlying production process is assumed to be separable, and the factor prices are assumed to be independent of input quantities, at least for transportation. A more general approach to microeconomic demand modeling is the structured choice approach introduced earlier in the context of urban passenger transportation. The choices available to the firm include location, level of output, substitution among inputs, and a series of choices relating directly to the transportation of commodities, such as origins or destinations, modes, shipment size, and frequency of orders. For this the application of choice models such as the ones described in Chap. 5 is common.

Choices in Freight Transportation

The types of choices mentioned in the previous section can be classified into three classes. First are the choices relating to a firm's location of its production and marketing activities. The second class includes choices related to the nature of the production process adopted, to the level of output, and to the marketing of the product, particularly its pricing. The third class of choices is related to the logistics of transportation of both inputs and outputs in terms of packaging, transportation modes, and levels of inventory. Chiang et al. (1980) have defined these classes of choice as long-run, intermediate-run, and short-run. Clearly most demand models of transportation are capable of dealing with the short-run logistics choices. Production and location analysis extends beyond the scope of transportation. Most commodity transport demand models are therefore conditional on the long-term locational choices and intermediate-term production decisions.

In describing the logistics choices that underlie commodity transport demand we can think of a firm that is located at a given point in space and that follows a given production process to produce a given level of output. Inputs are needed for this process from locations other than that where the firm is located, and these inputs must be transported.

This situation can be considered a good model of a potential user of commodity transportation. If the firm is a shipper rather than a receiver of a commodity, then the picture is reversed but the nature of the choices remains essentially the same.

The following are the important choices that must be made by the user of commodity transportation:

1. *Total quantity.* This is represented by the demand function and results from the optimization of the production process taking into account the costs of transportation and associated logistics, and the nature of the market in which the products are marketed.
2. *Supplier.* For each input, the firm has a choice among suppliers that are located at different points in space. Factor prices offered by different suppliers may be different; or they may be the same but with different suppliers offering

different logistics, level of service such as lead time for orders, and supply reliability. This choice is analogous to destination choice in passenger travel.

3. *Mode*. Different modes will in general offer different levels of service and result in different costs for commodity transportation, so the firm will in general choose among available modes in an effort to minimize the total generalized cost of transportation.

4. *Shipment size*. The firm has a choice of shipment size associated with any given total quantity of commodity shipped. More frequent shipments result in smaller shipment size and vice versa. The size of shipment is an important factor in logistics decisions, for it affects the levels of inventory that must be kept on hand in order to meet the needs for the commodity during the time between shipments. It will also affect the choice of mode.

5. *Frequency of shipments*. Closely related to the choice of shipment size, this choice will depend on the handling costs involved in making orders. It will also affect inventory levels.

6. *Reorder point*. This is the firm's choice of the point at which to have a shipment planned to arrive in relation to the point at which available inventories are expected to run out. Usually as a safety measure reorder points are sooner than stock-out points; how much sooner will depend on inventory costs.

To illustrate the interaction between the choices of shipment size and frequency of shipments, consider the following situation: a firm requires a total of T tons of a certain commodity per year. The firm has a choice of frequency of orders and shipment size. Let the handling cost per order be h and the frequency of shipments be f, so that average shipment size is $S = T/f$. The warehousing cost per ton and per unit time is w. Figure 10.1 shows the levels of inventory that have to be maintained by the firm for a given value of f or S. It can be seen from the

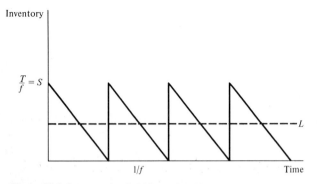

Figure 10.1 Inventory levels with regular shipment schedule.

figure that the average inventory level, not including any safety stocks for emergencies, is given by

$$i = \frac{1}{2}S = \frac{T}{2f}$$ (10.19)

The total warehousing cost is then given by

$$W = wi = \frac{wS}{2} = \frac{wT}{2f}$$ (10.20)

The firm has a choice between infrequent large shipments, which would raise the total warehousing costs, or frequent small shipments, which would raise the handling costs. The optimal combination of shipment size and frequency can be derived by minimizing the sum of these two costs, which we shall refer to as logistics costs L:

$$L = \frac{wT}{2f} + hf$$ (10.21)

where, as defined before, h is the handling cost per shipment, and W is the unit cost of warehousing. The optimal frequency of shipments can be found from

$$\left.\frac{\partial L}{\partial f}\right|_{f*} = 0$$ (10.22)

and combining Eqs. (10.21) and (10.22) yields the optimal frequency and shipment size:

$$f^* = \sqrt{\frac{wT}{2h}}$$ (10.23)

and

$$S^* = \sqrt{\frac{2hT}{w}}$$ (10.24)

for which the total logistic cost is given by

$$L^* = \frac{wT}{2f^*} + hf^*$$

$$= \sqrt{2hwT}$$ (10.25)

It should be noted that this model represents only the trade-off between warehousing costs and handling costs. Other considerations can influence the choice of shipment size, and hence frequency, such as transport rates and mode levels of service. It should be clear that the appropriate size of shipment is not independent of the mode considered. It is also interesting to note that a given shipment size S will result in a given logistics cost L. Hence the use of shipment size as a factor in a transport demand function such as the Friedlaender and Spady model described in the previous section is as a proxy for logistics costs. Whether the demand has a positive or negative elasticity with respect to shipment size will depend on the relative values of w and h. It will normally be negative except when the handling cost per shipment is unusually high.

This simple example can also be used to illustrate the firm's choice of reorder strategy in order to deal with uncertainties either in the transportation system performance or in the use rate of the commodity. Figure 10.1 shows the evolution of inventory levels when every shipment of size $S = T/f$ arrives precisely on time, that is, at precisely the point in time when stocks on hand run out. It also depicts a situation in which the rate at which the commodity is used up is precisely S tons per time period between shipments $1/f$, i.e., precisely T tons per year. If for some reason the commodity is used up at a faster rate, such as due to an unexpected upsurge in the demand for the firm's output, then the inventory will run out before a shipment arrives. Both of these events, the delayed arrival of a shipment and the early depletion of inventory, will result in what is called a *stock-out*, at potentially high opportunity costs to the firm. In order to avoid stock-out the firm will usually maintain a safety stock by adjusting the reorder schedule and the scheduled arrival times of shipments in such a way as to limit the risk of stock-out to a certain level. Figure 10.2 illustrates how a delay of

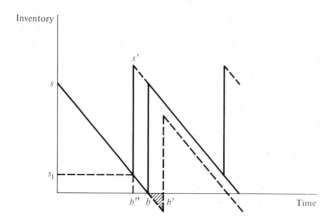

Figure 10.2 The effect of shipment delay on inventory level.

shipment arrival can result in stock-out and how the firm can avoid that by having shipments scheduled to arrive earlier. In the figure a shipment arrival delay from b to b' can cause a stock-out as indicated by the crosshatched area. In order to avoid that, the shipment can be scheduled to arrival earlier than b, resulting in a maximum expected inventory level S' and a safety stock of S_1 which will be used up if the shipment is now delayed and arrives at time b rather than b''. Clearly, the maintenance of a safety stock will increase inventory costs. Hence the selection of the appropriate level of that stock would depend on the warehousing cost and on stock-out and the uncertainties about the transportation system and the estimates of the demand for the firm's output. For some commodities it is possible to keep safety stocks to a minimum if it is possible to use a fast mode of transport such as air for quick response to emergencies and imminent stock-outs. Analyses of safety stock using methods of inventory theory have been done by Roberts et al. (1976) and by Baumol and Vinod (1970). Safety stocks are usually made proportional to the sum of the time between shipments $1/f$ and t the travel time. Baumol and Vinod suggested, for example, the following simple rule for determining safety stock S_1:

$$S_1 = K\sqrt{\left(\frac{1}{f} + t\right)T} \qquad (10.26)$$

where the proportionality factor K would depend on the unreliability of the transport system as measured, e.g., by the standard deviation of the travel time, or the unreliability of the estimate of the firm's rate of use of the commodity, also as measured by the standard deviation of that estimate.

Modeling Choice in Commodity Transportation

The general transportation choice models introduced in Chaps. 4 and 5 can be used to model the process of making the choices mentioned in the previous section. The choice analysis can be structured in a simultaneous or a sequenced manner.

Most applications to date have concentrated on sequenced, or conditional, choice models. Mode choice has been analyzed rather extensively in the literature, using predominantly logit models [see, for example, Sasaki (1978) and Hashemian (1981)]. Recently in a study by Chiang et al. (1980) logit models of choice were developed to describe the joint choice of mode and shipment size for different classes of commodity.

Most choice models of commodity transportation are based on choice functions that represent the generalized cost of transportation and logistics. Before describing some of these models a discussion of commodity transport costs is appropriate.

Commodity transportation costs As mentioned earlier in this chapter, the challenge in modeling commodity transportation demands lies in understanding all the factors that make up the total cost of transportation. It can be said that the cost of transportation depends on three major factors: (1) the transportation technology used, (2) the logistics of shipment scheduling and sizing, and (3) the commodity characteristics. These three factors are not independent, for its easy to see that the cost of using a particular technology depends, among other things, on the size and the frequency of shipments as well as on the type of commodity being carried.

The following are the components of the total cost of commodity transportation:

1. *Shipping cost.* This is the rate charged by the carrier per unit of the commodity. It is usually dependent on the shipment size and on the length of haul. The shipping rate charged by a carrier will often include many of the components of commodity transportation, other than simply the cost of operating the carrier's system. These components will include insurance, handling costs, sometimes packaging costs, and often a provision for reimbursement for delays in transit that might cause the receiver to incur stock-out costs. The shipping cost will depend predominantly on the mode of transportation used. Handling costs as well as packaging costs will also depend primarily on the mode used. Packaging costs will often be influenced by the costs of loss or damage that may be caused by poor packaging.

2. *Time cost.* The travel time component contributes to commodity transport cost in two ways. First is the potential loss of value of the commodity due to its limited shelf life either because of perishability, as in the case of fruits and vegetables, or because of its time value, as with newspapers and fashionable clothes. Second is the cost of the tied up capital represented by the value of the shipment while it is in transit. For high-value commodities or for very large shipments this can add up to a significant cost component.

3. *Warehousing cost.* This cost usually depends on the type of commodity stored. It also depends on the overall general level of inventory. As discussed in the previous section the deterministic level of inventory, not including safety stock, will depend on the frequency and size of shipments. The warehousing or inventory cost will also include the cost of the capital tied up in the inventory. This will usually encourage shippers or receivers of high-value commodities to maintain minimum inventory levels and to depend on emergency, fast transportation such as by private truck or by air in order to avoid stock-outs.

4. *Ordering cost per shipment.* This cost usually depends on the mode used and on the nature of the process by which the carrier in question operates. Frequent long-term orders from the same supplier will understandably result in lower ordering costs than when the supplier choice is constantly changed. Emergency orders will also tend to cost more.

5. *Unreliability costs.* These costs are reflected in two ways. First, in response to unreliability in the logistics process, higher safety stock levels must be kept, resulting in higher warehousing costs. Second, frequent emergency orders and disruptions in the receiver's or the shipper's inventory control system, or even production and marketing processes, will all result in higher costs.

Deterministic mode choice Deterministic mode choice in commodity transportation follows directly from the minimization of the total transportation cost function. A simplified model from Baumol and Vinod (1969) illustrates the application of the concept of abstract modes and abstract commodities to mode choice. Ignoring safety stock and stock-out costs, the choice between two modes A and B can be done on the basis of a simple cost function of the form

$$C_i = r_i + \theta t_i \qquad (10.27)$$

where C_i = cost per unit by mode i
$\quad\quad r_i$ = freight rate per unit
$\quad\quad t_i$ = travel time
$\quad\quad \theta$ = cost of time, incorporating the deterioration rate and the value of tied-up capital

Note that none of the other cost factors are included in Eq. (10.27), for they are predominantly commodity-dependent and are assumed not to depend on the mode. Also note that in this cost model only r_i and t_i are mode-dependent and θ is commodity-dependent. This model can be considered a mode and commodity abstract model. It states that given two models characterized by r_A, t_A and r_B, t_B, and given a commodity whose time value is θ, then the deterministic choice process results in mode A being chosen if $r_A + \theta t_A < r_B + \theta t_B$. For any given value of θ a set of indifference curves between modes with given values of r and t can be developed. This is done by setting the value of the cost at a constant and then varying r and t. In order to develop meaningful indifference curves, it is convenient to transform r and t into mode attributes for which the utility can be assumed positive. This can be done by reciprocal transformations:

$$e = \frac{1}{r}$$
$$s = \frac{1}{t} \qquad (10.28)$$

where e might stand for economy and s for speed.

The equation of the indifference curves can be derived for constant levels of total cost C_o:

$$C_o = r + \theta t$$
$$= \frac{1}{e} + \theta\left(\frac{1}{s}\right)$$

which gives
$$\frac{1}{e} = C_o - \left(\frac{1}{s}\right) \qquad (10.29)$$

This gives a family of hyperbolic indifference curves for different values of C, as shown in Fig. 10.3. The exact shape of these curves will depend on the value of θ. For example, given two modes A and B, with A being an inexpensive but slow mode and B a rapid but expensive mode, it would be possible to compare these modes by locating them on the indifference map. Figure 10.3 shows a situation where mode B is preferred to A, suggesting a high θ value for the commodity in question.

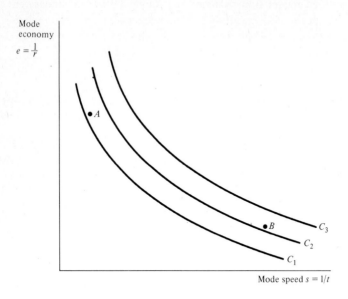

Figure 10.3 Indifference between modes for commodity shipment.

To consider θ purely a commodity characteristic is a simplification that may be relaxed in some cases. Indeed, the mode used can often affect the commodity value depletion while in transit. For any given perishable commodity, θ is expected to be significantly lower when the mode has refrigerated vehicles than when it does not. The indifference between modes can still be analyzed in this case, although the indifference map will be three-dimensional. A simple graphic representation of indifference for a two-mode case can be used to visualize the impact of mode and commodity attributes on mode choice. For two modes A and B the indifference is given by

$$r_A + \theta t_A = r_B + \theta t_B$$

or
$$r_A - r_B = \theta(t_B - t_A) \tag{10.30}$$

for which the indifference plane is shown in Fig. 10.4. On the front side of the plan, A is preferred to B and vice versa. Any combination of the variables of Eq. (10.30) including θ that results in a point on the plane would result in a tie between the two modes. Simple indifference analysis, such as is shown in Fig. 10.4, can be useful in determining the combination of service attributes needed in order to attract a particular commodity into the domain of a given mode. This can be done by adjusting the rate, the travel time, or θ itself by improving the packaging or by refrigeration for perishable commodities.

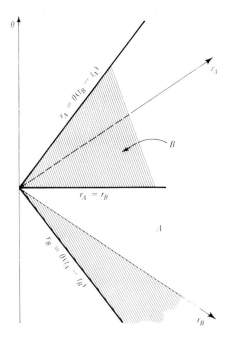

Figure 10.4 Indifference plane between two modes A and B.

Stochastic mode choice Stochastic choice of mode for commodity transportation can be postulated for basically the same reasons as in passenger transportation. Even though the shipper or receiver is assumed to choose according to the minimum cost principle, randomness in the choice function arises due to inaccuracies in the way costs are perceived or measured. The stochastic choice models of Chap. 5 can be applied to commodity transport in the same manner they are applied to passenger transport. Depending on the choice set available and the situation being modeled, binary or multinomial choice models can be applied. Aggregate calibrations are usually based on general commodity flow data [Hashemian (1981)], while disaggregate calibrations are based on individual shipper data [Chiang et al. (1980)].

Most applications of stochastic choice models have centered on the logit model, probably due to its simplicity. However, because many of the alternative modes available for commodity shipments are overlapping, the probit model would in general be a more suitable model. Examples of overlapping modes would be rail carload service and rail with less than carload shipments, and truck on flatcar (TOFC) rail service.

An interesting recent application of multinomial logit modeling to commodity mode choice is a study by Chiang et al. (1980). Using data from the

Commodity Transportation Survey of the Census of Transportation, a choice set containing 32 mode and shipment size combinations was developed. The set is shown in Table 10.1 and is based on four transport technologies: rail, common carrier truck, private truck, and air. These four are articulated on the basis of shipment sizes into 11 different modes. A logit model was then calibrated with a choice function containing 22 variables including 13 choice-specific dummy variables. Table 10.2 shows the model variables.

Some of these variables warrant some discussion. The distance variable for private truck is obviously a mode-specific variable and is included in order to represent the medium- and long-run decision by the shipper or the receiver to

Table 10.1 Mode and shipment size combinations used by Chiang et al. (1980)

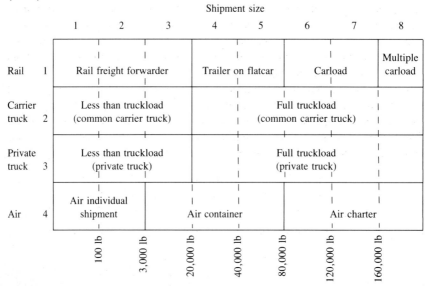

Table 10.2 Variables used in the Chiang et al. model of mode and shipment size choice

1. Transport charges
2. Capital carrying cost in storage
3. Capital carrying cost in transit, or tied up in loss and damage claims in emergency shipments
4. Same as 3, but with regular shipments
5. Ordering costs
6. Loss of value in transit or in storage
7. Distance variable for private truck
8. Value variable for air shipments
9. Use rate for rail shipments
10–22. Mode size class dummy variables

acquire a private truck, the implication being that the private truck will be acquired only if distances are not very large. Private truck as a mode of commodity transportation has been observed to be common only in short-haul transportation. The impact of this variable on the choice function should then be expected to be negative. The value variable for air shipments is another mode-specific variable included in order to represent the fact that the logistics process for high-value commodities is not the same as bulk commodities: they are usually shipped via fast modes, in small shipment sizes, and their inventory levels are kept to a minimum. This suggests that air transportation will have a particular attractiveness in this case. Hence the impact of this variable on the choice function is expected to be positive. The use rate variable for rail shipments is intended as a mode-specific variable for this mode. As use rate increases, bulk handling of commodities becomes attractive. This limits the choice of modes to those suitable for high volumes and with specialized handling technologies, thereby increasing the attractiveness of the rail modes. The effect of this variable is also expected to be positive. The specification of the choice model with such a large number of alternative-specific dummy variables suggest that a number of factors affecting choice are not explicitly accounted for in the other variables of the model. Indeed, the calibration results obtained by Chiang et al. suggest that most of the explanatory power of the choice model comes from these alternative-specific variables. Of course, use of dummy variables may increase the explanatory power of a model, but it will also make it that much less policy sensitive. Multinomial choice models of the type illustrated here remain, however, the most powerful and most promising tool for analyzing commodity transportation behavior and demand.

A number of other applications of choice modeling to commodity transportation can be found in the literature. Most applications have centered simply on mode choice and used the logit choice model. Kullman (1973) calibrated a binary logit model for choice between rail and truck using freight rate, mean and standard deviation of transit time, value of commodity, mileage, and annual tonnage as explanatory variables. Boyer (1977) introduced shipment size as an additional variable in the binary choice model. Levin (1978) calibrated a multinomial logit model for choice between three modes: truck, rail, and piggyback. Other types of choice analysis have also been applied to commodity mode choice. Winston (1978) applied a binary probit to the analysis of choice between truck and rail, and Sasaki (1978) used a discriminant function to allocate coal movements in the Ohio River Basin between rail and barge.

10.3 SPATIAL INTERACTION MODELS OF COMMODITY FLOW

This is an aggregate approach in which the demand for commodity flows between regions is derived directly from some measure of the economic interaction between them. In its most common application the approach results in models of the gravity type, in which the volume of commodity flowing between a pair of regions is proportional to a product function of the measures of economic activity in the regions and proportional to a decreasing function of the total cost of commodity transportation. In addition to the gravity method, models of optimization also belong to this general approach. These can be placed in two classes, differing primarily in the objective function used in the optimization process. One group of models optimizes by minimizing the total transportation cost involved in moving a given quantity of commodities between a set of origins and destinations. Another group optimizes on the basis of maximizing the overall net profit involved not only in the transportation of the commodities but in the whole process of manufacturing, marketing, and distribution.

Gravity Models

Gravity models have been common in the analysis of commodity flows. The basic structure of a gravity model in this case is not different from its structure in the passenger case (Chap. 6). The simplest gravity model is one such as developed by Black (1972), where the flow between two regions is proportional to the total excess supply in the region of origin and the total excess demand in the region of destination and is inversely proportional to some measure of the cost of transportation. For example, Black's model is of the form

$$T_{ij}^k = \frac{S_i^k D_j^k F_{ij}^k}{\sum_i D_j^k F_{ij}^k} \tag{10.31}$$

where T_{ij}^k = total tons of commodity k produced in region i and shipped to region j

S_{ij}^k = total shipments of commodity k from region i

D_{ij}^k = total demand for commodity k in region j

F_{ij}^k = a friction factor which is equal to a $1/d_{ij}^\lambda$, where d_{ij} is the euclidian distance between region i and region j, and λ is an empirically derived exponent which may vary depending on the commodity group being examined

Black found that the gravity formulation is not seriously affected by disaggregation of commodity flows. He also investigated the effects of changes in (1) the areal extent of the study area in square miles, and (2) the numbers of regions examined or dells in the flow matrix. He found study area size to be unimportant. This is not a surprising result when one considers the high level of aggregation at which this type of model is estimated. The values of λ obtained by Black varied considerably between commodities (from over 2.0 to less than 0.02), causing one to wonder whether a simple gravity model can offer any explanation of the forces that underlie the demand for transportation of commodities.

A more elaborate formulation of the gravity model is one that is explicitly multimodal in structure, thereby allowing the estimation of flows by mode. This formulation is analogous to the simultaneous model of urban passenger demand discussed in Chap. 4. Perle (1965) and Mathematica, Inc. (1967–1969), both proposed models of this general structure. The Mathematica model is essentially an abstract mode model and follows the general structure of the passenger abstract mode model described in Chap. 8:

$$V_{ijm} = a_o P_i^{a_1} P_j^{a_2} Y_i^{a_3} Y_j^{a_4} M_i^{a_5} M_j^{a_6} N_{ij}^{a_7} (T_{ij}^b)^{b_o} (T_{ij}^r)^{b_1} (C_{ij}^b)^{d_o} (C_{ijm}^r)^{d_1} \quad (10.32)$$

where
$\quad V_{ijm}$ = volume of freight flow from i to j by mode m
$\quad P_i, P_j$ = population of the origin and destination
$\quad Y_i, Y_j$ = gross regional product of the origin and destination
$\quad M_i, M_j$ = industrial character indexes
$\quad T_{ij}^b$ = least shipping time from i to j
$\quad T_{ijm}^r$ = travel time by mode m divided by the least travel time
$\quad C_{ij}^b$ = least cost of shipping from i to j
$\quad C_{ijm}^r$ = cost of mode m divided by the least cost from i to j
$\quad N_{ij}$ = number of modes serving i and j

This model was not calibrated due to the extensive data requirements it posed. Perle's model with a similar structure was calibrated using data on five commodity groups: agriculture products, animals, mining products, forestry, and manufactured goods. Nine regions were used to provide a sample of origin-destination flows. Perle's model was a mode-specific model in which the transportation cost in each mode was explicitly specified.

Gravity models have limited value for the microscopic analysis of commodity demands. The models of the type used by Black (1972) are too aggregative to provide more than an approximate estimate of total flows between regions. Their value for forecasting or policy analysis is by necessity rather limited. On the other hand, models such as Mathematica's cannot adequately deal with all the determinants of demand and mode choice with the simple gravity structure they adopt. The behavioral approach to commodity transportation choice analysis, an example of which was discussed in the previous section, is a more appropriate approach giving models that are more policy sensitive and less demanding of data than gravity models.

Optimization Models

The simplest form of optimization in the analysis of commodity flow demands is the classic transportation problem. In this problem a set of origins and destinations is given. The origins represent points of excess supply, and the destinations represent points of excess demand. Unit transportation costs are given between each origin and destination and are assumed fixed and unaffected by the volume of traffic. The flows of commodities between origins and destinations are then derived in such a way as to minimize the total transportation cost expended in the system, in the same way Wardrop's second principle is applied to the traffic assignment problem (see Chap. 7). The procedure used to derive the flows is linear programming, and the formulation of the model is as follows.

Let S_i be the excess supply in location i, and D_j be the excess demand in location j. Let c_{ij} be the transportation cost between i and j per unit of commodity. The linear programming formulation is to find the commodity flow between i and j, X_{ij}, such that the total cost of transportation is minimized.

Minimize
$$C = \sum_i \sum_j c_{ij} X_{ij} \qquad (10.33)$$

subject to
$$\sum_j X_{ij} \leq S_i \qquad (10.34)$$

$$\sum_i X_{ij} \geq D_j \qquad (10.35)$$

$$X_{ij} \geq 0 \qquad \text{for all } i, j \qquad (10.36)$$

The linear programming approach to commodity flow analysis has been used extensively in transportation planning, particularly at the macroscopic regional level [see, for example, Roberts and Kresge (1968)]. It has two major restrictions that severely limit its applicability to demand analysis. One is that in order to apply the rather simple techniques of linear programming, the assumption of constant unit transport costs must be made. In reality this assumption is quite strong and could lead to significant distortions in flow estimates. Unit costs in commodity transportation can vary for a number of reasons, not the least important of which is the quantity discounts that carriers often will offer to shippers of large quantities. These discounts imply that average transportation costs decline with quantity, resulting in concave total cost functions. Practical mathematical programming techniques are not readily available for dealing with concave cost functions.

It is interesting to note the difference between this case and the case of urban traffic assignment discussed in Chap. 7. In the urban case congestion effects cause the average cost to increase with volume, leading to a convex total cost function, for which solutions by mathematical programming are possible. The difficulty in the case of commodity flows from the concavity of the cost function; but if a combination of congestion effects and scale economies balance out to result in a nonconcave total cost function, then the solution of the optimal flow problem by mathematical programming becomes feasible.

The other limitation of linear programming is one that is common to all optimization methods of demand analysis, since optimization implies that there is one central decision-making unit that decides on the distribution in the whole system. While this will occur within large firms that are major users of the transportation system, it does not in the case of small-volume users who must adapt to transportation services that are made available to them, nor does it necessarily represent the sum total of the optimization processes that may take place within all the firms in the system. Hence, the optimization methods may be appropriate for estimating the behavior of individual shippers or receivers, but not necessarily as models of total system behavior.

Spatial Equilibrium and Optimization

Recalling the problem of traffic assignment, we can note that the flow can be estimated either by the optimization principle (Wardrop's first) or by seeking equilibrium between demand and supply at the individual rather than the system level (Wardrop's first). In commodity flow analysis, there is a connection between the two principles. To see this, we consider a simple multiregion example where the excess supply in each region is an increasing function of its price in that region and the excess demand a decreasing function of the price in the region. Commodity flow will occur between any pair of regions if the price at the destination less the price at the origin equals the transportation cost. The flows between regions have to satisfy the conservation property that the total net export from any region be limited by the excess supply in that region and that the total net import be limited by the excess demand. The problem can be simply solved for the two-region case, but it will require an equilibrium model for the multiregion case. If the decision process is one of maximizing net benefit and if the net exports in each region are fixed, then the problem resolves to the linear programming problem.

The simple two-region case was illustrated by Chiang et al. (1980) using a graphical solution. In a two-region system we let S_1 be the excess supply in the first region and D_2 the excess demand in the second. These values are related to the prices p_1 and p_2 in the two regions, as shown graphically in Fig. 10.5, where

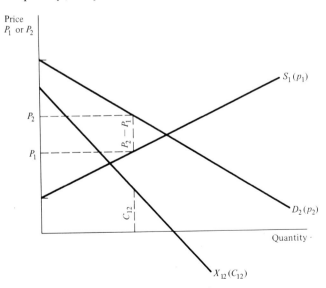

Figure 10.5 Transport demand function in a two-region system.

D is a decreasing function of p_2 and S_1 an increasing function of p_1. Flow from region 1 to region 2 will occur if the cost of transportation c_{12} is equal to the price difference $(p_2 - p_1)$. Equilibrium requires that the quantity shipped between the two regions x_{12} be equal to S_1 and to D_2 at any given transportation cost. In other words, if the demand curve for transportation is given by $X_{12}(c_{12})$, then the following equality must hold:

$$X_{12}(c_{12}) = X_{12}(p_2 - p_1) = S_1(p_1) = D_2(p_2) \qquad (10.37)$$

Graphically this is shown by the transportation demand curve X in Fig. 10.5, where for each value of transportation cost c_{12} the amount shipped is such that $S_1 = D_2$ and $(p_2 - p_1) = c_{12}$.

Optimization and microeconomic analysis of the firm combine when the approach used is to incorporate a spatial element into the firm's production cost function. The process of deriving commodity transportation demands then becomes a straightforward application of the microeconomic theory of the firm, but one that contains an element of spatial interaction and transportation.

10.4 MACROECONOMIC MODELS OF COMMODITY TRANSPORTATION

In the application of macroeconomic analysis to transportation demands transportation is considered one of the many sectors of an economy, exchanging inputs and outputs with the rest. Macroeconomic models attempt to deal, at an aggregate level, with the intersectoral flows of goods and services. Every sector of an economy needs inputs from other sectors in order to produce its own output. By considering transportation explicitly as one of the sectors it becomes possible to analyze the transportation requirements or demands of the other sectors of the economy. It is then possible to convert these requirements into flows by commodity or commodity group, depending on the sector in question and the type of transportation technology used.

Two approaches to macroeconomic modeling have been applied to transportation demand analysis. The first is an econometric approach in which systems of simultaneous equations are used to relate the intersectoral requirements and flows. The second is the input-out approach which is based on certain simplifying assumptions regarding the relationships between intersectoral flows. These assumptions permit significant simplifications of the analysis and reductions in the data requirements. Consequently input-output models have been much more extensively used in transportation demand analysis than econometric simultaneous equation systems. The two are related in principle, and we shall limit our discussion in this section to input-output models as they apply to the analysis of commodity transportation demands.

Input-Output Models

The idea of organizing intersectoral flows as inputs and outputs goes back over two centuries, although its formulation as input-output matrices can be credited to Leontief (1936). The basic structuring of an input-output model begins by identifying the flows of goods and services X_{ij} between sectors of an economy, where i is a producing sector and j is a purchasing sector. These flows are measured in money terms, although under some conditions they could be measured in physical terms. The total output of any given sector of the economy is then given by

$$X_i = \sum_{j \in E} X_{ij} \tag{10.38}$$

where E refers to the set of all sectors that constitute an economy. The sectors whose demands can be assumed to be exogenous to and not affected by the flows within the production sectors of the economy are then identified and separated out. These sectors would include primarily government, net exports to the outside of the region in question, the accumulation sector (investments), and in some cases the households (consumers). The requirements of all these sectors are grouped together and referred to as *final demand*. Equation (10.38) is then modified so that the total output of any sector i is considered the sum of the flows between it and all other production sectors in the economy, and made up of the amount needed to meet the final demand, in addition to the requirements of all the other production sectors of the economy:

$$X_i = \sum_{j \in P} X_{ij} + Y_i \qquad \text{for all } i \in P \tag{10.39}$$

where P represents the set of all the producing sectors in the economy, Y_i is the final demand for the output of sector i, and X_{ij} is flows between production sectors as defined earlier. The methodological advances in input-output analysis were made possible by a set of simplifying assumptions:

1. Each sector produces a set of homogenous products that for the purposes of the analysis can be considered one, and each product is produced by only one sector.
2. All firms within a sector have sufficiently similar production technologies that they can be adequately represented by an average technology.
3. An equilibrium between total supply and total demand for production outputs can be achieved.
4. The technology of production does not change rapidly and can therefore be assumed constant over a short period of time.

Some of these assumptions were later relaxed to develop more general, albeit more complex, input-output models. Using this set of assumptions the development of the input-output model proceeds by the definition for each pair of sectors of what is called the *technical coefficient* a_{ij} as the amount of flow between sector i and sectior j per unit of the total output of sector j. In other words

$$a_{ij} = \frac{X_{ij}}{X_j} \qquad (10.40)$$

The technical coefficients a_{ij} are also referred as the *direct requirements* since they describe the direct requirements of each sector j from all other production sectors i. Combining Eqs. (10.39) and (10.40) yields

$$X_j = \sum_{i \in P} a_{ij} X_j + Y_j \qquad \text{for all } j \in P \qquad (10.41)$$

which can be better stated in matrix notation as

$$\mathbf{X} = \mathbf{AX} + \mathbf{Y}$$

or $$\mathbf{Y} = (\mathbf{I} - \mathbf{A})\mathbf{X} \qquad (10.42)$$

in which $\mathbf{Y}$ represents a vector of final demands, $\mathbf{X}$ a vector of outputs, $\mathbf{A}$ the matrix $\{a_{ij}\}$, and $\mathbf{I}$ the identity matrix.

Assuming that the $(\mathbf{I} - \mathbf{A})$ matrix is nonsingular, it is possible to convert Eq. (10.42) into a model that predicts the output on the basis of a given (or forecast) final demand:

$$(\mathbf{I} - \mathbf{A})^{-1}\mathbf{Y} = \mathbf{X} \qquad (10.43)$$

where $(\mathbf{I} - \mathbf{A})^{-1}$ is the inverse of the $(\mathbf{I} - \mathbf{A})$ matrix and is referred to as the *matrix of direct and indirect requirements*. Each entry, say b_{ij}, in the inverse matrix will give the amount of output required from sector i in order to meet one unit of final demand on sector j. Thus when i and j are the same, b_{ij} is a direct requirement, and when they are not, it is an indirect requirement.

We illustrate this model by a simple example as follows. Consider an economy with three production sectors: transportation, manufacturing, and services. The flows between the sectors and to final demand are given as follows:

				Final demand	Total output
Transportation 1	4	10	8	18	40
Manufacturing 2	3	9	6	42	60
Services 3	3	15	20	12	50
External input	30	26	16		
Total inputs	40	60	50		

Note that the external inputs to each sector are the difference between the total input (which must be equal to the total outputs) and the internal inputs (which are equal to the column sums of the flow table). The value of these external inputs is sometimes called the *value added* in the economy due to the economic activities represented in the table. The technical coefficients can be calculated for this table using Eq. (10.40) to give the following **A** matrix:

$$\mathbf{A} = \begin{bmatrix} 0.100 & 0.167 & 0.160 \\ 0.075 & 0.150 & 0.120 \\ 0.075 & 0.250 & 0.400 \end{bmatrix}$$

The corresponding values of $(\mathbf{I} - \mathbf{A})$ and $(\mathbf{I} - \mathbf{A})^{-1}$ are as follows:

$$(\mathbf{I} - \mathbf{A}) = \begin{bmatrix} 0.900 & -0.167 & -0.160 \\ -0.075 & 0.85 & -0.120 \\ -0.075 & -0.250 & 0.600 \end{bmatrix}$$

$$(\mathbf{I} - \mathbf{A})^{-1} = \begin{bmatrix} 1.1713 & 0.3416 & 0.3810 \\ 0.1318 & 1.2884 & 0.2928 \\ 0.2013 & 0.5795 & 1.8363 \end{bmatrix}$$

Equation (10.43) can be verified with these numerical values as follows:

$$\begin{bmatrix} 40 \\ 60 \\ 50 \end{bmatrix} = \begin{bmatrix} 1.1713 & 0.3416 & 0.3810 \\ 0.1318 & 1.2884 & 0.2928 \\ 0.2013 & 0.5795 & 1.8363 \end{bmatrix} \begin{bmatrix} 18 \\ 42 \\ 12 \end{bmatrix}$$

Note that the diagonal entries of the $(\mathbf{I} - \mathbf{A})^{-1}$ matrix are all above unity. This is expected since these values represent the output of each sector per unit of its final demand, and since to meet one unit of final demand, any sector must produce that unit in addition to an amount it will sell to others that need it to produce the inputs the sector in question needs to produce its output and to meet its final demand requirements.

The transportation requirements of the economy can by analyzed by looking at the total output of the transportation sector and at the row and column values for that sector in the input-output table. Using Eq. (10.43) it is possible to predict the transportation requirements that are caused by any change in the economy, such as an increase in the final demand for some product. To illustrate this, suppose that the economy described by the numerical example undergoes a 10 percent increase in the final demand for manufactured goods and no other changes in final demand. The effect of this increase on transportation requirements can be estimated by applying the model with the new value of Y_2. The new output vector $\mathbf{X}'$ can be calculated using Eq. (10.43):

$$\mathbf{X}' = \begin{bmatrix} 1.7130 & 0.3416 & 0.3810 \\ 0.1318 & 1.2884 & 0.2928 \\ 0.2013 & 0.5795 & 1.8363 \end{bmatrix} \begin{bmatrix} 18 \\ 42 \times 1.1 \\ 12 \end{bmatrix}$$

$$= \begin{bmatrix} 51.190 \\ 65.411 \\ 52.434 \end{bmatrix}$$

The complete intersectoral flow table can also be generated for the estimated new output vector. This is done by multiplying the **A** matrix with a diagonalized output matrix: a matrix with diagonal entries equal to the output of each vector. In other words,

$$\mathbf{X}'_{ij} = \mathbf{A}(\mathbf{X}'_j)^* \qquad (10.44)$$

where $\mathbf{X}'_{ij}$ is the new intersectoral flow table, **A** is the table of technical coefficients a_{ij}, and $(\mathbf{X}')^*$ is a diagonalized new output matrix constructed as follows:

$$(\mathbf{X}')^* = \begin{bmatrix} X'_1 & 0 & 0 \\ 0 & X'_2 & 0 \\ 0 & 0 & X'_3 \end{bmatrix} \qquad (10.45)$$

Applying Eqs. (10.44) and (10.45) to the numerical example we obtain

$$\mathbf{X}'_{ij} = \begin{bmatrix} 0.100 & 0.167 & 0.160 \\ 0.075 & 0.150 & 0.120 \\ 0.075 & 0.250 & 0.400 \end{bmatrix} \begin{bmatrix} 51.19 & 0 & 0 \\ 0 & 65.411 & 0 \\ 0 & 0 & 52.434 \end{bmatrix}$$

$$= \begin{bmatrix} 5.1 & 10.9 & 8.4 \\ 3.8 & 9.8 & 6.3 \\ 3.8 & 16.4 & 21.0 \end{bmatrix} \quad \begin{array}{l} \text{Transportation} \\ \text{Manufacturing} \\ \text{Services} \end{array}$$

It is possible therefore with this model to estimate the impact of a change in the final demands, and hence the outputs of the economy on transportation requirements. Comparing $\mathbf{X}'_{ij}$ with $\mathbf{X}_{ij}$ we can see that the increase in the final demand for manufactured goods has increased the transportation requirements of that sector from 10.0 to 10.9 units. It has also increased the transportation requirements of the service sector from 8.0 to 8.4 units, since this sector has to increase its production in order to meet the increased demands of the manufacturing sector for inputs. The transportation sector's own transportation requirements increase from 4.0 to 5.1 units.

The simple input-output model illustrated in this example has limited applications in transportation demand and policy analysis. Its single-region structure and the simplifying assumptions implied in it limit its applicability to macroscopic aggregate forecasts of transportation requirements at the gross national or regional levels. If the purpose of transportation planning is to prepare for changes that might imply modifications of the technologies of production, then it is clear that the constant technical coefficient assumption must be relaxed. Furthermore, if the main cost of transportation is due to the spatial separation between origins and destinations, and if industries do not have perfectly inelastic demands for transportation, then it is clear that a multiregional structure must be given to the input-output model in order to improve its usefulness for transportation demand analysis.

However, despite its limitations, the single-region input-output model has been applied to numerous transportation studies both at the regional and the national level. Its application has been typically aimed at a broader purpose than simply the analysis of transportation demand and extends into economic planning and impact analysis. Notable among the applications are the Columbia Transportation Study by Roberts and Kresge (1969), and the Sudan Transport Study by the ADAR Corporation (1974).

Multiregional input-output The extension of the input-output model to the multiregional level was first proposed by Isard (1951). Since then considerable developments have been made by Leontief (1970), Chenery (1967), Moses (1955), and Polenske (1970). The multiregional input-output model is structured basically by introducing the spatial dimension into the intersectoral flow tables. Consider a system divided up into n subregions for the purpose of the analysis. Consider an economic model with m production sectors. The intersectoral flows can be arranged for each region in a simple input-output table resulting in n regional tables. A systemwide input-output table is also constructed in the same way to serve as a control total for intersectoral flows among all the regions. The set of tables is illustrated in Fig. 10.6. Next interregional trade flows are arranged

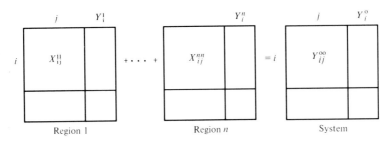

Figure 10.6 Regional input-output tables.

separately for each commodity or sector, resulting in m flow tables of dimension $n \times n$ each, and a summation table showing the sum total of all the commodity flows. These tables are illustrated in Fig. 10.7. Fundamental properties of these

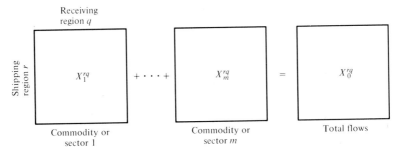

Figure 10.7 Interregional trade flows.

tables can be used to construct the multiregional input-output model. The total amount of a commodity i consumed in a region r, that is, the row sum of the ith row in the input-output table for region r, must be equal to the total amount of that commodity shipped to the region (including from within it) as given by the column sum for region r in the trade flow table for commodity i. Likewise, the total amount produced as given by the column sum in the regional input-output matrix must equal the total quantity shipped out of the region (including to the region itself), as given by the row sum of the corresponding trade flow table. This relationship is illustrated in Fig. 10.8. Letting X_{ij}^h be the intersectoral flow

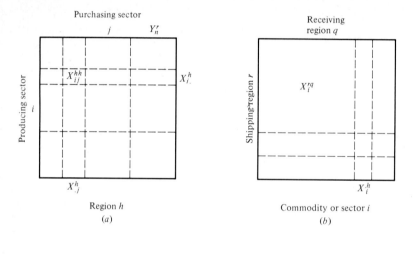

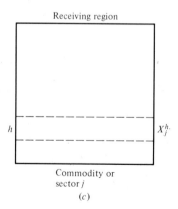

Figure 10.8 Relation between trade flows and regional inputs and outputs.

between sectors i and j in region h, and X_i^{rq} be the trade flow of commodity (or sector) i between regions r and q, then the property can be written as follows:

$$X_i^h = \sum_{j\in E} X_{ij}^h = \sum_{r=1}^{n} X_i^{rh} = X_i^{\cdot h} \tag{10.46}$$

and

$$X_{\cdot j}^h = \sum_{i\in E} X_{ij}^h = \sum_{q=1}^{m} X_i^{hq} = X_i^{h\cdot} \tag{10.47}$$

The construction of a multiregional input-out model proceeds from this basic formulation by constructing the multiregional matrices for the whole system. The first is a matrix of intersectoral technical coefficients. This matrix is shown in Fig. 10.9 and has only diagonal entries that are constituted by the technical

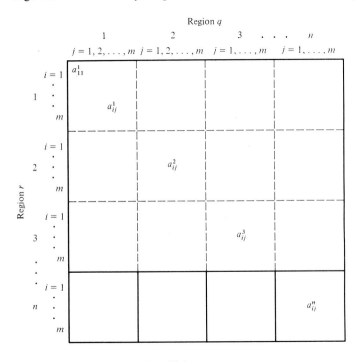

Figure 10.9 Regional technical coefficients.

coefficient tables for each region. The second is the interregional trade flow matrix which is made of $n \times n$ submatrices of dimension $m \times m$ each. Each of the submatrices is a diagonal matrix including only the trade flow for a given commodity (or sector) between the part of the regions indicated by the location of the submatrix in the overall interregional trade matrix. This is shown in Fig. 10.10

To construct an input-output model relating output to final demand three methods have been applied. The first is a gravity method by Leontief (1970), the second is the column trade coefficient method by Moses (1955) and Chenery (1967), and the third is a variant of the second and is referred to as the *row trade coefficient method*.

The gravity method Here the trade matrix of Fig. 10.10 is taken as a starting

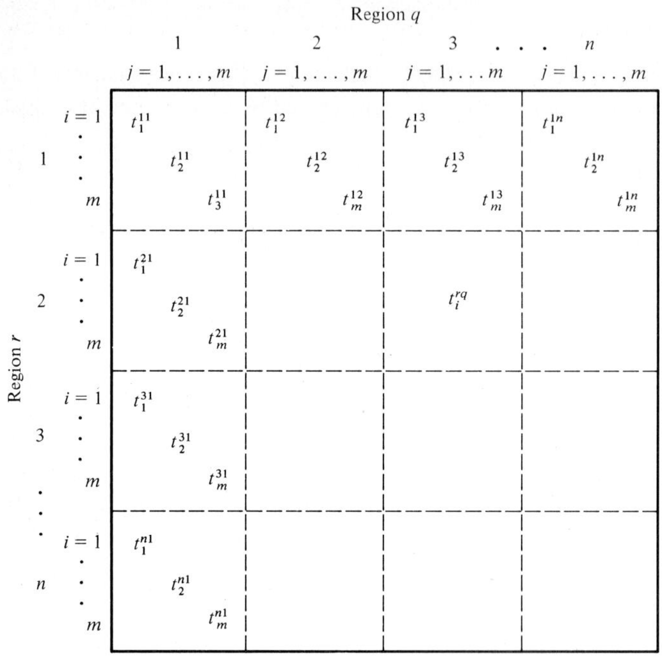

Figure 10.10 Interregional trade coefficients.

point. The row and column sums of this matrix represent, respectively, the total production and the total consumption of each commodity in each region. To estimate the flow of commodities between regions a proportional flow model is used modified by a gravity coefficient for each region pair and commodity. This gravity coefficient reflects the cost of transferring one unit of each commodity between the two regions in question. Letting $\mathbf{S}$ be a diagonal matrix of the flows of each commodity into each region we have

$$\mathbf{S} = \{S_{i.}^{rq}\}$$

where
$$S_{i.}^{rq} = \mathbf{X}_{i}^{r\cdot}(1 - G_{i}^{rq}) \tag{10.48}$$

where G_{i}^{rq} is a gravity coefficient incorporating the effects of transport cost and, if appropriate, the relative attractiveness of region r as a supplier of commodity

i to region q. Also, letting **T** be a matrix of flows of each commodity from each region then:

$$\mathbf{T} = \{t_i^{rq}\}$$

where $$t_i^{rq} = X_i^{\cdot q}(1 - G_i^{rq}) \tag{10.49}$$

Combining these equations with the conservation rules spelled out in Eqs. (10.46) and (10.47), it can be shown that the complete input-output model can be written in the following form [see, for example, Polenske (1970)]:

$$X = (\mathbf{S}^{-1}\mathbf{T} - \mathbf{A})^{-1}Y \tag{10.50}$$

Changes in transportation costs, reflecting in changes in the values of G_i^{rq} for each commodity and region pair, will result directly in changes in the flows to and from the transportation sector, and thus allow the estimation of transport demands.

Other interregional input-output models Additional simplifications have been proposed in order to reduce the magnitude of the computations in an interregional input-output model. One method that has been used is the so-called column coefficient method [Moses (1955)]. In this method it is assumed that for each region the fraction of the total consumption of a commodity that is imported from another region is the same for all commodities or sectors. This assumption results in the creation of a diagonal matrix of regional trade coefficients for each commodity and region pair. These coefficients t_i^{rq} are obtained by dividing the entry in the large interregional trade matrix by the column sum of that matrix:

$$\mathbf{T} = t_i^{rq}$$

where $$t_i^{rq} = \frac{X_i^{rq}}{X_i^{\cdot r}} \tag{10.51}$$

The input-output model is then written as

$$\mathbf{X} = (\mathbf{T}^{-1} - \mathbf{A})^{-1}Y \tag{10.52}$$

While this model greatly simplifies the analysis of interregional commodity flows, it lacks the capability of directly estimating the impacts of changes in the transportation system since it does not have an explicit reference to transportation cost. An interesting application of this model can be found in Hill (1975). For our purposes a simple numerical example will suffice.

> **Example** This example is of a system of two regions and an economy of two sectors. The regional intersectoral trade flows are given in the following matrices, one for each region:

Region 1

Sector	$j = 1$	$j = 2$	Final demand	Total consumption
$i = 1$	5	4	10	19
$i = 2$	3	6	7	16
Value added	4	10		
Total production	12	20		

Region 2

Sector	$j = 1$	$j = 2$	Final demand	Total consumption
$i = 1$	2	2	8	12
$i = 2$	3	2	5	10
Value added	14	2		
Total production	19	6		

The interregional trade flows by commodity are also given in the following matrices:

Commodity 1

Shipping region	Receiving region		Total production
	1	2	
1	10	2	12
2	9	10	19
Total consumption	19	12	

Commodity 2

Shipping region	Receiving region		Total production
	1	2	
1	12	8	20
2	4	2	6
Total consumption	16	10	

The regional input-output matrices show the total consumption and production of each commodity (or sector) as the row and column sums for each region. Note that according to Eqs. (10.46) and (10.47) these should be equal to the totals of each commodity received and shipped by each region, respectively.

Thus in this example

$$X_{1.}^1 = X_{.1}^1 = 19$$
$$X_{2.}^1 = X_{.2}^1 = 16$$
$$X_{1.}^2 = X_{.1}^2 = 12$$
$$X_{2.}^2 = X_{.2}^2 = 10$$

and
$$X_{.1}^1 = X_1^{1\cdot} = 12$$
$$X_{.2}^1 = X_2^{1\cdot} = 20$$
$$X_{.1}^2 = X_1^{2\cdot} = 19$$

and finally
$$X_{.2}^2 = X_2^{2\cdot} = 6$$

The regional technical coefficients a_{ij} can be computed for each region and pair of commodities by dividing $X_{ij}^h/X_{.j}^h$. They are arranged in a multiregional matrix **A** as follows:

$$
\mathbf{A} = \left\{ \begin{array}{l} \text{Region 1} \begin{cases} i = 1 \\ i = 2 \end{cases} \\ \text{Region 2} \begin{cases} i = 1 \\ i = 2 \end{cases} \end{array} \right.
\begin{array}{c}
\overbrace{\begin{array}{cc} \text{Region 1} \\ j = 1 \quad j = 2 \end{array}}^{} \quad \overbrace{\begin{array}{cc} \text{Region 2} \\ j = 1 \quad j = 2 \end{array}}^{} \\
\begin{bmatrix}
0.417 & 0.200 & 0 & 0 \\
0.250 & 0.300 & 0 & 0 \\
0 & 0 & 0.105 & 0.330 \\
0 & 0 & 0.158 & 0.330
\end{bmatrix}
\end{array}
$$

Next, the column trade coefficients $t_{i.}^{rh}$ are calculated for each commodity and pair of regions by dividing the entries of the trade matrices by the column sums: $X_{i.}^{rh}/X_{i.}^{.h}$. The values are obtained in one table for each commodity (or sector):

Shipping region	Commodity 1		Commodity 2	
	Receiving Region		Receiving Region	
	1	2	1	2
1	0.530	0.167	0.750	0.800
2	0.470	0.833	0.250	0.200

These are arranged into the multiregional trade coefficient matrix T as follows:

$$
\mathbf{T} = \left\{ \begin{array}{l} \text{Region 1} \begin{cases} i = 1 \\ i = 2 \end{cases} \\ \text{Region 2} \begin{cases} i = 1 \\ i = 2 \end{cases} \end{array} \right.
\begin{array}{c}
\overbrace{\begin{array}{cc} \text{Region 1} \\ j = 1 \quad j = 2 \end{array}}^{} \quad \overbrace{\begin{array}{cc} \text{Region 2} \\ j = 1 \quad j = 2 \end{array}}^{} \\
\begin{bmatrix}
0.530 & 0 & 0.167 & 0 \\
0 & 0.750 & 0 & 0.800 \\
0.470 & 0 & 0.833 & 0 \\
0 & 0.250 & 0 & 0.200
\end{bmatrix}
\end{array}
$$

Note that both **T** and **A** have the same dimension and format. Also note that the column sums of **T** equal unity.

With these matrices prepared it is possible now to apply the multiregional input-output model of Eq. (10.52). To do this we obtain the following matrices:

$$
\mathbf{T}^{-1} = \begin{bmatrix} 2.2948 & 0 & -0.4600 & 0 \\ 0 & -4 & 0 & 16 \\ 1.2948 & 0 & 1.4601 & 0 \\ 0 & 5 & 5 & -15 \end{bmatrix}
$$

and

$$
(\mathbf{T}^{-1} - \mathbf{A}) = \begin{bmatrix} 1.8778 & -0.2 & -0.4600 & 0 \\ -0.25 & -4.3 & 0 & 16 \\ -1.2948 & 0 & 1.3551 & -0.33 \\ 0 & 5 & -0.158 & -15.33 \end{bmatrix}
$$

for which we obtain

$$
(\mathbf{T}^{-1} - \mathbf{A})^{-1} = \begin{bmatrix} 0.7502 & 0.1959 & 0.2778 & 0.1985 \\ 0.3374 & 1.1925 & 0.2590 & 1.2391 \\ 0.74177 & 0.28121 & 1.0215 & 0.2715 \\ 0.10239 & 0.2860 & 0.0739 & 0.3361 \end{bmatrix}
$$

Applying Eq. (10.52) we verify with

$$
\mathbf{X} = \begin{bmatrix} 12 \\ 20 \\ 19 \\ 6 \end{bmatrix} \quad \text{and} \quad \mathbf{Y} = \begin{bmatrix} 10 \\ 7 \\ 8 \\ 5 \end{bmatrix}
$$

that

$$
\mathbf{X} = \begin{bmatrix} 0.7502 & 0.1959 & 0.2778 & 0.19849 \\ 0.3374 & 1.1925 & 0.259 & 1.2391 \\ 0.7418 & 0.2812 & 1.0215 & 0.2715 \\ 0.1024 & 0.3860 & 0.0739 & 0.3361 \end{bmatrix} \begin{bmatrix} 10 \\ 7 \\ 8 \\ 5 \end{bmatrix} = \begin{bmatrix} 12 \\ 20 \\ 19 \\ 6 \end{bmatrix}
$$

The effect of a change in the final demand can now be traced back to the output vector and to the flows of commodities between regions.

Changes in transportation system Changes in the transportation system can affect the trade coefficients as well as the technical coefficients. In order to be able to trace the effects of such changes on commodity flow demands it is necessary to modify these coefficients before reapplying the multiregional input-output model. A number of methods have been proposed for this. Liew and Liew (1979) proposed a method in which the relationship between the technical coefficients and trade coefficients, and the cost of transportation are derived from assumptions about the production processes underlying the various sectors production systems. Specifically by assuming Cobb-Douglas production functions they proposed the following model for updating the interregional technical coefficients:

$$(a_{ij}^{rq})' = a_{ij}^{rq} \exp (\delta \ln p_j^q - \delta \ln c_i^{rq} - \delta \ln p_i^r) \qquad (10.53)$$

where a_{ij}^{qr} is the interregional technical coefficient defined as the product of the regional coefficient and the interregional trade coefficient:

$$a_{ij}^{rq} = t_i^{rq} a_{ij}^q \qquad (10.54)$$

In Eq. (10.53) the $(')$ notation indicated a new coefficient; p_j^q and p_i^r are the prices of the commodities j and i in regions q and r, respectively, and c_i^{qr} is the unit transportation cost of commodity i between the two regions q and r. With this model, changes in a transportation system can be translated into changes in transport cost, and their effects on commodity flows can be estimated.

Multiregional input-output models provide a powerful tool for analyzing commodity transport demands at the macroeconomic level. Despite their many restrictive assumptions, they remain the most feasible models for application in national and regional planning. Considerable research is still necessary in order to permit further development of this approach and to relax more of the restrictive assumptions made.

PROBLEMS

10.1 Given is a city in which there is demand for a particular agricultural commodity. The demand is given by the following function:

$$Q = a - bP$$

where Q is the quantity purchased, P is the unit price, and a and b are positive parameters. All land surrounding the city can be put to production of the commodity, and the area is sufficiently large to permit approximating the city by a single point.

The cost of production per hectare is S and the yield per hectare is H tons. The transport cost to the city of the commodity is Cd per ton, where C is a constant and d is the radial distance from the production area to the city.

Assume that all land can be used for production and that production will occur wherever it is *profitable* to do so. Find

(a) The total area of production and quantity produced

(b) The selling price of the commodity in the city (the commodity can be sold at only one price)

10.2 Given the following economy with four sectors and the following interindustry transactions:

	1	2	3	4	Final demand	Total gross output
1. Manufactured primary products	1	2	0	4		60
2. Transportation	11	5	3	15		45
3. Labor	20	5	1	20		60
4. Services	4	3	10	10		55

(a) What are the final demands in the table as given? What are the total outlays of each of the four sectors? What are the corresponding values added for each sector?

(b) During a forecasting period, it is anticipated that there will be a 5 percent growth in the final demand for manufactured goods. Assuming that the final demand for services and for transportation increases in the same proportion as the amount paid to labor, find the impact of the growth on transportation.

10.3 Interpret the economic meaning of the column sums in the table of direct and indirect requirements of an input-output model. Would you expect the value of this sum for transportation to be high or low? Why?

10.4 A shipper of mangoes must decide which of two route alternatives to choose for a shipment of 5 t of mangoes. The first alternative is to use a conventional truck on a route that requires 3 days of travel time, and which charges $23/t. The second alternative is a refrigerated truck but on a route which requires 5 days of travel time and which charges $30/t. The market value of mangoes is $1500/t. The deterioration of mangoes is given by the following two functions:

Unrefrigerated:
$$p = 6.25 \text{ x } 2^{t-1} \qquad t \leqslant 5$$

Refrigerated:
$$p = 1.25 \text{ x } 2^{0.5t-0.5}$$

where t is time in days, and p is the percentage deteriorated.

(a) Find the choice of mode of the shipper.

(b) If the total annual demand for the mangoes is estimated at 18,000 t and if the handling cost per shipment is $400 and the storage cost is $50/t per day, what would be a good shipment size and how much would be the total value of mangoes that will deteriorate in storage?

REFERENCES

Baumol, W. J., and H. D. Vinod: An Inventory Theoretics Model of Freight Transportation, *Mgmt. Sci.*, vol. 16, pp. 413–421, 1970.

Boyer, K. O.: Minimum Rate Regulation, Model Split Sensitivities and the Railroad Problem, *Journal of Political Economy,* vol. 85, pp. 493–512, 1977.

Black, W. R.: Interregional Commodity Flows: Some Experiments with the Gravity Model, *J. Region. Sci.*, vol. 12, no. 1, pp. 107–118, 1972.

Chenery, H. B.: Interdependence of Investment Decisions, American Economic Assoc., *Readings in Welfare Economics,* pp. 336–371, 1967.

Chiang, Y. S., P. O. Roberts, and M. Ben Akiva: "Development of a Policy Sensitive Model for Forecasting Freight Demand," Center for Transportation Studies, Cambridge, Mass., report CTS81-1, 1980.

Friedlaender, A. F., and R. H. Spady: *Freight Transportation Regulation*, The MIT Press, Cambridge, Mass., 1981.

Hashemian, H.: "Mode Choice between Air and Truck in Short Haul Market," Institute of Transportation Studies, Berkeley, PhD dissertation, 1981.

Hill, E.: "Calculation of Trade Flows and Income Multipliers Using the Multiregional Input-Output Model," MIT Dept. of Urban Studies, Cambridge, Mass., working paper MRIO-3, 1975.

Isard, W.: Interregional and Regional Input-Output Analysis: A Model of A Space Economy, *Rev. Econ. Stat.,* vol. 33, no. 4, 1951.

Kullman, B.: A Model; of Rail Truck Competition in the Intercity Freight Market, in "Studies in Railroad Operations and Economics," MIT Dept. of Civil Engineering, Cambridge, Mass., report R74-35, vol. 15, Chap. 6, 1973.

Lefeber, L.: "Allocation in Space: Production, Transportation and Industrial Location," North Holland, Amsterdam, 1968.

Leontief, W.: Quantitative Input-Output Relations in the Economic System of the United States, *Rev. Econ. Stat.,* vol. 18, no. 3, 1936.

Leontief, W.: *Input-Output Economics*, Oxford University Press, New York, 1970.

Levin, R. C.: Allocation in Surface Freight Transportation: Does Rate Regulation Matter? *Bell Journal of Economics,* vol. 9, pp. 18–45, 1978.

Liew, C. K., and C. J. Liew: Use of Multiregional Variable Input-Output Model to Analyze the Impacts of Transportation Costs, *Transp. Res. Rec.,* no. 747, pp. 5–12, 1979.

Mathmetatica, Inc.: *Studies in the Demand for Freight Transportation,* Princeton, N.J., vols. 1–3, 1967–1969.

Miernyk, W.: *The Elements of Input-Output Analysis,* Random House, New York, 1965.

Moses, L.: The Stability of Interregional Trading Patterns and Input-Output Analysis, *Am. Econ. Rev.,* vol. 45, no. 5, pp. 803–831, 1955.

Perle, E.: Estimation of Transportation Demand, papers of the *Region Sci. Assoc.,* vol. 15, pp. 203–215, 1965.

Polenske, K. R.: "A Multiregional Input-Output Model for the United States," Harvard Economic Research Program, Cambridge, Mass., 1970.

Roberts, P. O., and D. Kresge: Simulation of Transport Policy Alternatives for Columbia, *Amer. Econ. Rev.,* vol. 58, pp. 341–393, 1968.

————, et al.: "Models of Travel Time and Reliability for Freight Transport," Center for Transportation Studies, Cambridge Mass., report CGS 76-16, 1976.

Sasaki, B.: Predicting Transporter's Choice of Mode, Transportation Research Board Annual Meeting, 1978.

Shephard, R. W.: *The Theory of Cost and Production Functions,* Princeton University Press, Princeton, N. J., 1953.

The ADAR Corporation: "Econometric Models of the Sudan," Philadelphia, Penn., 1974.

Winston, C.: Mode Choice in Freight Transportation, Berkeley Dept. of Economics, Berkeley, 1978.

INDEX